**Development control:
policy into practice**

In memoriam
H. W. M.

Development control: policy into practice

Peter H. Morgan, BA(Leics), PhD(Wales)

Susan M. Nott, LLB(Wales), BCL(Durham)

Butterworths
London
1988

United Kingdom	Butterworth & Co (Publishers) Ltd, 88 Kingsway, LONDON WC2B 6AB and 61A North Castle Street, EDINBURGH EH2 3LJ
Australia	Butterworths Pty Ltd, SYDNEY, MELBOURNE, BRISBANE, ADELAIDE, PERTH, CANBERRA and HOBART
Canada	Butterworths. A division of Reed Inc., TORONTO and VANCOUVER
New Zealand	Butterworths of New Zealand Ltd, WELLINGTON and AUCKLAND
Singapore	Butterworth & Co (Asia) Pte Ltd, SINGAPORE
USA	Butterworths Legal Publishers, ST PAUL, Minnesota, SEATTLE, Washington, BOSTON, Massachusetts, AUSTIN, Texas and D & S Publishers, CLEARWATER, Florida

British Library Cataloguing in Publication Data

Morgan, Peter, H.
  Development control: policy into practice.
  1. England. Environment planning
  I. Title   II. Nott, Susan M.
  711'.0942

  ISBN Hardcover 0 406 50250 1
    Softcover 0 406 50251 X

Printed and bound in Great Britain by
Mackays of Chatham PLC, Chatham, Kent

Preface

The idea for this work emerged from the continuing attempt of one of the authors to explain to disparate groups of students, studying in various environmental disciplines, what was actually meant by the development control system. Clearly, it is a system that depends on the law for its structure, but equally clearly, it cannot be understood by a study of the law alone. Policy from a wide range of sources has to be taken into account and an appreciation gained of its place within the system. Only then is it possible to begin to comprehend the forces at work in the development control process that, to most people, is represented by the making of an application for planning permission. This work attempts to analyse that process by presenting an examination of the development control system that includes references to planning theory, philosophy, policy and practice as well as planning law. Given the legal content of the work and the fact that one of the authors is a lecturer in law, it is perhaps worth stressing that this work is in no way an attempt to add to the books on planning law. As has already been said, the development control system is inextricably linked to the legal system but this work is very much an attempt to examine the former with reference to the latter.

The authors would like to thank each other for all the contributions, comments and criticisms that each made on the other's work, particularly the criticisms, in which nothing was spared, as may possibly be common between husbands and wives who choose to write together! Thanks must also be given to 'Joyce' without whom the greater part of the manuscript would not have been prepared, and to Sweet & Maxwell, for their permission to quote from the Journal of Planning and Environment Law. Finally, thanks are due to our publishers who had the confidence that we could write this book.

May 1988

P.H.M
S.M.N

Contents

Preface   v
Table of statutes   xi
List of cases   xv

Chapter 1   **Introduction to development control**   1
Development control   2
The development control system at work   5
Two examples of development control   11
   The first example   11
   The second example   18
The decision   22
Planning appeals   23
Judicial challenge   25
Enforcement   26
Compensation   27
Exceptions   30
Conclusion   32

Chapter 2   **The personnel of planning**   33
The Department of the Environment   35
Other government departments   41
Local government   45
   Organisation   45
   Planning   47
   The role of local government in development control   49
The developer   54
Members of the public   56
Other groups   59
   Development corporations   60
   Statutory undertakers   61
   Bodies charged with protecting the environment   61
The courts   62
The ombudsmen   63

Contents

Chapter 3 Planning permission – the application	65
The meaning of development	66
Development as interpreted by the courts	72
Operations	74
Material change of use	78
Interpretation of development in planning appeals	83
Circulars and their interpretation of development	89
General Development Order and Use Classes Order	91
The General Development Order	92
The Use Classes Order	99
Application for planning permission	101
Publicity and consultation	104
The development plan	109
Material considerations	110
Chapter 4 Development plans	114
Development plans as policy documents	115
The concept of land policy	116
Development plans and The Town and Country Planning Act 1947	118
Development plans and the Town and Country Planning Act 1971	123
Formation and structure	125
Development plans under the 1947 Act – the 'old style' plan	127
Development plans under the 1971 Act	130
Development plans and the law	160
Judicial review under section 244	160
Judicial comment under section 245	165
The future of development plans	169
Chapter 5 Local policy and special controls	173
Local authority policy	177
Central government	177
Local planning officers	180
Local councillors	182
The public	183
The forms and functions of local planning authority policy	187
Specific policies supported by statute	190
Non-specific policies supported by various sources	214
Chapter 6 Department of the Environment policy	222
The origins of policy	223
Making policy known	225

Circulars 228
  The production of circulars 229
  The content of circulars 229
The legal significance of circulars 232
Development control policy notes 239
Other sources of policy 241

Chapter 7 **The development site** 243
The site defined 243
The development plan and other material considerations 244
The planning history 246
The significant features 248
  The form of the development 248
  The function of the development 250
  The location of the development 261
Some common issues 266
  Visual issues 266
  Local impact 268

Chapter 8 **Planning permission – the decision** 272
Planning conditions 275
Planning agreements 287
  Town and Country Planning Act 1971, section 52 290
  Local Government Act 1972, section 111 293
  Highways Act 1980, section 278 295
  Local Acts of Parliament 296
Planning gain 297

Chapter 9 **The last resort – appeals and enforcement** 300
Planning appeals 301
  Why appeal? 301
  Appeal to whom? 304
  The conduct of appeals 309
  The decision 313
Enforcement 314
  Why do breaches occur? 314
  How are breaches discovered? 315
  The enforcement process 316
Stop notices 324
Injunctions 326

Contents

Chapter 10   **The courts: their role in the process of develop-**
               ment control   328
The function of the courts   329
  Reviewing the administration   330
  Application for judicial review   341
Ombudsmen   346
Other functions of the courts   351

Index   353

Table of statutes

PAGE

Artisans and Labourers
   Dwellings Improvement
   Act 1875 2
Artisans and Labourers
   Dwellings Improvement
   Act 1879 2
Caravan Sites and Control of
   Development Act 1960 .. 95, 193,
                                194
   s 2 195
   Sch 1 195
Caravan Sites Act 1968 193
   s 6 195
Civic Amenities Act 1967
   Pt III 212
Control of Pollution Act 1974: 213, 214
   Pt I 213
Countryside Act 1968 215
   ss 6–10 215
Glamorgan County Council Act
   1973
   s 7 296
Health and Safety at Work Act
   1974 213
Highways Act 1959
   s 82 201
Highways Act 1980 210
   s 1(1)(a) 210
   10(2) 210
   16(8) 210
   18 210
   24 210
   38 212
   278 .... 287, 290, 295, 296, 298
Historic Buildings and Ancient
   Monuments Act 1953 305

PAGE

Housing of the Working Classes
   Act 1890 2
Housing Act 1985 36
Housing and Planning Act
   1986 147,
                    200, 225, 228, 287
   s 25 200
   48 44
   49 83
   Sch 6 200
   Sch 10 147
   Sch 11 83
Housing, Town Planning, Etc
   Act 1909 2
Inner Urban Areas Act 1978 151
Local Government Act 1894 45
Local Government Act 1972 .. 45, 47,
                    131, 134, 150
   s 1 46
   (1) 46
   20(4) 46
   101 50
   111 .... 287, 293, 294
   ss 124–127 211
   s 124 47
   125 47
   194 46
   222 326
   Sch 14
   para 27 47
   Sch 16
   para 32 48
   Sch 19 46
   para 19(1) 108
   (2)(a) 108

PAGE

Local Government Act 1974 .. 63, 347
  Pt III 63
  s 25(1) 348
    26(1) 347
      (2) 348
      (4) 348
        (b) 348
      (6) 348
    29 349
    31(2) 349
Local Government Act 1978 64
Local Government Act 1985 36,
      114, 146, 157, 158, 195
  s 3(3) 195
    5(2)(a) 159
  Sch 1 .... 48, 158
    para 2(1) 5
      12 49
Local Government, Planning
  and Land Act 1980 ..... 31, 136,
    146, 151, 152, 153, 198,
                199
  Pt IX 151
  Pt XVI 31, 60
  s 86 .... 48, 102
    (3) 109
  ss 134–171 31
  s 136 198
    140 60
  ss 148–150 .... 60, 198
  s 179 .... 19, 198
  Schs 26–31 31
  Sch 29 .... 60, 198
  Sch 32 19
    Pt I 198
    para 17(1) 199
        23 199
        27 199
London Government Act 1963 46
Mines and Quarries (Tips) Act
  1969 213
Minister of Town and Country
  Planning Act 1943 37
  s 1 37
National Heritage Act 1983 61
National Parks and Access to the
  Countryside Act 1949 .... 20, 215
  s 89 201
  Pt V 215
Nature Conservancy Council Act
  1973 61
New Towns Act 1946 60
Opencast Coal Act 1958 197

PAGE

Parliamentary   Commissioner
  Act 1967 63
  s 4(1) 348
    5(1)(a) 348
      (2) 348
    6(3) 348
    8 349
    10(3) 349
    12(3) 347
  Sch 2 348
Public Health Act 1875 2
Public Health Act 1936 93
  s 269 93
Supreme Court Act 1981 62
  s 31 62
Town and Country Planning Act
  1947 .... 2, 5, 12, 66,
    114, 115, 118, 119, 120,
    121, 126, 127, 128, 246
Town and Country Planning Act
  1962 114
Town and Country Planning Act
  1968 123,
    131, 149, 150, 319
Town and Country Planning Act
  1971 .... 2, 12,
    34, 38, 42, 54, 61, 67, 70,
    72, 73, 90, 104, 115, 123,
    128, 129, 130, 142, 150,
    151, 162, 163, 172, 174,
    177, 201, 212, 213, 215,
    216, 218, 220, 225, 226,
    227, 233, 235, 238, 281,
    316, 319, 328, 330, 333,
    334, 339, 340, 341, 344,
    345, 346, 351, 352
  s 2B 97
    6 .... 130, 131, 132
    (3) 132
  ss 7–15 12
  s 7 11
    (1) 5
    (1A) 133
    (4) 136
    (6) 136
    (6A) 136
    8 .... 11, 143
    (1) 57
    9 .... 11, 134
    (1) 143
    (3) 134
    (3b) 143
    (5) 144

PAGE

Town and Country Planning Act
  1971—*contd*
s 10 144
  10C 146
  11 .... 146, 149
    (1) 146
    (7) 146
    (10) 146
  12 155
    (1) 57
  13(1), (2) 156
  14(3), (4) 38, 156
  15B 116
  19 48
  20(1) 158
    (2) 157
  21[7A] 130
  22 .... 54, 66, 69, 72, 74,
          75, 76, 77, 78, 79, 80,
                     248, 329
    (1) 5, 243
    (2)(a) 67
       (b) 67
       (c) 67
       (d) 68
       (e) 68
       (f) 68
  22(3) 213
       (a) 69, 80
       (b) 69
    (4) 69
  23(1) 6
  25 34
  26 .... 105, 250
    (7) 17
  28(3) 17
  28(2B) 192
  29 .... 10, 109, 110, 114,
          173, 219, 228, 238, 275,
          278, 280, 281, 283, 293
    (1) 4, 5, 10, 110, 165,
          166, 245, 272, 283, 329
  30 219
    (1)(a) 283
       (b) 282
  31A 287
  32(1)(b) 286, 287
  34 .... 105, 246
  35 .... 38, 104
  36 .... 38, 72, 274, 301, 311
  37 .... 38, 104, 272, 301
  41 .... 14, 246, 278
  42 14

PAGE

Town and Country Planning Act
  1971—*contd*
s 51 341
  51A 341
  52 .... 218, 287, 290, 291,
          292, 293, 296, 297,
          298, 332, 337
    (1) 218
    (2) 291
    (3) 225, 292
  53 .... 70, 71, 72, 306, 351
ss 54–58 .... 13, 225
s 54 .... 13, 67, 174, 202
    (2) 226
  54A(1) 206
  55 .... 63, 77, 206, 315, 318
    (1) 226
    (2) 226
  56 .... 174, 206
    (6) 226
  56A 206
  58 .... 174, 202
  60 .... 16, 176, 201, 341
  61A 193
  63 .... 176, 207
  64 207
  65 212
ss 66–86 44
s 84 291
  87 .... 27, 71, 73, 318, 322
    (1) 316, 317, 319
    (4) 318, 320
    (5) 320, 321
    (9) 317
    (10) 320
  88 .... 27, 306, 323
    (1) 320
    (2) 319, 324, 326
  88A(1) 321
     (3) 321
  89 324
    (4) 324
    (5) 324
  90 .... 27, 325, 326
    (1) 325
    (2) 325
    (3) 325
    (7) 325
  95 306
  101 206
  102 .... 63, 318
  109 207
  112 215

PAGE

Town and Country Planning Act
1971—*contd*
s 113 215
121 216
122 216
124 217
173(3), (4) 202
177 326
180–187 29
190 206
235 340
242(2) 341
(3) 341
244 .... 26, 62, 160, 161,
165, 332, 333, 336, 339,
340, 341, 343, 345, 346
(1) 160, 161, 165, 330
(2)(b) 62, 162, 165, 346
(3) 340
(4) 340
(5) 340
245 .... 25, 62, 72, 165,
166, 282, 311, 323, 332,
333, 336, 339, 340, 341,
343, 345, 346
(1) 330
(4) 346
(b) 312, 339
246 323
247 351
266 .... 43, 220
270 217
277 .... 67, 175, 190, 292, 328
(6), (6A), (7) 192
(10) 190

PAGE

Town and Country Planning Act
1971—*contd*
s 277A 77, 192, 292
277B(1) 175
290 .... 61, 69, 74, 75,
78, 86, 87, 88,
89, 320
(1) 31, 220
Pt II 130, 158
VII 28
VIII 28
IX 29
X 340
Sch 4 .... 48, 157
5 .... 127, 130
Pt I 129
Sch 9 .... 305, 307
11
Pt I 226
Town and Country Planning Act
1984 232
s 1 232
Town and Country Planning
(Minerals) Act 1981 ..... 96, 195,
196
s 1(1) 76
Town and Country Planning
(Scotland) Act 1972 42
Tribunals and Inquiries Act
1971 339
s 12 339
Wildlife and Countryside Act
1981 .... 59, 215
ss 28–33 68
53–58 215

List of cases

PAGE

A

Abbey Homesteads (Developments) Ltd v Northamptonshire County
    Council (1985) 291
Alderson v Secretary of State for the Environment (1984) 183, 284
Anisminic Ltd v Foreign Compensation Commission (1969) 332
A-G v Wilts United Dairies Ltd (1921) 299
Avon County Council v Millard (1986) 293

B

Barnham v Secretary of State for the Environment (1985) 162, 168, 237
Barvis Ltd v Secretary of State for the Environment (1971) 75, 86
Bedfordshire County Council v Central Electricity Generating Board (1985) 77
Bendles Motors v Bristol Corpn (1963) 79, 86
Bizony v Secretary of State for the Environment (1976) 331
Bradford Metropolitan District Council v Secretary of State for the Environ-
    ment (1977) 67
Bradley (E H) & Sons Ltd v Secretary of State for the Environment (1984) ... 161
British Oxygen Co Ltd v Board of Trade (1971) 292
Bromley London Borough Council v Greater London Council (1983) 345
Brooks and Burton Ltd v Secretary of State for the Environment (1978) 80
Buckinghamshire County Council v Callingham (1952) 74
Buckinghamshire County Council v Hall Aggregates (Thames Valley) Ltd
    (1985) 56, 161, 164, 165, 197, 334
Bullock v Secretary of State for the Environment (1980) 201
Burdle v Secretary of State for the Environment (1972) 82, 244
Buxton v Minister of Housing and Local Government (1961) 330

C

Camden London Borough Council v Secretary of State for the Environment
    (1980) 340
Chelmsford Borough Council v Secretary of State for the Environment
    (1986) 236, 308, 314, 331
Cheshire County Council v Woodward (1962) 75, 86
City of Bradford Metropolitan Council v Secretary of State for the
    Environment (1986) 289, 295
Coleshill and District Investment Co Ltd v Minister of Housing and Local
    Government (1969) 76, 77, 90, 233, 339
Council of Civil Service Unions v Minister for the Civil Service (1985) 344

List of cases

PAGE

Covent Garden Community Association Ltd v Greater London Council
(1981) 343

D

Davy v Spelthorne Borough Council (1983) 352
Dimes v Grand Junction Canal Co Proprietors (1852) 336
Dimsdale Developments (South East) Ltd v Secretary of State for the
Environment (1986) 241, 314

E

East Barnet Urban District Council v British Transport Commission (1962) ... 244

F

Fayrewood Fish Farms Ltd v Secretary of State for the Environment (1984) 75
Fourth Investments Ltd v Bury Metropolitan Borough Council (1985) .. 164, 165,
285, 334, 346
French Kier Developments Ltd v Secretary of State for the Environment
(1977) 339
Franklin v Minister of Town and Country Planning (1948) 336

G

Gouriet v Union of Post Office Workers (1978) 326
Grampian Regional Council v City of Aberdeen District Council (1984): 290, 296
Gransden (E C) & Co Ltd v Secretary of State for the Environment (1987) .. 233,
234, 307
Great Portland Estates v Westminster City Council (1985) 56, 111, 112, 139,
161, 162, 163, 165, 331, 334
Greater London Council v Secretary of State for the Environment (1983) ... 104,
166, 238
Greater London Council v Secretary of State for the Environment (1985) 331
Grenfell-Baines v Secretary of State for the Environment (1985) 314
Griffiths v Secretary of State for the Environment (1983) 333

H

Hall & Co Ltd v Shoreham by Sea Urban District Council (1964) 282
Halifax Building Society v Secretary of State for the Environment (1983): 313, 336
Hilliard v Secretary of State for the Environment (1979) 81, 82
Hussain v Secretary of State for the Environment (1971) 81

I

Iddenden v Secretary of State for the Environment (1972) 78
Inland Revenue Comrs v National Federation of Self-employed and Small
Businesses Ltd (1982) 342, 343

J

Jagendorf and Trott v Secretary of State for the Environment (1987) 338
James v Brecon County Council (1963) 74
James v Minister of Housing and Local Government (1965) 104
James v Secretary of State for Wales (1966) 104
Jones v Secretary of State for Wales (1974) 53

K

Kent County Council v Batchelor (1976) 201
King and King v Secretary of State for the Environment (1981) 318

xvi

PAGE
L
Lavender (H) & Son v Minister of Housing and Local Government (1970) . . . 338
Lord Advocate v Strathclyde Regional Council (1988) 41

M
Mason v Secretary of State for the Environment (1984) 308, 338
Metallic Protectives Ltd v Secretary of State for the Environment (1976) 318
Metropolitan Properties Co (F G C) Ltd v Lannon (1969) 336
Mid-Bedfordshire District Council v Secretary of State for the Environment
   (1984) 235

N
Newbury District Council v Secretary of State for the Environment (1981) . . . 282

O
O'Reilly v Mackman (1983) 341

P
Parkes v Secretary of State for the Environment (1979) 72
Penwith District Council v Secretary of State for the Environment (1986) . . . 239,
                                                                               334
Philglow Ltd v Secretary of State for the Environment (1984) 167
Poyser and Mills Arbitration, Re, (1964) 161
Pye (J A) (Oxford) Estates Ltd v Secretary of State for the Environment
   (1982) 168, 234, 235

R
R v Amber Valley District Council, ex p Jackson (1984) 294
R v Camden London Borough Council ex p Comyn Ching & Co (1984) 343
R v Carlisle City Council and the Secretary of State for the Environment
   (1985) 294
R v Chief Constable of Merseyside Police, ex p Carveley (1986) 345
R v City of London Corpn ex p Allen (1980) 110, 169
R v Greenwich London Borough Council, ex p Cedar Transport Group
   (1983) 344
R v Hillingdon London Borough Council, ex p Royco Homes Ltd (1974) . . . 281,
                                                                              285, 345
R v North Hertfordshire District Council, ex p Sullivan (1981) 343
R v St Edmundsbury Borough Council, ex p Investors in Industry
   Commercial Properties (1985) 217, 294, 337
R v Secretary of State for the Environment, ex p Ostler (1977) 332
R v Sevenoaks District Council, ex p Terry (1985) . . : 217, 294, 337
R v Stratford on Avon District Council, ex p Jackson (1985) 343
R v Worthing Borough Council, ex p Burch (1983) 232, 233
Rann v Secretary of State for the Environment (1980) 79, 100
Reading Borough Council v Secretary of State for the Environment (1986) . . . 340
Rhymney Valley District Council v Secretary of State for Wales (1985) . 318, 323
Rhys Williams v Secretary of State for Wales (1985) 104
Rockhold Ltd v Secretary of State for the Environment (1986): 234, 235, 237, 308
Royal London Borough of Kensington and Chelsea v Secretary of State for
   the Environment (1981) 80

PAGE

Runnymede Borough Council v Ball (1986) 326, 327, 345
Runnymede Borough Council v Smith (1986) 326, 327

S

Sears Blok v Secretary of State for the Environment (1980) 236, 308
Shanley (M J) v Secretary of State for the Environment (1982) 282, 283
Simmons v Secretary of State for the Environment (1985) 336
Sinclair-Lockhart's Trustees v Central Land Board (1950) 68
Sosmo Trust v Secretary of State for the Environment (1983) 112
Steeples (J J) v Derbyshire County Council (1984) 103, 288, 294, 295
Stringer v Minister of Housing and Local Government (1971) 338
Surrey Heath Borough Council v Secretary of State for the Environment
  (1987) 236

T

Thanet District Council v Secretary of State for the Environment (1978): 84, 339
Turner v Secretary of State for the Environment (1973) 331

W

Waverley Borough Council v Secretary of State for the Environment (1987) .. 167,
  168, 237
Wells v Minister of Housing and Local Government (1967) 72
Western Fish Products v Penwith District Council (1981) 72
Westminster Renslade Ltd v Secretary of State for the Environment (1984) ..112,
  299
White and Collins v Minister for Health (1939) 338
Windsor and Maidenhead Royal Borough Council v Brandrose Investments
  Ltd (1983) 225, 288, 292, 337
Winton v Secretary of State for the Environment (1982) 83
Wivenhoe Port Ltd v Colchester Borough Council (1985) 73
Wycombe District Council v Secretary of State for the Environment (1988) ...237

Y

Ynys Môn Borough Council v Secretary of State for the Environment (1981) ... 167

Chapter 1

Introduction to development control

> Quick they were whirled over long, straight, hopeless streets of reg-
> ularly-built houses, all small and of brick. Here and there a great oblong
> many-windowed factory stood up, like a hen among her chickens, puffing
> out black 'unparliamentary' smoke, and sufficiently accounting for the
> cloud which Margaret had taken to foretell rain. As they drove through
> the larger and wider streets, from the station to the hotel, they had to stop
> constantly; great loaded lurries blocked up the not over-wide
> thoroughfares.[1]

Town and country planning has been defined as the:

> ... art and science of ordering the use of land and the character and
> siting of buildings and communication routes so as to secure the
> maximum practicable degree of economy, convenience and beauty.[2]

Judged on these criteria, the Victorian city, realistically rather than
romantically or dramatically described by a contemporary novelist,
was clearly unplanned. Free market forces dictated the form and
location of all development, creating the bewildering mixture of
functions and qualities of environment that typified the Victorian
city. The result was an environment, which, at the turn of the
century, was unacceptable on several grounds. Firstly, it was disor-
ganised in layout which had the effect of producing inefficiencies in
communication. Secondly, its buildings were of variable quality and
age. Thirdly, it contained levels of social and economic deprivation
that were totally unacceptable, not only for those that had to suffer
them, but also for those whose task it was to administer the environment. Finally, it was evident that the free market was possibly
unwilling and probably unable to redevelop the environment in
either the manner or on the scale that was required. Naturally, this

1 Gaskell E *North and South* (first published 1854–55, republished 1970, Penguin)
 p 96.
2 Keeble L *Principles and Practice of Town and Country Planning* (4th Edn, 1969)
 p 1.

1

state of affairs stimulated debate[3] on what constituted the ideal environment, how it could be achieved and who should be responsible for instigating the change.

Gradually there emerged the concept of a planned and ordered environment with the emphasis on the importance of pleasant housing conditions. Strategies were evolved for the ordering and controlling of land uses, transport networks and the wholesale redevelopment of the then existing urban areas. Implementation of this vision was seen to depend on legislation, as only by utilising the force of the law did it seem possible to control and direct free market forces. The scheme was to be orchestrated by the local authorities, since they already had limited practical experience in urban development.[4] The first piece of legislation – the Housing, Town Planning, etc Act 1909 – gave local authorities additional powers to prepare schemes to control the development of new housing areas.

From these modest beginnings the planning system slowly started to develop, and this development has been well documented elsewhere.[5] It only needs to be said that by 1947 the modern system of town and country planning had emerged. The means by which its philosophy would be put into practice was provided by the Town and Country Planning Act 1947. Subsequent legislation, the Town and Country Planning Act 1971, for example, has changed the details of the system, but its underlying characteristics remain undisturbed. It is that system which forms the focus of this book.

Development control

Until this point, reference has been made to the emergence of town and country planning as a discipline charged with securing an orderly and pleasant environment. This book, however, is concerned not with town and country planning in general, but with one specific aspect of that discipline, namely, an analysis of the develop-

3 For example: Geddes P *Cities in Evolution* (1949); Howard E *Garden Cities of Tomorrow* (Reprint 1985).
4 For example, the Public Health Act 1875 gave local authorities not only the power to ensure the provision of public health facilities, such as sewers, but also to control building densities and the width of streets. The Artisans and Labourers Dwellings Improvement Acts 1875 and 1879 allowed local authorities to undertake slum clearance, while the Housing of the Working Classes Act 1890 allowed them to build housing.
5 For example: Cherry G E *The Evolution of British Town Planning* (1974); Cullingworth J B *Peacetime History of Environmental Planning* (1978–80); Ashworth W *The Genesis of Modern British Town Planning* (1954).

ment control system in England and Wales. Scotland and Northern Ireland are excluded from that analysis as the arrangements for town and country planning, and consequently development control in those countries, are somewhat different from those experienced in England and Wales. To have attempted to take account of these differences would, it was felt, have made the analysis unnecessarily complex, whilst at the same time, obscuring the principles of development control that it is the intention of this work to explore.

As the first step in this analysis, therefore, the relationship which exists between town and country planning and development control in England and Wales will be explained. Town and country planning consists, according to those commentators who have ventured an opinion on the matter, of a philosophy on the use of land which seeks to attain an environment which is most pleasing to the community as a whole. Ideas and opinions on the practical changes which are necessary to achieve this utopia vary with the times. Densely packed terraced housing set in a gridiron pattern of streets constituted the standard form of housing up to the Second World War. In post-war Britain this form of housing was no longer considered appropriate, and the concrete high-rise tower blocks of the 1960s were seen as the ideal replacement. Within a decade, however, these were seen as unacceptable and the low-rise, high density blocks were produced as an alternative. Today these are seen as inadequate in terms of the housing environment they provide, and the trend is towards more traditional housing at a low density, preferably with gardens. If town and country planning can, therefore, be taken to represent the search for the unattainable ideal environment in the form in which it is currently perceived as most obtainable, what is the process of development control?

The Department of the Environment,[6] which at present is responsible for administering the planning system, frequently employs the term 'development control' but never adequately defines it. This may be because the term is self-explanatory, simply denoting the process of controlling development. If this is true, then the key issue is those principles on the basis of which control is exercised. At this stage in the argument it is essential to appreciate the derivation of the goals of town and country planning, since development control represents a means of realising schemes which are judged to advance these goals at any particular time, whilst restricting those that do not. The problem is that there may be considerable

6 The Department of the Environment was established in 1970 (SI 1970 No 1681). Prior to that planning had been the responsibility of the Ministry of Housing and Local Government, established in its initial form in 1951. Its predecessor, the Ministry of Town and Country Planning, was established in 1943.

disagreement on what those goals are and how they can best be achieved.[7] In addition, the price that has to be paid for attaining the ideal environment through the process of development control is seen in some quarters as a heavy one. In a recent White Paper entitled 'Lifting the Burden'[8] the view was expressed that the notion of controlling development could stifle enterprise and the creation of jobs.

In the past, books have been devoted to individual aspects of what is undoubtedly the multi-faceted process of town and country planning. There are, therefore, books to be found on the law of town and country planning,[9] the philosophy of planning[10] and the practice of planning.[11] Yet each of these does not tell the whole story. Take, for example, section 29(1) of the Town and Country Planning Act 1971. This provides that:

> ... where an application is made to a local planning authority for planning permission, that authority, in dealing with the application, shall have regard to the provisions of the development plan, so far as material to the application, and to any other material considerations...

To understand fully the terms of this particular subsection it is not enough to know what constitutes a development plan or its purpose, or simply to appreciate the legal meaning of 'other material considerations'. To understand these aspects of development control more completely it is also necessary to have some insight into the philosophy of town and country planning. What the succeeding chapters of this work will seek to illustrate, therefore, is this integrated approach, an approach which is, moreover, focused on this particular facet of the system – development control. The reference to policy into practice found in the title is also a comment upon the purpose of the work, which is to demonstrate how these integrated

7 Disagreement seems to focus on the prioritisation of the goals, that is, should the main goal be to improve society or to improve the environment and hope that society will consequently also improve? One means of prioritising the goals is by weighting them according to their ability to be achieved. This then produces the argument that only the easiest goals will be aimed for, rather than the most important. For two good discussions of this view of planning, see Chadwick G *A Systems View of Planning* (1971); McLoughlin J B *Urban and Regional Planning: A Systems Approach* (1969).
8 Cmnd 9571.
9 For example: Grant M *Urban Planning Law* (1982, updated 1986); Telling A E *Planning Law and Procedure* (7th Edn, 1986); Heap D *An Outline of Planning Law* (9th Edn, 1987).
10 For example: MacAuslan P *Land, Law and Planning* (1975) and *The Ideologies of Planning Law* (1980); Faludi A *A Reader in Planning Theory* (1973); Harvey D *Social Justice and the City* (1973).
11 For example: *Keeble*; Cullingworth J B *Town and Country Planning in Britain* (1972); Burke G *Town Planning and the Surveyor* (1980).

ideas and subsequent policies of town and country planning are transformed, through the process of development control, into an environmental reality. Not that this transfer from concept to practice has always been successfully achieved. Witness, for example, the transformation of Le Corbusier's[12] cities in the sky, surrounded by acres of unspoilt countryside, into high-rise tower blocks set amid a sea of urban decay. The purpose of this book, however, is not to pass judgment on such individual policies; instead, it aims to demonstrate exactly how the development control system takes such policies and makes them into a reality.

The development control system at work

The development control system effectively works on two levels. An indication is given by the local planning authority of what it considers to be the ideal environment for a particular area in a document called a development plan. It is a legal requirement that local planning authorities prepare such a plan.[13] In addition, a local planning authority is given the power, by virtue of the 1971 Act, to control development in its area by making sure that any development proposed will be in accordance with the development plan and other material circumstances.[14] What constitutes development is defined in section 22(1) of the 1971 Act as:

> ... the carrying out of building, engineering, mining or other operations in, on, over or under land, or the making of any material change in the use of any buildings or other land.

The correct legal interpretation of this definition is an extensive topic for consideration in its own right, and has formed the basis for much comment.[15] Indeed, the importance of understanding what development is thought to mean in law will be considered in Chapter 3, but initially it is sufficient to realise that the local planning authority considers, in the first instance, whether or not a particular activity does constitute development. If development is thought to

12 Le Corbusier *Concerning Town Planning* (1947).
13 The term 'development plan' covers a range of plans that can date from the Town and Country Planning Act 1947. At present it is a requirement by virtue of s 7(1) of the Town and Country Planning Act 1971 that county authorities in England and Wales prepare structure plans. By virtue of the Local Government Act 1985, Sch 1, para 2(1), each of the London borough councils and each of the metropolitan district councils must prepare a unitary plan.
14 1971 Act, s 29(1).
15 See, for example, *Grant*, ch 4; *Telling*, ch 5.

be involved, the individual contemplating such activity requires planning permission.[16]

Even at this early stage the complexity of the development control system should be apparent, as should be the various forces which are at work. On the one hand, there is the local planning authority's plan for an ideal environment in its administrative area. On the other, there is the individual who wishes to undertake an activity which might have an impact on the environment. The proposed activity and the plan are thus compared, and their compatibility assessed, provided the activity in question constitutes development, for if it does not, no matter how considerable its impact may be on the environment, it cannot be controlled through the system of development control. Perhaps this situation is best illustrated by an example.

The owner of a fine old Victorian pier at a popular seaside resort wishes to attract more visitors onto his pier. Consequently, he purchases an inflatable pink elephant, thirty feet high and forty feet long, which he attaches to the roof of the pier's concert hall. The local authority immediately indicates to the pier owner that planning permission is necessary before the elephant can be displayed, as its erection constitutes development. In these circumstances the likelihood is that planning permission will be refused, since such a device is hardly in keeping with the architectural character of the Victorian pier. Probably, therefore, there will be a direct conflict of interest between the local planning authority's view of an appropriate environment, the pier owner's need to make a profit, and the legal question of whether such a device constitutes development. Does the erection of an inflatable and thus intrinsically non-permanent pink elephant constitute a 'building, engineering, mining or other operation in, on, over or under land'? If it does not, then the pier owner can display the elephant, however out of keeping with the environment the device may be.

It is the application for planning permission that is the deceptively simple process which lies at the heart of the development control system. It marks the start of the attempt to turn policy into practice. What follows, therefore, is a general description of that process in order that its salient points may be appreciated and the chief actors emerge. Before proceeding, however, a word needs to be said about this choice of starting point. As will become evident as the system is analysed in more detail, one of the major problems in attempting to explain the development control system is its essentially circular nature. Consequently, it is difficult to decide where to break into that circle at the point that will be most appropriate in

16 1971 Act, s 23(1).

introducing the whole system. Names and labels have already been used that mean a great deal to the reader who understands something of the organisation of planning, and the legal system within this country, but which, to the total novice, may mean little or nothing at present. In this introduction, therefore, the intention is to present the whole system in outline, while the details will be expanded upon in the rest of the work. This still leaves the problem of the chosen starting point – the application for planning permission. This is chosen as the most obvious starting place since, in reality, it represents the point from which many would-be developers start in their own attempts to comprehend, and, indeed, comply with the planning system. Having established this pragmatic justification, therefore, it is possible to return to the consideration of an application for planning permission.

Essentially anyone, either an individual or a corporate body,[17] who intends to undertake some activity that constitutes development, must apply to the local planning authority for planning permission. An application is made in writing on the appropriate form supplied by the local planning authority. This requires either a broad description of the proposed development or detailed drawings of what is proposed, depending on whether the application is for 'outline' or 'full' planning permisssion.[18] When the authority receives the application it is considered first by the planning officers, whose job it is to examine the proposals in the light of how they may affect the building or buildings, if any are involved, the surrounding area, and any planning policy, particularly in the form of development plans. This analysis is undertaken, not only by taking into account physical and land use factors, but also by considering less tangible factors that relate to the social and economic criteria of the location and its containing area. The planning officers do not usually take the final decision on the planning application, however, as this is a matter for the local planning authority in the form of the elected representatives[19] on the planning committee who are guided by the planning officers, but are,

17 An individual member of the public, a group of people forming some type of organisation, a company either public or private, a local authority or any form of local or central government organisation – all can apply for planning permission.
18 An outline application may be made in respect of a development involving a building operation only. It effectively establishes the principle of the right to develop, if it is allowed. The application consists only of the site plan and a brief description of the proposed development. A full application involves providing far more detail regarding the proposed development, including plans and drawings. See the Town and Country Planning General Development Order 1977, SI 1977 No 289, articles 5, 6 and 7.
19 The councillors elected to sit on the council also comprise the planning committee which makes the decisions regarding the planning applications.

7

nevertheless, free to reach their own decision.

At this stage, the parties involved in the planning system possibly need some introduction. Effectively, two principal parties have been introduced, in the form of the developer, who is seeking planning permission, and the local planning authority, which is considering the application with a view to approving or rejecting it. These parties in no way represent all the actors involved in the development control process, as will be fully explained in Chapter 2. Furthermore, the developer and the local planning authority do not represent structurally simple entities. To show them as such, even at this stage, would be a gross over-simplification, as the developer and the local planning authority are both potentially rather more complex.

A local planning authority has certain specified legal duties to undertake in its area of administration. Amongst these duties there is the requirement to control development, but on the basis of what criteria is not very clear. Theoretically, the present planning system was created as a means of ensuring that central government policy concerning land use and development was translated down to a local level, with local planning authorities acting as the main control mechanism. In reality, however, it can justifiably be argued that central government land use policy has never materialised in a cohesive form and that, as a consequence, local planning authorities have had to establish their own criteria for judging what constitutes appropriate development. Elements of central policy undoubtedly do exist to control, to a certain extent, the actions of local planning authorities. These include the structure plan,[20] which has to obtain central government approval, and Department of the Environment circulars,[1] but effectively the majority of development control decisions are made by the local planning authority in whose area the development is proposed. What criteria do local planning authorities, therefore, employ in reaching their decisions?

In order to fully answer this question it must first be understood that the term 'local planning authority' is potentially a misleading term. Within any local planning authority, two groups of individuals have a contribution to make whenever a development control decision is taken. On the one hand, there is the chief planning officer and his professional planning team, on the other, there are the local councillors. A planning officer is apolitical, giving his opinion as a professional planner on the positive or negative effects

20 Structure plans are a particular form of development plan described fully in Chapter 4.
1 Department of the Environment circulars are a particular form of central government policy advice and are considered fully in Chapter 6.

on the local community of a proposed development. The councillors, on the other hand, who are unlikely to be professional planners, may take account of the political implications of a particular application. Where, for example, an application involves industrial development, the planning officers might recommend that the application should be refused for some perfectly valid planning reasons – the road network is unsuitable for the increased flow of heavy goods traffic that the development would produce; the proposal is too large and unsightly in an area designated for inclusion in a green belt. The councillors may accept the truth of these criticisms, but may still decide to give their approval to the development as it will bring new jobs and investment to the area at a time of recession. It is difficult to say in these circumstances who has made the right decision, as each party has a perfectly valid point of view.

This increasingly intricate pattern of decision-making is further complicated when that other major actor, the developer, is included. It should not be imagined that the local planning authority is the most significant element within the planning system, simply because the discussion so far has concentrated on that body. Arguably, the role of the developer is the more important, as without his desire to undertake what constitutes development, there would be no role for the local planning authority to perform. Developers effectively fall into two groups – the public and the private developer – and the motivations of each group tend to be distinctive. The public developer, that is, a local authority or some branch of central government, is normally motivated by the public need for a particular development, without undue concern for the eventual profitability of the investment. This is, of course, not to suggest that public bodies undertake development with a total disregard to costs, which is very far from the truth, but rather, that the motivation for the development is more related to public need, or possibly a perceived public need, than an eventual profit. In contrast, the private developer, whilst also being concerned with public needs in the form of market demands, is normally concerned with the potential profitability of a proposed development.

At this point it becomes necessary to reconsider more fully the role of the planning committee, and its relationship with the planning officers, as it is the committee, rather than the officers, that usually takes the decisions on planning applications. The planning committee comprises a number of local councillors placed on the committee as the nominees of the different political parties they represent. Political representation on the committee is in proportion to a party's political strength on the council as a whole, with the chairman usually being a member of the majority party. As with all forms of local authority work, the councillors are advised by a permanent professional staff of local government officers, whose additional duty it is to carry out the instructions of the duly elected council.

With the exception of certain minor planning applications, all planning applications are brought before the planning committee, usually on a monthly basis. Among the documents which accompany each application will be the recommendation of the chief planning officer, who is responsible for presenting the applications to the committee. The committee may call upon the chief planning officer or some other member of his team, to explain any recommendation more fully, as well as hearing the comments of the applicant. Any member of the public also has the right to make representations[2] regarding the application, but usually they have to be content with submitting any such comments in writing. Having taken account of all these opinions, the committee then normally reaches one of four possible decisions. Firstly, they may consider that the application is important enough, or indeed is contentious enough, to be brought before the full council of the local authority and a decision will be deferred. Secondly, they may choose to reject the application outright. Thirdly, they may accept the application as it stands. Finally, they may approve the application subject to certain conditions.[3] The important point to realise at this stage is that the planning committee can reach any of these decisions regardless of any advice offered, or recommendation made, by the planning officers. This simple fact obviously raises many questions that lie at the very foundation, not only of the planning system, but of the system of local government in England and Wales, and aspects of this complex question will be considered in subsequent chapters.

At this point, however, the general outline of the procedures involved in an application for planning permission may usefully be illustrated by way of two examples. In these, an attempt will be made to illustrate in some detail the range of issues that have to be taken into account before the local planning authority reaches its decision. These issues are very broadly defined in section 29(1) of the 1971 Act as comprising the provisions of the development plan and any other material considerations. As will now become apparent, however, the phrase 'other material considerations' is a catch-

2 The operation of development control is undertaken in public, for the public good, so it follows that any member of the public may make his opinions known.
3 Planning permission may be subject to various conditions attached by the local planning authority as it thinks fit (s 29). These conditions must fulfil certain specific criteria, however, which are examined fully in Chapter 8.

all concept that is of fundamental importance to the effective working of the development control system. It enables the planning officers, in the first instance, to take into account any factors that are thought to be relevant to the application and its potential effect on the neighbourhood.

Two examples of development control

THE FIRST EXAMPLE

The intention is to consider an application for planning permission to convert a large Victorian villa into six separate flats. Such a villa would probably be located in the inner residential suburbs of a substantial town or city, in an area that contains buildings that are similar in both size and age. Faced with such an application, therefore, what factors are taken into account by the local planning officers before they recommend to the planning committee whether planning permission should be granted or refused?

Local planning policy All factual development control issues would be considered against a background of both local and national planning policies, and the forms these policies take can now be considered. At the local level, the planning officers would have to consult two basic policy sources – the development plan and any additional informal policy documentation. The development plan is not usually a simple document. In fact, the term 'development plan' can refer to a collection of plans that are likely to have been prepared by different local authorities.[4] Firstly, there will be a structure plan,[5] which will have been prepared by the county planning authority and approved by the Secretary of State for the Environment. This deals in broad outline with planning issues that concern the whole county. In the example under consideration, the structure plan may be consulted for information on the county-wide projections of housing need, or possibly some general policy relating to the redevelopment of old inner-city housing. The structure plan will not be site specific however, that is, it will not mention any specific location beyond the area or district. For a level of detail that may include specific planning policies and guidelines for the actual area within which the proposed development is situated, the planning officers will have to consult either a local plan,[6] or what is

4 Circular 22/84, Memorandum on Structure and Local Plans, para 1.6, gives the full definition of what may comprise the development plan.
5 1971 Act, ss 7–10.
6 1971 Act, ss 11–15.

termed the 'old style' development plan.[7]

The local plan will be a recent planning document prepared and approved by either the county or district planning authority. It sets out in considerable detail local planning policies that are drawn from the broad policies of the structure plan. These local policies will offer some specific advice, both about the area as a whole and the actual site of the proposed development. The land use of the site will be indicated, for example, together with the suggested housing density for that area. Policies will also be found concerning multiple occupation, social mix and public transport, and all can be referred to by the planning officers when considering the proposal. If such a local plan does not exist, however, it should be possible to consult the 'old style' development plan, which will contain far less information but will indicate the acceptable land use for the specific site, and may indicate what were considered to be the acceptable housing densities at the time the plan was approved.[8] Finally, attention must be paid to any revisions which are in hand to the content of either the structure or local plans, since these revisions might affect the proposed development.

All these plans, therefore, comprise what is known as statutory planning policy and have to undergo legally prescribed procedures before they become official planning documents.[9] It must not be thought, however, that these plans have to be followed slavishly in every detail, as it is acknowledged by all parties involved that the plans cannot take account of every local variation. Consequently, local planning officers would use these documents as a guide only in their consideration of the application. These plans are, nevertheless, obviously of fundamental importance in the development control system and are therefore considered in detail in Chapter 4, where their practical impact on the planning system is assessed.

Apart from statutory planning policy, other forms of local planning policy might exist and furnish additional guidance on whether or not to allow the villa to be converted into flats. Some of this policy may be in the form of informal policy. Informal planning policy means that the policy in question, although it has been produced by the local planning officers, has not gone through all the

---

7 Plans prepared under the Town and Country Planning Act 1947.

8 Plans prepared under the Town and Country Planning Act 1947 were to be regularly revised but in many instances this did not occur. After the 1971 Act came into operation such existing plans could not be revised, only superseded, and this has still not happened in many parts of the country. Consequently, the old plan may still remain as a valid planning document.

9 The procedures for approval of both structure and local plans are to be found in the 1971 Act, ss 7–15 and the Town and Country Planning (Structure and Local Plans) Regulations 1982, SI 1982 No 555.

legal procedures that are used to create development plans. As a consequence, documents containing such policy are used only as an indication of, rather than an actual specific guide to, local planning policy. In some instances, however, this informal policy elaborates upon some of the information in a local plan, indicating, for example, what are regarded as appropriate window or door designs when refurbishing old houses in particular districts. Although these documents would therefore be consulted by the local planning officers, they would not be given as much weight as the proposals in the local plan.

Many other forms of local policy will also be found to exist which have a formal basis within the planning system. Indeed, the range and form of this type of policy is enormous and whilst not, in theory, having the same importance as the development plan, it still plays a vital part in the development control process, especially when it is realised that all forms of development plans will not necessarily exist for, or, indeed, cover the site of the planning application. With this in mind, therefore, such local policy will be examined in detail in Chapter 5 where its different forms with their varying impact upon the system will become apparent.

National planning policy Having consulted these local policy documents and related their contents to the particular application, the planning officers would then consider any policy guidance available from the Department of the Environment. This comes in two forms, either as policy notes[10] and circulars, or as Acts of Parliament and their related statutory instruments.

Taking these legal materials first, the local planning officers may, for example, consult sections 54 to 58 of the 1971 Act which deal with listed buildings, since, given the age of the building in the example, it may have been given this special protection.[11] In order to understand more fully the consequences of a proposal to alter a listed building, the planning officers might then consult the Town and Country Planning (Listed Buildings and Buildings in Conservation Areas) Regulations 1987[12] which stipulate the mandatory procedures relating to these specially protected buildings. These legal sources of reference, however, usually deal with the procedures that have to be followed by the local planning authority,

10 Policy notes are a form of central government advice on general planning issues. They are published infrequently at present but, despite the fact that some are nearly 20 years old, they still stand as policy advice.
11 1971 Act, s 54 gives the Secretary of State the power to protect buildings. The implications of this are fully explained in Circular 8/87, Historic Buildings and Conservation Areas – Policy and Procedures.
12 SI 1987 No 349.

rather than giving any guidance on matters of policy or interpretation. They are therefore important as they, among other things, supply the framework within which the planning system operates.

Of far more help probably to the planning officers at this stage is that other form of Department of the Environment guidance – the circular. If indeed the building is listed, the planning officers could turn to the advice to be found in Circular 8/87,[13] which gives comprehensive general guidance. The importance, for example, of discovering a suitable use for a listed building is emphasised, and residential uses are especially mentioned.[14] The significance of the setting of the building is examined and it is even suggested that local authorities should seek expert advice on the quality and potential of the building from bodies such as the Historic Buildings and Monuments Commission for England.[15] All this general advice would be taken into account when considering the specific proposals for the particular building used in this example if it were listed, and it would be interpreted in relation to all the local factors. Clearly this aspect of the Department of the Environment's input into the planning system is especially significant. As Sir Desmond Heap states in the preface to *An Outline of Planning Law*:

> . . . Government comment in this sphere is important because in matters of planning control it is not so much the letter of the law which counts as the manner in which the law is going to be administered.[16]

Chapter 6 of this book will, consequently, assess Department of the Environment policy, taking into account its use by all parties concerned with development control, as well as considering the forms this policy can take.

Other factors The local planning officers' search for information is not yet complete, however, as other sources of published data still remain. Of major importance would be the planning history, if any, of the site in question. This is the record of any previous planning applications and their outcome. If permission had been given in the past for a similar development on the site this would have to be taken into account by the planning officers, even if, as would obviously be the case, the old permission had expired.[17] Details of similar applications in the area would also be of interest, but it

13 Historic Buildings and Conservation Areas – Policy and Procedure.
14 Circular 8/87, paras 19–24.
15 Circular 8/87, paras 12–18.
16 8th Edn, 1982, p ix.
17 Full planning permission normally lasts for five years from the date of the approval – 1971 Act, s 41. Outline planning permission lasts for three years – 1971 Act, s 42.

should be realised that the legal concept of precedent[18] does not apply to a planning application. In other words, if approval has recently been given for a similar development only a few yards away in the same road, this does not mean that approval will also be given for this application. The reasons for this are obvious, since the planning officers have to take into account whether there is a need for such a development, or whether there are already too many developments of this kind in the area. In addition, the unique location of every site produces different problems relating, for example, to traffic and access.

This argument usefully introduces the other all-important task that has to be undertaken by the planning officers in taking into account material considerations. This involves a detailed examination of the proposals in the light of how they might affect both the building, the site and the immediate locality. The significance of these factors is considered in Chapter 7 where a sequence of possible sites and forms of development are examined.

In the context of the example being considered, the most obvious factors are probably those that relate to the effect of the proposals on the building itself. The existing condition of the building would be likely to be taken into account. If, for example, the building is in a run down or even a semi-derelict condition, then the planning officers may be inclined to favour the proposals, as this would result in the elimination of an 'eyesore' from the area. If, on the other hand, the building is still being used as a single family dwelling and is in good condition, then this might militate against the proposals. The planning officers would also assess what physical effects, if any, the proposals would have on the fabric of the building. Would the new flats require a new entrance, or even entrances, to be formed, possibly at first and second floor levels? Such additions would clearly have a marked effect on the building's outward appearance, so attention would have to be paid to their proposed position, whether or not they could be seen from adjacent properties or roads, their design and the materials to be employed in their construction. Having considered the effect of the proposals on the fabric of the building, the planning officers would then turn their attention to the immediate site. Would the proposals necessitate either the removal of existing out-buildings, or possibly the building of new ones, such as garages? If buildings were removed, would this

18 Precedent in a judicial context means that inferior courts are bound to follow a decision of a superior court on a legal issue such as the interpretation of a statute. In the context of development control there is no such concept, though if an inspector chooses to disregard the decisions of other inspectors brought to his attention, it is important that he give his reasons for so doing.

affect the privacy of the site or surrounding sites, and if new buildings were constructed how might this affect the visual appearance of the site? The interest of planning officers extends beyond buildings to the protection of mature trees,[19] especially if any trees would have to be felled, as well as to any minor man-made features, such as old garden walls or stone gateposts.

Besides taking the physical effects of the proposals into account, the planning officers would also turn their attention to the wider implications of the proposed development. Since, for example, it is proposed to intensify the use of the building, this will produce more vehicular and pedestrian traffic. Consequently, an examination should be undertaken of how these increases might affect existing local traffic. What level of traffic already uses the road onto which the 'new' traffic will exit? What is the exact position of this exit in relation to other existing exits and road junctions? Is there any possibility that the exit point is likely to be dangerous, or will the increase in traffic produce levels of noise that are unacceptable? Again, there are likely to be local and national planning policies on these matters which would have to be considered in conjunction with the local factors.

Another issue might be the demand for the accommodation proposed and the likely effect its provision might have on local facilities, such as shops and schools. The conversion of the house into flats might be seen as a benefit if, as was mentioned, the house was in a poor structural condition, and there was a local need for accommodation of this nature. There may be many reasons, however, why such accommodation is not suitable for all types of family – too small, no garden, no play area for children, too many stairs and no lift – and so local need would have to be judged on detailed information indicating the types of household seeking accommodation. Account would also be taken of whether the flats were for sale or for rent, not because of the financial implications of the two forms of tenure, but rather in order to assess the likely effect on the locality. If the house was in a poor condition, while all other houses were in a good condition and were owner-occupied, then the conversion of the property into flats for sale would probably be the planners' first choice, flats for rent being slightly less acceptable as this could alter the social mix[20] of the area. On the other hand, if this was the first such conversion proposed, the alteration in the social mix would be so slight as to be unimportant, but if many of the older

19 Specified trees can be protected by the making of a tree preservation order under the 1971 Act, s 60.
20 A sociological term that refers to the mixture of social classes within an area, for example, the number of manual workers to the number of clerical workers to the number of professionals.

houses in the area have already undergone such alteration, then the planning officers have to decide if the social mix of the area should continue to change.

Then there is the related issue of the possible impact of the development on facilities in the area, which would depend, in turn, on whether or not the proposals are the first of their kind, or the latest of many. Concern will focus on the local shops, primary school, public facilities and public transport, and whether they can cope with the increased demand. Naturally, the form of demand is related to the type of occupier likely to be attracted to the proposed development, and this fact would be taken into account. Clearly, one of the concerns could be the age of the likely occupiers, as different age groups place different demands on different local services – young families with children need schools, older people may need a wide range of medical services. Another factor might be the social class of the inhabitants, and whether they are private car users, as this could have an effect on the demand for public transport facilities.

Finally, two remaining sources of information need to be considered. Firstly, colleagues within the department may be consulted on a formal or informal basis, as may colleagues from departments representing other aspects of the local authority's duties, such as the architects' department or the estates and valuers' department. Indeed, in some cases it may be a statutory duty to consult adjacent local authorities or even civil servants representing other forms of administrative or policy body.[1] Secondly, the planning officer, or rather his planning authority, is under a duty to consult the public. Exactly how this is done varies depending on the nature and location of the proposed development,[2] but at the very least, a notice of the application for planning permission is usually published in the local newspapers, which gives any member of the public an opportunity to contact the local planning authority with comments on the scheme.

The planning officers then take all the information they have accumulated and reach a conclusion, accompanied by their reasons, whether or not, in their opinion, planning permission should be granted. This conclusion is then presented, as has already been outlined, in the form of a recommendation to the local councillors who sit on the planning committee of the local council, and it is these elected representatives who actually make the decision in each instance.

1 Consultations are normally prescribed by the Town and Country Planning General Development Order 1977, SI 1977 No 289, article 15.
2 For example, as prescribed for unneighbourly development – 1971 Act, s 26(7); or for development in conservation areas – 1971 Act, s 28(3).

Before returning to a consideration of the next stage in the possible progress of a planning application, it is undoubtedly useful to illustrate the many factors which have to be taken into account, by way of another contrasting example. This will not only ensure that the procedure is clearly understood in outline, but will also allow the introduction of other aspects of the planning system that would have been inappropriate in the first example.

THE SECOND EXAMPLE

By way of contrast, it will now be assumed that a planning application has been received with a proposal to develop a new factory on the outskirts of a large town. The proposed development will cover 25 acres of land which at present is being used as arable pasture. The plan is to build 15 one-storey industrial units together with related delivery and parking spaces.

As in the previous example, the planning officers will have to consider a wide range of information and they can assess this in any order they think fit. Arguably, the procedure adopted in the first example is the most logical, that is, the working 'inwards' from the broad policy issues that are invariably documented, concluding with a site analysis. Naturally, the specific site of the proposed development will have to be borne in mind at all times, as the broader policy issues have to be related to the particular application, but it is often easier to consider the wider implications of the application first, because if these are totally unacceptable, there is little point in considering the site in any detail.

Local planning policy In considering this second example, the planning officers can start their assessment by referring to the development plan. Immediately several broad issues may be raised by policies to be found within both the structure and local plans. The structure plan, for example, will almost invariably contain policy proposals relating to industrial development and employment, and both of these will probably be encouraged in general terms. It is also likely, however, that the plan will contain proposals concerning the need to prevent the incursion of urban areas into the countryside, with the resulting loss of high grade agricultural land. When applied to the proposed development, therefore, it may well be that these policies appear contradictory and in the circumstances it is only the planning officers 'on the spot' who can begin to unravel the problem. Obviously, the next step would be to consult the local plan, if one exists, as this will show any planning proposals for the site in considerably greater detail. The local plan may indicate that the area is part of a green belt,[3] in which case the proposed industrial development is likely to be regarded as inappropriate, unless, of course, other planning policies exist, demonstrating that there is a very specific local need for employment. Alternatively, the planning officers may discover that no land has been allocated within the local plan as appropriate for industrial development of the type proposed, as part of a deliberate policy to relocate such development in another part of the county. On the other hand, there may be clear statements within the local plan emphasising the need to keep existing industry within the area. If this is so and the application has been made by a local industrialist who wishes to expand his business, but is unable to do so on his existing site, the situation may not be as clear cut as it first appeared. Effectively, therefore, the planning officers have to weigh up all the relevant policies within the statutory development plans in order to form at least a broad impression of the general policy as it affects the application.

The planning officers could then turn to a consideration of any other policy documentation that may exist locally and that relates in any way to the application. There may, for example, be no informal statements regarding industry, but advice notes may well exist on the form of landscaping which is desirable when industrial developments of this nature are proposed. The planning officers may also look to organisations, other than central and local government, for relevant information, such as annual reports from local Chambers of Commerce and Industry. Such information is obviously less important than formally established planning policy, but would form part of the total information package that the planning officers are seeking to create in relation to the application.

National planning policy In the case of this type of development, however, there may be other important policies apart from development plans, which may be of crucial importance in the deliberations of the planning officers. Industrial development plays a key role in the national land policy of the present government, as indeed it has done with previous governments. As a result of some quite specific legislation,[4] this government has sought to encourage industry by creating enterprise zones.[5] If the proposals under discussion were to relate to land within one of these designated zones, almost thirty of which are scattered over England and Wales, then plan-

3 A particular form of planning policy designed to prevent the undue outward spread of an urban area into the countryside. See Circular 14/84, Green Belts.
4 Local Government, Planning and Land Act 1980, s 179, Sch 32.
5 An enterprise zone is a designated area within which various benefits, such as exemption from certain taxes and planning controls, are allowed with the aim of encouraging commercial development.

ning permission for the industrial proposals would be virtually certain, as the prime policy objective in establishing these zones is to encourage just such development. Other special areas of various kinds also exist (a product of national land use policy) and whilst some of these are designed to encourage industry, others, such as the National Parks,[6] are founded on policies that would actively discourage industrial development, except in very specific locations. In practice, therefore, various 'official' policy statements may have to be taken into account in relation to the proposed development.

Recourse will then be had to the advice proffered in the policy notes and circulars from the Department of the Environment. As in the previous example, there may well be specific notes and circulars that relate directly to the proposed development, for example, Policy Note 3, Industrial and Commercial Development, or Circular 16/84, Industrial Development. In addition, there may be circulars which contain advice on a wider topic, such as Circular 14/85, Development and Employment, which also relate to the proposals. In every instance, however, it is important to stress that such documentation is nothing more than advisory and must be interpreted in the light of local policy and conditions.

Other factors   The next stage would involve a consideration of the planning history, if any, of the site, as well as an examination of any similar developments that may have been undertaken in the local authority area in the immediate past. Again, it must be appreciated that the planning officers are not looking for any binding precedents, but are simply trying to establish a background of information against which to consider the particular application that is before them.

Ultimately, therefore, their examination will concentrate on the area within which the development is proposed, and on a detailed consideration of its possible effects. As with the first example, there are two levels to such an investigation: the possible effects on the area in the immediate vicinity of the site as well as the possible effects on the site itself. In this example, an obvious concern would be the volume of traffic that such a development could conceivably generate, which would be on a very much greater scale than the traffic generated by the small residential development considered in the first example. In this instance, not only the quantity but also the nature of the traffic would be relevant, as industrial developments are likely to generate heavy goods traffic as well as cars and vans.

6 The National Parks and Access to the Countryside Act 1949 established National Parks with a view to protecting the natural beauty of the area for the enjoyment of the public.

Calculations of the likely numbers and type of vehicles, as well as the rate of vehicles per hour would therefore be attempted, probably with the help of the local authority's own transport planning section and traffic engineers. Substantial increases in traffic would have an impact, not merely in the vicinity of the proposed development, but over a much wider area, especially at junctions and at any accident black spots. In reality, however, it would be surprising if the developer who had proposed such a scheme, had not already taken these important factors into account and ensured that the site was well situated, with a connection to either a main trunk road, or preferably a motorway. This might not be attributable to the developer's concern over the environmental implications of his proposal, but is more likely to be linked to commercial considerations which demand good transport links for industrial developments.

Apart from its impact upon the existing road network, the proposed development might have implications for other services, such as housing. On the question of housing provision, the type of industrial development intended would be crucial, as different groups within the workforce might require different forms of housing. Clearly, many related factors are involved. For example, if it is assumed that the proposed development intends to concentrate on high technology industry, then it can also be assumed that the workforce will consist of either highly technically skilled, or highly qualified individuals. If this development will represent a move into the area by an existing company, then a proportion of its present workforce may wish to move with it, and will require housing. If the workers belong to a relatively high socio-economic class,[7] it may be assumed that they will enter the private housing market, so that the planning officers will have to take account of the availability of such housing within this area. In addition, given the workers' socio-economic class, the planning officers would also be aware that they probably have a high level of car ownership and could consequently journey to work over a considerable distance, thus distributing the likely housing demand. If, on the other hand, it is assumed that the proposed development will be made up of mixed, small-scale industrial enterprises, with a workforce consisting mainly of semi-skilled or unskilled workers, then the need would be for public-sector rented accommodation, situated in the near vicinity and enjoying good public transport links with the site.

Once the implications which the proposal may have for the wider area have been evaluated, attention can be focused on the site.

7 Socio-economic classes are a means of classifying the population according to their income and the status of their job. Class 1 would be a professional with an above average income, class 5 would be a manual labourer with a minimum wage.

Many factors will have to be considered, including the density of buildings covering the site, the internal road layout, the proposed access points and the design of the development. On the question of design, the planning officers are likely to be concerned, not only with the appearance of the industrial units, their size, height, colour and the materials to be used in their construction, but also with the visual impact of the development as a whole. In these circumstances the inclusion of proposals to landscape the perimeter of the site, or their omission, may be crucial, given that the location is in the countryside immediately adjacent to an urban area.

Finally, public reaction to the proposals will be sought, and any views expressed should be taken into account by the planning officers in drafting their recommendation on the application. At this juncture, the planning committee will reach a decision on the planning application for the proposed industrial development. This is the same stage at which the first example was concluded. In using these two distinct examples, it has been possible to illustrate some of the diverse forms of policy and information that have to be considered in resolving any application for planning permission. In the subsequent stages of this introductory examination of the development control process, however, it is no longer necessary to refer in any detail to either example. This is because the procedures involved are either administrative, and thus take no account of the particular facts of an application, or are likely to cover the same information about policy and site detail already considered in the examples.

The decision

When the planning committee takes a decision on a planning application, it has a number of options open to it. The major options are either to refuse a grant of planning permission, or to grant planning permission with or without conditions. It is also possible for a planning committee to approve a proposed development in principle, leaving detailed matters to be resolved at a later date. This is the effect of granting outline planning permission. It is not necessary at the introductory stage to consider these different forms of decision in any greater detail, as they will be fully examined in Chapter 8, except to note that where the planning committee approves an application, that approval is subject to time limits within which a start must have been made on the development. A refusal of planning permission can, however, set in motion another aspect of the development control system that neeeds to be outlined in this introduction.

If planning permission is refused or if the applicant is unhappy with any of the conditions attached to a grant of planning permission, he can appeal against the decision of the local planning authority, by using an appeals procedure that is a fundamental and important part of the whole system of planning and development control. The applicant initiates the procedure with a written notice of appeal to the Secretary of State for the Environment. Only the applicant may make such an appeal. No right of appeal exists against the grant of planning permission. Consequently, the appeals procedure is a means whereby only the disgruntled applicant can have his application for planning permission reassessed. The disgruntled member of the public, worried by the noise, traffic or loss of amenity that an approved development may represent, has no second chance to seek reappraisal of the local planning authority's decision.

Planning appeals

Once an appeal is launched, the Secretary of State usually appoints an inspector to determine the case or, in certain circumstances, determines it himself. Planning inspectors are employed by the Department of the Environment to adjudicate on planning appeals. Their suitability for this task rests on the fact that they have an extensive knowledge of the planning system, often holding one or more professional qualifications. Their task is to assess the merits of the case put before them by the applicant and by the local planning authority, a procedure which involves exploring the workings of the development control system.

An appeal is conducted either in the form of a public inquiry, or if both parties agree, by written representations. At present, the majority of appeals are resolved with an exchange of written representations, since this procedure saves both time and money. Public inquiries are normally reserved for the more significant planning applications, though the choice of procedure is entirely a matter for the parties. A planning appeal allows both parties to set out their arguments aimed at persuading the inspector to either allow the appeal, or uphold the original decision. The information likely to be presented in the course of such arguments is the same as would have been taken into account when the original application for planning permission was determined. All aspects of the proposals would, therefore, be examined, both in relation to any policy and the standing of that policy, and in relation to the possible effects of the development on the whole environment.

The procedures adopted at a public inquiry are partially at the discretion of the inspector but usually follow an established pattern[8] that allows both parties to argue their case, as well as question each other on their suggested interpretation of relevant policy and the possible effects that the proposed development may have. Expert witnesses may be called by either side in order to make a specific point, especially in a technically complex area involving, for example, transport. At the same time other interested parties, such as amenity societies,[9] other public bodies and, indeed, ordinary members of the public, are usually given an opportunity to express their views. In contrast to a court of law, the atmosphere at a public inquiry is as informal as possible, the sole purpose of the inquiry being an attempt by each party to convince the inspector that their case is right. Finally having heard all the arguments, and after seeking clarification on any points, the inspector visits the site in question accompanied by both parties.

In making a decision, the inspector treats the application as if he were determining it afresh. Effectively this means that he can reach any conclusion that he thinks fit. For example, it has been mentioned that conditions can be attached to a grant of planning permission if the local planning authority thinks that they are needed in order to allow the development to proceed. This could mean that in the case of the example given of an industrial development, planning permission would be granted, but subject to conditions, such as a requirement that the boundary of the site be landscaped by the industrial developer in a manner acceptable to the local planning authority before the industrial operations commenced. If this condition was unacceptable to the applicant, however, and there was an appeal, the inspector can then follow any course of action he thinks appropriate. He could strike out the offending condition, but he could also discharge other conditions attached to the grant of planning permission. Alternatively, he could uphold the condition or attach new ones, or even recommend that planning permission not be granted. In short, he can do whatever he thinks appropriate.

In determining an appeal, the Secretary of State or the inspector must give reasons for their decision. Usually, therefore, a decision letter will summarise the arguments presented during the course of the appeal, together with the decison maker's findings and conclusions, as well as the reasoning which supports them. It should be

8 The Town and Country Planning (Inquiries Procedure) Rules 1974, SI 1974 No 419.

9 These come in various forms, but all consist of organised groups that have an informed interest in some aspect of development and the environment. They are more fully explained in Chapter 2.

made clear, however, that only a very small percentage of planning applications are the subject of an appeal, because the majority are either approved, or the developer, refused planning permission, decides to take no further action. The appeals procedure is, nevertheless, an important aspect of the planning system and as such is examined fully in Chapter 9.

In terms of the appeals process, all decisions are final, since each represents the opinion of an impartial adjudicator who has considered in detail all the development control issues involved in each unique case. It has been suggested that a distinction can be drawn between inspectors' decisions and those made in the name of the Secretary of State.[10] Inspectors, it is argued, are politically impartial, being guided only by government policy, usually in the form of circulars, and there is evidence to suggest that they make every effort to retain this impartiality and independence. The Secretary of State, on the other hand, is a politician, and although he would be guided in his decision by the advice of the inspector, his decision remains his own and must therefore be open to the suggestion that it has been politically influenced.

Judicial challenge

Under the terms of section 245 of the 1971 Act the decisions of the inspector and the Secretary of State are open to challenge in the High Court. This process will be considered in detail in Chapter 10 where the impact of the courts on the development control process will be fully assessed. At this stage it is sufficient to make two important points about the task performed by the courts. Firstly, section 245 sets out very clearly the grounds on which decisions may be challenged. These include the failure to observe the correct procedure when processing an appeal, and exceeding the powers conferred in the 1971 Act, by omitting, for example, to give reasons for a decision, or breaching the rules of natural justice.[11] What needs to be emphasised at this stage, however, is that it is not the court's business to re-examine the various development control issues which were relevant to the case. This was the task of the inspector or the Secretary of State at the appeal stage, and should not be repeated by the court. The court's only role is to determine whether or not the law has been observed. What, however, in

10 Healey P *Local Plans in British Land Use Planning* (1983) p 76.
11 There are two rules of natural justice. The first requires impartiality of a decision maker. The second requires that before a decision is taken an individual should be given a chance to put his point of view. Failure to comply with the rules of natural justice can result in a decision being set aside by the court.

theory seems a straightforward distinction is in reality much harder to draw, as will become apparent in Chapter 10.

The second point which needs to be appreciated, is that, compared to the number of planning applications and planning appeals, very few cases reach the courts.[12] There may be many explanations for this, including the cost of litigation and the limited objectives which a litigant can achieve by adopting this course of action. If a developer has been refused planning permission, has appealed to the Secretary of State and lost, has challenged that decision in the High Court and won on the grounds that, for example, the rules of natural justice have been breached, he does not then end up with planning permission. The individual responsible for the legal error can simply correct it and still arrive at the same conclusion.

Two further processes within the planning system remain to be outlined in order to complete this introductory examination. They are enforcement and compensation.

Enforcement

Enforcement procedures are the powers possessed by a local planning authority to control unauthorised development. These powers are used when a development has been carried out either without planning permission, or in breach of a condition attached to the grant of planning permission. It should be noted, however, that they are not resorted to lightly. In many cases the local planning authority will content itself with informing the developer that planning permission should have been obtained, whilst agreeing to consider a retrospective application, or, in the case of a breach of a condition, draw the developer's attention to the fact, and suggest that the condition should be observed. If these warnings do not achieve the desired result, then the enforcement procedures can be brought into use. Effectively, these require that the development or breach of planning permission cease, and that specified steps be taken to restore the property to the condition it was in prior to the breach, all of which are to be undertaken within a specified period.

At this stage it is possible for the developer to appeal to the Secretary of State against the enforcement notice. The procedures

12 Basically this is because the powers of the courts in relation to development control decisions are very specific. The court usually acts as a review body determining whether a local planning authority, an inspector or the Secretary of State has acted in accordance with the powers given to them by statute. For example, in the case of the 1971 Act, s 244, which allows challenges to be made to the validity of a development plan, less than twenty such challenges have been made for the many hundreds of development plans which exist.

adopted for hearing an enforcement appeal resemble those used in a planning appeal. An inspector is appointed to hold a public inquiry or assess, in the form of written representations, the arguments put forward by the appellant and the local planning authority. Section 88 of the 1971 Act specifies the grounds for appealing against an enforcement notice, and these will be considered in greater detail in Chapter 9. It is worth noting at this stage that one of those grounds is that planning permission should have been granted. Where this is relied on, all the usual development control factors will be considered, with the result that the enforcement appeal will be almost identical to a planning appeal. Other grounds for appeal rely very heavily on issues of fact, such as the assertion that the breach of development control has been continuing for more than four years.[13]

When the enforcement appeal is in progress the enforcement notice itself is suspended, and, depending on the outcome of the appeal, the notice can be quashed as being invalid, planning permission can be given, or the appeal can be dismissed and the enforcement notice upheld. Whilst the appeal is in progress, however, the local planning authority can issue a stop notice[14] to prevent the continuation of the alleged breach of development control. This action highlights exactly what this very complex procedure seeks to achieve, namely, to allow the local planning authority to act in its role as development controller, seeking to protect the whole community from any inappropriate developments.

If the enforcement notice is upheld, then it will be acted upon by the local planning authority with the result that a failure to comply can lead to a criminal prosecution. It is also possible for the developer to institute an appeal on a point of law to the courts, during which time enforcement proceedings would again be suspended, but the development could continue to be restrained by the stop notice.

Compensation

It should be stressed that the development control process does not normally take account of financial matters. In other words, the cost of a proposed development is not normally a planning issue, nor is the cost to the developer of a refused planning permission, nor,

13 The four-year rule, which states that enforcement must be instituted within four years of the breach of planning control, applies with one exception only to operations, see 1971 Act, s 87.
14 1971 Act, s 90.

indeed, the cost of implementing a planning condition. Development control is, therefore, purely a question of whether or not the proposed development is suitable for its specific location at that particular time, and the question of the profits or losses that may or may not be made in relation to the development are not usually considered relevant. It must be mentioned, however, that in certain contexts the economic implications of a proposed development can be significant, such as the extra employment it would bring to the area, but in normal circumstances the question of direct costs will not be considered.

Distinct from the financial implications of a proposed development is the issue of compensation. This is a complex and extremely specialised aspect of the planning system[15] which has only indirect relevance for the development control process. There are various situations where a developer may attempt to claim compensation from a local authority. While it would take more than a few paragraphs to list all those situations, as well as to explain the manner in which the amount of compensation is calculated, it is possible to give some examples which will illustrate why compensation is available and its relevance for the development control process.

Consider the situation described in the second example where a local planning authority is faced with a planning application to develop industrial units. It was mentioned that the proposed site was presently being used as agricultural land – obviously the value of the site as an industrial development would be far greater than its agricultural value. If the application for planning permission were to be refused, would the local planning authority then be liable to a claim for compensation for the loss of development value of the land? This question would depend on a whole host of factors, some of which are listed in Parts VII and VIII of the 1971 Act, and include such considerations as the use proposed for the land in any statutory plans. If the local planning authority were to seek advice on its liability for compensation, it would probably be advised that in circumstances such as the ones described, compensation would not be payable, as the land was still capable of its original use and thus retained its original value as farm land, so nothing had been lost.

If this were the case, therefore, the question of compensation would be unlikely to affect the local planning authority's decision regarding planning permission. If, on the other hand, the land had been acquired by the developer as land designated for industrial

15 For example: Department of the Environment Consultation Paper, *Compensation provisions in the Town and Country Planning Acts*, 16th April 1986; Davies K *Law of Compulsory Purchase and Compensation* (4th Edn, 1984); Corfield F & Carnworth R J A *Compulsory Acquisition and Compensation* (1978).

development in a development plan, and then there was a change of planning policy which had the effect of including the land in a green belt, then there would be a much greater probability that compensation would be available in these circumstances. The question the local planning authority would have to ask itself, would be whether a refusal of planning permission in order to preserve the green belt was sufficiently in the public interest to risk the possibility of a compensation claim. The decision would obviously involve wide issues, such as local politics and finance, as well as the planning aspects. If the decision was to award planning permission, despite good planning reasons to the contrary, then it is obvious that the question of compensation has indeed affected the development control process. It should be stressed, however, that circumstances such as the ones described arise only infrequently.

Far more common is the serving of the local planning authority with a purchase notice as a consequence of an adverse planning decision or action. The purpose of such a notice is to compensate the property owner whose property has, as a consequence of the planning action, become incapable of reasonably beneficial use, as defined in Part IX of the 1971 Act.[16] In these circumstances, the compensation takes the form of the local planning authority being compelled to purchase the property in question. In similar vein is the blight notice, which is served on the local planning authority by the land owner whose property has been adversely affected by a planning decision. Here financial compensation is sought as recompense for the adverse effects of the planning decision. From these examples it is possible to determine that the award of compensation depends on there being a fall in the value, or potential value, of property. For any form of compensation to be gained the cause of such a fall must be directly attributable to a planning decision reached by the local planning authority. The important question is, therefore, whether the possibility of being served with such notices will, in any way, affect the development control decisions made by the local planning authority. Limited research suggests that this does sometimes occur,[17] but normally the local planning authority seems unaffected. For example, when roads are under construction, circumstances can arise which often lead to purchase or blight notices being served, but most local authorities seem to take them in their stride. This suggests that when a planning decision can clearly be shown to be in the public interest, the possibility of

16 1971 Act, ss 180–187.
17 The personal experience of one of the authors, who is involved in several local amenity societies, suggests that this may have occurred very occasionally in relation to some local planning decisions with which he is familiar.

financial claims against the authority interferes little, if at all, with the normal processes of a development control decision. Since, therefore, the availability of compensation is not a factor normally taken into account when development control decisions are reached, no attempt has been made in this book to consider the subject in any detail. This is not to deny its importance. Its omission simply serves to emphasise the theme of this book, namely an examination of the process whereby development control policy is put into practice. Only when this has been achieved does compensation become an issue.

Exceptions

To conclude this introductory chapter, passing reference will be made to those aspects of the planning system that may be considered as being exceptions to the development control process described so far. Despite the impression which might have been given, it should be mentioned that it is not always obligatory to obtain planning permission for development in the manner and form described in these pages. Planning permission is not needed for developments on Crown land, for example, where a process of 'consultation' is sufficient. What constitutes Crown land is more comprehensive than land held by the Crown and the Duchies of Lancaster and Cornwall, since it includes land held by government departments. What is all-important is that the land must be owned by the department, and not simply controlled by it. So, for example, British Steel, although a nationalised industry and thereby controlled by the government, is not regarded as a government department and thus is not exempt from the need to apply for planning permission. In contrast, National Health Service land, which is directly vested in the Department of Health, is Crown land. The effect that this and similar exceptions have on the development control system is usually slight for several reasons, not least of which is the fact that, in the case of disagreement between the local planning authority and the government department over a proposed development, the matter may be referred to the Secretary of State. This can result in a public inquiry being held as for any other planning dispute. Such public airings of differences of opinion between what are, in effect, public servants, supposedly acting for the public good, are not occurrences that either party welcomes. Consequently, the consultation which is required when developments on Crown land are proposed, will in most circumstances serve as an adequate alternative to the normal development control procedures.

Other exceptions are made in the case of local authorities and statutory undertakers[18] carrying out development on their own land, but again there are mandatory procedures that effectively substitute for development control when needed. Indeed, the number of special instances when the normal planning controls are in some way modified, or even dispensed with altogether, are increasing, as there has been a trend since 1980 for the government to introduce a variety of special areas in which development is controlled by unique systems. The Local Government, Planning and Land Act 1980 was responsible for creating urban development corporations[19] and enterprise zones. In each of these areas, the system of development control employed differs in some respect, be it large or small, from what has already been described. With all of these areas two important points must be appreciated in order to understand their impact on the development control system in general. One is that the areas have quite specific boundaries, so that there should be no debate over the system of development control in operation in any specific location. More important still are the implications that their existence may have for the area in which they are located, an aspect that will be considered further in later chapters.

The list of anomalies can be added to by mentioning the fact that in certain cases specific forms of development will require not only planning permission but additional authorisation from a government department. A good example of extra departmental control is provided by the additional safeguards that relate to any form of mineral development, while another example is found in relation to highways, both of which will be considered fully in Chapter 5. Other forms of anomaly within the development control system can be found in relation to some special local planning authority powers which can have a very marked effect on the development of an area. For example, it is possible for a local authority to compulsorily acquire property[20] in order to undertake development that it considers necessary. It is also possible for that same authority to enter into an agreement[1] with a private developer regarding the actual construction and management of the development.

18 See definition in 1971 Act, s 290(1).
19 Part XVI, ss 134–171, Schs 26–31.
20 A complex area of planning law and valuation that is of secondary interest to the subject matter of this work. For a specialist work see, for example, Denyer-Green B *Compulsory Purchase and Compensation* (1985).
 1 Planning agreements can take several forms and they are examined in Chapter 8.

Conclusion

In concluding this introductory chapter, the hope is to have succeeded in giving a simple and straightforward account of the development control system. What should have become apparent is that, in order to understand the system, certain points need to be appreciated. They are why the development control system exists and what it seeks to achieve, as well as how it goes about achieving it. The brief answer is that the development control system exists for the benefit of the community at large to protect it from development which is a response solely to market forces, rather than to the well-being of that community. The system's goal is an environment which offers the greatest good to the greatest number of people. How that is achieved, if it ever can be, is the subject matter of this book. The remaining chapters will be devoted to a detailed analysis of many of the issues briefly mentioned in the course of this chapter. The question will always be to what extent the procedures of the development control system can help transform the dream into reality, the policy into practice.

Chapter 2

The personnel of planning

It seems a relatively straightforward task to describe the personnel of planning. Nothing seems simpler than to list those individuals and organisations whose task it is to administer the planning system in England and Wales. Yet the simplicity of the task is deceptive for reasons which are implicit in the planning system itself. At the heart of that system is the notion of development control which insists that the use to which a particular piece of land or a building is put must be regulated. The nature of that regulation varies. It can take the form of plans which, in varying degrees of detail, offer a blueprint for future development in a particular area. It can take the form of a grant or refusal of planning permission for a specific development. It can take the form of designating buildings as of particular historic or architectural interest in order to preserve them. In all these ways, as was intimated in the introductory chapter, development can be controlled.

It is the fact that development control is a comprehensive term involving many separate processes which makes the task of describing the personnel of planning harder than it might otherwise be. The role, not to mention the importance, of the individuals and organisations discussed in this chapter can vary depending on the particular process being described. An example may illustrate this point. The Department of the Environment is the central government department responsible for formulating current central government policy on development control and publicising it to those who might be affected. Powers are given to the same Department to review and amend local planning authority policy on development control. The Department of the Environment also has responsibility for resolving planning appeals. In this role it can, for example, overturn local authority decisions to refuse planning permission. Indeed, should the issue be of sufficient importance, the initial application for planning permission can be dealt with directly by the Department of the Environment. These functions apart, the Department also has a role to play as a developer, since the Property Services Agency, which is responsible for acquiring and building office accommodation for government Ministries, is an adjunct of the Department. Therefore, far from having a fixed role in the development control process, the Department of the Environment has several, very distinct, roles to play.

With this in mind, the next problem is how to determine exactly who is involved in the making of development control decisions. The simple answer is to consult the relevant legislation. The Town and Country Planning Act 1971, for example, provides that an application for planning permission is to be made to the local planning authority.[1] Yet the matter does not rest here. The 1971 Act and its associated legislation[2] make it plain that there are individuals and organisations who have a right to be consulted so that they may, if they wish, express their views on an application for planning permission. Sometimes the legislation names the specific individuals[3] and organisations,[4] while on other occasions it simply provides for the application to be given publicity.[5] Much depends on the exact terms of the application. In contrast to those individuals who must be given an opportunity to participate in the decision-making process, there are others who are invited to have their say, merely because it is thought desirable. Some local planning authorities make it their practice to consult many more individuals than they are legally required to when they receive an application for planning permission.[6] Consequently, the legislation alone is not always able to provide a sure indication of who will be involved in a development control decision. Additional information may be found in sources such as Department of the Environment circulars or what is termed 'usual practice'.[7]

Apart from those directly involved in making development control decisions, there are certain individuals included among the personnel of planning whose task is to contribute only when something has gone amiss with the way in which the process has been administered. Such individuals are not, therefore, a part of the decision-making process. Instead, theirs is a supervisory role which has its limits determined by statute. In short, that role is to intervene when a decision-maker has not acted fairly and, if possible, set

1 Town and Country Planning Act 1971, s 25.
2 Town and Country Planning General Development Order 1977, SI 1977 No 289.
3 Ibid, article 15.
4 Ibid, article 17.
5 Ibid, article 8 and Sch 3, Part II.
6 The necessary consultations are prescribed in Town and Country Planning General Development Order 1977, SI 1977 No 289, article 15.
7 Circular 71/73, Publicity for Planning Applications, Appeals and Other Proposals for Development.

the decision aside.[8] There are two bodies entrusted with this supervisory role, the courts and the ombudsmen system. They represent the community's guarantee that those individuals entrusted with decision-making powers do not abuse them, and, as such, those bodies will be discussed in this chapter.

What these opening paragraphs are attempting to emphasise, therefore, is that 'development control' is a comprehensive term which, when analysed, can consist of many processes. The performance of those processes will involve, to a greater or lesser degree, the individuals and organisations described in the remainder of this chapter.

The Department of the Environment

The Department of the Environment is the central government department responsible for administering the planning system in England. Separate arrangements are made for Wales. The Department was created in 1970 when the Ministries of Housing and Local Government, Public Building and Works, and Transport were amalgamated.[9] The merger was considered desirable because of the links which existed between these Ministries and the functions each performed. Broadly stated, the Ministry of Housing and Local Government was responsible for land use planning and the protection of the environment, while the other Ministries, including the Ministry of Housing, were responsible for initiating major public sector developments, such as the building of roads. The creation of the Department of the Environment was seen as essential in order to provide administrative and policy co-ordination of what were often conflicting functions. This point was clearly made in the White Paper which suggested that the Department of the Environment be established.

> It is increasingly accepted that maintaining a decent environment, improving people's living conditions and providing for adequate transport facilities all come together in the planning of development. These are among the main functions of local authorities and are having an ever-

8 While it is possible for the courts to set aside a decision, an ombudsman has more limited powers. On some occasions it may be feasible for a decision to be reconsidered. If not, the ombudsman may be able to secure an apology or an ex gratia payment. It is also possible for a body to refuse to act on an ombudsman's findings.

9 All the functions of the Minister of Public Buildings and Works, the Minister of Housing and Local Government and the Minister of Transport were transferred to the Secretary of State for the Environment by the Secretary of State for the Environment Order 1970, SI 1970 No 1681.

increasing impact on ordinary people, in town and country and especially in and around the larger urban areas. Because these functions interact, and because they give rise to acute and conflicting requirements, a new form of organisation is needed at the centre of the administrative system . . . the new department will be responsible for the whole range of functions which affect people's living environment. It will cover the planning of land – where people live, work, move and enjoy themselves. It will be responsible for the construction industries, including the housing programme, and for the transport industries, including public programmes of support and development for the means of transport. There is a need to associate with these functions responsibility for other major environmental matters: the preservation of amenity, the protection of the coast and countryside, the preservation of historic towns and monuments, and the control of air, water and noise pollution, all of which must be pursued locally, regionally, nationally and in some cases internationally. And it will have the leading responsibility for regional policy; . . . It will also have the particular responsibility of ensuring that people's rights are adequately protected wherever they are affected by the proposals of their neighbours or of public authorities. Local authorities are profoundly involved in these fields and the new department will, therefore, carry responsibility at the centre for the structure and functioning of local government as well as for regional affairs.[10]

The Department of the Environment is still performing the role outlined for it in the White Paper. Its task may not have been made any easier by the creation in 1976 of a separate Department of Transport.[11] Hence, although of necessity close ties exist between the two, they function once more as separate Ministries.

To describe the functions performed by the Department of the Environment is, as the extract from the White Paper makes clear, no easy task. Although the major interest of this book is planning in general, and development control in particular, the Department of the Environment is by no means a Ministry of Town and Country Planning under another name. The Department has overall responsibility for many matters. They include local government, conservation, environmental protection, and housing as well as town and country planning. For example, the Department of the Environment initiated the legislation which secured the abolition of the metropolitan counties.[12] The same Department distributes finance, via the rate support grant, among local authorities. Housing too is within this Department's remit, and the legislation giving council tenants the right to buy council housing originated in the Department of the Environment.[13]

10 *The Reorganisation of Central Government* (Cmnd 4506) paras 30–31.
11 Secretary of State for Transport Order 1976, SI 1976 No 1775.
12 Local Government Act 1985.
13 Housing Act 1985.

Given the range of responsibilities entrusted to the Department of the Environment, the logic of including town and country planning among them might appear open to question. It is possible, however, to advance a simple justification. Town and country planning is a function of both central and local government. Therefore, it is sensible that the government department which has the responsibility for local government should have this additional responsibility. Consequently, when changes are made in the system of local government, necessary changes can be made in the planning system. More important still, such an arrangement allows central government to initiate policy in relation to land use planning which it can then communicate to local planning authorities for implementation in their areas.

If the reason for including planning within the remit of the Department of the Environment is the opportunity it offers for policy co-ordination, then practical evidence might be expected of this process at work, with the Secretary of State as the key figure in the Department of the Environment, having a leading role to play. Indeed, it is interesting to note that predecessors of the Secretary of State were charged with a particular statutory responsibility which is now apparently defunct. This was to secure 'consistency and continuity in the framing and execution of a national policy with respect to the use and development of land throughout England and Wales'.[14] Reference to the planning system in its current form shows that devices exist which can make such 'consistency and continuity' a reality. The first of these is the development plan.

The evolution of the development plan will be described in detail in Chapter 4. At present it is sufficient to state that development plans, which may assume several forms, are documents prepared by local planning authorities which set out an individual local planning authority's policy for the future use of land in its area. Included in the development plan may be a local planning authority's strategy for encouraging industry in its area, its policy on the conservation of buildings of architectural interest, as well as the designation of land for specific purposes, such as residential development. The Secretary of State has overall responsibility for approving development plans, although under the present system he generally only approves the upper tier, called structure plans.[15] These, in turn, are intended to shape the policy contained in the second tier, known as local plans, which are not usually directly approved by the

14 The Minister of Town and Country Planning Act 1943, s 1, repealed by the Secretary of State for the Environment Order 1970, SI 1970 No 1681.
15 That approval includes the power to modify policies in a structure plan. For a description of the Secretary of State's role, see Chapter 4 and Circular 22/84, Memorandum on Structure and Local Plans.

Secretary of State. On his instructions, however, specific policies may be removed from any development plan.[16] By entrusting this task to the Secretary of State, the Department of the Environment can, if it wishes, ensure that development plans are consistent with each other and that nothing in them impedes the implementation of central government land use policy.

Apart from scrutinising development plans, the Secretary of State is also responsible for resolving planning appeals. The 1971 Act permits an individual refused planning permission by a local planning authority, or unhappy with the terms upon which he has been granted planning permission, to appeal to the Secretary of State.[17] The process of determining such appeals gives the Department of the Environment yet another opportunity to monitor the performance of local planning authorities. Consistency with the development plan as well as central government policy can thus be assessed, and a decision can be reversed on appeal if this is felt to be warranted.

In short, there appears to be the potential within the Department of the Environment to allow it to direct generally land use planning in England. This is confirmed by the fact that other legislative provisions exist which give significant positive powers to the Secretary of State to further such a process. These include the power to 'call in' certain decisions.[18] For example, if a development is proposed which will have far-reaching consequences both at a local and at a national level, then the Secretary of State, by calling in the application for planning permission, can make the decision rather than leaving it to the relevant local planning authority. Last, but by no means least, is the power of the Secretary of State to introduce legislation which can radically alter the face of land use planning, providing such legislation is approved by Parliament. It is such legislation which defines permitted development, that is, development which can proceed without the need to secure planning permission.[19]

Having briefly outlined the various powers possessed by the Department of the Environment, it only remains to assess the effectiveness with which the Department performs its role. Before

16 Policies may be deleted when the structure plan is approved or a local plan is 'called in'. The power to call in a local plan for approval is given to the Secretary of State for the Environment in the 1971 Act, s 14(3), (4). For an example of this power at work see [1986] JPL 399.
17 1971 Act, ss 36 and 37.
18 The Secretary of State has the power under the terms of the 1971 Act to call in planning applications (s 35) and planning appeals (ss 36 and 37) for his determination.
19 Town and Country Planning General Development Order 1977, SI 1977 No 289.

forming an opinion, some appreciation is necessary of the administrative organisation within the Department of the Environment. In overall charge is the Secretary of State. In addition, there are two Ministers, one responsible for Local Government and Environmental Services, the other for Housing and Construction. These three leading figures within the Department are, of course, politicians and therefore their stay in the Department is unlikely to be lengthy. As should already be apparent, the Secretary of State is responsible for taking many key decisions. Yet to say this is to risk misunderstanding the way in which the Department of the Environment functions. The day-to-day business of the Department is obviously conducted by civil servants employed in the Department's London and regional offices. The bulk of the decision-making will be delegated to them. In this respect, the Department of the Environment is no different from any other government department. It is clear that no Secretary of State would have the time to give every decision his personal attention. All he can hope to do is to make sure that any possibly contentious item is brought to his attention. That said, the Secretary of State is, of course, answerable in Parliament for any of his Department's shortcomings whether or not he personally took the decision.[20]

Given the emphasis on delegation within the Department, it is possible that it may have adverse effects on its ability to monitor and co-ordinate land use planning. The dangers involved are possibly best illustrated by considering the Secretary of State's responsibility to decide planning appeals and how this task has been gradually delegated to a body of individuals known as the Planning Inspectorate who function as a self-contained unit within the Department. The Planning Inspectorate is made up of planning inspectors. They perform a variety of functions on the Secretary of State's behalf, including hearing appeals against the refusal of planning permission or objections to planning conditions. When hearing an appeal, the inspector's role has judicial overtones since he will be receiving evidence from opposing parties and reaching a conclusion based on that evidence. This judicial flavour to the work has led to demands in the past that the Inspectorate should cease to be associated with the Department of the Environment in order to avoid the appearance of functioning under the direction of the Department.[1]

This reasoning has been systematically rejected on the basis that inspectors are performing not a judicial but an administrative function. By this is meant that the role of an inspector, once he has determined the local situation, is to apply Departmental policy on

20 This is the doctrine of Ministerial responsibility.
1 *The Franks Committee Report* (Cmnd 218) para 303.

land use planning to the particular circumstances of the situation. Therefore, it is vital that the Inspectorate remains within the Department, since it is in this fashion that it is kept in touch with such policy. What gave added weight to this argument was the fact that, in the past, the inspector would compile his report together with his recommendations, which would then be passed on to the Secretary of State. The Secretary of State was then free to accept or reject his inspector's recommendation as long as he gave reasons for his decision.

That situation has changed, with the majority of planning appeals now being determined by the inspector himself without any recourse to the Secretary of State.[2] The consequences of this change, which was designed to speed up the planning process, are many. It stresses the judicial nature of the inspector's role and so, in the eyes of some, may reinforce the argument for removing the Inspectorate from the Department of the Environment. More important still, however, it may have serious consequences concerning the implementation of Departmental policy. It was argued in the preceding paragraphs that one of the reasons for setting up the Department of the Environment was to secure a co-ordinated land use policy with the Department at its centre, disseminating central government policy and, in various ways, ensuring that that policy was observed. The centralisation of the planning appeal system within the Department of the Environment was one of those ways. Whether this is a satisfactory method is open to doubt, since an individual refused planning permission may choose not to appeal, though the chances are that any sizeable and, therefore, significant development which is refused planning permission will be the subject of an appeal.

If there is an appeal this would seem to give a golden opportunity to ensure Departmental policy is observed. Arguably, however, the greater delegation to inspectors of the power to make decisions is undermining the Department's policy co-ordination in a variety of ways. There may be inconsistency between inspectors, with certain inspectors acquiring a reputation for favouring or opposing certain developments. Since they are not the originators of the policy they may have to apply, inspectors may not appreciate its true significance, nor be able to create the necessary exceptions to a policy, as the Secretary of State would theoretically be able to do. In addition, there is the possibility that inspectors may be applying policies which are totally at variance with Departmental policy. That these

2 Town and Country Planning (Determination of Appeals by Appointed Persons) (Prescribed Classes) Regulations 1981, SI 1981 No 804; Town and Country Planning (Determination of Appeals by Appointed Persons) Regulations 1986, SI 1986 No 623.

dangers are inherent in the process of delelgation cannot be denied. To what extent the decisions show this is happening remains a matter for speculation, particularly since inspectors' decisions can hardly be described as freely available.[3] A further anomaly is introduced by the fact that a grant of planning permission, as opposed to the conditions attached to it, cannot be appealed.[4] This presents local planning authorities with the opportunity to ignore or re-interpret central government policy on a particular issue, and grant planning permission to a development totally at odds with Department of the Environment development control policy. In these circumstances, there is little chance for central government to reinstate its policy.

Perhaps as a final comment on the role of the Department of the Environment it is appropriate to refer to the Property Services Agency. This is a unit within the Department with the task of providing accommodation for government departments. Its presence is mentioned to give an indication of the contradictions which are apparent within the Department. It is a curious notion that within the government department responsible for land use planning, a unit functions which designs, builds and acquires office accommodation on behalf of central government and yet is spared the necessity of complying with the development control regulations which the Department of the Environment is responsible for producing. The reason is that development on land owned by the Crown – which includes central government – is exempt from planning control, an issue that will be raised again in the following section.[5]

Other government departments

Although the Department of the Environment is the central government department responsible for the administration of the land use planning system in England, it is necessary to mention briefly the involvement of other Ministries in the process. That involvement varies in character. The Department of the Environment has little or no responsibility for land use planning in either

3 Selected decisions are reported in the Journal of Planning and Environment Law and in Planning Appeals Decisions. Copies of individual decisions may be obtained from the Department of the Environment.

4 The remedy open to those who unsuccessfully oppose a grant of planning permission is the application for judicial review.

5 On this topic see Circular 18/84, Crown Land and Crown Development. For a contrasting Scottish view on this point, see *Lord Advocate v Strathclyde Regional Council* (1988) Guardian, 16 February.

Scotland or Wales. In those areas, the Scottish Office and the Welsh Office respectively, handle planning and environment matters. In reality, policies applied by the Department of the Environment in England tend also to be applied by the Welsh Office in Wales. This is borne out by the fact that legislation, such as the Town and Country Planning Act 1971, is as relevant in Wales as it is in England. In addition, circulars offering guidance to those engaged in the planning process tend to be issued jointly by the Department of the Environment and the Welsh Office.[6] That said, it is the Welsh Office which administers the planning system in Wales. Therefore, functions performed by the Secretary of State at the Department of the Environment in England, are normally performed in Wales by the Secretary of State in the Welsh Office.[7] With this division of labour, therefore, comes the possibility that policies jointly agreed upon will not be applied with the same degree of consistency as they would be if one Minister were responsible.

In contrast, Scotland and the Scottish Office enjoy greater autonomy. Legislation is often passed which applies only to Scotland.[8] Therefore, the planning system is distinct from that in England and Wales, though the policies underpinning it may be similar. As has been pointed out in Chapter 1, the Scottish system is outside the scope of this book. The responsibilities of the Scottish Office are noted merely to make it plain that the Department of the Environment has no administrative responsibilities in Scotland.

The relationship between other Ministries and the development control process is a two-fold one. On the one hand, Ministries such as the Department of Transport will engage directly in development. There is no denying the impact that the Department of Transport's road building programme has on the environment and on individuals living in the vicinity. That said, there is an apparent anomaly in the fact that government departments are outside the system of development control. In contrast with the private developer, government departments are free to proceed with whatever development they choose, without the need to secure the permission of the relevant local authority.[9] The justification for this freedom arguably lies in the desire to prevent individual local

6 Whether a circular applies equally in England and Wales is apparent from the heading to the circular. One example of separate circulars is Department of the Environment Circular 15/84, Land for Housing and Welsh Office Circular 47/84, Land for Housing in Wales.
7 For example, the approval of structure plans.
8 See, for example, the Town and Country Planning (Scotland) Act 1972, which is the Scottish equivalent of the 1971 Act.
9 Government departments must, however, consult with local planning authorities before undertaking development.

authorities from blocking schemes of national importance and benefit. In addition, government departments are seen as representing the Crown, and it is a matter of tradition that the Crown is not subject to the systems which it is itself responsible for creating, unless specific provision is made for this.[10]

However, since government departments cannot be left totally free to ignore the development control system, the duty to consult is placed on such departments.

> Development by the Crown does not require planning permission. But Government Departments will consult local planning authorities before proceeding with development . . . which would otherwise require planning permission.[11]

As well as consulting local planning authorities, government departments must publicise their proposals so that members of the public may object.[12] If as a consequence objections are received, it is the Department of the Environment which determines the dispute.[13] This scheme has no statutory authority to back it. It is simply the practice followed when government departments undertake development.

Secondly, apart from initiating development, development proposals from private citizens can have a considerable impact on the activities of certain Ministries. Provision has been made, therefore, to keep such Ministries informed. The Ministry of Agriculture, Fisheries and Food, for example, must be alerted to developments which will result in the loss of ten acres or more of agricultural land.[14] Its objections, if it has any, will then be taken into account when the local planning authority decides whether or not to let the proposed development go ahead. Bearing in mind that 'development and agriculture are competitors for land',[15] local planning authorities are instructed to involve the Ministry of Agriculture in other aspects of the development control process. Most particularly, when local planning authorities are drawing up plans

10 So far as the 1971 Act is concerned some of its provisions can affect Crown land. For example, a policy in a development plan can relate to Crown land and buildings on Crown land can be listed. See 1971 Act, s 266.
11 Circular 18/84, Crown Land and Crown Development, Part IV, para 4.
12 Publicity will usually be given to the proposal by the local planning authority acting on their behalf. See Circular 18/84, para 18.
13 Circular 18/84, paras 23–25. The local planning authority is responsible for collecting objections.
14 Town and Country Planning General Development Order 1977, SI 1977 No 289, article 15(1)(i).
15 Circular 75/76. The government's current policy on development and agriculture is to be found in Circular 16/87, Development involving Agricultural Land.

for the future use of land in their area, discussions should be held with the Ministry over the impact their proposals will have on the supply of agricultural land.[16]

This involvement of the Ministry of Agriculture in the development control process is hardly exceptional. The Department of Transport also has the right to be consulted, since proposed developments, especially residential or retail developments, can greatly increase the flow of traffic on a particular road. Consequently, the Department of Transport must be informed by a local planning authority of any proposed development which, for example, involves new or altered access to a motorway or trunk road on which speeds of more than 40 mph are permitted.[17]

It should be apparent, therefore, that government departments, apart from the Department of the Environment, can have an impact on the development control system in very distinct ways. Local planning authorities may canvass their opinions on proposed private developments. Alternatively, given their position outside the formal system of development control, government departments may canvass the opinions of local planning authorities on developments which those departments propose to undertake. There is, however, one remaining way in which the process of development control assumes a significance beyond the confines of any particular government department.

At the present time, for example, much attention is focused on the high levels of unemployment in the United Kingdom. The solution to this problem may seem far removed from the planning responsibilities of the Department of the Environment. In practice, the desire to create more jobs and, in particular, jobs in certain parts of the United Kingdom may have an impact on planning policies. In the past, attempts were made to disperse offices and industry into particular parts of the country with policies involving the allocation of office development permits and industrial development certificates.[18] The former scheme was administered through the Department of the Environment and has now been abolished.[19] The latter scheme was the responsibility of the Department of Industry and has also been abolished.[20] At present, the desire to create jobs has led to suggestions for simplifying planning controls

16 Circular 22/84, Memorandum on Structure and Local Plans, Annex C.
17 Town and Country Planning General Development Order 1977, SI 1977 No 289, article 11(2).
18 1971 Act, ss 66–86.
19 Housing and Planning Act 1986, s 48.
20 Control of Office Development (Cessation) Order 1979, SI 1979 No 908.

in certain areas in an attempt to create employment.[1] This serves as an example of how the policies related to land use planning can be significant in attacking the economic ills which face the United Kingdom. As a consequence, therefore, the thinking of the Department of the Environment can clearly have an effect on and equally be affected by the thinking of many other central government departments. Direct legal or policy relationships are thus not always needed, as will be illustrated in later chapters.

Local government

ORGANISATION

In order to appreciate the role played by local government in the development control process, attention has initially to be focused on the way in which local government in England and Wales is organised. The logical starting point would appear to be the Local Government Act 1972 which reorganised local government on a two-tier basis, that of counties and districts. It is, however, necessary to mention briefly the situation which existed prior to the passage of the 1972 Act, since reference will be made, on occasions, to the planning functions performed by local authorities prior to local government reorganisation.

Before 1st April 1974 when the 1972 Act took effect, the pattern of local government in England and Wales varied. Leaving aside Greater London, there were some areas where there was a single tier of local government. These were the county boroughs whose councils exercised all the relevant local government functions.[2] In contrast, other areas had two tiers of local government. These were the administrative counties which were further subdivided into county districts – that is municipal boroughs, urban districts and rural districts.[3] Functions were divided between the tiers.

Given these complications, it might be thought that the objective of any local government reform would be uniformity. To a certain extent this was achieved in the 1972 Act when England and Wales were divided into counties and those counties subdivided into dis-

---

1 For recent government thinking see, for example, the White Paper 'Lifting the Burden' (Cmnd 9571), aspects of which are implemented in the Housing and Planning Act 1986, and the White Paper 'Building Businesses not Barriers' (Cmnd 9794).
2 In order to qualify as a county borough a certain level of population was required. In the Local Government Act 1894, which established county boroughs, this was 50,000, but it increased over the years.
3 This arrangement originated in the Local Government Act 1894.

tricts. Those new counties did not necessarily correspond with the old counties. Wales, for example, is divided into eight counties for the purposes of the 1972 Act, as opposed to the traditional thirteen. The functions allocated to the counties include responsibility for such matters as education, personal social services and libraries. As for the districts, responsibility was allocated to them for items such as housing and environmental health. It has to be said that this allocation of functions is perhaps not as clear cut as might first appear. The management of services such as parks, playing fields and car-parking provision was left to local negotiation between district and county councils;[4] while on issues such as housing, which is in the remit of district councils, county councils were given reserve powers.[5]

This scheme of county and district councils was not, however, uniformly applied across England and Wales. Six areas in England were given the title of metropolitan counties.[6] These were large conurbations, such as Merseyside, and the responsibilities of metropolitan county councils were more limited than those of non-metropolitan county councils.[7] In contrast, the functions of metropolitan districts were more extensive than those of their non-metropolitan counterparts. These six areas apart, Greater London was also the subject of special arrangements. The Greater London Council was created in 1965 when the London Government Act 1963 came into operation. Also created in that Act were thirty-two London borough councils, with only the City of London remaining unaffected by these changes. This arrangement was left in place by the 1972 Act.[8]

To add to an already complex picture, reference must also be made to a third tier of local government. The 1972 Act made provision for parish councils in England, where they are confined to rural areas,[9] and community councils in Wales.[10] Their powers and functions are strictly limited, however, being mainly consultative,

---

4 See the Local Government Act 1972, Sch 19, for the complex arrangements made in relation to car parking.
5 Ibid, s 194.
6 Greater Manchester, Merseyside, West Midlands, West Yorkshire, South Yorkshire and Tyne and Wear.
7 Education and social services were the responsibility of county councils in non-metropolitan areas, but of the district councils in metropolitan areas.
8 Local Government Act 1972, s 1(1).
9 Ibid, s 1. Rural parishes already in existence when the Act came into force remained. Additional parishes were added to their number by the Local Government (Successor Parishes) Orders 1973 and 1974, SI 1973 No 1110, No 1939, and SI 1974 No 569.
10 Local Government Act 1972, s 20(4).

with few positive activities to perform such as the provision of recreational space.[11]

The picture which has emerged so far of local government re-organisation is of an essentially two-tier system with the tiers being in no sense hierarchical. Functions are divided between those tiers with adjustments in the division being made in the metropolitan and Greater London areas. This situation, however, changed with the publication of the White Paper 'Streamlining the Cities'[12] and the passage of legislation to abolish the Greater London Council and the six metropolitan county councils. On 1st April 1986 these councils disappeared. The justification advanced for this step was that since these councils were responsible for so few services – as compared with non-metropolitan counties – yet consumed much in the way of resources, abolition was the only sensible solution. Opposition was expressed to this view, but to no avail. The func-tions previously exercised by the metropolitan counties have, where possible, been taken over by the districts. Alternatively, special non-elected boards have been created to cope with matters which cannot conveniently be handled at the district level, for example, the fire service.

PLANNING

The business of land use planning is an important function of local government. It is at this level that policies can be adapted to suit the realities of a particular situation. From the description in the pre-vious section it should be apparent that the norm is for two tiers of local government. Functions are assigned between the tiers accord-ing to opinion on the best and most efficient way to deliver a particular service. Prior to reorganisation under the Local Govern-ment Act 1972, planning was a function of the counties in those areas where two tiers of local government existed. They were responsible for producing the development plan in the form then required. County councils could, and did, delegate some of their authority for carrying out planning functions to the district councils.

After reorganisation in 1972, planning still remained a function for which responsibility was shared. The task of preparing the new style development plans was divided between the counties and districts.[13] This was the situation even in the metropolitan counties

11 Ibid, Sch 14, para 27. Parish councils also have the power to acquire land for the purpose of their functions under ss 124 and 125.
12 Cmnd 9063.
13 Structure plans were prepared by the county planning authorities and local plans were normally drawn up by district planning authorities.

and Greater London.[14] In addition, two categories of application for planning permission were created. Where the application involved 'county matters' – for example the mining of minerals – then the county council was responsible for processing the application.[15] The remaining applications for planning permission, and by far the greater number, were handled by the district councils. Yet in January 1981, this allocation of functions was revised by virtue of the Local Government, Planning and Land Act 1980, section 86.

> From that date district planning authorities will be responsible for determining all planning applications which were formerly classified as county matters by paragraph 32(d) of Schedule 16 to the Local Government Act 1972.[16]

As matters stand at present, county councils are therefore responsible for formulating the general strategy for land use in their area, normally in the form of a structure plan. In contrast, detailed matters such as applications for planning permission, the enforcement of the planning system and the preparation of detailed development proposals for a particular area – local plans – are the responsibility of district councils.

It should perhaps be mentioned at this point that parish and community councils have no specific role to play in this planning system. All aspects of decision-making are undertaken by the county and district councils, leaving the third tier simply to comment upon any proposals which might affect their area.[17] In this respect these councils have little more impact on the planning system than members of the public.

There remain, of course, those areas where two tiers of local government no longer exist, the metropolitan counties and Greater London. Since it was the metropolitan county councils which were abolished and the metropolitan district councils which survived, the responsibility for development control is largely undisturbed. It is only in respect of the preparation of development plans that some adjustments have had to be made. A new style of development plan, called a unitary plan, has been devised.[18] The metropolitan

14 In the case of Greater London, the system was adapted somewhat in the 1971 Act, s 19, Sch 4.
15 What constituted county matters was set out in the Local Government Act 1972, Sch 16, para 32.
16 Circular 2/81, para 2. Effectively this reallocation of functions means that with the exception of those planning applications mentioned in the remainder of paragraph 32 – mineral working, for example – all planning applications are determined by the district planning authority.
17 Town and Country Planning General Development Order 1977, SI 1977 No 289, article 17.
18 Local Government Act 1985, Sch 1.

district councils and the London borough councils are each responsible for preparing a unitary plan. If it seems sensible, a number of metropolitan district councils or London borough councils can join forces to prepare a joint unitary plan,[19] and this process is fully examined in Chapter 4.

From what has been said on the subject of local government, certain points should be clear. Central government decides how local government is organised, and the hope is that any decisions are arrived at with an eye to efficiency, rather than political advantage. Central government also allocates responsibility for development control. Arguably, this too should be done on the basis of which body is best able to perform a particular development control function. Most functions, at present, are concentrated in the hands of the district councils. Development plans are the exception since the feeling is that policies for the future land use are best devised at county rather than district level. Yet this may not always be the strategy of central government. Unitary plans can be seen as offering the opportunity to allocate even this function to the district councils. There is evidence in the consultation paper 'The Future of Development Plans'[20] that such a move is being contemplated, though it is meeting with opposition. Whatever the future may hold, it is vital to understand that development control is not a single process, but, as this book will demonstrate, a number of procedures. The important question is what particular expertise is called for in the performance of these procedures and which tier of local government possesses that expertise.

THE ROLE OF LOCAL GOVERNMENT IN DEVELOPMENT CONTROL

While it is obvious from what has been said so far that local authorities have a role to play in the process of development control, attention now needs to be focused on what exactly that role is. Central government, in the shape of the Department of the Environment, is responsible for formulating policies on how land should be used, which are in turn communicated to local authorities. In addition, central government has at its disposal ways of monitoring how closely those policies are adhered to, not to mention the means of completely transforming the role local authorities play in the process of development control. What needs to be examined, therefore, is the relationship between central and local government.

What needs to be appreciated is that local authorities are not

19 Ibid, Sch 1, para 12.
20 A Consultation Paper issued by the Department of the Environment in 1986.

agents for central government, in the sense that they do exactly what central government wants. A local authority consists of elected representatives, the local councillors. This may appear a rather obvious statement but it gives a clue to some of the dilemmas currently facing local government. In 1965, the Maud Committee, in a survey of local authorities, found that 50% were controlled by a political party or coalition of parties.[1] More recently a report on the conduct of local authority business, popularly known as the Widdicombe Report, found that in 1985, the proportion of councils in political control had risen to 84%.[2] This was attributed, in part, to local government reorganisation reducing the total number of councils. Another contributing factor was the decline of councils dominated by independent councillors who owe allegiance to none of the major political parties. In short, local government is becoming more political and the likelihood is that local councillors will belong to one of the major political parties and their decisions will reflect the policies of that party. To quote from the Widdicombe Report:

> The sharpening of political intensity is reflected in relations between the parties or individual authorities, relations between councillors and officers, and relations between authorities and central government.[3]

From this development flow several significant consequences. When a local authority is discharging whatever development control functions have been assigned to it, the practice is not for the whole council to take every decision.[4] This would be impossible and not in the interests of good administration. Instead, the power to take such decisions is quite legitimately delegated to a committee, the planning committee.[5] It is this committee which will take decisions, such as whether or not to grant planning permission. There is no legislation governing the composition of these committees. In theory, therefore, the majority political party on a particular council, if there is one, could, if it chose, allot all the seats to members of its party. In reality, seats are allocated according to the political parties' strength on the council as a whole. This means that the

1 Quoted in *The Conduct of Local Authority Business* (Cmnd 9797) para 2.39. The 50% is an average. For example, at that time 100% of London boroughs were politically controlled but only 20% to 40% of counties.
2 *The Conduct of Local Authority Business* (Cmnd 9797) para 2.40.
3 Ibid, para 2.45.
4 The power of a local authority to delegate the exercise of specific functions to a committee is to be found in the Local Government Act 1972, s 101.
5 This does not prevent particularly controversial or complex planning applications being referred to the full council for a decision with simply a recommendation from the planning committee.

political views and tensions in the council as a whole may be reflected on a committee such as the planning committee.

Much of the business transacted by the planning committee will not be politically contentious. The decision whether or not to grant planning permission for a kitchen extension is hardly the stuff of high political drama. Faced with plans for large scale developments, however, political views can, and do surface. Certain political parties may see particular forms of development as more in line with their political aspirations than others. Each of the major political parties has a policy on the environment. When that policy is put into practice at local government level, it may result in certain forms of development being favoured at the expense of others. This mix of politics and planning can be a dangerous one. On the one hand, it may mean that the development control policy being favoured by a particular local authority is totally at odds with central government policy. Consequently, appeals may proliferate as applicants attempt to have decisions reversed and central government policy reinstated. In addition, development control decisions must be taken for good planning reasons, not good political reasons. If they are not, then the courts may have grounds for saying that a decision has not been lawfully reached.

In relation to development control, a local authority will have a planning department which will administer the planning system for that particular area. It will be this department which receives applications for planning permission and processes them, in the meantime ensuring that anyone who wishes to see the application and comment upon it is given an opportunity to do so. The personnel within a planning department will vary depending on the administrative structure, but a considerable number will be professional planners holding professional qualifications from either the Royal Town Planning Institute, the Royal Institute of British Architects, or the Royal Institution of Chartered Surveyors. This signifies that these individuals have received a professional training, usually at least to first degree level, in some aspect of planning or design. Persons such as these will be employed as planning officers, and their role within the department is a difficult one to describe. Besides administering the planning system, these individuals will obviously have an expertise in land use planning. Therefore, the senior members of the department will offer advice and guidance on the consequences of their actions, to members of the council.

It is difficult to articulate how influential individual planning officers are in determining the actions of their particular local authority. A great deal will depend on the personalities of the individuals involved. It emerged as part of the research conducted on behalf of the Widdicombe Committee that 59% of councillors agree, rather than disagree, that council officials have too much influence over decision making.[6] This feeling was particularly strong among councillors in parties in the minority on the council. This view may reflect the fact that where there are majority and minority parties on a council, contact between councillors representing the majority party and council officials is going to prove more frequent, thereby possibly exaggerating the amount of influence such officials possess. It is interesting to note that in a research study conducted some years ago in a London borough, planning officers did not feel that their influence was particularly strong.[7]

Therefore, rather than engage in speculation it is perhaps sensible to consider what positive statements can be made regarding the relationships between councillors and their officials. The most important of these is the fact that although planning officers can and do offer advice and although that advice may frequently be taken, ultimately the decision-making power rests with the council and its committees. As long as they comply with the law, local councillors can have whatever land use policy they choose. The fact that it does not meet with the approval of their planning officers is immaterial.

It is obvious that the constraints imposed by the law and the willingness of councillors to be guided, will guarantee that a council's approach to land use planning is not totally frivolous. What is worth noting, however, is the more important politics become in local government, the less prepared local councillors on the majority party may be to heed the advice they have been given. This was a general trend noted in the Widdicombe Report and there is no reason to believe that it would be any less pronounced in that area of local government concerned with land use planning.[8]

Another point which needs to be emphasised is that although councillors are responsible for taking decisions, the day-to-day management of the planning department is a matter for the planning officers. This raises the question of how well this division of responsibilities is observed. The Widdicombe Committee noted some complaints on this score, especially on the subject of councillors attempting to influence officers.[9] While complaints of interference are far from new, what is new is:

> ... the combination of administrative intervention and political objectives. This can occur in particular where the majority party has an ideological view on a management issue, such as the role of the direct

6 Cmnd 9797, para 2.52.
7 Underwood J *Town Planners in Search of a Role* (1980).
8 Cmnd 9797, ch 6.
9 Cmnd 9797, ch 6.

labour organisation or the decentralisation of services. There can be no doubt that this has caused tensions in many authorities.[10]

The pervasive influence of politics has also led to allegations regarding the appointment of council officials. Local councillors are invariably involved in the appointment of senior officials. This has led to allegations that some officials are no more than political appointees. While the Widdicombe Committee affirmed that appointments should be made on merit and not as a consequence of political opinions held,[11] it is obvious that in appointing officials, local councillors will favour officials who seem likely to implement their policies rather than oppose them. It is a matter for argument whether or not this is a political appointment.

The role which local authorities have to play in the development control process is therefore a complex one. It involves making specific decisions on how most appropriately to utilise land and property within their area. In reaching those decisions various forces may be at work. These include the views of central government on appropriate development control policy, not to mention the opinions of the local authority's own planning officers on such matters. Nor will local councillors be without their own views, influenced by their party politics or the opinions of their constituents. It is in this context that local authorities take their development control decisions. While those decisions undoubtedly have an impact on the environment, it is an impact which is limited by one particular factor. A local authority can suggest in the development plan how it wishes land and property to be developed. It can grant and refuse planning permission in accordance with those aspirations. Yet a local authority has no positive way to ensure that its suggestions are followed, apart, that is, from engaging in development itself.

On occasions, local authorities do act as developers.[12] They build houses, schools and sports centres. Nor is it uncommon for a local authority to enter into partnership with a private developer to redevelop a shopping centre,[13] for example. Yet, this is the exception rather than the rule. The development control system exists to regulate development. Unfortunately the ideas of the developer on what is appropriate development may be totally at odds with those of the local authority. A national supermarket chain may want to

10 Cmnd 9797, para 2.54.
11 Cmnd 9797, paras 6.180–6.200.
12 As is more fully discussed in Chapter 4, one of the basic concepts of the Town and Country Planning Act 1947, and of every subsequent Town and Country Planning Act, is that local planning authorities shall act as developers. Powers, such as powers of compulsory purchase, are proof of this fact.
13 See, for example, *Jones v Secretary of State for Wales* (1974) 28 P & CR 280.

build a store and create jobs. The problem is that the site which the company considers ideal may not be the one designated by the local authority for such a development. In such a situation, the local authority cannot force the company to build on the site it considers appropriate. The aspirations of potential developers may therefore act as powerful constraints on the development control policy of a local authority.

The developer

The term 'developer' normally conjures up images of large companies with grandiose schemes to build shopping centres or office blocks. In reality, developers come in many shapes and forms. Literally, a developer is any individual or organisation which wishes to undertake development as defined in the 1971 Act.[14] As has already been mentioned, development may be undertaken by central government departments and agencies, such as the Property Services Agency. Local authorities and nationalised industries, such as the National Coal Board (now British Coal), undertake development. The development undertaken by public bodies is, however, in certain ways distinguishable from that undertaken by private developers. When a local authority builds a school or the Department of Transport constructs a road, that development is seen as for the greater good of the community. Even the decision of a government department, such as the Inland Revenue, to build office accommodation, may be an attempt to bring jobs to a region where there is high unemployment. In deciding whether to undertake development, public developers may place less emphasis on the financial implications of their decisions than private developers. Local authorities, for example, may build housing to high standards on land that is available to them. A private developer will want to build houses in an area where people wish to live and at standards which are acceptable. Most of all, the private developer will wish to make a profit.

Motives apart, development by public bodies may not appear to be the subject of the same rigorous scrutiny as that undertaken by private developers. It has already been mentioned that central government departments do not have to apply for planning permission, though they consult with local authorities. As for local authorities, they apply to themselves for planning permission,[15]

14 1971 Act, s 22.
15 For the procedure see the Town and Country Planning General Regulations 1976, SI 1976 No 1419, regs 4 and 5.

while nationalised industries have the power to undertake certain developments, described as permitted development, without securing planning permission.[16] In comparison, the private developer may find his plans subject to considerably greater levels of scrutiny. In addition, even if those plans are approved, conditions may accompany the approval which can severely limit the developer's freedom of action. Conditions may, for example, be used to restrict the companies who can occupy industrial units to local companies.[17]

As a group, private developers are not alike. They can range from the individual householder who wishes to improve his house by extending it or to run a business from it, via the small builder, to international property developers. Development is undertaken by the private sector for a purpose, and more often than not that purpose will be to make a profit. At the level of the individual householder the profit motive may be at its weakest and may be accompanied by other motives, such as the desire to improve the neighbourhood or make changes which are in keeping with the character of the area. Yet even individual householders may think ahead to the day when they sell their property and recoup the cost of the improvement. Given the importance which profit may assume, the need to apply for planning permission and the conditions which may accompany a grant of planning permission seem no bad thing. They can be used to prevent the worst excesses of the developer, such as building houses at a density which is totally unsuited to a site or destroying trees so as to build an extra house.

The profit motive of the private developer should not assume distorted proportions, however, but rather should be viewed in the context of any normal business organisation seeking to make a reasonable profit. Consequently, property development is also guided by common business standards, such as the quality of the product, which the better developer will continually seek to improve in order to uphold his reputation, and thus ensure a future share of the market. A distinction must also be made between those who fund property developments and those who organise and undertake the development. In some instances this may be the same organisation, but more usually the development is undertaken on behalf of a funding organisation, a pension fund for example, by professional developers. These individuals are often drawn from the ranks of the same professional institutions as those that furnished the planning officers mentioned above. In this instance,

16 Town and Country Planning General Development Order 1977, SI 1977 No 289, Sch 1, Class XVIII (statutory undertakers), Class XX (National Coal Board).
17 See Loughlin M *Local Needs Policies and Development Control Strategies* School for Advanced Urban Studies, Bristol (1984) for a detailed study.

however, the Royal Institution of Chartered Surveyors is likely to be the major source, while other professionals, such as accountants, lawyers and engineers may also be involved in the complex development process. These individuals may be considered as forming a distinct sub-group, as they constitute what can be termed as the professional advisers to the private developer. As such, their services are available throughout the whole range of private developments, from the simple house extension to the major office development, and consequently, they play an important role in the development control system.

Whatever sort of private developer is applying for planning permission, his is a vital role, as without him there would be little development to control. The development control system exists to prevent his worst excesses, for example, to prevent factories being built too close to residential development, or farmland being indiscriminately developed with housing. Yet, the system also responds to the developer's needs and demands. Policies are formulated on out-of-town shopping developments and the density of residential development because these are matters which concern the developer. Nor is the developer simply concerned with that aspect of the development control system which grants or refuses planning permission. Indeed, it is interesting to note that of the few judicial challenges which have been made to development plans, most have involved private developers.[18] This shows that developers have a contribution to make when policy for future land use is being formulated, since such policies can seriously restrict their plans for future development.

Members of the public

It might be tempting to dismiss in a few sentences the role which members of the public play in the planning process as being simply the ability to comment on proposals for development. Once an application for planning permission is made, members of the public may be able to comment on that initial application.[19] Should there be an appeal, either because the application for planning permission is refused, or exception is taken to a condition, members of the public may make representations during the appeal proceed-

18 *Great Portland Estates v Westminster City Council* [1985] AC 661, [1984] 3 All ER 744; *Buckinghamshire County Council v Hall Aggregates (Thames Valley) Ltd* [1985] JPL 634.
19 This is by virtue of the fact that all planning applications are available for public inspection. New applications are normally printed in local newspapers.

ings.[20] When proposals are made regarding the shape of future development in an area, comment is sought from members of the public before including those policies in the development plan.[1] This right of members of the public to comment is sometimes provided for in the relevant legislation, sometimes encouraged by a local planning authority.

Elsewhere in this book where specific features of the development control process are considered, it will be made clear if members of the public have to be consulted. What follows is an attempt to assess how influential members of the public can be within the planning process. The right of individuals to comment upon proposed developments would, at first sight, appear to be an important right. Yet, members of the public, although they might express general disquiet over developments in their community, are unlikely to make specific comments on particular developments within that community. There may be many reasons for this apparent apathy. They include the need to know when a particular development is proposed, the ability to gain access to and understand exactly what the suggested development entails, as well as sufficient confidence to express an opinion on the scheme if this is felt necessary. Although an individual may be prepared to do this if particularly affected by a development, such as a proposal to build a public house in the vicinity of his home, an interest in the community as a whole is harder for the individual to maintain.

It is, therefore, as a member of an organisation that an individual is better able to influence the planning process. The logic underlying this statement is that, as a member of a group, an individual will have access to the resources of that group, whether financial or in the shape of specialist knowledge. In addition, local government is more likely to take notice of an organisation which represents hundreds of individuals than a lone member of the public. Indeed, in certain circumstances a local planning authority is bound to ask community groups for comments concerning proposed developments. Where the local planning authority creates a conservation area for example, it will be expected to encourage the formation of an amenity society, and ask for their comments on proposed developments in the area.[2] An amenity or civic society will be locally based and has as its objective the protection of the environment in

20 The appeals procedure is discussed in Chapter 9. The Town and Country Planning (Inquiries Procedure) Rules 1974, SI 1974 No 419, rule 7(2) leaves it to the discretion of the inspector whether members of the public can appear at a public inquiry.

1 1971 Act, ss 8(1) and 12(1).

2 Circular 8/87, Historic Buildings and Conservation Areas – Policy and Procedures, para 68.

that locality. On the positive side, it can be seen as a vehicle to encourage individuals to take an interest in their environment. The criticism has sometimes been made, however, that membership of such groups is confined to middle class professionals who resist change, not for the sake of the community as a whole, but to protect the residential environment which caused them to live in that locality.[3]

Apart from groups formed to take an interest in a specific locality, there are national groups whose business it is to protect and conserve the environment. This emphasis on protection is important, since these bodies will, in the main, comment upon development which threatens the well-being of the item they aim to protect. The National Trust, for example, is concerned with the preservation and management of important historic buildings and their grounds, as well as areas of the countryside and coast. The National Trust owns the buildings and the land which it administers and will, therefore, for the most part, be able to resist development on its property which it considers undesirable. In contrast, other groups with an interest in the preservation of buildings, such as the Georgian Group, which is dedicated to preserving Georgian architecture, will not normally own property, but simply act as pressure groups whenever property of the kind in which they have an interest is threatened, either by unsympathetic renovation or by demolition.

There are many national and international groups of this nature dedicated to preserving a particular aspect of the environment. They range from the Victorian Society to Greenpeace. Their membership varies in size and for a great many of those members, membership signifies not an active wish to participate but a general concern with the environment and what may adversely affect it. Obviously proposed development may appear damaging, depending on the perspective the particular organisation adopts. A plan to build a nuclear power station might be unacceptable to members of Greenpeace because of their objections to nuclear energy, to members of the Society for the Protection of Rural England because of the countryside which will disappear and to members of the general public because they will be unhappy living near a nuclear power station. That opposition, for whatever reasons, may make its mark through the opportunity given in the development control system for members of the public to make their views known.

In addition to their ability to mobilise opposition to what are seen as damaging developments, national groups can use their resources

3 Lowe P & Goyder J *Environmental Groups in Politics* (1983). This work contains a study of a local amenity group, the Henley Society.

to press for legislation. This can be either legislation designed to better protect that group's particular interests, such as the Wildlife and Countryside Act 1981, or legislation simply to aid the management of the group, such as improvements in the tax position of charities. In addition, national groups have the ability to attract the attention of the media to a particular cause and this may again make it easier to resist development. A recent study on environmental groups concluded:

> There are nearly a hundred national environmental groups and several thousand local ones. Some are quite old, dating from the 19th century, but many others have emerged during the past two decades. Their concerns range from global issues to do with the future of industrial society, the extinction of species and even human survival, down to local issues such as preserving neighbourhood amenities. These concerns have been taken into the political arena; since the 1960s, environmental groups have emerged as a significant force, enjoying contacts with local government, Parliament and the civil service, and using the media to mount campaigns. Not only have they influenced legislation and official policy, but they have also gained considerable public sympathy.[4]

What can be added to this is that their impact on land use, whether direct or indirect, is undeniable, since they represent not downright resistance to change, but the desire not to wantonly destroy the environment.

Other groups

The organisations considered in this section are bodies whose impact on the development control process is spasmodic, yet none the less significant for that. Such bodies are brought into being by central government in order to perform a specific task. In fulfilling their objective they can have an impact on the development control process in two ways. Organisations of this nature may either undertake development or else protect certain aspects of the environment from the encroachment of developers. In addition, central government funds may be allocated to these bodies, which they then distribute at their discretion. The organisations which could feature in this section are distinct from central government departments, local authorities, pressure groups and members of the public, and to deal with them all in detail would require a separate book. Some specific examples have been selected, therefore, in the hope of illustrating the range of organisations which can sometimes be involved in the development control process.

4 *Lowe & Goyder* p 1.

DEVELOPMENT CORPORATIONS

These are bodies created by legislation to direct development in certain parts of the country.[5] They take two forms – new town development corporations and urban development corporations. New town development corporations are being disbanded as their task of creating the new towns is reaching completion. The task of the urban development corporations, that of regenerating existing urban areas, is, however, just beginning. The Merseyside Development Corporation, for example, was created to promote development and regeneration in Merseyside's declining dock areas. Urban development corporations are directly financed by central government. They engage directly in development, either alone or in partnership with private developers. On Merseyside, part of Liverpool's historic south docks have been refurbished by the Merseyside Development Corporation, then developed by a private developer as shops, offices and private accommodation. The point to note about urban development corporations is that they possess all the planning powers which would, in normal circumstances, be exercised by the local planning authority. Prospective developers within their area will apply to the development corporation for planning permission and not to the relevant local planning authority.[6] The procedures used and the rights of appeal will be exactly the same as with a local planning authority.[7] Where the development corporation intends to undertake development, it will apply to itself for planning permission, taking care to consult with interested parties, including the neighbouring local authority, with regard to its proposals.[8] The body responsible for taking the decisions to grant or refuse planning permission is comprised of the non-elected members of the development corporation's board. The members of the corporation are appointed by central government. Therefore, the political pressures discernible in the case of local government are not apparent here.

5 The New Towns Act 1946 authorised the setting up of new town development corporations in those areas selected for new town development. The Local Government, Planning and Land Act 1980, Part XVI established urban development corporations.
6 An urban development corporation may take on the functions of a local planning authority by virtue of the Local Government, Planning and Land Act 1980, ss 148–150, Sch 29.
7 The only distinction is that there is no equivalent of the local planning authority's planning committee. The applications for planning permission are discussed by the officers and the members of the corporation. All other procedures involving publicity and consultation with the public and interested parties are the same.
8 Local Government, Planning and Land Act 1980, s 140.

STATUTORY UNDERTAKERS

Statutory undertakers are in a unique position as they are permitted to embark on certain forms of development without securing planning permission. They are not totally outside the scope of the development control system, however, unlike central government departments. Nor are they subject to the full rigours of the system as a private developer would be. Their special status is emphasised by the fact that the term statutory undertaker is specifically defined. According to the 1971 Act a statutory undertaker means:

> ... persons authorised by any enactment, to carry on any railway, light railway, tramway, road transport, water transport, canal, inland navigation, dock, harbour, pier or lighthouse undertaking, or any undertaking for the supply of electricity, gas, hydraulic power or water ...[9]

Falling within that definition are such bodies as electricity boards.

BODIES CHARGED WITH PROTECTING THE ENVIRONMENT

The organisations discussed to date represent peculiarities in the development control system, since development undertaken by them may not be subject to the usual planning procedures. In contrast, bodies, such as English Heritage or the Nature Conservancy Council, exist to protect a particular aspect of the environment. In the case of the Nature Conservancy Council it is areas of countryside which are of special scientific interest.[10] The Council has powers to designate such areas and to protect them from adverse development such as drainage. English Heritage, on the other hand, was constituted in order to manage sites of historic interest[11] such as Stonehenge, which were formerly the responsibility of the Department of the Environment.

Bodies of this kind need to be mentioned because they have an undoubted impact on development control. Their task is to keep a watching brief on certain important features of the environment and safeguard them from unsympathetic development. Described in this way, the task they perform may seem similar to that undertaken by a body such as the National Trust. There are distinctions, however, since the Nature Conservancy Council and bodies like it are quangos, that is quasi non-governmental organisations. They have a statutory status and their membership is appointed by government. In contrast, the National Trust draws its membership from the general public and its governing body is elected from that

9 1971 Act, s 290.
10 Nature Conservancy Council Act 1973.
11 National Heritage Act 1983.

membership. The National Trust's major sources of revenue, therefore, are its membership subscriptions, entrance fees to its properties, bequests and investment income. Bodies such as English Heritage, however, receive funds from central government, some of which are available for distribution to voluntary organisations.

Whether the different constitutions of organisations such as English Heritage and the National Trust, lead to different attitudes on such matters as proposed development is a matter for speculation. What is important is that the reader is familiar with organisations of this nature, representing, as they do, a particular interest, whose views will have to be taken into account by potential developers as well as central and local government.

The courts

Until this point it might have appeared obvious what role the various individuals and organisations mentioned have to play in the development control process. This may not be the case with the courts, yet for all that, their role is one worth mentioning. Briefly stated, it is the business of the courts to ensure that those most closely concerned with the development control process, that is the decision makers, behave lawfully. By virtue of various statutory provisions,[12] the courts have the power to decide whether the Secretary of State, his planning inspectors or the local planning authority have exceeded the powers given to them by law or ignored a procedure set out in the relevant legislation. If, for example, a local planning authority fails to give the necessary publicity to its proposed development plan or refuses an individual planning permission, not on planning grounds, but because it disapproves of his political views, these will be grounds for applying to the courts to set aside the decisions in question. While, therefore, it is the business of the courts to make legal as opposed to planning judgments, there is no denying that such judgments can and do have an impact on the planning process.[13] Failure to comply with the relevant procedure to constitute a valid development plan can result in parts or indeed the whole of the development plan being rendered inoperative.[14] Refusal of planning permission on irrelevant grounds can force the local planning authority to consider the application afresh.

12 1971 Act, ss 244 and 245; Supreme Court Act 1981, s 31.
13 That impact is usually not a direct impact but an indirect one, in the sense that the courts will indicate the parameters within which development control decisions are made.
14 1971 Act, s 244(2)(b).

Consequently, the courts have a significant role to play and it will be dealt with in Chapter 10 in much greater detail, since it raises many important questions, including whether the courts can and do refrain from commenting on the planning merits of the issue before them. All that needs to be appreciated at present is the power of the courts to upset what appears to be a perfectly valid decision on the grounds that it has been improperly made.

Apart from this power to review decisions, the courts have another role to play. They are the body with responsibility for ensuring that the development control system is respected and observed by professionals and public alike. If, therefore, an individual demolishes a building designated to be of particular historic or architectural significance without consent,[15] or turns his land into a caravan site without planning permission, it is to the courts that the local planning authority charged with administering the planning system may ultimately look. Under various statutory provisions it is a criminal offence to flout the planning system, and the courts have the job of deciding whether an offence has been committed and what punishment to impose.[16]

The ombudsmen

The ombudsmen are another group of individuals whose role within the development control system is not immediately apparent. They act in a supervisory capacity, ensuring that satisfactory standards of administration are observed. In this respect, ombudsmen differ from the courts, since it is not their task to determine whether a particular action is lawful. There are two categories of ombudsmen. Local commissioners are ombudsmen responsible for ensuring good administration in local government.[17] The Parliamentary Commissioner for Administration oversees the administrative activity of central government.[18] If an ombudsman finds that either central or local government departments have been guilty of maladministration, then he will seek a remedy for the individual

15 Consent known as listed building consent is needed by virtue of the 1971 Act, s 55.
16 It is an offence, for example, to fell a tree which is the object of a tree preservation order by virtue of the 1971 Act, s 102. Normally, however, a breach of the development control system does not automatically render the offender liable to prosecution.
17 The powers of the local commissioners are set out in the Local Government Act 1974, Part III.
18 Parliamentary Commissioner Act 1967.

affected. The term 'maladministration',[19] is an open-ended concept and covers such failings as delay, ineptitude and carelessness on the part of the administration. The significance of the ombudsman system for the development control process lies in the fact that both central and local government have a role to play in the administration of the planning system. If, therefore, they perform that role badly and, for example, fail to inform an individual of an application for planning permission which may affect him then the ombudsman may decide that this amounts to maladministration causing injustice to the individual.[20] While the ombudsman has no power to set a decision aside as the courts can do, an ex gratia payment may be secured from the local authority to compensate for its carelessness.[1]

The ombudsman appears to have little direct impact on the development control system.[2] Yet, by ensuring that both central and local government observe high standards of administration, this has the indirect effect of ensuring that the planning system is administered as efficiently as possible. In addition, if something does go wrong, the ombudsman system may offer the opportunity of securing a remedy where none previously existed, since the shortcomings the ombudsman investigates are not normally of the sort which would attract a remedy from the courts.[3]

19 The term is not defined in either of the relevant Acts. The best description of what amounts to maladministration was given in a Parliamentary debate. It was said to consist of ' . . . bias, neglect, arbitrariness and so on'.
20 According to the relevant Acts, maladministration, if it has occurred, must have caused injustice. Sometimes, therefore, an ombudsman will feel that no remedy is necessary since no injustice has been caused.
 1 Local authorities are empowered to make such payments by the Local Government Act 1978.
 2 This may not always be so. See Hammersley R 'Plans, Policies and the Local Ombudsman: the Chellaston case' Journal of Planning and Environment Law, 1987, p 101.
 3 For an assessment of the overlap between the courts and the ombudsman see Macpherson M 'Local Ombudsman or the Courts?' Journal of Planning and Environment Law, 1987, p 92.

Chapter 3

Planning permission – the application

The purpose of this chapter is to examine the notion of planning permission. Yet, before the chapter involves itself with the minutiae of the subject, it is as well to concentrate on two very basic questions – essentially, why and when does an individual have to apply for planning permission? If a start is made with the 'why', then it appears that the need to obtain planning permission rests on the notion of restricting what the individual may do with either land or buildings. The desirability of such controls is a comparatively recent phenomenon. In the past, few cities and towns have been planned. Instead, market forces and other forces of change have been allowed to take command, producing what has been termed the 'organic town'. Therefore, in the descriptions which exist of seventeenth and eighteenth century town life, a picture is presented of mixed uses, including residential and industrial uses, existing side by side or even within the same building. In addition, there were irregular narrow streets and no uniformity of building height or style, the crescents of Bath and squares of London being an exception rather than the rule. In short, the picture that emerges is of haphazard development which, rather than being planned, simply responded to the various forces at work within developing cities and towns.

When controls were finally introduced in the nineteenth century their primary aim was to improve public health rather than the built environment, and any effect that such legislation had on the environment was indirect. Gradually, however, theories began to emerge which canvassed the possibility of planning cities and towns in order to provide a better, as well as a more healthy, environment. As has been explained in Chapter 1, the concept of the ideal or utopian town was developed, and a body of town planning theory and practice grew up from the turn of this century. This growth in town planning together with its related statutory developments has been extensively analysed in other works,[1] and as it does not form

1 Cherry G E *The Evolution of British Town Planning* (1974); Cullingworth J B *Peacetime History of Environmental Planning* (1978–80); Ashworth W *The Genesis of Modern British Town Planning* (1954).

the main theme of this work, that analysis need not be reiterated.

It is expedient, therefore, to move on to the Town and Country Planning Act 1947 in order to observe the concepts and practices of town planning being presented in a fully mature form for the first time. The legislation itself can be viewed as a socialist measure, in that its basic aim was to provide the greatest good for the greatest number of people. In future, communities would be planned with incompatible uses separated from one another, with a co-ordinated transport system designed to meet the needs of the inhabitants, and with the integrated provision of community facilities, such as schools and open spaces. Moreover, the period immediately after the Second World War appeared an ideal time to contemplate such a venture, due to the pressing need to restore devastated city centres and provide homes fit for heroes. In order to achieve this ideal environment the 1947 Act and all subsequent Acts up to the present day, are based on a simple premise; in order to undertake development it is necessary to secure planning permission. As currently defined in section 22 of the Town and Country Planning Act 1971, development constitutes 'the carrying out of building, engineering, mining or other operations in, on, over or under land, or the making of any material change in the use of any buildings or other land'.

Having briefly dealt with why planning permission may be needed, it is now possible to consider when it is needed. Since the need to obtain planning permission depends on there being development, it is obviously important to understand exactly what is meant by the term. In order to do this there are a number of factors which have to be considered and any notion that there is a single easy answer should immediately be abandoned. Yet, this is not to suggest that the issue of whether or not a particular activity constitutes development is constantly open to debate. In most instances it is obvious right from the outset that the particular activity does or does not constitute development. For example, the intention to build a house, or a superstore, or an office block, or to mine for coal or gravel are obvious instances of the 'carrying out of building, engineering, mining or other operations in, on, over or under land'. Alternatively, a plan to turn a dwelling-house into a fish and chip shop, or a warehouse into a hotel would appear to qualify as a 'material change in the use of any buildings or other land'.

The meaning of development

Apart from defining development as 'the carrying out of building, engineering, mining or other operations in, on, over or under land, or the making of any material change in the use of any buildings or other land', the 1971 Act enlarges upon that definition. In particular, the 1971 Act emphasises that certain activities which might appear to be included in that definition can go ahead without the need to obtain planning permission. Briefly, the following activities fall into this category.

(i) Internal or external improvements or maintenance works none of which materially affects the external appearance of the building so treated.[2]

The purpose of this exception is to make clear that routine maintenance, such as painting and decorating or installing a new kitchen, will not require planning permission. If, of course, the purpose of the alterations is to change the use of a building, then the answer is very different. In addition, there are certain buildings called listed buildings, or buildings within a conservation area, which may not be treated in this manner.[3] Alteration to them may require special permission, not planning permission but listed building consent, before the alteration is undertaken.[4] Obviously, the question as to what materially affects the external appearance of a building and, therefore, may require planning permission by virtue of falling within the definition of development, is open to argument. It could include the fitting of replacement windows or stone cladding, or even painting the building in a particular distinctive colour.[5] A final point to note about this first exception is its reference to works for the alteration of a building by providing additional space in the building below ground level. This can constitute development though it may not alter the external appearance of a building.[6]

(ii) Maintenance or improvement works carried out by a local highway authority to, and within the boundaries of, a road.[7]

(iii) The breaking open of streets for the inspection, repair or renewal of sewers, mains, pipes, cables by a local authority or statutory undertaker.[8]

Exceptions (ii) and (iii) make it clear that maintenance work on

2 Town and Country Planning Act 1971, s 22(2)(a).
3 1971 Act, s 54 (listed buildings), s 277 (conservation areas). See Chapter 5 for details.
4 Town and Country Planning (Listed Buildings and Buildings in Conservation Areas) Regulations 1987, SI 1987 No 349, reg 3.
5 See, for example, *Bradford Metropolitan District Council v Secretary of State for the Environment* (1977) 35 P & CR 387.
6 1971 Act, s 22(2)(a).
7 Ibid, s 22(2)(b).
8 Ibid, s 22(2)(c)

the highway or a statutory service will not require planning permission. Exception (iii) appears a sensible provision given that many holes in the road have to be dug in an emergency, and that their impact on the environment is limited, since they are only temporary. More contentious, perhaps, is the exception in relation to the local highway authority. In an environmentally sensitive area, a conservation area for example, the repairing of a York stone pavement with concrete flags may cause considerable resentment because of what is perceived as its adverse effect on the environment. Despite this, such actions would appear to fall under the heading of maintenance and not require planning permission.

(iv) The use of any buildings or other land within the curtilage of a dwelling-house for any purpose incidental to the enjoyment of the dwelling-house as a dwelling-house.[9]

(v) The use of land for agriculture or forestry and the use for such purposes of any building occupied with land so used.[10]

Exception (v) appears to sanction the use of any land for agricultural purposes or forestry without the need for planning permission. At first sight this seems acceptable, since the production of food and timber are admirable objectives. On further consideration, it would appear worthwhile to examine the impact each undertaking may have on the landscape. In order to make land viable for farming it may be necessary to drain marshlands, clear trees and remove hedges, all of which can have a considerable effect on the visual qualities of an area, besides destroying the habitat of animals and birds. The same is true of using land for forestry, particularly if the trees to be grown are all of one type which may not be a native species of the area. Indeed, the scope of this particular provision has been limited by other legislation, such as that concerned with tree preservation orders and sites of special scientific interest.[11] While this legislation does not reimpose the need to apply for planning permission, it does impose other duties on the owner.[12]

(vi) In the case of buildings or other land used for a purpose of any class specified in an Order made by the Secretary of State, the use thereof for any purpose in the same class.[13]

9 Ibid, s 22(2)(d). As for what constitutes the curtilage of a dwelling-house, see *Sinclair-Lockhart's Trustees v Central Land Board* (1950) 1 P & CR 195.
10 Ibid, s 22(2)(e).
11 Wildlife and Countryside Act 1981, s 28.
12 Ibid, ss 28–33.
13 1971 Act, s 22(2)(f).

Exception (vi) is probably the most important exception of those listed. From time to time, and most recently in 1987, a revised Use Classes Order[14] is produced by the Secretary of State for the Environment. Briefly, since the Use Classes Order will be considered in greater detail at a later stage, the Order lists sixteen classes of use, for example, Shops (Class A1), Business (Class B1) and Assembly and leisure (Class D2). The idea is that if buildings or land are functioning within a particular class of use, then their use for some different purpose within the same class is not to be deemed as involving development, and planning permission will not be required. The logic behind this exception is, that if premises are being used as a shop, for example a newsagent's, then the individual should be free to change the shop to, say, a chemist's, without being put to the time and expense of applying for planning permission. In this way the planning system will not be clogged with unobjectionable proposals, while it is usually to the overall benefit of the economy that premises should be left vacant for as short a time as possible.

Besides listing those activities which do not constitute development, section 22 of the 1971 Act provides that the following activities do constitute development.

(i) The use of a single dwelling-house for the purpose of two or more separate dwellings.[15]

(ii) The deposit of refuse or waste materials on an existing dump if either (a) the superficial area of the dump is extended or (b) the height of the dump is extended and exceeds the level of the land adjoining the dump.[16]

(iii) The display of advertisements on the external part of a building not normally used for such a display.[17]

It is not to be imagined, however, that section 22 is the only section with guidance to give on what constitutes development. Many of the terms referred to in the course of that section are defined elsewhere in the 1971 Act, and most particularly in section 290, the interpretation section. Words such as 'agriculture', 'building', 'advertisement' and 'local highway authority' have particular meanings assigned to them as indicated in section 290. As it would require too much space and would serve little purpose to reproduce section 290 here, it is sufficient to refer to the interpretation of 'agriculture' given in section 290 by way of an example.

14 SI 1987 No 764.
15 1971 Act, s 22(3)(a).
16 Ibid, s 22(3)(b).
17 Ibid, s 22(4).

'agriculture' includes horticulture, fruit growing, seed growing, dairy farming, the breeding and keeping of livestock (including any creature kept for the production of food, wool, skins or fur, or for the purpose of its use in the farming of land), the use of land as grazing land, meadow land, osier land, market gardens and nursery grounds, and the use of land for woodlands where that use is ancillary to the farming of land for other agricultural purposes, and 'agricultural' shall be construed accordingly.

As is no doubt abundantly clear from the above, the interpretation section aims to give a very precise definition of what certain terms mean, adding to an overall concept of what does or does not constitute development.

The term development is clearly a key concept so far as the 1971 Act is concerned, since the fact that an operation or change of use constitutes development makes it necessary to apply for planning permission. Equally obviously, the description of development given in the 1971 Act is a general description. It would be foolish to expect anything else, as a more precise definition would undoubtedly exclude activities which the legislators would wish to include. Yet the 1971 Act has itself gone some way to expanding that definition, by dealing with specific instances as well as defining, in their turn, some of the key terms. In addition, supplementary rules, called delegated legislation have been issued, whose purpose is to exclude certain activities from the definition of development where they would otherwise be included. The two main bodies of such rules are known as the General Development Order[18] and the Use Classes Order.

Yet, for all the guidance given in primary and delegated legislation, difficulties are undoubtedly bound to arise. An individual may contemplate using a half-acre of land he owns, and which is presently not used for any purpose but is simply waste land, as a place to breed Alsatian dogs. There may be outbuildings on the land where the dogs will be locked at night and where puppies can be kept. The question is, therefore, whether the landowner will need planning permission before he goes ahead with his scheme. The issue will be drawn to the attention of the local planning authority, either because the prospective dog-breeder seeks their advice before embarking on his scheme, or because he simply goes ahead, not knowing or caring whether he needs planning permission, and neighbours complain to the local planning authority.

The landowner may seek advice, either informally from the staff of the planning department, or from a private planning consultant. Alternatively, the machinery exists under section 53 of the 1971 Act

18 Town and Country Planning General Development Order 1977, SI 1977 No 289.

for him to ask for a formal determination from the local planning authority as to whether the activity contemplated constitutes development and requires planning permission. The request for such a determination may form part of an application for planning permission. In giving advice, either on a formal or on an informal basis, the local planning authority will presumably take account of the general definition of development, as well as any exceptions to it. In the example given, it might be argued that there has been a change of use, but is the land, as a consequence, being used for agriculture? The extended definition of agriculture has already been noted and it includes the keeping and breeding of livestock. The local planning authority is therefore left with the task of deciding whether dog breeding fits this description. If it does, then planning permission is not necessary. In reaching a decision the local planning authority may be aware of other instances where this or a similar problem has arisen and take account of this.

Eventually, the would-be dog-breeder will be given a decision indicating whether or not planning permission is required. What it is important to note about this decision is that it constitutes a piece of statutory interpretation on the part of the local planning authority. Its task is to take the general terms of the Act and decide whether they apply to the specific situation before it. The development control issue of whether or not it favours having a dog-breeder on that piece of land is irrelevant for these purposes, and only becomes relevant if and when an application for planning permission is made.

Once the local planning authority has reached a conclusion it will be passed on to the person making the inquiry. If the local planning authority has been consulted on an informal basis, the individual concerned can choose to follow its advice or ignore it. If, however, the local planning authority does believe that the activity in question constitutes development, it may be tempted to take action against an individual who ignores its advice.[19] Where a local planning authority has been asked to give a formal ruling on the matter under the terms of section 53, then the situation is somewhat different. Its decision must be in writing and be given within eight weeks of being requested unless there is some agreement to the contrary.[20] If this decision is to the effect that the action contemplated does not constitute development, then this has been held

19 A local planning authority has the power under s 87 of the 1971 Act to issue an enforcement notice requiring a breach of planning control to be remedied. This power is discussed in Chapter 9.
20 Town and Country Planning General Development Order 1977, SI 1977 No 289, article 7(6).

to be the equivalent of unconditional planning permission.[1] Alternatively, should an applicant wish to challenge a determination made under section 53 or the failure of a local planning authority to reach a decision, he can appeal to the Secretary of State by virtue of section 36 of the 1971 Act. The decision of the Secretary of State can, in its turn, be subject to review by the courts under the terms of section 245 of the 1971 Act.

The introduction of the courts into the picture at this stage is timely, since statutory interpretation is looked upon as their particular task. Yet, strangely, the opportunities which the courts have for interpreting the terms of the 1971 Act are limited. Because going to law costs time and money and remedies are only available in certain situations, there may be a marked reluctance on the part of the individual to turn to the courts for relief. This is not to deny that there have been numerous occasions in the past, when the courts have interpreted a particular section of the 1971 Act. So far as section 22 is concerned, the definition of development and its application has frequently been considered by the courts, with the result that considerable attention is paid to these decisions in those texts which are devoted to an analysis of planning law.[2]

Development as interpreted by the courts

As is pointed out in the majority of planning law texts, there are two aspects to the definition of development set out in section 22; the undertaking of an operation or the making of a material change of use. Reference is normally made to the comment of Lord Denning in *Parkes v Secretary of State for the Environment*[3] where he compared the two activities:

> ... the first half, 'operations', comprises activities which result in some physical alteration to the land, which has some degree of permanence to the land itself, whereas the second half, 'use', comprises activities which are done in, alongside or on the land but do not interfere with the actual physical characteristics of the land.[4]

This observation raises a number of questions. The first of these is whether the distinction matters in practice. For the purposes of the

---

1 *Wells v Minister of Housing and Local Government* [1967] 2 All ER 1041. Note the comments on this case in *Western Fish Products v Penwith District Council* [1981] 2 All ER 204.
2 For example: Telling A E *Planning Law and Procedure* (7th Edn, 1986) ch 5; Grant M *Urban Planning Law* (1982, updated 1986) ch 4.
3 [1979] 1 All ER 211.
4 Ibid, 213.

1971 Act it can, since the distinction is important elsewhere in the Act.[5] In the case of an individual applying for planning permission, however, it is unnecessary to specify whether the activity in question constitutes an operation or change of use. Instead, the emphasis focuses on full disclosure of what exactly that individual proposes to do. The local planning authority has the power to require further particulars in order that, when the development control decision is taken, it is an informed decision where everything possible has been taken into account.[6] It is also the case that many activities for which planning permission is sought will involve both a change of use and operations. A proposal to turn a warehouse into a superstore might involve building operations, such as the construction of a customer car park, as well as the change of use.

Where both aspects of the definition are involved it is conceivable that problems might arise. If the example just mentioned is considered, then it is possible that an application for planning permission might concentrate on the change of use from warehouse to superstore and not mention any related operations that would have to be undertaken. It is probable that such an oversight or omission would be revealed when the planning implications of the change of use were considered by the local planning authority. If this were not so, can it be assumed that planning permission for the change of use, by implication, includes any related development? This point was considered by the courts in *Wivenhoe Port Ltd v Colchester Borough Council*.[7] Here, planning permission was granted for a change of use to warehousing in a manner described as a less than satisfactory example of clear and accurate draftsmanship. On the question whether this permitted the construction of warehouses, the Court of Appeal held that it did not. Given the fact that the 1971 Act distinguishes between a use and an operation, and that the application for planning permission when considered by the court showed no evidence that permission to construct warehouses had been sought, the planning permission was no more than an agreement to allow land to be used for warehousing. If this decision does nothing more, it highlights the need for an applicant for planning permission to make clear what he wishes to do and for a local planning authority to be precise in what it is willing to permit.

5 In the context of enforcement, for example, where the unauthorised development has been in existence for four years or more it is safe from enforcement proceedings. This applies in the main to operational development. The only change of use included is the change of use of any building for use as a single dwelling-house. See the 1971 Act, s 87.

6 Town and Country Planning General Development Order 1977, SI 1977 No 289, article 5(1).

7 [1985] JPL 396.

OPERATIONS

Apart from acknowledging the distinction drawn in section 22 between operations and change of use, the courts have also concentrated on interpreting the essential qualities of each contrasting activity. In interpreting the term 'building operations', the approach of the courts appears to be to inquire whether the end product of the enterprise under scrutiny is a building. If it is, then, by implication, the activities involved will in the normal course of events, constitute building operations. There appears to be an inevitable logic to this, since the purpose of building operations would seem to be the production of buildings. Indeed, in section 290, the interpretation section, building operations are linked with buildings.

> 'Building operations' includes rebuilding operations, structural alterations of or additions to buildings, and other operations normally undertaken by a person carrying on business as a builder.

As for the term 'building', that too is considered in section 290. For the purposes of section 22, it states that the term includes 'any structure or erection, and any part of a building, as so defined, but does not include plant or machinery comprised in a building'.

Using this framework, the courts have given further indications of what may be considered a building. Normally they have done this when asked whether a particular structure constitutes a building for the purposes of the 1971 Act, and its erection, building operations. Bearing in mind that each case turns on its own particular facts, such cases can still prove important for the specific and general guidance which they provide. The factors which appear crucial in distinguishing a building are size, permanence and physical attachment. The smaller an item is, and the fact that it is brought on site complete, the less likely it is to be considered a building. As most commentators point out, a model village was considered a building in *Buckinghamshire County Council v Callingham*,[8] whereas in *James v Brecon County Council*[9] a set of fairground swingboats was not. A conclusive factor in the latter case was not so much their size, and their lack of resemblance to what may conventionally be thought of as a building, but their lack of permanence, since they could simply be carried away when the need arose. Lack of permanence also relates to the final characteristic of a building highlighted by the courts, namely physical attachment to the land. This may have influenced the court in the swingboats case, though it may not always be decisive, as shown by a contrasting pair of cases, *Cheshire*

8 [1952] 2 QB 515, [1952] 1 All ER 1166.
9 (1963) 15 P & CR 20.

County Council v Woodward[10] and *Barvis Ltd v Secretary of State for the Environment*.[11] In the former, the installation of a wheeled coal hopper with a conveyor sixteen to twenty feet high did not constitute development, while in the latter case a tower crane eighty-nine feet high running on rails did constitute a building and hence development. The decisive issue is perhaps the overall impact of any installation, movable or otherwise, on the land.

While buildings and building operations have been the subject of considerable judicial comment, the same is not true of engineering operations. In section 290 of the 1971 Act, engineering operations are said to include 'the formation or laying out of means of access to highways'.[12] Means of access include 'any means of access, whether private or public, for vehicles or for foot passengers, and includes a street'. In normal usage the term engineering tends to be associated with the construction of roads, bridges, canals and railways, and this sort of activity is implied by the definition given in section 290. When the courts have had occasion to consider the term, the emphasis has been on the connection between engineers and engineering operations. That connection does not necessarily mean that engineering operations have to be supervised by a qualified engineer according to plans drawn up by him. This point was made in *Fayrewood Fish Farms Ltd v Secretary of State for the Environment*[13] where engineering operations were said to be 'of the kind usually undertaken by engineers, ie, operations calling for the skill of an engineer'.[14] The court emphasised, however, that this 'did not mean that an engineer must actually be engaged on the project'.[15] Though the engineering operations being considered in this case were those mentioned in the General Development Order,[16] the likelihood is that the courts would take the same approach to the term when it is used in section 22. Besides the more obvious road and bridge building, engineering operations may therefore involve large scale earth-moving and excavations, the latter possibly as part of a mining or building operation, but not automatically.

Mining operations are in direct contrast with building and engineering operations. On the one hand, there is no mention of mining operations in section 290 of the 1971 Act. Normally, the term is

10 [1962] 2 QB 126, [1962] 1 All ER 517.
11 (1971) 22 P & CR 710.
12 This should be considered in conjunction with the classes of permitted development sanctioned by the General Development Order.
13 [1984] JPL 267.
14 Ibid, 268.
15 Ibid, 268.
16 Town and Country Planning General Development Order 1977, SI 1977 No 289, Sch 1, Class VI.

associated with the winning of minerals from the land. This is reinforced by other statutory references to mining operations, where the term is defined as 'the winning and working of minerals in, on, or under land, whether by surface or underground working'.[17] Another point of contrast is the nature of the operations involved. Building and engineering operations take place over a specified period, which can be long or short depending on the complexity of the project involved. Although mining operations will also be concluded when supplies of the mineral in question have been exhausted, or can no longer be economically extracted, this can take decades if not hundreds of years. Consequently, the impact of mining operations on the environment is much more long-term. Added to this is the fact that building and engineering operations normally involve construction resulting in an end product capable of use. Whilst there is also an end product of mining, the nature of the extraction process is likely to produce little that is of positive benefit and a great deal that may be environmentally detrimental.

One point the courts have not been called on to consider, however, is the activities of businesses which extract minerals from waste tips, in particular, coal from slag heaps. There have been planning decisions in the past that suggested that this did not constitute development, presumably on the basis that it was not a mining operation, since the minerals had already been extracted from the ground. Such an anomaly has now been rectified, however, under the terms of the Town and Country Planning (Minerals) Act 1981, section 1(1). As a result, from 19th May 1986 when the section entered into force, such reclamation activities constitute development and planning permission is required in order that they may be legitimately undertaken. This immediately brings into question the position of those individuals who engaged in such activities without planning permission, believing that it was not necessary prior to this date. Their situation is specifically dealt with in the General Development Order.[18]

The final types of operation mentioned in section 22 are 'other operations'. What exactly is included in this expression was considered by the House of Lords in *Coleshill and District Investment Co Ltd v Minister of Housing and Local Government*.[19] When the courts are called upon to interpret an expression used in a statute, certain rules are said to exist indicating how they should go about this task. One of these rules is termed the *eiusdem generis* rule.

17 Ibid, article 2.
18 Town and Country Planning General Development Order 1977, SI 1977 No 289 (amended by SI 1985 No 1981) Sch 1, Class XXVII.
19 [1969] 2 All ER 525.

Essentially this means that where a series of specific terms are used – building, mining, engineering – followed by a general phrase – or other operations – then that general phrase should be interpreted in such a way that it reflects the specific activities. When this argument was put to the House of Lords in the *Coleshill* case it was rejected on the basis that it was impossible to discover a common denominator between the various activities. The expression 'other operations' could therefore be given an exceedingly wide meaning in order to bring the maximum number of activities under control, provided, that is, that they do not amount to permitted development. In practice,[20] this does not seem to have occurred, perhaps because the accompanying expressions are so broad that little which would seem to merit the attention of the development control process will not be covered by them.

In bringing to a close this discussion of the various types of operation listed in section 22, one activity remains to be discussed, that of demolition. Demolition is a process which can have a considerable impact on the physical environment, yet it has always been a matter for conjecture whether it constitutes development within the terms of section 22. Indeed, the very terms 'development' and 'demolition' appear incompatible, the one positive, the other negative. If a building is listed or is in a conservation area, then special arrangements have been made to control demolition.[1] This is logical, since such buildings may have special architectural features or be an essential element of the townscape. Their demolition cannot therefore be undertaken without due consideration. Beyond these special cases, however, the attitude to demolition appears ambivalent. This stems, perhaps, from the fact that there is no specific reference in the statutes to demolition and what constitutes demolition. In the past it has been suggested that this omission be remedied but no such move has been made to date.[2]

There appears no logical reason, given the current definition of 'development', why demolition could not amount to an engineering or other operation or, indeed, be part of a building operation. There is, in fact, judicial authority to this effect in *Coleshill and District Investment Co Ltd v Minister of Housing and Local Government*. Here, the House of Lords refused to state categorically that demolition did or did not constitute development. To quote Lord Pearson,

20 Very few decisions, either planning appeal decisions, or judicial decisions refer to an activity as constituting 'or other operations'. On this point see [1983] JPL 618 (planning appeal decision) and *Bedfordshire County Council v Central Electricity Generating Board* [1985] JPL 43.

1 1971 Act, ss 55, 277A.

2 Dobry G *Control of Demolition* (1974).

> Notwithstanding that an operation is a demolition or removal operation, one still has to see whether it comes within the scope of development as defined . . . It may be within the definition of 'building operations', eg, because it constitutes a structural alteration of a building or because it is such an operation as to be normally undertaken by a person carrying on business as a builder. It may be an engineering operation.[3]

What is clear is that as there is no general principle, each situation will have to be judged on its own particular facts. The truth of this is shown by *Iddenden v Secretary of State for the Environment*[4] where the demolition of Nissen huts was said not to constitute development. Factors such as the scale of the operation and whether the demolition is simply part of a more extensive undertaking, may all prove important.

MATERIAL CHANGE OF USE

Apart from operations, the other limb to the definition of development is a material change of use. Section 290 of the 1971 Act says of the term 'use' that 'in relation to land, it does not include the use of land for the carrying out of any building or other operations thereon'. From this it can be deduced that a use of land involves activity on the land which is not of a type that would be covered by the operational limb of the definition of development. Section 22 makes it clear that in order to constitute development there must be not merely a change of use, but a material change of use. It does not take a great deal of insight to appreciate that the term 'material' is important and likely to give rise to difficulties. Consequently, it is hardly surprising that there has been a considerable amount of litigation regarding this particular aspect of the definition of development.

Before considering the guidance given by the courts as to what constitutes a material change of use, some preliminary points need making. In many cases there is no doubt on the matter, since the change of use contemplated is included in the Use Classes Order. The Use Classes Order will be discussed in detail at a later stage. It is sufficient at this stage simply to reiterate that its purpose is to establish certain classes of use and state that, as a general rule, a change that remains within a class is permitted development, subject, of course, to any other legislative provisions. That said, it might be thought that by setting out the various classes of use, such as Shops, Business and General Industrial, the Use Classes Order

3 [1969] 2 All ER 525 at 543.
4 [1972] 3 All ER 883.

provides valuable evidence as to what constitutes a material change of use. Could it not be argued that a change from a Class A1 use, Shops, to a Class C1 use, Hotels and hostels, is obviously a material change of use? In many cases this might be true but it is not automatically so. In *Rann v Secretary of State for the Environment*,[5] the pitfalls inherent in this approach were illustrated. Here planning permission had been granted for a house to be used as a guest house. Instead, the owners used it to provide holiday accommodation for the mentally handicapped. When the local planning authority took enforcement proceedings, an appeal was made to the Secretary of State who found that the house was being used as a home or institution as defined in Class XIV of the then current Use Classes Order. The court rejected his finding and stressed that the purpose of the Order was to indicate what is permitted. It may be unwise to use the classes to show that a material change of use has occurred. Some uses are very specific and it will be hard to accommodate them successfully in the Use Classes Order.

In order, therefore, to be considered a material change of use, some important, as opposed to trivial, alteration in the use to which a building or land is put, must have occurred. Whether this is so is a question which will be answered, in the first instance, by the local planning authority and, if there is an appeal, by an inspector or the Secretary of State for the Environment. Only in a minority of cases will the issue come before the courts, enabling them to give general advice on how the term 'material change of use' should be interpreted. Yet that advice can only be general since, as has been pointed out on numerous occasions,[6] whether there has been a material change of use is 'a question of fact and degree'.[7]

Until this point, the material changes of use under discussion have been those where a building or land ceases to be used for one purpose, and is put to some totally different use. Obviously this frequently occurs in practice, yet if this were all that was meant by a material change of use, then many activities with a considerable impact on the environment could take place without being subject to development control. The 1971 Act itself gives due consideration to this aspect in section 22. Here, the use of what was previously a single dwelling-house as two or more separate dwelling units is

5 (1980) 40 P & CR 113.
6 In reality, in almost every one of the decisions mentioned in this section.
7 What is implied by this is that the courts acknowledge the right of the Secretary of State to make appropriate development control decisions on the facts as they appear to him. They will intervene only if there is no evidence, or his decision is totally outrageous or based on facts which are immaterial. The courts' tolerance is illustrated by a case such as *Bendles Motors v Bristol Corporation* [1963] 1 All ER 578.

specifically said to constitute a material change of use.[8] This would seem to be on the basis that, although the use remains residential, the character of that use has materially altered by virtue of its intensification.

At what stage the intensification of a use is so considerable as to amount to a material change of use, is a difficult issue. That it does occur is borne out by decisions in cases such as *Brooks and Burton Ltd v Secretary of State for the Environment*.[9] Here a shed was used for the manufacture of concrete blocks which were then dried in the open air. The site was acquired by a firm who increased the number of concrete blocks being manufactured by installing specialist machinery, 25 feet high, in the open air. The local planning authority issued an enforcement notice which was upheld on appeal. One of the Secretary of State's findings was that there had been an intensification of use resulting in a material change of use. The Court of Appeal said on this point:

> We have no doubt that intensification of use can be a material change of use. Whether it is or not depends on the degree of intensification. Matters of degree are for the Secretary of State to decide. He did so in this case. There was ample evidence to support his decision on this point.[10]

Yet, mere intensification of the use is not normally sufficient. This can be demonstrated by using as an example a garage visited by 200 cars a day. If that garage begins selling exceedingly cheap petrol the number of cars visiting it may increase to 600 a day. There may be queues of cars impeding the free flow of traffic along the road, and the residents of houses nearby may find the traffic noise has increased. Here there can safely be said to have been an intensification of the use. However, according to the terms of section 22 there must be a material change of use, and in the example it can be argued that the use has not changed, merely intensified. This was the conclusion reached by the court in *Royal London Borough of Kensington and Chelsea v Secretary of State for the Environment*.[11] Here, the use of a garden adjoining a restaurant for dining was not an intensification of use. Of that expression the court said:

> In ordinary language, intensification meant more of the same thing or possibly a denser composition of the same thing. In planning language, intensification meant a change to something different. It was much too late no doubt to suggest that the word 'intensification' should be deleted

8 1971 Act, s 22(3)(a).
9 [1978] 1 All ER 733.
10 Ibid, 744.
11 [1981] JPL 50.

from the language of planners, but it had to be used with very considerable circumspection, and it had to be clearly understood by all concerned that intensification which did not amount to a material change of use was merely intensification and not a breach of planning control.[12]

There may be good reason for the court to criticise the use made of the expression intensification of use. In particular, it impedes an appreciation of those situations where changes in emphasis are occurring which could result in a material change of use.

This often occurs where premises or land may have primary, as well as ancillary, uses. Normally, such ancillary uses are tolerated, and need not be the subject of an application for planning permission as long as they are linked to the primary purpose.[13] Therefore, in an ordinary family house the primary use is residential. Yet, in that house there may be a room set aside as a workshop where furniture is made for the home, an office where one of the family who is a teacher marks essays, a garage where the family car is repaired and a garden where hens are kept. Such ancillary uses would, in normal circumstances, be regarded as ancillary to the main use of the house as a residence.

Circumstances can occur, however, when an ancillary use grows to such a degree that it becomes the primary use. When this happens, what was previously tolerated as incidental may have grown to such a degree as to constitute a material change of use. The owner of a smallholding may be able to sell crops that are surplus to his requirements at the farm gate or in a farm shop. Where, however, the smallholder begins to buy in produce from neighbouring smallholders and sells items, such as washing powder or tinned food, as well as fresh produce, it can be argued that a material change of use has occurred. In *Hilliard v Secretary of State for the Environment*,[14] produce was sold on a farm which had been grown there and elsewhere. A building was erected with planning permission supposedly for the storage of farm implements. In reality it was used to store fruit and vegetables which were then sold wholesale to hospitals and schools in the area. The local planning authority served an enforcement notice which was confirmed on appeal by the Secretary of State. This was on the basis that the sale of fruit and vegetables had so intensified as to represent a material change of use. The Court of Appeal rejected the Secretary of State's finding. In their judgment, since no evidence had been produced on the amount of fruit and vegetables bought in and distributed from

12 Ibid, 51.
13 See, for example, *Hussain v Secretary of State for the Environment* (1971) 23 P & CR 330.
14 (1979) 37 P & CR 129.

the farm, there was no material on which this conclusion could be reached. The only evidence was that of a building not being put to the use intended. Arguably, here the expression intensification is misleading as it obscures the real issue – namely was this no longer a farm but a fruit and vegetable wholesale business?

In this discussion no mention has been made to date of the planning unit. According to one source,

> ... the planning unit is a concept which has evolved as a means of determining the most appropriate physical area against which to assess the materiality of change, to ensure consistency in applying the formula of material change of use.[15]

In other words, when asking whether one primary use has succeeded another, or whether an ancillary use has become a primary use, the question must be answered, not in the abstract, but with full knowledge of the extent of the physical surroundings where the activities occur. In *Burdle v Secretary of State for the Environment*,[16] it was indicated that a useful working rule in determining what was the appropriate planning unit was to assume that it was the whole unit of occupation, unless some smaller unit could be recognised as the site of activities which amounted, in substance, to a separate use both physically and functionally. Therefore, in this case and in *Hilliard*'s case, considerable emphasis was placed on choosing the correct planning unit before concluding whether or not there was a material change of use.

When dealing with the question of material change of use, the first step is to isolate the unit of occupation, which will be a building or piece of land. Once the unit has been identified, its primary and ancillary uses can be assessed and any subsequent changes in use, or between the balance of uses, can be monitored. That said, it should be apparent that the larger the planning unit, then the more difficult it will be to show a material change of use. If planning permission is granted to use a warehouse for the sale of carpets to the public, for example, the primary use of the planning unit would appear to be a retail use. If, in the years to come, a portion of the warehouse becomes an office for handling customers' accounts, and another part, a staff rest room, it would seem difficult to argue that the primary use has changed, as these additional uses would appear to be ancillary uses related to the primary use of a large unit.

According to the judgment in *Burdle v Secretary of State for the Environment*, the way in which a unit of occupation can be

15 *Encyclopedia of Planning Law and Practice*, para 2–817.
16 [1972] 3 All ER 240.

regarded, not as a single planning unit, but as several planning units, is for there to be physical and functional separation. If, therefore, the carpet warehouse of the above example were partitioned, with two-thirds being used for retail purposes and the other third as a staff canteen and rest room, would there be a material change of use? In reality, each case will depend on its own particular facts, and especially, whether two separate planning units have been created.[17] In *Winton v Secretary of State for the Environment*,[18] a building used originally for the manufacture of concrete blocks was divided into two. It was agreed that this had the effect of creating two planning units, one used for metalworking and the other to convert motor cars to right-hand drive. The local planning authority served an enforcement notice which was confirmed on appeal by the Secretary of State. In this case the court held that a division of a building does not automatically constitute development. This occurs only if the division has planning consequences, amounting to a material change of use. That is a question of fact and degree for the Secretary of State and here he had held that it was a material change of use.

Interpretation of development in planning appeals

As the heading to this section indicates, the term development is interpreted not only in the courts, but also in the course of planning appeals. Local planning authorities, as a prelude to taking enforcement action[19] or to granting or refusing planning permission, may have to decide whether the activity in question constitutes development. The point may still be in contention on appeal to a Department of the Environment inspector whose decision will settle the matter.[20] These decisions are important, since they may be considered to represent the working definition of development as used by one of those parties who operate within the development control system on a daily basis. To appreciate the true content of

17 Some light has been thrown on this issue by the Town and Country Planning (Use Classes) Order 1987, SI 1987 No 764, para 4; Circular 13/87, Changes of Use of Buildings and Other Land, para 9; Housing and Planning Act 1986, s 49, Sch 11.
18 (1982) 46 P & CR 205.
19 Enforcement is described in Chapter 9. If an individual undertakes development without planning permission, the local planning authority has the right to try to remedy that breach of the development control system by instigating enforcement proceedings.
20 It is, of course, possible, as has already been made clear, that the issue will then be referred to the courts. Yet, the majority of disputes over the term 'development' will be settled by an inspector or the Secretary of State for the Environment.

that working definition would, however, require a great deal of research. In the case of a local planning authority, it would require the analysis of its planning decisions over the years in order to build up a picture of what, in its opinion, did or did not constitute development. Nor would an analysis of one local planning authority's working definition of development necessarily be the same as that of another local planning authority. A considerable degree of consistency could be expected but not complete uniformity.

The task of analysing the interpretation put on the term 'development' in planning appeals would be less onerous in certain respects. Written copies of inspectors' decisions are available from the Department of the Environment. In addition, selected decisions are published in specialist journals, and a series of planning appeal reports exists.[1] Should a situation arise where there is doubt over whether the activity in question constitutes development, such decisions may represent a source of guidance. If, for example, the owner of a public house decides to erect items in the garden adjoining the public house for children to play on, will this amount to development? Given that there is no direct judicial authority on the point, a recent inspector's decision on this very issue might appear relevant. Such a decision exists[2] and in it, the distinction was made between objects anchored to the ground, which did constitute development, and free-standing items which did not.

The question is, therefore, if this decision were drawn to the attention of another inspector or a local planning authority, what would be its standing? There is no rule that local planning authorities must follow such decisions, nor, indeed, need other planning inspectors.[3] This, of course, gives scope for diverging practices among local planning authorities and inspectors, and, in the case of a planning appeal, the decision may consequently depend on the opinions of the inspector allocated to the case.

Whilst the judicial system itself can, on occasions, be equally prone to inconsistency, this is normally eliminated once the High Court is reached. In the same way, one might expect such inconsistency to be eliminated at the planning appeal stage. While in theory this could be achieved if every planning appeal decision were to be scrutinised by officials of the Department of the Environment, in reality, this does not occur. Apart from the more important plan-

---

1 Selected decisions are to be found in the Journal of Planning and Environment Law and the Estates Gazette. Recently, a series of Planning Appeal Decisions has been published.

2 *Thanet District Council and Host Group Ltd* 1986, I PAD 364.

3 There is likely to be a great deal more consistency on what does or does not amount to development than on pure development control issues, such as whether or not to grant planning permission.

ning appeals,[4] inspectors are authorised to take planning appeal decisions on the Secretary of State's behalf and without his having the opportunity to review them. Consequently, there can be inconsistency between planning inspectors. In a paper analysing the difficulties arising from the delegation of the Secretary of State's powers to the Planning Inspectorate, this problem was referred to, though there is no published research on the extent of the problem.[5]

As the purpose of this section is to consider the interpretation given to the term 'development' in planning appeals, what has been said may seem to suggest that the task is not worth pursuing. Indeed, in the majority of planning appeals the question of what constitutes development will not be an issue but attention will be focused on whether, on planning grounds, planning permission should be granted or refused. The decision by one planning inspector to allow a building society to open an office in one town's prime shopping location, will offer little guidance if the same situation were to arise in a town hundreds of miles away. On the other hand, a finding that a particular activity does amount to development, may fruitfully be followed if similar circumstances arise elsewhere.

Therefore, subject to these qualifications, it might be thought appropriate to summarise the findings of either inspectors or the Secretary of State on what, in their view, does or does not constitute development. Attempts have been made to do this in the past by analysing the views expressed, either in planning appeals, or in appeals against an enforcement notice.[6] Such decisions, whilst they lack the depth of analysis which is normally to be found in a judicial decision, are of interest, since they reflect how a key term, such as 'development', is interpreted in practice. That said, the effort required to undertake such an analysis is beyond the scope of this book. All that can be done is to highlight the significance of these decisions and provide a single example by way of illustration.

It will be recalled that what exactly constitutes a building has already been considered, together with the judicial opinion expressed on the matter. From this it emerged that a building was normally constructed on site rather than transported there readymade. It had a degree of permanance, though the fact that the

---

4 These are likely to be determined by the Secretary of State for the Environment on appeal.

5 Sullivan J M 'The Implementation of Ministerial/Departmental Policy Objectives' Journal of Planning and Environment Law Occasional Papers *Contemporary Planning Policies*.

6 Brown H J 'Operations within the Definition of Development' Journal of Planning and Environment Law, 1973, p 642; 'Material Change of Use within the Definition of Development' Journal of Planning and Environment Law, 1974, p 180.

object in question was not attached to the site, and could be moved around, did not automatically mean that the item could not be considered a building. Over the years, therefore, the courts have declined to interfere with the Secretary of State's findings that, for example, the installation of a coal hopper and conveyor did not constitute development while the erection of a mobile tower crane did.[7]

By reviewing the planning decisions on this single point – what does or does not constitute a building for the purpose of the definition of development – the hope is to isolate those features which inspectors and the Secretary of State see as significant. This is allowing for the fact that a particular structure may not be considered a building and its introduction onto the land may not represent building operations, but that development will have taken place as a consequence of a material change of use. This was the situation in *Bendles Motors Ltd v Bristol Corporation*[8] where the court declined to interfere with the Minister's finding that the installation on a garage forecourt of a free-standing egg-vending machine was a material change of use, since it introduced a shop use where planning permission existed for a garage and petrol filling station.

From an analysis of reported planning and enforcement appeals, it appears that the ministerial approach to what constitutes a building is substantially the same as that of the courts. On various occasions, the introduction of the following items onto land has been held to amount to building operations. Those items are a slide, portable cabins, polythene tunnels used for growing plants, and an incinerator used for disposing of the remains of dead pet animals. By way of contrast, neither a lorry body used as a workshop, a playhouse in the shape of a boot, metal pegs interlaced with two strands of nylon rope nor an inflatable whale constituted buildings, nor did their installation constitute a building operation. The reasoning underlying such findings seems to be based on the following principles. An item fixed to the land is likely to be considered a building and covered by the definition of building given in section 290 of the 1971 Act. Therefore, it was said of a slide erected on Felixstowe Pier:

> . . . it took ten days to erect and would take three days to dismantle and is secured to the pier decking by 64 bolts.[9]

7 *Cheshire County Council v Woodward* [1962] 2 QB 126, [1962] 1 All ER 517; *Barvis Ltd v Secretary of State for the Environment* (1971) 22 P & CR 710.
8 [1963] 1 All ER 578.
9 [1979] JPL 547 at 548.

In a separate instance,[10] involving an appeal against an enforcement notice, the owners of a hotel had installed play equipment in a pub garden. Whilst it was conceded that a slide, climbing frame and swings, which were set in concrete, required planning permission, the same was not true of a plastic playhouse in the shape of a boot. The latter was distinguished on the basis that it was secured to the ground by four metal pegs and could be removed by one man in a matter of minutes. Therefore, in the opinion of the inspector

> ... the installation of the boot did not itself constitute operational development requiring planning permission.[11]

The fact that an item is not securely fixed to the land and can be moved is not, however, decisive. An incinerator, installed in the garden of a veterinary surgery, measured four feet by two feet by four feet high and was made from sheet metal. It stood on four legs on concrete, and was connected to some nearby gas cylinders. In an appeal against an enforcement notice,[12] it was argued that the incinerator was portable and, therefore, planning permission was not required. In rejecting this argument, the point was made that

> the fact that a structure is physically capable of being moved and is not affixed to the ground does not of itself determine whether development is involved: account must be taken of the degree of permanency of the structure on the land which is affected by that structure and indeed of all the circumstances concerning the matter.[13]

On this basis the incinerator was found to constitute a building as defined in section 290 of the 1971 Act, since it had not been moved from the time when it had been constructed, nor was there any indication that it would be moved in the future. In addition, the incinerator was not thought to be easily portable and would have to be dismantled before it could be moved.

The same reasoning was adopted in relation to a portakabin being used as an office. In what was a complex appeal against an enforcement notice,[14] the inspector concluded that, since the portakabin was not fixed to its concrete base, its installation was not a building operation. In commenting on the inspector's conclusion, the Secretary of State felt that the fact that the structure was not fixed to the ground was not decisive. It was important that the portable office had not been moved in the past nor were there plans to move it. Indeed, since telephone wires and electricity cables were

10 1986, 1 PAD 364.
11 Ibid, 366, 5.1.
12 [1978] JPL 487.
13 Ibid, 488.
14 [1978] JPL 571.

attached to the portakabin, moving it was no easy task. The Secretary of State concluded, therefore, that the installation of the portakabin was a building operation, which required planning permission.

Apart from the issue of ease of movement, it might be thought that size is a factor in determining whether an item constitutes a building. The items considered so far have been substantial objects. The same description does not appear true of polythene tunnels or ropes and metal pegs. In the case of the tunnels[15] they were 20 feet by 40 feet and consisted of polythene sheeting over metal hoops. In finding that the siting of such tunnels on land constituted building operations, the Secretary of State drew attention to their substantial size and the manner of fixing them to the ground. Although it was conceded that they could be moved, it was felt that a considerable amount of work would be involved in their repositioning. In contrast, the marking out of plots with metal pegs and nylon rope did not amount to development.[16] It was stated that 'the works involved in driving into the ground these 12 small pegs . . . and the stringing between them of two strands of thin nylon rope'[17] did not constitute a building within the terms of section 290 of the 1971 Act nor an operation of the type amounting to development. They were so insubstantial that they could be disregarded.

In view of the decisions just mentioned, there might appear to be a correlation between size and what may or may not constitute a building. It would seem, however, that matters are more complex than this. Reference has already been made to the playhouse in the shape of a boot. On another occasion,[18] a lorry body used as a garden shed was described as 'a chattel and not a structure' though no further explanation was given for this description. Perhaps the most vivid illustration that size is not the only consideration involved an inflatable whale.[19] The whale was 80 feet long, 15 feet wide and 15 feet high. It was stationed on Felixstowe Pier where it was secured by ropes. When inflated, on most days from April to October, it served as a children's playroom. Deflated, it was stored on the pier. The question which had to be resolved in this case was whether the inflatable whale could be considered a building within the terms of the section 290 definition. The conclusion reached on this point was that it could not. The following extract from the inspector's report shows how this conclusion was reached.

15 1986, 1 PAD 237.
16 [1977] JPL 122.
17 Ibid, 123.
18 [1982] JPL 202.
19 [1979] JPL 547.

By virtue of section 290 of the 1971 Act, 'building' is defined as including 'any structure or erection'. The fact that a structure may be physically capable of being moved or is not permanently fixed to the ground does not of itself determine whether its installation involves the carrying out of operations constituting a development for the purposes of the Planning Acts. However, in this particular case, the whale is only inflated for relatively short periods for use as a type of enclosed trampoline for children and the view is taken that, when inflated, it is more in the nature of a piece of equipment.[20]

From the series of decisions discussed in the preceding paragraphs, certain generalisations are possible about the nature of a building for the purposes of development control. The list of decisions is by no means comprehensive, yet certain points are constantly stressed. These include whether or not the item in question is fixed to the ground. If it is not, this is not conclusive, since questions will then be raised concerning the ease with which the item can, and indeed has in the past, been moved. Size appears immaterial except where the item in question is so small that it can safely be ignored. A combination, therefore, of considerable size with ease of removal, may convince an inspector that the item in question is outside the scope of the definition of development. The inflatable whale is a case in point. In this context, the purpose for which an item is used and the fact that it is intended to be stored when not in use, may be an important factor.

Circulars and their interpretation of development

The significance of circulars in the planning process has already been mentioned in an earlier chapter. The intention here is merely to consider what guidance is given in the circulars on the question of planning permission in general, and development in particular. What has constantly to be borne in mind is that once it has been established that development is involved, a whole new set of considerations then arise on the issue of whether or not to grant planning permission. These development control considerations, which form the core of this work, have yet to be discussed. Circulars, however, as opposed to judicial decisions, have a great deal to say on development control. This is in the very nature of circulars, since they are essentially vehicles for the dissemination of central government policy. Judicial decisions, on the other hand, can only ever be indirectly concerned with planning policy, in theory at least. The court's task is to interpret legislation and decide whether the

20 Ibid, 548.

powers and procedures laid out in the legislation have been observed.

Given this analysis of the situation, it might be expected that circulars would have little to say on the appropriate definition of development, since this is not their task, nor would any opinion expressed on this matter appear to carry much authority. While many circulars do refer to current legislation, the purpose is normally to alert those who might have an interest in such legislation to its existence, and what it seeks to achieve. In Circular 11/86,[1] for example, reference is made to the term 'development' and the meaning to be attached to it. This is because one of the objectives of the Circular is to make it plain that certain undertakings, such as the removal of material from mineral working deposits, constitute development within the meaning of the 1971 Act.

What needs to be borne in mind, however, is that despite the interpretation of development offered by this or any other circular, such interpretation is irrelevant, if the words of the relevant Act cannot bear that particular meaning.[2] The court's analysis of legislation, therefore, is the only authoritative interpretation, and whatever a circular says must be read with this fact in mind. In the majority of cases the circular will be accurate in its assessment of legislation, but the possibility remains that a circular can be the source of disinformation.

Bearing this in mind, it appears that what slight reference there is in circulars to the term 'development' is concerned, for the most part, with reiterating what is said in relevant legislation. There is little, if any, attempt in the circulars to amplify the terms used in the legislation. There may be various explanations for this. They include the fact that the language used in the 1971 Act is deliberately left open-ended, so that as and when cases arise, decisions can be made as to whether or not development is involved. The whole object of this would be defeated if circulars were to try to anticipate such decisions. In addition, on those very rare occasions when a circular has attempted to do just this, the advice it contains has not always met with the approval of the court.[3] The contribution, therefore, that circulars make to the analysis of the term development is exceedingly limited. The reason for this is rooted in the nature of circulars and the role which they play in the development control process. The approach to what constitutes development is a pragmatic approach. A minimum of guidance is given in the legis-

1 Circular 11/86, Town and Country Planning (Minerals) Act 1981.
2 Circulars are not binding in the sense that primary and delegated legislation are binding. They merely offer advice.
3 *Coleshill and District Investment Co Ltd v Minister of Housing and Local Government* [1969] 2 All ER 525.

lation. Instead, problems are resolved as and when they arise, with a maximum use being made of common sense.

General Development Order and Use Classes Order

Although this chapter is entitled 'Planning permission', so far it has mainly been devoted to analysing the notion of development. This is unavoidable, however, as the concepts of development and planning permission are inextricably linked. As can now be appreciated, the concepts of 'building, engineering, mining or other operations' and 'material change of use', which are the corner-stones of the definition of development, cover a whole range of activity from the comparatively trivial domestic development to major undertakings, such as the redevelopment of city centres.

This fact that certain types of development will have the minimum of impact on the environment has led to the creation of the General Development Order and the Use Classes Order, both of which have already been referred to in passing. These Orders work on the basis that certain developments may be permitted without the need to obtain planning permission beforehand. In this fashion, the administrative machinery of the development control process does not become overloaded with what are relatively trivial matters. Instead, time can be devoted by officials to those developments which will have a substantial impact on the environment and the community at large.

If the logic of this concept is sound, therefore, those categories of development permitted without the need to secure planning permission should be selected using planning policy criteria. The aim should be to ensure that the activities specified in either the General Development Order, or the Use Classes Order, will be those which have the minimum impact on the environment in terms of traffic generated, noise produced or buildings erected. It is equally logical that there may be areas, perhaps of outstanding natural beauty or architectural interest, where even the smallest amount of development may have a disproportionate impact. It may be necessary, therefore, to exclude such areas from the scope of the General Development Order or Use Classes Order.

In the analysis of the General Development Order which follows, these opening remarks should be borne in mind in order to detect whether there is such a logic underlying the terms of the Order. The impact of the permitted development on the environment should be assessed in the hope of determining whether the General Development Order successfully balances administrative convenience with a proper regard for the environment, and the normal issues of development control.

THE GENERAL DEVELOPMENT ORDER

The General Development Order opens with the following statement:

> Subject to the subsequent provisions of this order, development of any class specified in Schedule 1 to this order is permitted by this order and may be undertaken upon land to which this order applies, without the permission of the local planning authority or of the Secretary of State.[4]

From this extract it is clear that there are two aspects to the Order. On the one hand, there is the list of permitted development in Schedule 1. In addition, there are restrictions on this permitted development, which are set out in the body of the Order. This analysis will begin with what constitutes permitted development.

Schedule 1 of the General Development Order lists 30 classes of permitted development, together with their corresponding conditions, if any exist. The general description of each class of development is as follows:

Class I Development within the curtilage of a dwelling-house This allows a house to be extended or a garage to be built, provided the original cubic capacity of the house is not increased beyond certain specified limits. There are also other restrictions covering matters of height, projection and site coverage. Also included in this class are porches, animal enclosures and satellite antennas, all of which are the subject of size restrictions.

Class II Sundry minor operations Minor operations include the erection of means of enclosure, such as fences and walls, the construction of access to certain highways and the exterior painting of buildings. Restrictions are imposed here on matters such as the height of walls or fences.

Class III Changes of use Obviously this has to be read in conjunction with the Use Classes Order. According to the terms of the Use Classes Order a change of use within a class – for example from an insurance office to a solicitors' office – is not deemed to involve development. In Class III of the General Development Order the change permitted is from one class of use to another entirely separate class which might, in normal circumstances, amount to development. The criterion being exercised is clearly that the permitted change is to a use that is likely to be less environmentally damaging,

4 Town and Country Planning General Development Order 1977, SI 1977 No 289, article 3.

thus creating fewer development control problems. Therefore, premises being used for the sale of food and drink (Class A3) or for the sale or display of motor vehicles can be used as shops (Class A1). Other changes between business (Class B1), general industrial (Class B2), and storage and distribution (Class B8) are permitted subject to restrictions on floor area.

Class IV Temporary buildings and uses   This permits temporary buildings to be erected in order to facilitate the performance of building or engineering operations for which planning permission has been granted. Mining operations are specifically excluded. Once the operation has come to an end, the buildings must be removed. In addition, land, excluding buildings and the curtilage of a building, can be put to a particular use without planning permission for not more than 28 days of a calendar year, subject to certain restrictions.

Class V Uses by members of recreational organisations   The class permits the use of land, provided it is not within the curtilage of a dwelling-house, but not buildings, for recreational purposes, provided the users belong to an organisation with a certificate of exemption.[5]

Class VI Agricultural buildings, works and uses   This permits building and engineering operations to be carried out on agricultural land with an area exceeding one acre. There are various restrictions on the height, size and siting of buildings. The operations in question must be related to the agricultural purposes to which the land is put. The extraction of minerals is also permitted, subject to restrictions, but the construction of dwelling-houses is specifically excluded. Permission is also given for the construction of fish ponds as well as other engineering operations related to fish farming. The permission is, as always, subject to various restrictions.

Class VII Forestry buildings and works   Where land is being used for the purposes of forestry, building and other operations are permitted, provided they are relevant to the forestry industry. Restrictions are imposed, including a prohibition on the provision of dwelling-houses.

Class VIII Development for industrial purposes   Where land is used with planning permission for industrial purposes, development, such as the erection of machinery and the alteration of

5 That certificate must be granted under the terms of the Public Health Act 1936, s 269.

machinery can be undertaken. This is subject to restrictions on the height of machinery, the increase in floor space of a building, and provisions designed to ensure that the external appearance of buildings is not materially altered.

Class IX Repairs to unadopted streets and private ways Repairs of this nature can be undertaken provided the works are carried out on land within the boundaries of the street or way.

Class X Repairs to services This permits the inspection and repair of services such as sewers and electricity cables.

Class XI War damaged buildings, works and plant Rebuilding work can be undertaken provided the cubic content of the building is not increased beyond the levels permitted in Classes I and VIII. The original external appearance must be maintained unless permission is given to alter it.

Class XII Development under local or private Acts, or orders Development authorised in this fashion is permitted provided that if it includes the construction of a building or means of access to the highway, the approval of the local planning authority is sought. This can be refused only in certain specified circumstances.

Class XIII Development by local authorities This permits local authorities to provide such items as bus shelters and refuse bins, as well as allowing them to undertake small-scale construction operations on their property for purposes related to those for which the property is used.

Class XIV Development by local highway authorities Works can be undertaken to improve or maintain the highway on land which borders the highway.

Class XV Development by drainage authorities Works can be undertaken by drainage authorities to improve or maintain water courses or drainage works.

Class XVI Development by water authorities Water authorities can, without planning permission, undertake such works as the laying of pipes. Buildings and equipment can also be constructed in order to facilitate the conduct of surveys, provided that the land is restored to its original use and appearance at the end of six months.

Class XVII Development for sewage and sewage disposal Water authorities may carry out works below the ground to maintain, improve and construct sewers.

Class XVIII Development by statutory undertakers Statutory undertakers, such as electricity boards, are allowed to undertake specified development related to their particular statutory functions. For example, the electricity boards can lay cables and construct buildings on their land to protect machinery. Statutory undertakers include not only those obvious examples already mentioned, but some less obvious bodies such as the Post Office and the Civil Aviation Authority.

Class XIX Development by mineral undertakers In order to benefit from this class of permitted development certain quite detailed conditions have to be satisfied. For example, the mining operations in question must have been commenced on or after 1st January 1946 and before 1st July 1948. The type of development which can be undertaken is related to the erection, alteration or extension of buildings, plant or machinery, subject to certain restrictions.

Class XX Development by the National Coal Board A range of activities is permitted subject to certain restrictions. These activities include the deposit of waste and the erection of buildings in the vicinity of the pit-head.

Class XXI Uses of aerodrome buildings Buildings on an aerodrome which is under the control of the Civil Aviation Authority can be used for purposes connected with air transport or other flying activities at that aerodrome.

Class XXII Use as a caravan site Land can be used as a caravan site if the circumstances specified in the Caravan Sites and Control of Development Act 1960 are satisfied. The use must cease when those circumstances no longer exist.

Class XXIII Development on licensed caravan sites Where a site licence issued under Part I of the Caravan Sites and Control of Development Act 1960 is in existence, development required under that licence is permitted.

Class XXIV Development by telecommunications code system operators Subject to restrictions on size, work is authorised to install the communications equipment an individual will need in order to function as a telecommunications code system operator. Such operators have to be licensed under the relevant legislation.

Class XXV Other telecommunications development Installation of microwave antennas on buildings other than dwelling-houses is authorised where such permission is not available under Class XXIV. There are restrictions on the size of antennas and efforts are made to minimise their effects on the appearance of buildings.

Class XXVI Mineral exploration   Operations, such as drilling boreholes, are permitted in order to facilitate the exploration for minerals. Many restrictions are imposed in order to protect the environment. Trees cannot normally be felled and at the end of the period allotted for exploration all buildings and equipment must be removed and the land restored.

Class XXVII Removal of material from mineral-working deposits   A complex provision which authorises this activity, either on a temporary basis until planning permission is obtained under the Town and Country Planning (Minerals) Act 1981, or on a more permanent basis where the operation is on a relatively small scale.

Class XXVIII Warehouses   Subject to restrictions on size, buildings used as warehouses can be extended or altered.

Class XXIX Amusement parks   Where land or a seaside pier is used as an amusement park, certain operations can be undertaken. These include the erection of booths or stalls, which are going to be used to provide amusement or entertainment for the public. Restrictions are imposed on size.

Class XXX Development by the Historic Buildings and Monuments Commission for England   Development can be undertaken to preserve buildings or monuments in the care of the Commission.

From this brief and far from comprehensive survey of the General Development Order it is to be hoped that a picture has now emerged of what constitutes permitted development. Before that picture is complete, however, mention has to be made of certain restrictions set out in the body of the Order. Although a detailed analysis of such restrictions is beyond the scope of this book, an attempt will be made to give an impression of what these restrictions involve. One of the most important allows a local planning authority with the approval of the Secretary of State,[6] or the Secretary of State himself,[7] to direct that either all permitted development, or alternatively certain classes of permitted development, cannot take place in a designated area. Instead, planning permission must be obtained in the normal fashion. In certain special circumstances,[8] the local planning authority may make a direction itself; although operative immediately, that direction will expire at the end of six months unless it has been confirmed by the Secretary of State.

6 Town and Country Planning General Development Order 1977, SI 1977 No 289, article 4(1) and (2).
7 Ibid, article 4(1).
8 Ibid, article 4(3).

Powers to prevent the undertaking of permitted development are also vested in mineral planning authorities.[9] Here, the powers are a great deal more restricted, since they relate only to two very specific forms of permitted development. These are Class XXVI.2 – operations and excavations in order to ascertain the presence of minerals – and Class XXVII.2 – the removal of materials from a stockpile or mineral-working deposit which exceeds certain stated dimensions. A mineral planning authority[10] may make use of this power to require an application for planning permission to be made in the ordinary way, only if what would have been permitted development is seen to pose a threat. That threat must, according to the terms of the General Development Order, take certain stated forms. The land on which the development is to be carried out must be within a National Park, an area of outstanding natural beauty, a site of archaeological interest or a site of special scientific interest. Alternatively, the development must be seen as posing a serious detriment to the amenity of the area in which it is to be carried out, or to the setting of a grade 1 listed building, or to the inhabitants of nearby residential buildings, or would endanger aircraft using a nearby aerodrome.[11] Any direction made by a mineral planning authority in pursuance of these powers can be disallowed by the Secretary of State within 28 days.[12]

From the description given of the General Development Order, together with the restrictions on its operation, certain comments may legitimately be made regarding its effectiveness. It was suggested that the premise behind the General Development Order was that some activities, whilst undoubtedly constituting development, will have such a limited impact on the environment that they can safely be permitted without the need to apply for planning permission. That this is indeed the logic underpinning the General Development Order is emphasised by the nature of the restrictions on its operation. As has been demonstrated, where a mineral planning authority issues a direction restricting permitted development it will be because of the sensitive nature of the environment. Local planning authorities have even wider powers to restrict permitted development, and it might be expected that they too will use those powers to protect environmentally sensitive areas. Indeed, even the classes of permitted development take account of discrete environmental areas, such as National Parks and conservation

9 Ibid, article 4A.
10 For a definition of mineral planning authority, see the 1971 Act, s 2B.
11 Town and Country Planning General Development Order 1977, SI 1977 No 289, article 4A(2).
12 Ibid, article 4A(5).

areas, by restricting even more severely in these areas what can be regarded as an acceptable level of permitted development.[13]

On the other hand, if it is true to say that there are areas of such outstanding natural beauty or historical interest in which either all development must be specifically authorised or, at the very least, lower levels of permitted development can be tolerated, it appears to call into question the accuracy of the premise that permitted development can be allowed because it has little impact on the environment. Undoubtedly, it can have a very considerable impact. In some situations that impact may be aesthetic. The proliferation of porches, house extensions, satellite receiving dishes and fences may do little in the opinion of some to improve the visual amenity of a particular area. Visual amenity is therefore sacrificed, in order to allow the individual the fullest possible enjoyment of his property. Consequently, only if the visual amenity of the area is outstanding will the individual's freedom to deal with his property be restricted.

Yet, closer examination of the classes of permitted development show that any potential effect may go far beyond the purely visual. Class XVIII, for example, which deals with development by statutory undertakers, such as electricity boards or the Post Office, permits the listed authorities to erect on their land buildings or items, such as phone boxes, which relate to the particular function that the body performs. Besides their visual impact, such structures may have other effects on neighbouring property, producing noise, fumes or extra traffic. Even something as comparatively trivial as the erection of a phone box or bus stop may have a considerable impact on the domestic environment of the surrounding property owners.

Yet another aspect to the classes of permitted development is those classes which allow the performance of routine maintenance work. Class X, for example, authorises repairs to services, such as sewers, pipes and cables. This seems eminently sensible, since it allows vital services to be maintained, while the impact on the environment will hopefully be minimal and temporary. In contrast, Class VI, which deals with agricultural buildings, works and uses, allows those who own agricultural land to erect buildings and win minerals from their land. These activities can be engaged in only if certain restrictions are observed, yet there is no denying their impact especially on the visual amenity of rural areas.

It appears, therefore, that there may be no single explanation for the thirty classes of permitted development listed in the General

13 See, for example, Class 1 of the Town and Country Planning General Development Order 1977, where the amount by which a house can be enlarged is restricted in such areas as compared to other localities.

Development Order. Whilst it may be acceptable that the reasons for the inclusion of classes may vary, the question remains as to what those reasons should be. Should the General Development Order be used only to permit development where the environmental impact is minimal? Alternatively, should it be used as a much more radical instrument of policy, designed to boost the economic well-being of the community at large by removing the restrictions on planning control, and retaining them only when there is a proven need so to do. As it presently stands, the General Development Order appears to represent a compromise between those two extremes.

USE CLASSES ORDER

The Town and Country Planning (Use Classes) Order 1987[14] is a provision which seems at first glance to have little connection with the General Development Order. Rule 3(1) of the Order provides as follows:

> ...where a building or other land is used for a purpose of any class specified in the Schedule, the use of that building or that other land for any other purpose of the same class shall not be taken to involve development of the land.

The Schedule lists the sixteen classes of use in four parts which provide a useful means of summarising the Order.

PART A
Class A1 Shops This gives a list of nine uses, including such examples as post offices and travel agents, which are all to be classed as shops.
Class A2 Financial and professional services These are effectively all office uses that 'it is appropriate to provide in a shopping area' such as banks and solicitors' offices.
Class A3 Food and drink This includes fish and chip shops and other shops which provide hot food for consumption off the premises, as well as those premises where food is consumed, such as cafés and restaurants.

PART B
Class B1 Business This is a wide class including offices, other than those found in Class A2, research establishments and industry, provided that the use 'can be carried out in any residential area without detriment to the amenity of that area'.
Class B2 General industrial This is to include all industry that

14 On the operation of the new Use Classes Order see Circular 13/87, *Changes of Use of Buildings and Other Land*.

does not fall within Class B1 or Classes B3 to B7. The best general description would be light industry on a moderate scale.

Class B3 to B7 Special Industrial Groups A-E Specific industries and industrial processes are included in these classes. Examples range from galvanising via boiling linseed oil to breeding maggots from putrescible animal matter.

Class B8 Storage or distribution This includes both buildings and land.

PART C

Class C1 Hotels and hostels Specifically excluded from this class are establishments where care is provided, for example, old persons' homes.

Class C2 Residential institutions Apart from the obvious examples of hospitals, colleges and boarding schools, this class specifically includes residential homes where care is provided.

Class C3 Dwelling-houses Apart from including what might be termed a typical family house, this class also includes a house where up to six residents can live together, for example, students, or alternatively old people in a small residential home.

PART D

Class D1 Non-residential institutions Eight uses are listed which include museums, schools and libraries.

Class D2 Assembly and leisure A list of five uses is supplied, ranging from cinemas and dance halls to outdoor sports centres.

The Use Classes Order differs from the General Development Order in a number of ways. As can be seen from the extract quoted from rule 3(1) of the Use Classes Order, the change of use of a building or land to another use in the same class is deemed not to constitute development of the land. This contrasts with the General Development Order where the activities listed in the various classes are said to constitute development, but development which is permitted, subject, of course, to various restrictions. It appears, therefore, that the underlying purpose of the Orders is different. On the one hand, the General Development Order permits development for reasons, such as expediency, or the minor nature of the change. In contrast, the Use Classes Order indicates activity which is not to be thought of as development. In addition, it cannot be presumed that a change of use from one class to another does automatically constitute development.[15]

The next distinguishing feature between the two Orders is the language used. The Use Classes Order uses general terms whilst the

15 *Rann v Secretary of State for the Environment* (1980) 40 P & CR 113.

General Development Order is much more specific. In one sense the generality of the language of the Use Classes Order is illusory, since definitions are supplied of some of the key terms used in the Schedule such as 'care'. The Use Classes Order is therefore more restricted in its operation than would first appear to be the case. Yet, the underlying purpose of the two Orders is remarkably similar, namely, the liberalising of the development control system. As was remarked earlier, the General Development Order represents the balancing of two very contradictory forces – the desire to protect the environment and the desire to promote the economic well-being of the community. Since the General Development Order is a statutory instrument, changes can and have been made to its content with comparative ease, in order to promote one or other of these aims.

The Use Classes Order represents the balancing of the same contradictory forces and can be altered with the same comparative ease, most recently in 1987. Despite this, many uses of a building or land exist which are not covered by the Order. The problem is that by setting out the uses in general terms, there is a difficulty in including new uses as and when they arise. Should a new use class be invented for them or can they safely be amalgamated with an existing use? Is a recording studio, for example, the equivalent of a professional service or a business in the matter of noise produced, traffic generated, structural alteration required or individuals working on the premises? Since every class should contain uses which are roughly compatible, it is no easy task to add to, or subtract from, the use classes list. Indeed, any plan to expand, or in any way change, that list, must once again balance those competing forces of amenity and economic well-being. Any attempt to strike a balance between the two forces is both difficult to achieve and unlikely to please everyone.

Application for planning permission

Once it has been established that the activity in question does constitute development for which planning permission is required, then the procedure examined in the following pages has to be observed. To begin with, an individual or a company seeking planning permission must submit their application to the local planning authority. Details regarding the procedure to be followed are given in the General Development Order. An application must be made on the form supplied by the local planning authority, and, as well as giving the particulars required by this form, plans and drawings must also be provided so as to enable the land which is the subject of the application to be identified, and to illustrate the nature of the proposed development.[16] All this information is then submitted to the local planning authority, which can ask for additional information if this is thought necessary.[17]

Even at this early stage, it is as well to clarify some points. The first of these relates to the identity of the local planning authority. In most instances the local planning authority is the district planning authority.[18] The second point is that the applicant for planning permission does not have to be the owner of the land or building in question. The chances of an individual applying for planning permission when he does not own the property in question, may well seem remote. Yet, on reflection, it is perfectly logical for a prospective purchaser of land to ascertain whether a local planning authority will allow a house to be built on it and, moreover, a house of the type the prospective purchaser desires, before he invests his money. To ensure that this comparative freedom to apply for planning permission is not abused, however, a fee is charged by the local planning authority for processing each application.[19] The scale of fees chargeable varies according to the nature and size of the development and the fee scale that is currently in operation.

It is possible, in certain circumstances, to make an application for outline planning permission, when the application relates to the erection of a building.[20] It is not possible, however, to make an outline application for a change of use. The procedure used to apply for outline planning permission is identical with that already described. If granted, outline planning permission is usually subject to the condition that certain matters, referred to as reserved matters, have to be approved by the local authority before the development can go ahead. The General Development Order defines reserved matters as items such as siting, design, external appearance, means of access and landscaping of the site, details of which have not been given in the original application.[1] While an application for outline planning permission allows an individual to judge how his proposals

---

16 Town and Country Planning General Development Order 1977, SI 1977 No 289, article 5(1).
17 Ibid.
18 Local Government, Planning and Land Act 1980, s 86. Of the planning applications still dealt with by the county planning authority, these concern, in the main, mineral workings and land in National Parks.
19 Town and Country Planning (Fees for Applications and Deemed Applications) Regulations 1983, SI 1983 No 1674 (amended by SI 1987 No 101).
20 Town and Country Planning General Development Order 1977, SI 1977 No 289, article 5(2).
1 Ibid, article 2.

for development will be received without incurring the expense of architect's drawings to show how the building will look, the process has its disadvantages, particularly in areas where the external appearance of a building may be very important, such as in conservation areas. The General Development Order, therefore, provides that a local planning authority can refuse to entertain an application for outline planning permission, if it believes that information on such matters as external appearance is essential before it can reach a proper development control decision.[2] The applicant may, in these circumstances, either provide the information required, or appeal to the Secretary of State.[3]

Finally, circumstances may arise where a local authority wishes to undertake development on land which it owns. If this is so, a local authority may be in the position of applying to itself for planning permission, since it is the local planning authority. A special procedure has to be observed if, and when, this occurs.[4] Basically this requires the local authority to pass a resolution seeking permission for the development which it may intend to carry out itself or which may be carried out on its behalf. Once the resolution is passed, persons affected by the development have to be notified to give them a chance to object. A copy of the resolution must be placed in the register of planning applications.[5] Twenty-one days after a copy of the resolution has been placed in the register the local authority may pass a second resolution affirming its intention to carry out the development, provided the Secretary of State has not decided to consider the application himself.[6] The planning permission obtained in this fashion is referred to as deemed planning permission.

After the application for planning permission has been submitted to the local planning authority, it must reach its decision on whether or not to grant this permission. The General Development Order states that a local planning authority has eight weeks to arrive at a decision once a valid application has been received.[7] The parties, that is, the local planning authority and the applicant can, however, mutually agree to extend the period.[8] If a planning application fee is

2 Ibid, article 5(2).
3 Ibid.
4 Town and Country Planning General Regulations 1976, SI 1976 No 1419, regs 4 and 5.
5 Ibid, reg 4(3). On the importance of observing this and other procedural requirements, see *J J Steeples v Derbyshire County Council* [1984] 3 All ER 468.
6 Town and Country Planning General Regulations 1976, SI 1976 No 1419, reg 4(5).
7 Town and Country Planning General Development Order 1977, SI 1977 No 289, article 7(6).
8 Ibid.

payable, but is not sent with the rest of the information required, then this eight week period does not begin to run until the fee is paid.[9] After eight weeks, if no decision has been reached or an extension agreed to, the applicant can treat his application as if it has been refused, and appeal to the Secretary of State.[10] From a purely practical point of view, the 1971 Act sets out a deadline, within which a decision must be made in order to ensure that applications for planning permission neither accumulate nor grow stale. That said, the fact that a local planning authority reaches a decision after, say twelve weeks, rather than eight, does not rob the applicant of his right to appeal against a refusal of a planning permission or a condition he considers unreasonable.[11]

Before considering the all-important material considerations which a local planning authority has to take into account in reaching its decision, it is worth mentioning that the Secretary of State for the Environment has the power, under the terms of the 1971 Act, to 'call in' an application for planning permission at any stage.[12] If he does so, then he will make the decision on the application, rather than leaving it to the local planning authority. The occasions when the Secretary of State chooses to take advantage of this power are few in number. In the past it has been used in circumstances where the application for planning permission is of national, rather than local, significance. The application by a property company to develop the Coin Street area in London is one such example.[13] When individuals feel that an application for planning permission raises issues of considerable importance, they can alert the Secretary of State to this fact in the hope that he will call in the application. The decision is, however, one for the Secretary of State to make.[14]

PUBLICITY AND CONSULTATION

Whilst the two parties most concerned with an application for planning permission are obviously the person or persons seeking planning permission and the local planning authority considering the application, other individuals may also want to comment on the

9 Ibid, article 7(6A).
10 1971 Act, s 37.
11 See *James v Minister of Housing and Local Government* [1965] 3 All ER 602, affirmed in *James v Secretary of State for Wales* [1966] 3 All ER 964.
12 1971 Act, s 35. Certain types of planning application, particularly those which, if approved, would conflict with the implementation of the development plan, have to be brought to the attention of the Secretary of State for the Environment to give him an opportunity to call them in. See Circular 2/81, Appendix D.
13 *Greater London Council v Secretary of State for the Environment* [1983] JPL 793.
14 He, in his turn, must act reasonably and not abuse his power. See *Rhys Williams v Secretary of State for Wales* [1985] JPL 29.

application. If, for example, planning permission is sought for a change of use from grocery shop to fish and chip shop, a whole range of individuals may wish to air their views. Some persons living in the area may regard the proposed shop as a useful extra amenity. Others may oppose the idea on the ground that it will generate extra traffic, noise and litter. Owners of similar shops in the vicinity may feel that another fish and chip shop will adversely affect their trade.

In order to ensure that the views which an application for planning permission may generate are taken into account, provision is made to publicise applications in addition to seeking comments from interested individuals. So far as publicity is concerned, all applications for planning permission must, within fourteen days of receipt, be entered by the local planning authority on its planning register.[15] The register consists of two parts. One part lists applications, together with relevant plans and drawings. The other part is intended as a permanent record of applications for planning permission and the fashion in which they were decided. The register can be inspected by members of the public during normal office hours.

Although the existence of a planning register ensures a certain level of publicity for planning applications, the onus is on members of the public to keep themselves abreast of developments in their locality. Since this will mean regular trips to wherever the planning register is held, the chances are that not many individuals will choose to avail themselves of this opportunity. Consequently, local newspapers can, and do, extract information from the planning register to keep their readers informed of proposed developments in the area.

Where it is predictable that an application for planning permission will have far-reaching effects, then additional efforts are made to publicise such proposals. Developments of this nature fall into a number of categories. There are, for example, the so-called 'bad neighbour' developments. These include developments that would produce noise, dust and smell or attract large numbers of people and cars, or simply those activities which, whilst they are necessary, most people choose to avoid. The General Development Order requires those bad neighbour developments that it lists to be actively publicised, so that public opinion can be canvassed before any decision is made.[16] The developments singled out are: (i) the

15 A local planning authority is under a duty to keep a register by virtue of the provisions of the 1971 Act, s 34. The Town and Country Planning General Development Order 1977, SI 1977 No 289, article 21, gives detailed directions on how that register is to be kept.
16 1971 Act, s 26; Town and Country Planning General Development Order 1977, SI 1977 No 289, article 8.

construction of public conveniences; (ii) the construction of buildings or use of land for disposal of refuse or waste materials, or as a scrap yard or coal yard, or for winning or working of minerals; (iii) the construction of buildings or use of land for the purpose of retention, treatment or disposal of sewage, trade waste or sludge, excluding operations such as the laying of sewers or the construction of septic tanks for individual dwelling-houses; (iv) the construction of buildings to a height exceeding twenty metres; (v) the construction of buildings or use of land for the purposes of a slaughter house or knacker's yard or for killing or plucking poultry; (vi) the construction of buildings and use of buildings as a casino, fun-fair, bingo hall, theatre, cinema, music hall, dance hall, skating rink, swimming bath or gymnasium (provided it is not part of a school, university or college) or Turkish or other vapour or foam bath; (vii) the construction of buildings and use of buildings or land as a zoo or for the business of boarding or breeding cats or dogs; (viii) the construction of buildings and use of land for motor car or motor cycle racing; (ix) the use of land as a cemetery.

Should the proposed development fall into one of the classes just described the applicant for planning permission must give notice of his application in a local newspaper. Until this has occurred, the local planning authority cannot consider the application. Besides the newspaper notice, details of the application must be posted by the applicant on the site for a period of not less than seven days in the month immediately preceding the making of the planning application. Where an applicant is unable to gain access to a site of which he is not the owner, the local planning authority should display a notice as near the site as possible. These measures are designed to ensure that a potentially contentious development is given considerable publicity so that individuals who will be directly affected, and members of the public in general, may comment, and those comments be taken into account by the local planning authority when a decision is reached.

Apart from the bad neighbour developments listed in the General Development Order, there may be other activities not listed which might cause an adverse reaction in near neighbours or members of the general public. A proposal for a large residential property to become a funeral home might not agree with everyone's notion of an ideal neighbour. Since, however, funeral homes are not mentioned in the General Development Order, there is no need to give the proposal the publicity which is required for a cemetery, though the impact of the two would appear similar. The problem is that any list of bad neighbour developments is always going to have omissions. Attempts to make it comprehensive are probably

doomed to failure. Responsible local planning authorities, therefore, will ensure that adequate publicity is given to developments
which, in their opinion, are likely to have a particular impact on the
neighbourhood in question. Advice to this effect is given to local
authorities in Department of the Environment Circular 71/73.[17]
This suggests that site notices should be posted when, for example,
in the local planning authority's opinion, the development would
bring crowds or noise into a generally quiet area.[18] The problem
with this advice is that it is not legally binding, and can be ignored by
applicant and local planning authority alike.

This raises a separate but related question about the usefulness of
publicising a proposed bad neighbour development, or indeed any
other kind, as there are yet other instances where an application for
planning permission will have to be publicised, either in the local
press, or by means of site notices.[19] While the notion of keeping
members of the public in touch with proposed developments in
their community appears to have much to recommend it, the usefulness of the opinions gained in this fashion may be questionable.
Members of the public, informed that a theatre is about to be built
in their neighbourhood, are likely to raise questions over the traffic,
parking problems, noise and generally increased activity that such a
development is likely to cause. Yet, these are the very planning
issues that any prudent local planning authority will consider before
reaching a decision on whether or not the proposed development
should go ahead. Notices in the newspapers and on the site are
hardly likely to alert a local planning authority to any development
control issue having a bearing on the proposed development apart,
perhaps, from the strength of public opinion. Even this evidence
may be illusory, since only a vociferous minority may have chosen to
comment. As to the weight which should be accorded public opinion
when making a planning decision, there is no simple answer.

As has been demonstrated, those instances where it is a legal
necessity to publicise a development are not very common. Some
local planning authorities, however, choose to go beyond what is
demanded by law, believing that individuals should be kept abreast
of developments in their community.[20] Another method of canvassing opinion is to consult certain individuals and organisations for

17 Publicity for Planning Applications, Appeals and Other Proposals for
Development.
18 Circular 71/73, para 7.
19 See, for example, Circular 2/81, Appendix D. This direction to local planning
authorities in England calls for planning applications which conflict with the
development plan and for which the local planning authority is not inclined to
refuse planning permission, to be advertised in the local press.
20 For a discussion of this and other issues see Eversley D *The Planner in Society*
(1973).

their views on a particular development. While publicity simply invites comment, consultation normally ensures that informed views are sought out, and taken into account once they have been given. Indeed, in certain instances, there is a statutory duty on local planning authorities to consult.[1] The organisations which they have to consult fall into three categories – other local authorities, government organisations and specialist bodies. District planning authorities, for example, should consult county planning authorities where a proposed development is likely to conflict with, or prejudice, a structure plan or local plan proposals or other determinations made by the county planning authority.[2] Parish and community councils, as well as neighbouring local authorities, may all have a right to be consulted in circumstances where a proposed development affects their locality.[3]

The number of governmental organisations which a local planning authority may have to consult is considerable. They range from the Secretary of State for the Environment to the Minister of Agriculture, Fisheries and Food, and include local water authorities, highway authorities and the Secretary of State for Defence. Who has to be consulted depends on the nature of the proposed development. The likely loss of agricultural land is a matter for the Minister of Agriculture,[4] while operations in the catchment of, or on the banks of a stream or river, require that the views of the local water authority be sought.[5] In addition, there are specialised agencies, such as the Nature Conservancy Council, whose opinions must be sought when the development proposed is in an area of special scientific interest.[6] The whole idea of imposing a duty to consult is to make sure that organisations which possess specialist knowledge, and which may also be responsible for establishing and administering policy at a national or regional level, are informed of current proposals and allowed to express their views on the likely impact of such proposals.

As should now be apparent, during the period between the receipt of an application for planning permission and the determination of that application, a local planning authority is required by law to act in a specific fashion. The aim of those legal requirements is to keep the general public, as well as specific agencies,

1 Town and Country Planning General Development Order 1977, SI 1977 No 289, article 15.
2 Local Government Act 1972, Sch 19, para 19(1), 19(2)(a).
3 Town and Country Planning General Development Order 1977, SI 1977 No 289, article 17.
4 Ibid, article 15(1)(i).
5 Ibid, article 15(1)(f).
6 Ibid, article 15(1)(g).

informed, besides accumulating views on the proposed development. These procedures should not be allowed to obscure the nature of the decision which the local planning authority is taking. The decision is a development control decision taken on sound planning grounds. The whole purpose of consultation and publicity is to have a variety of views expressed on the planning strengths and weaknesses of the proposed development. When the local authority planning committee comes to make its decision, it will have to take account of those views, in addition to any other material considerations, which will help it reach a determination. This is required by section 29 of the 1971 Act. This states that in reaching a decision on a planning application regard must be had to the development plan, if relevant, as well as any other material consideration. It is to this stage of the process that the chapter now turns.

THE DEVELOPMENT PLAN

Specific mention of the development plan is made in section 29 of the 1971 Act in order to stress its importance as a development control policy document. Even if it were not specifically mentioned it would undoubtedly be a material consideration. As it is, section 29 emphasises that the development plan cannot lightly be ignored, though the choice of wording 'have regard to' as opposed to 'shall follow' may be significant. The inference is that once a local planning authority has had regard to the development plan, as well as taking account of other material considerations, it can decline to follow the strategy indicated in the development plan.

The significance of development plans as a source of development control policy will be fully explored in the next chapter. As will be demonstrated, given the time and effort that is devoted to preparing such documents, it does not appear logical to allow them to be ignored. In general terms, the logic of this sentiment is unimpeachable. Reference has already been made to the need for a district planning authority to consult a county planning authority when an application for planning permission is received which conflicts with the structure plan. Provision is also specifically made for a local planning authority that intends to grant planning permission for development which, in its opinion, would conflict with or prejudice the implementation of the development plan, to publicise this fact in the local press.[7] Perhaps the relationship between the development plan and a determination whether or not to grant planning permission is best summarised in section 86(3) of the Local Government, Planning and Land Act 1980.

7 Circular 2/81, Appendix D, para 3.

> It shall be the duty of a local planning authority when exercising their functions under section 29 of the Town and Country Planning Act 1971 (determination of applications) to seek the achievement of the general objectives of the structure plan for the time being in force for their area.

Yet, having emphasised the significance of the development plan, it has to be appreciated that the policy which it contains can be ignored. The wording of section 29(1) makes this clear. What is not clear is when a local planning authority would wish to behave in this fashion. Perhaps the answer to this question lies in the very nature of the development plan as an instrument of development control policy. The specific circumstances of an application for planning permission may, for example, justify a departure from the general policy statements of a development plan. Even more significant is that fact that development plans may grow stale. Although provision is made for these plans to be revised or altered, this can be a lengthy process. A change in policy may therefore be decided upon which affects statements in the development plan without being incorporated into the plan itself. This might lead applications for planning permission to be treated differently than if the development plan were the sole consideration. As long as the local planning authority has had regard to the development plan, this is sufficient.

The other dilemma which may face a local planning authority in its efforts to have regard to the development plan is the fact that such a plan is often either in the course of preparation or revision. At this stage when choices are still being made about the appropriate policy to follow in the plan, an application for planning permission can necessitate choices being made before the consultation period, which precedes the making of a development plan, has occurred. On a purely practical level, the local planning authority must come to a decision or risk being deemed to have refused planning permission. Provided any decision arrived at takes account of all material considerations, which would, therefore, include a development plan in the course of preparation, that decision is unimpeachable.[8] This is the reasoning adopted by the courts and its logic is hard to fault since otherwise, the preparation or revision of a development plan would place an embargo on the consideration of planning applications affected by the embryonic plan.

MATERIAL CONSIDERATIONS

Apart from the specific reference to the development plan, section 29 gives little guidance to the local planning authority on what

8 Circular 22/84, Memorandum on Structure and Local Plans, para 1.12. See also *R v City of London Corporation, ex p Allen* (1980) 79 LGR 223.

amounts to a material consideration. Bearing in mind these qualifications, it is possible to compile a list of what may or may not be regarded as a material consideration. That list reflects the contents of this book and many of those matters briefly mentioned here are considered at length in forthcoming chapters.

Local policy It might be expected that a local planning authority's development control policy is, for the most part, to be found in the development plan. Although this is partly true, the statement needs qualifying in order that an accurate picture of the situation is obtained. A county planning authority must, as a matter of law, prepare a stucture plan. It is a matter of judgment whether local plans are prepared. If there is no local plan this is not to say that a local planning authority will have no policy on future development within its area. It is simply that that policy will not have attained the formality of a local plan. A local planning authority is able to take account of its development control strategy, whether formal or informal, in considering an application for planning permission. Indeed, a formal local plan is sometimes supplemented by informal guidelines, though the legality of this combination may be suspect after the decision in *Great Portland Estates v Westminster City Council*.[9] A full examination of the range and form of local policy is undertaken in Chapter 5.

Central government policy The Department of the Environment is the central government Ministry principally concerned with development control policy. That policy can be expressed in many forms; legislation, delegated legislation, circulars and even after-dinner speeches by the Secretary of State. In reaching its decision, a local planning authority should take into account any of this policy which is relevant to the particular circumstances of the application being determined.

Whether or not a local planning authority is forced to adhere to Department of the Environment policy depends on the manner in which that policy is expressed. Legislation, primary or delegated, is binding on any local planning authority to which it applies. The policy which is expressed in legislation tends to be general in character, designed to provide the framework within which actions are taken. Although, for example, a county planning authority is bound by law to prepare a structure plan, the contents of that plan are barely referred to in the relevant legislation.

The detailed strategy of the Department of the Environment's development control policy is normally revealed in circulars. As has

9 [1985] AC 661, [1984] 3 All ER 744.

already been explained, circulars are not binding in the sense that legislation is binding. Yet, it is equally true that a local planning authority which chooses to ignore the contents of a particular circular, must have convincing reasons for choosing to do so. Apart from the Department of the Environment's policy input, which is considered in Chapter 6, other government Ministries may have policies which have a bearing on development control. The Department of Transport and the Ministry of Agriculture, Fisheries and Food are the most obvious examples, and their influence is considered in Chapter 5.

The site   In resolving an application for planning permission, the site itself is a major factor. The nature of the site and the proposed development will indicate which central government and local planning authority development control policies are relevant. In addition, the past planning history of the site is a material consideration. Factors, such as the site's existing use and past planning permissions, are items which a local planning authority is entitled to take into account in reaching its decision. The weight to be attached to such matters in the process of development control is explored in Chapter 7.

Other circumstances   It is difficult to be categorical on what may amount to other material considerations. It very much depends on whether an issue is relevant to the development control decision being taken.[10] For example, reference can be made to the personal circumstances of an applicant for planning permission. In reality, it is necessary to qualify this statement, as much depends on which personal circumstances can be taken into account in a development control policy. Two cases need special mention. The first of these is the financial situation of the applicant. In general, it can be a material consideration that the applicant for planning permission is unable to finance the scheme in question.[11] However, the fact that a developer may make a considerable profit, should he be given planning permission, is irrelevant. Secondly, whether or not a developer is prepared to offer a planning gain is also, in theory, an irrelevant consideration in determining his application for planning permission.[12] The concept of planning gain is a vexed one. It refers to the willingness of developers to concede benefits, for example a

10 On this point of what amounts to a development control issue or planning policy see *Great Portland Estates v Westminster City Council* [1985] AC 661, [1984] 3 All ER 744.
11 *Sosmo Trust v Secretary of State for the Environment* [1983] JPL 806.
12 *Westminster Rensdale Ltd v Secretary of State for the Environment* (1984) 48 P & CR 255. See also Circular 22/83, Planning Gain.

car park for the use of the public, should their application for planning permission prove successful. Obviously, the availability of planning gain should neither delay the granting of planning permission where this is appropriate, nor cause it to be given where it is inappropriate. There is nothing to stop a developer voluntarily offering planning gain, but its availability should not be taken into account. What constitutes planning gain is dealt with in Chapter 8.

In listing the items which can amount to material considerations, two factors are seen as important. What is material will vary according to the specific circumstances of the case. Even when all the material considerations have been assembled, no single one is conclusive. A local planning authority has to balance them against each other and reach a decision. That decision must indicate the reasoning which lies behind it. If it appears that a material consideration has been ignored or an immaterial one taken into account, the decision can be challenged, either by appealing to the Secretary of State, or by seeking judicial review from the courts, as will be considered in Chapters 9 and 10.

Chapter 4

Development plans

As section 29 of the Town and Country Planning Act 1971 states:

> ...where an application is made to a local planning authority for planning permission, that authority, in dealing with the application, shall have regard to the provisions of the development plan, so far as material to the application, and to any other material considerations ...

The development plan is, therefore, clearly intended to be the first point of reference for the local planning authority when taking its development control decision on any planning application. Consequently, it is crucial to appreciate the form and function of development plans. There is no statutory definition of the term 'development plan'. It is, in fact, a collective term used to cover four types of plan that have emerged since the passage of the Town and Country Planning Act 1947. Department of the Environment Circular 22/84, Memorandum on Structure and Local Plans, contains the bulk of governmental guidance on these documents at the present time. This Circular indicates that the development plan for an area consists of the operative provisions of any structure plan, any local plan, any alterations to either or both of these plans, and the 'old style' development plan approved under the relevant legislation up to and including the Town and Country Planning Act 1962. Structure plans set out county planning authority policy, and as such, provide a framework for local plans which, when appropriate, develop these structure plan policies in relation to specific areas. The provisions of the 'old style' development plan remain operative until revoked, normally by the approval of a local plan covering the same area. To these is now added the unitary plan, introduced by the Local Government Act 1985, which within metropolitan counties and Greater London substitutes for both structure and local plans. These then:

> ...are the documents which comprise the development plan and contain the provisions to which a local planning authority should have regard when dealing with applications for planning permission.[1]

1 Circular 22/84, Memorandum on Structure and Local Plans, para 1.6.

114

Development plans are complex documents of fundamental importance in the development control system. Furthermore, this complexity is increased because the various forms of plan will have been produced at different times. These different forms of plan will also coexist within a local planning authority area and even overlap in some instances, which does little to aid any attempt to appreciate their function. For example, every county planning authority in England and Wales has a structure plan approved under the 1971 Act that covers the area of the county. This structure plan, however, does not supersede any existing 'old style' development plans approved under the 1947 Act that may also cover parts of the county area. The 'old style' development plans will only become 'redundant' when local plans, approved under the 1971 Act, have been adopted. As local plans do not have to cover the whole of a local planning authority's area, they can and do exist alongside the 'old style' plans.

If the development control process is to be fully understood a detailed knowledge of all forms of development plan is required. This is necessitated by the simple fact that the local planning authority must refer to the development plan in making a decision on any planning application, so clearly the plan is of some importance. The plan's main function is as a vehicle of policy, that is, it contains the approved and formally expressed ideas of the local planning authority regarding the future development of its area. These ideas may be expressed in general or quite specific terms, depending on the type of plan. Regardless of the type of plan, however, it is primarily a policy document and the significance of this will now be considered.

Development plans as policy documents

In relation to this all-important function there is no statutory guidance, and little explanation is forthcoming from Circular 22/84, except in continuing references to the need for plans to be '. . . a clear and concise statement of policies and proposals for development . . .'.[2] At the same time, no indication is provided as to exactly how these policies and proposals are to be produced. In some respects, the sources of such policies may be considered obvious. It is clear to any participant in the development control system that a considerable proportion of such policies will be derived from an analysis of local factors. Indeed, this type of policy is part of what development plans should contain, but related to elements of more general planning policy. What is the source of this general planning

2 Circular 22/84, introductory para 1.

policy? If this policy is derived solely from a local analysis, each plan is likely to stand apart from its neighbours, and relate only to its unique locality. This is contrary to the provisions of the 1971 Act, which requires that all such plans should be broadly compatible.[3] To gain a clearer picture of the derivation of this general planning policy, it is necessary to understand the basic concepts of planning philosophy that justify the use of development plans.

THE CONCEPT OF LAND POLICY

It is not the intention of this work to delve deeply into the more esoteric aspects of planning theory, especially when there is more than adequate coverage provided by a host of other sources.[4] Nevertheless, some aspects of the theory must be considered as they are fundamental to a better understanding of the whole planning system. Initially, it must be appreciated that a development plan was regarded as an essential part of those mechanisms created to impose elements of central government land policy at regional and local levels. Land policy is regarded as an element of central government development policy,[5] but opinions differ as to what exactly land policy includes.[6] Clearly, it must be concerned with the ways in which the government interrelates its development policies with those of a social or economic nature. Land policy may, therefore, be better understood if the government's overall purpose in terms of such policy is analysed. In this respect, the government's basic desire is obviously to control the development and use of land. This raises the question of what it may be hoping to achieve, and four suggestions have been made.[7]

Firstly, there is what might be termed the negative purpose of supplying some form of protection for any given area. This has the effect of protecting individual property owners from the actions of their neighbours if these actions could adversely affect their own property interests. As has been suggested elsewhere,[8] such protection exists in the shape of laws governing land and property, for example, the legislation relating to landlord and tenant. Nevertheless, it is a valid purpose for government intervention, and succes-

3 1971 Act, s 15B.
4 For example: Faludi A *A Reader in Planning Theory* (1973); Friend J K et al *Public Planning: The Intercorporate Diversion* (1974); Bailey J *Social Theory for Planning* (1975); McAuslan P *The Ideologies of Planning Law* (1980).
5 Lichfield N & Darin-Drabkin H *Land Policy in Planning* (1980).
6 See the discussions in *Lichfield & Darin-Drabkin,* and in Dunkerley H B et al *Urban Land Policies and Opportunities* (1978).
7 Healey P *Local Plans in British Land Use Planning* (1983) ch 1.
8 McAuslan P *Land, Law and Planning* (1975).

sive planning statutes have added to the existing protection offered by land law in a variety of ways. All such legislation, not only planning statutes, must, therefore, be considered as forming part of the government's development policy.

Secondly, it is suggested that the government's purpose is to compensate for the failure of free market forces to supply the development needs of the country in terms of land and property. This is an intriguing concept, as it involves the implicit assumption that the government is capable of ascertaining what, and indeed, where, such market shortcomings exist. This concept has provoked speculation,[9] since it not only draws on the assumption of welfare economics regarding the government's ability to ascertain need, but also raises questions of the government's own role. It is, however, apparent that such government attempts to ascertain land use needs, and broadly balance them against actual supply, may produce policy that will form a fundamental element in the preparation of a development plan.

Thirdly, the government's purpose can be seen as intervening to ensure that land is used in the general interest. This is quite distinct from the second suggested purpose, where the government is the supplier of what the market fails to provide. In this instance, the government is seen as operating more in the role of the arbitrator between development needs and market responses, although to complicate matters, it may also have participatory and managerial functions. This purpose can best be clarified by referring to some of the roles played by government in the planning system. For example, it can be argued that the government acts as a form of arbitrator in planning appeals, where it seeks to discover what is best in the general interest. In its participatory role, however, it is involved in the production of development plans, which themselves may be the subject of its arbitration at a public inquiry. Finally, its managerial role can be seen as extending from the highest official within the Department of the Environment, down to the local planning officer. All three roles can be viewed as combining to play a part in the government's intervention function.

The final purpose involves the government deliberately controlling the land and property market in a direct manner in the interests of the community. This can effectively take two forms. The first is where the government taxes private land development, nationalises land, or indulges in substantial public sector land ownership in order to deliberately structure the land market. The second is

9 For example: Castells M 'Towards a Political Urban Sociology' in Harloe M (Ed) *Captive Cities* (1977); Hallett G *Urban Land Economics* (1979); Hayward J & Watson M (Eds) *Planning, Politics and Public Policy* (1975).

where the government actively protects the environment in a variety of ways, so as effectively to constrain the operation of free market forces within the protected areas.

These four suggested purposes may be taken as a summary of the underlying motives of the government in its attempts to create an effective land use policy, and elements of each are clearly discernible in the planning system. Consequently, the next stage is to consider how this land use policy is translated into a form of land use planning and the role that development plans play in achieving this. By way of an introduction it is useful to examine the ideas that paved the way for the first truly comprehensive piece of planning legislation – the Town and Country Planning Act 1947.

DEVELOPMENT PLANS AND THE TOWN AND COUNTRY
PLANNING ACT 1947

An examination of the 1944 White Paper 'The Control of Land Use' reveals that a comprehensive national land use policy, forming part of an overall development policy, was very much in the minds of the authors. It is equally clear that the control of land use was to be a fundamental element in this development policy, and that it would take the appearance of a system of land use planning that would complement the national post-war exercise in social and economic restructuring. This restructuring was to take the form of a considered policy involving new housing, totally new layouts for bombed or blighted areas, new schools related to a new Education Bill, the balanced distribution of industry better to maintain active employment, well balanced agricultural production, national parks and leisure facilities and a modern transport system:

> ... all these related parts of a single reconstruction programme involve the use of land, and it is essential that their various claims on land should be so harmonized as to ensure for the people of this country the greatest possible measure of individual well being and national prosperity.[10]

The very essence of the government's land policy was that it formed part of a comprehensive scheme for national development. The resulting system of land use planning can only be fully understood in the context of this wider scheme. Support for such a scheme seems to have been almost total from the political, administrative, and economic sectors of post-war Britain, for reasons that are outside the scope of this book.[11] The land use planning system that emerged was, consequently, able to incorporate new and wide-

10 Cullingworth J B *Town and Country Planning in Britain* (1972) p 31.
11 See Hall P et al *The Containment of Urban England* (1973), for commentary on this aspect.

ranging controls over the development of land that, in different circumstances, may well have been unacceptable. At the heart of these controls, as set out in the Town and Country Planning Act 1947, was the need to apply for planning permission when undertaking development. Decisions on individual applications for planning permission were to be made in the light of land use policy, but clearly, such policy needed to be translated from its broad national nature into much more specific local policy for the concept to operate successfully. The main focus for this translation was a single mechanism – the development plan – which was to embody the essence of national land policy in a specific local context.

This concept of a development plan, and what actually emerged from the 1947 Act, is possibly the first instance of the ideas relating to policy and land use planning going fundamentally astray. In Cullingworth's analysis of the events and arguments which led up to the eventual form that development plans were to assume in the 1947 Act,[12] he makes the point that, from the very outset, such plans were seen as natural extensions of the relevant aspects of national policy. Central government, in the person of the Minister for Town and Country Planning, was to be given extensive powers to ensure that it would not only translate national development policy into land use policy, but would also be in a position to execute such policies. Consequently, the vehicle of land use policy, the development plan, as envisaged in the 1944 White Paper, was to be comprised of two levels. The first level was the outline plan. Outline plans were intended to set out the broad land use policy concepts, and were to be prepared by the local authorities for their districts. The plans were then to be submitted to the Minister for Town and Country Planning, who would consider them in relation to his national land use policies. Outline plans would deliberately be free from the complex mixture of land use detail that had so complicated the previous planning experiments of the 1930s. Once these outline plans had been considered and discussed by the Minister and other interested and responsible parties, they would then be approved as policy documents that set out the general land use principles, which, it must again be stressed, were derived from, and compatible with, national land use policy. Using the outline plan as a basis, the second level of plan, the detailed development plan, would then be created, taking into account the various detailed aspects of land use and development that concerned each area. In other words, there would have been a strictly logical policy and decision-making sequence. This would have led from the general principles of national development policy, as decided by the government,

12 *Cullingworth.*

through the national land use policy as interpreted by the Minister for Town and Country Planning, to the outline plans prepared by the local authorities. The outline plans would operate as the mechanism for reconciling national and local land use policy, whilst the detailed development plan would translate such policy into development proposals for a specific locality.

Such a logical sequence was not, however, to emerge from the procedures set out within the 1947 Act. Instead, the two levels of plan were merged into a single development plan. Quite why this occurred is open to debate,[13] but what cannot be disputed was that the development plan as represented in the 1947 Act fell far short of the translating mechanism it was originally intended to be. Not only was the plan deficient in this respect, but the problem was exacerbated by the fact that the 1947 Act allowed local authorities, which were to act both as plan producers and as plan enforcers, a considerable element of interpretative discretion regarding the principles embodied in the plan. As has been concluded:

> This discretion was unfettered by any requirement to stick rigidly to these principles. In the interests of a powerful and flexible policy-oriented planning system, no mechanisms other than political representation and central government overview were built in to ensure that these powers were not exercised arbitrarily. Similarly, no limitation was put on the range of matters which could be brought to bear on making decisions on future development.[14]

At this point, however, it should be realised that although this form of plan seems to be far removed from the specific policy mechanism originally conceived, its metamorphosis did not cause concern, as it was envisaged that the public sector would be the major property developer. In this scenario, therefore, government land use policy would be guaranteed by the fact that government itself would dominate the property market, not only ensuring suitable developments but also, by its very dominance, effecting a control over land values.[15]

Despite, or perhaps because of, these various concepts, the reality of development plans after their introduction in the 1947 Act was not what had been envisaged. Their failure was not due simply to the shortcomings of the plans themselves, but was attributable, in part, to the administrative system within which they had to operate. The problem started at the top with the new Ministry of Town and Country Planning. This was, in theory, the source, not only of the

13 *Cullingworth*, p 97.
14 *Healey*, p 25.
15 Neutze M 'Urban Land Policy in Five Western Countries' Journal of Social Politics, 1975, p 225.

all-important national land use policy, but also of overall development control. In this latter capacity the Ministry was expected to achieve policy consistency by approving plans and monitoring developments by way of planning appeals. As was observed as early as 1950, however, the Minister had in fact:

> ... only a general mandate for securing consistency and continuity in the planning of land. And this vague direction gives the Minister no real field in which his is the last word, or for which he must bear responsibility.[16]

The problem seemed to be that national development policy, of which land use policy was only one aspect, was being generated by a whole range of Ministries on a far from co-operative basis. The Board of Trade, for example, administered the all-important industrial location policy entirely separately from the land use policy of the Ministry of Town and Country Planning. This contrasted sharply with the function envisaged for the Ministry as the manipulator of a resource and policy base for many other established ministerial areas. The fundamental problem was that these Ministries were unwilling to be so manipulated, and there were two main reasons for this. Firstly, they believed it would undermine their own power structure. Secondly, there was reluctance to place a heavy burden of responsibility on the local authorities who, unlike the Ministries, were novices in implementing land use policies.

The second administrative problem centred on the local authorities, which, despite alternative suggestions, were eventually selected to function as local planning authorities under the 1947 Act. This decision produced numerous problems in achieving the implementation of national land use policy through the mechanism of the development plan. As has already been mentioned, the Ministry of Town and Country Planning was producing very little clear land use policy. This obviously left the local planning authorities with only one option when carrying out their duty to prepare development plans. As national policy guidance was not available they would have to use their discretion in preparing the plans. The problem with this exercise in discretion was that there was a shortage of qualified town planners at the local planning authority level who were capable of understanding '... either the thinking behind the legislation or the ideas of the evangelist town planning movement'.[17] Consequently, the development plan was either farmed out to private planning consultants, which was not necessarily a bad step since it would then be prepared by profession-

16 Haar C M *Land Planning in a Free Society* (1951) p 30.
17 *Healey*, p 26.

als who understood its underlying concepts, or it would be prepared by individuals within the local planning authority, many of whom lacked professional training. This second possibility, which was by far the more common, produced a development plan that tended to be rich in local land use detail, short on local land use proposals, and totally lacking in any concept of national or even neighbouring land use policy.

Despite these shortcomings the planning system lumbered into operation and continued largely unchanged until being reassessed in a major review undertaken by the Planning Advisory Group.[18] In this, the main shortcomings of development plans were summarised as:

(i) a misleading concentration on local detail;
(ii) a largely inflexible form that was difficult to adapt to new issues;
(iii) a general deficiency in the statement of policies, especially those not directly related to land use;
(iv) providing an inadequate guide for development control purposes;
(v) long delays in approval due to an overcentralised system.[19]

The Report blamed these failings on a wide range of factors, but undoubtedly the most significant was that the development plan had been sidetracked from its intended purpose, and its function altered as a consequence. This was due to central government losing interest in national and regional land policy, and consequently failing to ensure that the plans reflected national development policy. In addition, the local planning authorities were increasingly being placed under pressure by the unexpected increase in applications for planning permission from the private sector. The development plans that were created, were, therefore, hurried, unco-ordinated attempts to produce some local basis for the development control process, with no reference to the few policy concepts that might exist at regional or national levels. In these circumstances, the development plan became a negative means of controlling land use, rather than a positive policy document establishing general principles that could be used both to control and to promote development.

The Planning Advisory Group recommended changes in the planning system. In particular, the Group recommended that the main objectives of development plans should be:

18 The Planning Advisory Group *The Future of Development Plans* (1965).
19 *The Planning Advisory Group*, paras 1.2–1.29.

... providing more positive guidance for developers and development control, by widening the scope of plans in order to deal more fully with policy and also the promotion and quality of development.[20]

The system could, it was suggested, be made more efficient by:

... clarifying levels of responsibility, so that only major policies and objectives are brought before the Minister for approval, while matters of detail and local land use are settled locally.[1]

Their proposals culminated in the suggested reintroduction of a two-level development plan system that was practically identical to that envisaged in the White Paper of 1944. Effectively, there were to be structure plans, which set out the broad policy strategy for an area, whilst taking account of national land use policy, and local plans, that would translate the generality of the structure plans into detailed proposals for the control and development of land in specific parts of that area. Only structure plans, as the policy interpretation documents, would be sent to the Minister for approval.

DEVELOPMENT PLANS AND THE TOWN AND COUNTRY PLANNING ACT 1971

The proposals of the Planning Advisory Group were acted upon in the Town and Country Planning Act 1968, which was later repealed and its contents incorporated into the Town and Country Planning Act 1971, which forms the statutory basis of the present planning system. However, it must not be thought that the shortcomings of the development plan system have been eliminated, as it can be convincingly argued that the plans still fail to operate in the way originally conceived:

The identifiable failings of the current planning system ... are a direct result of conceptual deficiencies... These conceptual deficiencies failed to appreciate the purpose and hierarchical nature of strategic planning and failed to appreciate the implications of introducing public participation into planning.[2]

This indicates that the nature of the planning process is essentially hierarchical in which '... each level of planning performs a strategic function for the level below and conversely is constrained by the strategic planning of the level above'.[3] This hierarchy con-

20 *The Planning Advisory Group*, para 1.22.
1 *The Planning Advisory Group*, para 1.22.
2 Bruton M 'PAG Revisited' in *Report on the Policy Symposium on the Future of Development Plans*, Town Planning Review, 1980, p 137.
3 Diamond D 'The Uses of Strategic Planning' Town Planning Review, 1979, p 19.

sequently controls the relationships between the policy options produced at different levels, in allowing them to develop within a specific vertical framework. In other words, policy is produced at any given level as a response to the perceived needs at that level, but in a context that respects the policy decisions that have been made by the level above, and in the knowledge that its own policy will effectively define the general context of the policy produced at the level below. Furthermore, these levels will be represented by organisations which:

> .. may or may not be linked vertically through the different levels of planning activity. However, there is every likelihood that horizontally, at both higher and lower levels of planning, the organisations will be administratively separate and operating within a distinctive set of policy guidelines even though they may be concerned with the same problem or issue.[4]

How then does the British planning system relate to this conceptual model with its postulated logical flow of development policy?

At the national level, in general terms, development policy is probably at its most obvious, in the sense that government is always voicing a concern for the problems of society, the policies needed to solve them and the resources available to effect such solutions. Most departments, the more obvious being the Department of the Environment, the Department of Employment, the Department of Health and Social Security, the Department of Transport and the Department of Industry, are involved with providing the broad policy framework within which land use planning can take place. As has been noted:

> Although policies are clearly stated at this level, the extent to which co-operation and compatibility between the various sectors of central and local government is ever achieved is far from clear.[5]

At the regional level, a much wider range of agencies can be found, for example, the Land Authority for Wales, the ten regional Water Boards, the ten regional Health Authorities, the Countryside Commission, and the Manpower Services Commission. Within their fields of expertise, these agencies all perform a variety of co-ordinating and linking functions in relation to both policy and development, but only in a partial way, as each tends to relate only vertically, to the isolated policy of its national body, rather than horizontally, to other agencies. The only real attempt that was made to alter this system was seen in the foundation of the Regional

4 *Diamond*, p 19.
5 *Bruton*, p 138.

Economic Planning Councils between 1964 and 1965, which were to provide:

> ... a broadly based source of regional advice for central government and to assist in the commissioning and formulation of plans for regional economic and social development.[6]

A range of such plans was eventually produced whose value varied considerably, but the Councils were abolished in 1979, having arguably achieved little of real significance.

At the local level the system is formalised in the shape of structure and local plans. Here, the system clearly requires that the structure plan should provide a formal statement and explanation of the local policies, indicating both their derivation from policies at the higher levels, and their significance for land use policy at the local plan level. Equally clearly, it is at this point that the system is most likely to break down completely because the local planning authority normally lacks a clear statement of its own planning policy. This is compounded by central government's lack of clarity about its own land use objectives, the absence of a regional economic plan, and further confused by a host of regional agencies' policies, many of which are likely to be incompatible. It is hardly surprising, therefore, that structure plans tend to lack the clear and formal statements of policy that are expected of them. At the level of the local plan, the inadequate structure plan is paid little more than lip-service, when and if the local planning authority decides it needs to prepare a formal local plan.

Consequently, development plans are unlikely to be those '... clear and concise statements of policies and proposals for development...' demanded by Circular 22/84, but rather a somewhat vague and general collection of what might loosely be termed land use policies for a specific area. Despite this fact, these plans play a formal, and indeed fundamental, role in the development control process, even if their policy basis is less than sound, and so their structure and nature must be further explored.

Formation and structure

Having considered the derivation of the policy contained within development plans, it is now possible to turn to a more specific examination of the formation and structure of the plans themselves. At present, there are four types of development plan that can be found covering any particular area in England and Wales, with the

6 *Bruton*, p 139.

exception of Greater London where the system is slightly different.[7] They are: (i) the 'old style' development plans; (ii) structure plans; (iii) local plans; (iv) the newest type called unitary development plans. The description of a development plan found in Circular 22/84[8] and reproduced at the start of this chapter indicates the possible interrelationship between the first three types of plan. It is highly unlikely that all four types would be in existence at any one time in any one area. Indeed, some plans are intended to be mutually exclusive, and this is the case with unitary plans which are meant to replace the structure and local plans in Greater London and the six metropolitan counties, following the abolition of those authorities in April 1986. Consequently, it is impossible for both unitary plans and metropolitan structure or local plans to exist for the same district, but this does not take into account the time which will lapse before the unitary plan is prepared, as during this period all the existing plans will still operate in the development control system.

The picture is not as complex as it may first appear, however, and may be summarised as follows. Structure plans will exist for all non-metropolitan areas, normally covering the whole county. County planning authorities are constantly engaged in the process of updating and revising their structure plans, and the resulting amendments, once approved, also form part of the structure plan. After a structure plan has been approved, local plans may be produced by either the county or the district planning authority, but invariably these plans will not cover the whole area of either the district or the county, but only a part. Consequently, for those areas where no local plan has been adopted, the 'old style' development plans introduced by the 1947 Act and possibly subsequently revised, still apply. In other words, in any non-metropolitan area at the present time it may be possible to have as valid policy documents the following development plans – a structure plan, together with some revisions; a local plan with some revisions; and an 'old style' development plan in its latest revised form which cannot antedate the approval date of the structure plan. In any metropolitan area the same mix of plans can exist whilst the unitary plan is in preparation. However, once the unitary plan has been approved, it will supersede all other plans.

Given this situation, it is obviously necessary to explain what

7 The development plan situation in the Greater London area is somewhat different from elsewhere in England and Wales, mainly as a result of the Greater London Plan becoming the structure plan. The detailed differences in relation to each form of plan will be noted at the appropriate point in the chapter.
8 Circular 22/84, para 1.6.

each of these plans is, and the function it is supposed to perform within the development control process. As has already been made clear, the general intention of all such plans was to translate the principles of national land use planning policy down to the local level, but the four types of plan attempt to achieve this in different ways, largely as a result of chronological changes in planning ideology. Consequently, it seems logical to examine the 'old style' development plan first.

DEVELOPMENT PLANS UNDER THE 1947 ACT – THE 'OLD STYLE' PLAN

As conceived under the 1947 Act:

> Development plans were thus to provide principles for trans-lating... policy into spatial allocations and detailed development, co-ordinate the public sector development effort, and indicate the basis on which small scale private development would be regulated.[9]

Consequently, these plans were meant to be detailed, indicating precisely the boundaries of present or future land uses as determined by the local interpretation of national land use policy. Such precise interpretation could logically only take one form, so these plans are essentially map-based. The plans were created by taking the appropriate scale of ordnance survey map, which was then colour coded to indicate the various areas of appropriate land use and development opportunity.

A clear indication of the form and content of these plans is to be found in Schedule 5 of the 1971 Act and in the now superseded Development Plan Regulations 1965.[10] The Regulations repeat the original statutory requirement that the plan was to show the manner in which the land was to be used, and the time stages within which the developments shown on the plan were to be undertaken. They then list what topics the plan might be expected to cover, giving a clear indication of the planning policy that the local planning authority was expected to consider. For example, a plan might define the sites of proposed roads, public and other buildings; allocate areas of land for residential, industrial and other purposes; and designate areas of comprehensive development.[11] At a somewhat more mundane but practical level, the Regulations also indicated the scale of the ordnance survey base maps to be used for such an exercise, the most common being 'county maps', on a scale of one inch to one mile, and 'town maps', on a scale of six inches to one mile.[12] Other maps for particular forms of proposal were also

9 *Healey*, p 45.
10 SI 1965 No 1453.
11 Ibid, reg 4.
12 Ibid, regs 5 and 6.

specified,[13] while all plans submitted before 1965 had to be accompanied by a programme map indicating the dates within which the proposed developments might be expected to take place.

To constitute a complete development plan, these maps had to be supplemented with a written statement which provided additional information that did not lend itself to being indicated directly on the maps. Information would be provided, for example, indicating the policy on residential densities and the form of development permitted in rural areas. Development plans submitted after 1965 would also contain written information on the phasing of development, information that previously had been indicated on the maps. In addition, if an area had been indicated on the map as a comprehensive development area, the written statement would give some indication of the purpose of such proposals.

The 'old style' development plan, therefore, consists of the maps, of which there are normally many, and the written statement. This is inevitably a concise document that explains little regarding the planning concepts and policies, concentrating instead on details, such as development densities. Despite the fact that these plans are clearly map-based, the written statement is specified as taking precedence if there is a contradiction between it and the maps.[14] This can be explained only on the grounds that the Ministry of Town and Country Planning must have realised that if these plans were to be regarded as the local expression of national land policy, then that policy had to be presented in some form of written statement which indicated some logical reasoning. In reality, however, the plans were seen by both local planning authority and developer as simply a means of controlling land use.

The 1947 Act specified that the plans were to be based on a survey of the local authority area but, unlike the 1971 Act, did not indicate exactly what the survey was to include. In addition, the plans represented a local interpretation of national land use policy, but this policy was not particularly evident in the early 1950s when the plans were first being prepared. Consequently, the plans tended to reflect the findings of the local survey, which usually concentrated on the basic planning elements, such as land use patterns and densities of occupation. Given the belief that the public sector was to undertake the majority of development, and the supposition that the private sector would be making few applications for planning permission, the early plans were little more than graphic indications of existing land use patterns. This was probably recognised as being

13 Ibid, regs 7–10.
14 Ibid, reg 15.

somewhat less than what a development plan should be, but as the plans were intended to be revised on a regular basis every five years, local planning authorities simply concentrated on getting their first plan approved.

What actually happened is well recorded and is summarised in the Planning Advisory Group Report in 1965. Effectively, the original plans became, in many instances, frozen as the only approved planning control documents for an area. Even when they were revised, that was nothing more than a simple update of the first plan in terms of altered land use zones and new densities. Despite these shortcomings, in some areas these documents still remain the only approved detailed plan and, as such, must be referred to as the approved policy document when a planning application is made. They are no longer used in an attempt to ensure that all planning applications strictly conform to the specific land use zones, which was one of the main criticisms of their use in the 1965 Report. Problems also arose from the fact that once these plans had been approved,[15] they became akin to 'holy writ', representing, as they did, the only local manifestation of national land use policy that had been approved by the Minister. The fact that they had been prepared with reference only to local factors was conveniently forgotten. Consequently, when the unexpected demand from the private sector for planning permission started to increase, the approved plans were regarded as an essential policy document when determining an application for planning permission. Effectively this was by default, as little other written policy documentation existed at the time. This meant that when a development was proposed that did not correspond with the land use indicated on the approved plan, planning permission was inevitably refused. The plans effectively represented negative planning controls and, as such, bore little relationship to the original concept that created them. Although this is no longer the case with modern, post-1971 Act development plans, it is important to understand this usage of the 'old style' development plans, as it may help to place them in their correct perspective when they are encountered in dealing with a current planning application.

Some of these plans were revised, and in this state they may be regarded as having a somewhat greater contribution to make to an understanding of current local planning policy. This is due to the fact that in the 1960s local authority planning departments became more aware of the needs and limitations of the planning system. At the same time more policy guidance became available from central government. This central government policy took several forms but

15 The procedures for approval are retained in the 1971 Act, Sch 5, Part I.

most common were the planning bulletins.[16] However, it has been suggested that due to the review procedure these 'old style' development plans never achieved finality as:

> The plan is under constant review and in this way is better calculated to represent what, at any given moment, are the latest concepts of good planning.[17]

The plans had to be reviewed every five years, but this did not always occur and the plans, often in only their first revised state, have not been superseded in many areas, and will, therefore, be considered as valid planning policy.

On the question of when these 'old style' development plans are likely to be superseded in any particular area, it is helpful to note that the Secretary of State keeps an updated register indicating the local planning authorities' intention to compile new development plans under the 1971 Act, and the date when this process will commence.[18] This date is of considerable consequence as it indicates the significance that should be attached to an 'old style' development plan for the purpose of a development control decision. Prior to the date, it is the only development plan policy available at the local level, while after the date, the intention to create a new development plan containing current local planning policies as some form of local plan under the 1971 Act is established. This fact would naturally be taken into account when making a development control decision, as it is a clear indication that the policies within the 'old style' plan are under review and likely to be revised.

Finally, it should also be noted that all of what has been said in this section regarding the form and content of the 'old style' development plan is applicable to such plans found within the administrative area of Greater London and the London boroughs, subject to minor modifications.[19]

DEVELOPMENT PLANS UNDER THE 1971 ACT

The survey Part II of the 1971 Act is concerned with structure and local plans and section 6 deals exclusively with the survey that must precede the creation of both types of plan. Since the work involved

16 For example, Planning Bulletin No 1 'Town Centres – Approach to Renewal' included advice and direction on preparing a development plan review relating to the regeneration of town centres.

17 Heap D *An Outline of Planning Law* (8th Edn, 1982) p 44.

18 1971 Act, s 21(7A).

19 1971 Act, Sch 5, Part II; Town and Country Planning (Development Plans for Greater London) Regulations 1966, SI 1966 No 48.

in the survey has, in the past, always proved to be a major undertaking, it is generally acknowledged that the one major survey will serve the needs of both structure and local plans. The survey is normally undertaken by the county planning authority, since it has always been assumed that the survey is a specific procedure which will precede the formulation of the structure plan. Section 6 is not specific on this point.[20] It simply requires that every local planning authority must institute a survey of all or part of its area if it has not already done so. On the other hand, some commentators[1] are quite specific that this duty to undertake a survey refers to the county planning authority, and practice seems to support this contention.

The other point that needs clarification is the requirement to survey all or part of the area. This is not an attempt to save money, but rather this recognises that survey work has been an integral part of the planning process for some time. For example, a local planning authority could have been involved in carrying out relevant survey work, since it was made a requirement in the Town and Country Planning Act 1968. In addition, as a result of the Local Government Act 1972, local planning authorities could have been amalgamated. It could thus be expected that the initial survey work for the county would have been covered, or possibly partly covered, by these previous surveys. Consequently, the requirement for a survey for the purposes of structure plan preparation demands that only those areas as yet unsurveyed should be included in the new survey.

Section 6 also requires that any matters included in the survey be kept constantly under review. A local planning authority can institute a fresh survey at any time if it is thought appropriate. Realistically, the possibility of a new survey being conducted in anticipation of the revision of any structure plan is extremely unlikely, due to the heavy cost, the amount of time needed, and the levels of expertise required. This is acknowledged in Circular 22/84 where it deals with the review of structure plans. The Circular indicates that county planning authorities ' . . . may also, if they think fit, institute a fresh survey of the area, but should avoid unnecessary work'.[2]

The section also requires that the local planning authority must 'institute' such a survey, as distinct from the instruction in previous Acts to 'carry out' the survey. It has been suggested[3] that this

20 Section 6 refers neither specifically to the structure plan nor indeed to any form of development plan, nor to which level of local planning authority is expected to undertake the survey.
1 *Heap*, p 47.
2 Circular 22/84, para 2.3.
3 *Heap*, p 47.

change is deliberate, and reflects a more realistic and modern approach to the creation of planning policy, in that local planning authorities are thereby empowered to seek the help of outside planning consultants in the preparation of the plans. Given the complexity of some of the issues that may have to be included in structure plans, it would be unrealistic to assume that every county planning authority would have the necessary planning experts 'in house'. Consequently, the use of outside experts where necessary would have the important effect of strengthening the structure plan as a major policy document.

The section then notes that the local planning authority is under a duty to consider in the survey those matters which might be expected to affect the development of the area, and actually specifies those matters that must be included.[4] They are the principal physical and economic characteristics of the area, including the details of land use; the size, composition and distribution of the population; the whole of the communication infrastructure; and any other matters that are important to the full understanding of the area, or as may be prescribed by the Secretary of State. The most important requirement in planning terms, is that such a survey must also concentrate on the changes occurring or likely to occur in any of these matters. Finally, there is the additional requirement that, where necessary, the survey must take account of those neighbouring areas that are logically related to the subject being examined, but which actually lie outside the area of the county planning authority undertaking the survey.

The importance of section 6 cannot be overstated, as it makes what might be termed classic planning practice a statutory requirement for the first time. As such, the quality of the plans founded on this survey will be much higher than that of those 'old style' development plans. The information accumulated from these surveys represents a unique set of data relating to each county and its region. A synopsis of this information, moreover, is publicly available in the 'Report of the Survey'. The surveys, therefore, represented a major advance in the preparation of development plans, but as will now become clear, it was still a long and difficult step to bridge effectively the gap between a thorough survey and a meaningful structure plan.

Structure plans The concepts and definitions, both official and academic, of exactly what structure plans are supposed to be and do, has changed since they were first discussed in the Planning Advisory Group Report in 1965.[5] What remains constant, however,

4 1971 Act, s 6(3).
5 *The Planning Advisory Group*, para 2.5.

is the insistence that these plans are to supply the rationale that underlies the policies of the local planning authority. They must also avoid the determination of any detailed land use proposals in relation to specific areas. They are, in effect, to outline and explain the strategic planning policies for the area in both the county and regional contexts, but quite what this entails, and the manner in which it should be presented, has been redefined frequently since the 1965 Report. It is important, therefore, to examine these changes since they allow any structure plan to be seen in context, that is, in relation to the ideas that dominated its preparation during the years of its production.

Function The 1971 Act does not define the term structure plan but simply states that it must take the form of a written statement:

> ... formulating the local planning authority's policy and general proposals in respect of the development and other use of land in that area (including measures for the improvement of the physical environment and the management of traffic).[6]

This statement was considerably expanded upon in the Ministry of Housing and Local Government publication – Development Plans: A Manual on Form and Content, 1970.[7] The Manual sets out seven quite specific functions that a structure plan should perform.[8] These include interpreting national and regional policies in terms appropriate to the area, so they can be used as a basis for establishing aims, policies and general proposals. These aims, policies and proposals can then, in their turn, be used to set the general context for the production of local plans, and also specify where priority areas for intensive immediate action, called 'action areas', should be located. The structure plan is also seen as providing the basis for both the co-ordination and discussion of development control decisions, thus serving as a vehicle to bring the main planning issues before the public and the Secretary of State. Finally, as an interim measure, the structure plan could serve as a basis for development control in those areas that were not covered by an approved local plan. It was, in effect, to provide ' ... the planning framework for an area ... ' in relation to those matters ' ... so far as they are subject to planning control and influence'.[9]

These requirements gave rise to some practical and conceptual

6 1971 Act, s 7(1A)
7 A document produced specifically to aid plan preparers who would have to continue with structure plan preparation after the 1968 Act was repealed as structure plans remained in the 1971 Act.
8 Development Plans: A Manual on Form and Content, para 3.10.
9 Development Plans: A Manual on Form and Content, para 3.6.

problems, particularly in relation to the way in which structure plan policy was derived, and the detail in which it was expressed. The question of detail was an important issue that led to several changes, both in structure plan format and procedure. The problems perhaps stemmed from the function relating to development control, which naturally necessitated considerable levels of detail regarding land use decisions, and also from the fact that the 'old style' development plans were detailed map-based statements of land use policy. Consequently, the county planning authorities were uncertain as to how the structure plans could both guide local plans, and serve as a basis for development control, without including within them some considerable levels of detail. The district planning authorities, on the other hand, having lost some of their planning functions to the counties as a result of local government reorganisation under the Local Government Act 1972, saw both local plans and development control as being powers specifically allocated to them. They therefore criticised structure plans as being too detailed, whilst at the same time failing to supply the strategic policy framework that was supposed to be their main function.[10] This question of detail in structure plans gave rise in 1972 to an amendment of the 1971 Act[11] regarding the procedure to be followed in a public examination of the plan. It was already clear at this stage that the number of individuals seeking to make representations would unduly prolong the inquiry. Undoubtedly, this was attributable to the level of detail contained within the plans, which individuals rightly or wrongly saw as having a direct effect upon their property. Section 9 was, therefore, amended to allow the Secretary of State to choose who would be allowed to make representations at the Examination in Public. This did not overcome the problem of detail, but simply removed one of its consequences.

The problem was tackled more directly in 1974, however, in Circular 98/74, The Functions of Structure Plans,[12] and the Town and Country Planning (Structure and Local Plans) Regulations.[13] These attempted to redefine the functions and content of structure plans in a more succinct manner that emphasised their general strategic role, and stated more clearly the level of detail that should be included. The Circular cut down a structure plan's functions to three. Whether their order implies some sort of priority is open to

10 Finney J & Kenyon S 'Relationship Between Structure Planning and Local Plans in a Metropolitan Area' in *Structure Planning Practice and Local Planning Practice* (1976) p 57.
11 1971 Act, s 9(3).
12 This circular is no longer current but is useful in that it introduced what were to become almost the standard functions of structure plans.
13 SI 1974 No 1486.

debate. According to Circular 98/74, structure plans should explain the local planning authority's policies and proposals for development, thereby giving guidance on issues of structural importance. As to what constitutes such an issue, the following definition is supplied:

> ... an issue of structural importance is a matter on which the choice will affect either the whole, or a substantial part, of the area concerned.[14]

Secondly, structure plans must demonstrate the integration and utilisation of national and regional policies within the area. Finally, they were to provide the basis for local plans by establishing the local planning framework.

This precise description effectively laid the foundations for what were to become the established general functions of all structure plans. It has survived largely unchanged and can be found in the current circular on structure plans, Circular 22/84. Consequently, what might be termed the modern concept of structure planning emerged in 1974 and has influenced the form, content and scope of the majority of plans approved after that date. No plans were, in fact, approved until 1975, when the first four appeared,[15] while only three more gained approval in 1976,[16] and in these cases it is unlikely that the modern concepts were included. Approvals gained in pace from 1977 onwards, however, and in these later plans it should be assumed that the 1974 concepts were fully integrated.

Form Circular 22/84 not only confirms that the three functions of a structure plan remain unchanged, but also offers advice on what the plan should contain, namely, policies and general proposals of structural importance.[17] The emphasis is to be on 'broad detail' expressed in 'general terms' so as to avoid the old problem of excessive detail. On the same lines, the obligation to explain fully the content from within the plan, which might involve the introduction of details, has been abandoned in favour of a separate document which does not form part of the plan.[18]

The structure plan itself consists of a written statement, and a key diagram, which takes the form of a generalised map of the area, and

14 Circular 98/74, Structure Plans, para 3.
15 These were the Solihull County Borough Structure Plan, the Warwickshire Structure Plan, the Hereford and Worcestershire (Worcestershire) Structure Plan and the Coventry County Borough Structure Plan.
16 These were the Greater London Development Plan, the Hereford and Worcestershire (Herefordshire) Structure Plan and the Leicestershire (excluding Rutland) Structure Plan.
17 Circular 22/84, para 2.1
18 This is now called the explanatory memorandum which has to be submitted with, but does not form part of, the structure plan.

these documents must be accompanied by an explanatory memorandum.[19] It is important to note that the requirement for an explanatory memorandum was introduced by the Local Government, Planning and Land Act 1980.[20] Consequently, plans approved before 1980 will not have such a document, and the information normally to be found in the explanatory memorandum will be an integral part of the written statement.

As is specifically required by the 1971 Act, the written statement must formulate the policy and proposals of the local planning authority; state the relationship between these proposals and those of their neighbouring planning authorities if they may affect each other; and also contain any other matters as directed by the Secretary of State. Section 7(4) then requires that these policies and proposals must be justified by reference to the survey and additionally, have regard to any current regional economic planning policies that relate to the area, and to the availability of resources needed to carry out the proposals for the area. Section 7(6) requires that the whole statement must be illustrated by a key diagram and any other diagrams needed to explain the plan more fully.

Prior to 1980, the written statement would also contain a full justification of each and every policy that the planning authority saw fit to place within the plan. Therefore, once the plan was approved by the Secretary of State, not only the policies within it, but also, by implication, the reasons supporting those policies, were given authority. Arguably, in considering policies in a pre-1980 structure plan, of which there are seventy-one, it is far more difficult to dispute the justification or appropriateness of any policy in that plan, since both the policy and the reasoning to support it have been formally approved.

After 1980, however, this justification element has been removed to the explanatory memorandum. The reason for this change is difficult to understand, as the level of reasoning that has to be included in the memorandum is no less demanding than that which originally had to be included in the written statement. The memorandum, however, is not to be treated as forming part of the structure plan, despite being required as part of the formal submission. As has been noted:

> The change may be one of form rather than substance, but it means presumably that in approving the policies and proposals in the structure plan the Secretary of State does not necessarily approve the local planning authority's reasons.[1]

19 Circular 22/84, paras 2.9–2.19.
20 Introduced as an amendment to the 1971 Act, s 7(6A).
1 Telling A E *Planning Law and Procedure* (7th Edn, 1986) p 55.

It may now be possible to dispute the justifications for policies contained within the post-1980 plans as the justifications themselves are not subject to approval and cannot be regarded as 'faits accomplis'.

Content With regard to the written statement, it is now useful to consider what subjects are included, or indeed, have to be included within this part of the structure plan. As has been mentioned, the content will vary depending on whether the written statement is pre- or post-1980, but both forms of statement will indicate, in general terms, the county planning authority's policies and proposals for the development control of their area. Circular 22/84 also contains some quite specific advice on the subjects to be included in these statements. Before considering this advice in more detail, it is important to understand both the form and sources of the policies and proposals included, in order to appreciate what constitutes an acceptable or unacceptable proposal.

The fundamental problem seems to lie in the structure of the plans themselves, where the policies expressed have to be broad enough to specifically exclude their interpretation as detailed development control policies. This, together with the fact that the topics that the plans could include were wide-ranging in the extreme, gave the local planning authorities a scope which they apparently found difficult to cope with. As various commentators have noted,[2] the content of structure plans has shown some marked changes since the first were approved in 1975. The early plans attempted a comprehensive approach, being much influenced by the strategies of regional planning.[3] Furthermore, due to the impossibility of analysing the enormous quantities of data that covered every aspect of what were often large county areas, the actual analysis often failed to go beyond even the most elementary levels[4] and the resulting policies were very broad and vague. For example, the following are two examples of policy statements taken from the City of Coventry Structure Plan, 1975:

Transportation Policy
5. 5. 1 The Council will pursue an integrated transport policy involving improvement and extension to the existing road network and public

2 For example: Drake M et al 'Aspects of Structure Planning' (1975) Centre for Environmental Studies Report 20; Barras R & Broadbent T A 'The Analysis in English Structure Plans' Urban Studies, 1979, p 1; Eke J F 'Structure Plans' Public Finance and Accountancy, 1977, p 149.
3 Davies C 'Structure Plans: Theory and Practice' 1975, Midlands New Towns Society.
4 *Barras & Broadbent.*

transport services and restraint on the use of the private car during the peak period by means of selective parking controls and traffic management.

Shopping

5. 7. 4 Central Area

The Council will encourage the quality, variety and extent of central area shopping provision by selective floorspace increase, concentrating upon the possible provision of a further department store and additional small shop units to improve trade mix, to ensure the maximum use of the resources of the City and enhance the commercial attractiveness of the City while having regard to the success of other policies which aim to absorb under-utilised capacity of existing shops.

As can be seen, such statements are clearly capable of a wide interpretation, but it must be stressed that this does not negate in any way their standing as approved policy, providing that the structure plans from which they come are not in the process of being reviewed. Until such time, they remain a controlling force on the local planning authority, even if they no longer represent or indeed clearly state the policies of the authority.

Later plans, which were still in the process of preparation after the publication of the 1974 Circular,[5] all tended to concentrate on the advice which it contained, which was to isolate the key issues of the area rather than attempt the previous blanket approach. As a result, subsequent plans have tended to be somewhat more specific in highlighting policies that were seen as fundamental to the effective planning of the area, and this trend continued until the last plan was approved in 1985. This concentration on specific policies, however, has not narrowed the range of subjects covered in the structure plan, as different counties concentrated on different issues, which naturally raises the important question of how certain issues were chosen and others excluded.

The contents of some of the plans clearly related to issues that arose from the geographical nature of the county, as in the case of the Cambridgeshire Structure Plan, which focused on the problems caused to the inhabitants by rural inaccessibility. However, as has been pointed out,[6] although the issues in the Cambridgeshire instance stemmed from the physical nature of the settlement pattern, the suggested policy solutions were of a distinctly social nature, effectively involving the redistribution of certain resources to disadvantaged groups. This introduces the question of what constitute acceptable policies within these plans, and the criterion seems to be

5 Circular 98/74.
6 Bruce A 'Structure Plan Amendments Show Centralist Tendencies' Planning, 1980, 14th November, p 394.

that they must serve a genuine planning purpose. As to what exactly constitutes a planning purpose, this issue has been fully explored by the courts and will be considered in detail at the end of this chapter. At this stage it is sufficient to note that the House of Lords defined a planning purpose as that which related to the character of the use of the land.[7]

As to how such planning policies are produced, little research has been undertaken on the production of structure plans.[8] What should be clearly understood is that structure plans are compromises in the truest sense, in that they reflect the intermediate course between conflicting opinions. The opinions include those of the planning officers in the local planning authority preparing the plan. There are also other groups whose opinions the plan-preparing authority has a statutory obligation to canvass. These include the district authorities within the county area, and local pressure groups, such as amenity societies, not to mention national pressure groups and central government itself. Added to this is the fact that local councillors will also have ultimate control over the opinions that emerge as a result of the statutory consultation. This may produce an interesting explanation as to the level of compromise included within the plans, as it has been suggested that:

> Policy choices spelt out too explicitly might generate opposition from councillors, from the districts, and from other powerful interests.[9]

This view has been supported by research.[10] In terms of having their opinions incorporated as part of the plan, the most effective of these participating groups are probably the district councils and local pressure groups, followed by public agencies and central government departments who are motivated when policies touch on their specific interests. Least interested appears to be the private property sector, due possibly to the nature of these plans, containing, as they do, general rather than specific policies. These general policies tend to be non-site specific, insofar as, although they may be related to a particular part of the county area, such as a town centre, they do not, indeed must not, apply to any specific geographically definable parcels of land. Consequently, it is only when such parcels of land are considered as suitable areas for housing development by the

---

7 *Great Portland Estates v Westminister City Council* [1985] AC 661, [1984] 3 All ER 744.
8 Blowers A *The Limits of Power. The Politics of Local Planning Policy* (1980); Dare R 'Public Participation and State Power: the Case of South Yorkshire' Policy and Politics, 1979, p 337; 'The Dialectics of Policy-Making: Form and Content' in Healey P et al (Eds) *Planning Theory: Prospects for the 1980s* (1982).
9 *Healey*, p 58.
10 *Blowers*.

private sector, that concern would be shown regarding development policies within the structure plan. In taking this somewhat relaxed approach to structure plans, the private sector could be underestimating their significance within the planning system, and in the revisions of these plans which are now taking place, all potentially interested parties would do well to be involved at the policy formulation stages.

Scope Having established that the policies and justifications contained, either within the written statement, or in the written statement and the explanatory memorandum, are compromises between the views of the various parties concerned, it is possible to consider the actual topics included. Circular 22/84 devotes the whole of one section[11] to listing these topics. This section also comments on the content of local plans and effectively illustrates the differences between the two types of plan by continually stressing the generality of structure plan policies as contrasted with the specific nature of the policies found in local plans.

The Circular emphasises that non-land use matters such as ' . . . financial support, consultation arrangements and proposed methods of implementation . . . '[12] should not be included as policies within the structure plan itself, but could be included in the explanatory memorandum if forming part of the reasoned justification. Further comments indicate that the plans ' . . . should be precise but should not be over-detailed, particularly where they are quantified';[13] that the policies should not be limited to any specific time duration; and that in relation to any revision of a plan, the current national or regional policies should be considered and included where appropriate. The importance of taking account of resources is then stressed, together with the importance of clearly stating the assumptions upon which various resource allocations may be made.

This need to clarify any assumptions contained within the plan or its related documentation is again alluded to in the context of forecasting future levels of population and employment, but this is qualified by stating that ' . . . it should seldom be necessary to undertake elaborate forecasting exercises . . . '.[14] Such a statement is difficult to reconcile with the stress placed on the importance of clarifying the assumptions, but probably relates to two aspects of the government's view of these plans. Firstly, they should be prepared, or rather, at the present time, revised as quickly as possible

11 Circular 22/84, section 4, The Content of Structure and Local Plans.
12 Circular 22/84, para 4.2.
13 Circular 22/84, para 4.3.
14 Circular 22/84, para 4.12.

without wasting time on data analysis at unnecessarily sophisticated levels. Secondly, the present revision process is such that the plan itself has become a much more flexible, indeed, almost transitory document, that can be altered to reflect change whenever necessary. This view of the plans is supported by implication in a later statement to the effect that 'Existing planning permissions are not inescapable commitments and it is the function of structure . . . plans to reappraise the position . . . '[15] This point is further emphasised by the statement on phasing which suggests that plans:

> . . . should allow flexibility in the rate at which land is made available for housing, subject to the need to relate this to the provision of new services, roads etc. While the provision of major infrastructure and other services may affect the programming of development, phasing should not be used as an arbitrary rationing process governing the release of land available for development.[16]

The flexibility of the plan seems to be established, therefore, and this must be seen as an important point when taking account of the standing of policy contained within the plan.

The Circular then proceeds to cover the specific topics that will normally be included within structure plans. The first of these deals with Housing.[17] After stating that structure plans should give a general indication of the scale of allowance that has been made for housing, including, if necessary, actual numbers, and suggesting that the explanatory memorandum could indicate the different means whereby the housing could be supplied, the Circular indicates what would not be desirable in any such policy:

> However it is not in general desirable to seek to control the disposal of private houses through planning restrictions, and it is inappropriate to include . . . policies or proposals which might lead to the assessment of planning applications on the basis of the identity, personal needs or characteristics of individuals (for example the number of years a person has lived in the area).[18]

The next topic comes under the heading of Industry and Commerce and simply states that the structure plan policies should promote the regeneration of industry wherever possible. What is rather puzzling, however, is the suggestion that the plan should indicate proposals for major energy developments. The suppliers of such requirements, for example, the Central Electricity Generating Board, are not constrained in any way by structure plan policies, as

15 Circular 22/84, para 4.16.
16 Circular 22/84, para 4.17.
17 Circular 22/84, paras 4.18 and 4.19.
18 Circular 22/84, para 4.19.

will be fully explained in the next chapter. The only possible explanation for the suggested inclusion of these proposals, is that the government sees such policies as indicating a need for a particular resource which can then be taken into account when energy expansion plans are being discussed on a national basis. In this sense the plan can almost be regarded as an advocacy document.[19] It also brings into question the insistence that the plans be based on realistic resource estimates, which is hardly the case when the resource in question is not under the control of the local authority.

Shopping is the next topic, and relatively bland advice is offered in the Circular, including warnings that policies relating to large new shopping developments should be based on careful assessments of the traffic implications and existing retail patterns. The same uninformative approach is apparent when the next two topics, Transport Facilities and the Management of Traffic, are considered. Except here it is made clear that certain policies must be included in a structure plan, if, for instance, they are contained in a specific government policy document, such as a White Paper on roads. Comments then follow on Agriculture and Forestry, Minerals, Waste Disposal, Hazardous Development, Environment Improvement and Pollution Control, Environmental Protection and Conservation, Green Belts and Recreation and Tourism. Few significant points are raised, except to confirm the observation that policies within the plans may be reinforced by separate government policy or guidance.

The Circular then closes with some practical and detailed comments on the key diagram which must accompany the written statement. This diagram takes the form of a simplified map of the area of the plan which attempts to illustrate the physical location of the main policy proposals. Most important is the requirement that the diagram must not be overlaid on an ordnance survey map, as this could lead to an attempt to interpret the proposals in terms of specific locations. Furthermore, in the event of any contradiction between the diagram and the written statement, the latter will take precedence.

Approval Before a proposed structure plan is submitted to the Secretary of State for his approval, certain statutory procedures have to be observed. These are to be found in the 1971 Act, the

19 Struthers W A K & Williamson C 'Economic Development – Integrated Policy Planning and Implementation in Merseyside' Structure and Regional Planning Practice and Local Planning Practice, 1978, PTRC, p 1; Briscoe B 'The Implementation of Economic Policies in the West Yorkshire Structure Plan' Structure and Regional Planning Practice and Local Planning Practice, 1978, PTRC, p 11.

Town and Country Planning (Structure and Local Plans) Regulations 1982 and Circular 22/84.[20] As these documents go into considerable detail regarding all the various steps, it is sufficient simply to note their most significant aspects. There is a six-week period that runs from the publication of the draft plan and the explanatory memorandum within which interested parties can make representations to the local planning authority regarding its proposals. It is the responsibility of the local planning authority to make its proposals known, rather than simply advertise their existence. Apart from the requirement to consult the district councils within the plan area, it is also suggested that authorities will wish to make sure that particular efforts regarding publicity are made:

> ... (a) in areas on which the proposals ... are likely to have a particularly significant impact or where they provide for immediate change; (b) to bring the policies ... to the attention of identifiable groups of people who will be particularly affected by them; and (c) to bring the policies ... to the attention of sections of the community which, for example, because of language problems, may not be reached by the authority's normal publicity measures.[1]

Having left no stone unturned in publicising its proposals, the local planning authority is free to incorporate into the plan any comments and suggestions that it thinks appropriate. The structure plan is then submitted to the Secretary of State together with a section 8 statement which records the publicity that the local planning authority has afforded the plan. At the same time, the plan is made available by the local planning authority for inspection by any interested party and, providing that the Secretary of State is satisfied with the section 8 statement, there is a further period of six weeks during which any representations from the general public can be made directly to the Secretary of State. Assuming at this stage that the Secretary of State does not exercise his right to reject the plan outright,[2] he may choose to institute an Examination in Public[3] where issues are considered which, in the opinion of the Secretary of State, need further discussion. Such issues may include:

> ... conflicts between the submitted proposals and national or regional policies, or those of neighbouring planning authorities ... or where there are issues involving substantial unresolved controversy.[4]

20 1971 Act, s 8; SI 1982 No 555, part VII; Circular 22/84, paras 2.20–2.30.
1 Circular 22/84, para 2.25.
2 1971 Act, s 9(1).
3 1971 Act, s 9(3b).
4 Circular 22/84, para 2.36.

Since the Secretary of State selects the issues for discussion this gives him the right to select the people who will be heard at the Examination in Public.[5] A code of practice has been established by the Secretary of State regarding the Examination in Public.[6] Effectively, the procedure adopted is inquisitional, meaning that the inspectors, who are responsible for hearing the Examination in Public, question the interested parties invited to attend in an attempt to clarify the points at issue.

The whole plan approval procedure is concluded when the Secretary of State considers the inspector's report of the Examination in Public, together with all the other documentation and any other matters that he thinks may be relevant. The Secretary of State can then approve or reject the plan, or propose modifications to it, but he must give reasons for his decision. If he chooses to modify the plan, another period of consultation and public participation ensues. Ultimately, a point will be reached when the plan is considered satisfactory by the Secretary of State, and the plan will be approved and published in the prescribed manner.

The procedures outlined are, to a certain extent, of historic interest, as all structure plans have now been approved, but an understanding of the process is important, since the procedures may be relevant if substantial modifications and alterations of a structure plan are contemplated. It is a matter for the discretion of the Secretary of State[7] whether the full procedures will be followed for modifications to structure plans. An appreciation of the procedures also gives a better understanding of the ways in which the policies contained within the plan are derived and modified.

Some general comments can be added regarding the procedures for approval and modification. Little empirical research has been undertaken, but some commentators[8] remain convinced that central government interests predominate in any alterations that are made. The process of modification has been summed up as one dominated by:

> . . . 1. the strong sectoral patterns of government organisations overlaying the apparent 'pluralism' of the public sector development effort; 2. the political priorities of county authorities and their relations with districts; 3. the policy interests of central government ministers and the interpretation of these by central government officials; and 4. the way in

5 1971 Act, s 9(5).

6 Department of the Environment, 'Structure Plans: The examination in public – A guide to procedure' (1984).

7 1971 Act, s 10.

8 Jowell J & Noble D 'Planning as Social Engineering: Notes on the First English Structure Plans' Urban Law and Policy, 1980, p 293.

which the views of national industrial and development interests and local business and environmental lobbies filter into the thinking of ministers and local councillors on the one hand, and central and local government planners on the other.[9]

In part, therefore, structure plans may be seen as playing a strategic role of interpreting central government policy at a local level, the very role that planning philosophy has dictated they should play. But, as has correctly been suggested, there are far more interests involved than simply those of central and local government, so the structure plan represents a much broader and less well defined statement than would be the case if it were simply the vehicle for central government policy. A substantial body of criticism[10] has emerged regarding various aspects of the plans, and modifications have been introduced in relation to procedures for altering and updating the plans.[11] At present, however, the structure plan remains as the foundation policy document for all aspects of development control in England and Wales, and is likely to remain a constant source of reference.

Local plans   As Circular 22/84 succinctly states in its introduction:

> The structure plan sets out the county planning authority's policy and general proposals for the development and other use of land . . . and provides a framework for local plans. It is supplemented, as appropriate, by local plans which develop the policies and general proposals of the structure plan and relate them to precise areas of land.[12]

The Circular then indicates that local plans have four main functions:

> (a) to develop the policies and general proposals of the structure plan and relate them to precise areas of land defined on the proposals map; (b) to provide a detailed basis for development control; (c) to provide a detailed basis for co-ordinating and directing development and other use of land – both public and private; and (d) to bring local planning issues before the public.[13]

Clearly, these statements raise issues that need explanation. Some indication is necessary as to who produces such plans and how they have developed within the present planning system; their relationship with structure plans; and the nature of their form and content, as well as the means by which they gain approval.

9 *Healey*, p 63.
10 For example, see the various comments from the contributors to *The Future of Development Plans: PAG Revisited* in Town Planning Review, 1980, 51(2).
11 Current procedures are to be found in Circular 22/84 and SI 1982 No 555.
12 Circular 22/84, para 1.7.
13 Circular 22/84, para 3.1.

Function The first of these questions can easily be answered by referring to section 11 of the 1971 Act which deals with the preparation of local plans. In this section the phrase 'local planning authority' is frequently used in connection with local plan preparation, and no distinction is made between either county planning authority or district planning authority. This implies that either local planning authority can prepare a local plan, the criterion being simply the local planning authority's perceived need for such a plan. What is also made clear in the same section,[14] is that, unlike structure plans, the decision to prepare a local plan is at the discretion of the local planning authority. Although the Secretary of State may direct the matters to be included in such a plan, his power to insist that a local plan must be prepared is limited.[15]

Given this fact, it might be concluded that local plans are not expected to play a major role within the planning system, but in reality nothing is further from the truth. The fact that a local planning authority is under no duty to prepare such plans simply reflects the actual situation. This is that many areas are either already fully developed to a level of practical equilibrium, or are areas within which extensive development pressures are unlikely to occur. In these instances, a local plan would be superfluous to the needs of the local planning authority, and, given the lengthy procedures that have to precede its approval, its existence would be an unnecessary luxury.

Local plans are, therefore, usually optional,[16] but a considerable number have already been adopted, and many more have been designated, which means that a local planning authority has declared its intention to prepare a local plan. Those designations that occurred prior to 1987 can be discovered from an examination of the Development Plan Scheme held within each county of England and Wales. These schemes had to be prepared by county planning authorities,[17] in consultation with district planning authorities, indicating the local plans that were to be prepared within the county area. The information was not quite as comprehensive as might first appear, however, as schemes for certain areas, such as Greater London, were not included. The current situation has been altered somewhat as a result of the Local Government Act 1985 which, among other things, abolished the metropolitan county councils

14 1971 Act, s 11(1).
15 Ibid, s 11(7) and (10).
16 Any action area local plans indicated in a structure plan approved prior to 13th November 1980 must be prepared by the relevant local planning authority. This requirement has been removed by the Local Government, Planning and Land Act 1980.
17 1971 Act, s 10C.

and introduced a new form of development plan, called a unitary plan, which is not to be included in these schemes.[18] The Housing and Planning Act 1986 also introduced revised procedures for the schemes. A full explanation of the new schemes, now called Local Plan Schemes, is provided by Schedule 10 of the Housing and Planning Act 1986. Essentially, the new schemes are to be much more detailed, containing information regarding the nature and scope of the plan, as well as the area covered. The schemes will also provide a record of alterations to, and replacements of local plans, as opposed to simply recording the intention to prepare such a plan. The most important aspect of both the old and new style schemes is the fact that they are available for consultation by the public and, as such, provide an important calendar of potentially crucial policy and development decisions for specific areas of England and Wales.

Available statistics make it possible to gain an accurate indication of the trend towards local plan production over the last decade. From the date of the adoption of the first local plan in the City of Coventry (The Eden Street Action Area Plan) in 1975, production has been erratic. In 1976 it was estimated from the figures provided by the Development Plan Schemes that 3,543 local plans would be adopted in England by 1980, excluding the Greater London Council area.[19] Currently, it appears that only 526 or less than 15% of the estimated 3,543 have been prepared and only 304 adopted.[20] In 1982, Development Plan Schemes indicated a total of 1,382 proposed plans with 79 adopted.[1] This total of 1,461 means that over 2,000 of the plans proposed in 1976 had been abandoned. Suggestions can be made on why these plans should have been dropped. Local planning authorities were advised by the Department of the Environment in the past[2] that only plans which could be prepared and adopted within one year should be included in the schemes. Local planning authorities also undoubtedly made use of alternative non-statutory policy documents, or simply no longer saw a need for plans proposed in the first flush of enthusiasm. For whatever reason, the fact remains that the number of local plans proposed or adopted today is far less than originally anticipated.

18 The existing development plan schemes will remain in metropolitan areas, however, until such time as the unitary plans are approved.
19 Mabey R & Craig L 'Development Plan Schemes' The Planner, 1976, p 70.
20 Bruton M & Nicholson D 'Local Planning in Practice: A Review' The Planner, 1985, December, p 14; Coon A G 'Local Plan Coverage in the UK' The Planner, 1986, January, p 28.
1 Bruton M 'Local Plans, Local Planning and Development Plan Schemes in England 1974–1982' Town Planning Review, 1983, 54(1), p 34.
2 Circular 23/81, Local Government, Planning and Land Act 1980 – Town and Country Planning: Development Plans.

In an attempt to give some practical meaning to the coverage of the existing local plans, some research has been undertaken regarding the numbers of people affected by such plans.[3] It appears that prepared plans covered approximately 73% of the population of Greater London, 21% in the metropolitan counties and about 26% in the rest of England and Wales; adopted plans covered 44% in Greater London, only 7% in the metropolitan counties and about 12% in the rest of the country. Furthermore, on the basis of an analysis of the rate of plan production, it was calculated that it would be 1993 before half the population of England and Wales outside London would be covered by an adopted local plan. A better appreciation of what is actually occurring, or perhaps what is not occurring, in relation to the preparation of local plans, is likely to be attained if the forms that the plans take within the present planning system are now examined.

Form The concept of local plans is to be found in the Planning Advisory Group Report of 1965, where they were seen as the vehicles for the local detail that was needed to flesh out the broader planning policies expressed at county level within the structure plans. This idea caused no comment at the time, as it was envisaged that local plans would operate in much the same way as the 'old style' development plan but with one major exception – they would not need central government approval – an aspect which did indeed generate debate.[4] The Planning Advisory Group, however, seemed unconcerned over this point, possibly because the Group clearly had a view of the plan as performing more of an advisory than a controlling role:

> We would again stress the function of plans not primarily as a control mechanism but as a positive brief for developers, public and private, setting the standards and objectives for future development.[5]

Nevertheless, the local plan was described in their 1965 Report as being a detailed implementation document that not only laid down the basis for the control of all forms of development, both public and private, but also informed the public regarding the planning of their area. In order to enable this form of both positive and public planning to take place, three forms of local plan were suggested:

3 *Coon.*
4 For example, see: Heap D 'Exit the Development Plan: or the Shape of Planning Things to Come' Journal of Planning and Property Law, 1965, p 591; Town Planning Institute, 'Council's Observations on the Planning Advisory Group Report' Journal of the Town Planning Institute, 1966, 52(3), p 86.
5 *Planning Advisory Group Report* (1965) para 5.3.

(i) Action area plans. These were clearly seen as the most important. They were to be created for areas, implicitly urban, in
which a total scheme of large-scale comprehensive planning
action was to be undertaken within ten years.
(ii) District plans. These were intended for urban areas and were
effectively to relate the action area plans with each other,
while supplying a lower level of development control criteria
for the remaining area.
(iii) Town maps and village plans. These were for those non-
metropolitan areas in the counties, and effectively undertook
the same job as a district plan.

The Town and Country Planning Act 1968, however, simply
established a procedure for approval and a broad form of content
for local plans, but did not go into detail regarding the three types
proposed. It has been suggested that this lack of detail was due to a
desire to ensure that the plans remained flexible documents, thus
avoiding the pitfalls experienced by the 'old style' development
plans. More advice on the form of local plans was forthcoming in
the Development Plan Manual 1970 and related regulations.[6] This
advice reiterated the original Planning Advisory Group suggestions, with the exception of the idea for specific town and village
plans, which was thought to be unnecessary as these areas could be
covered by the district plan. Instead, the idea of a subject plan was
introduced. This was seen as a plan designed to concentrate on a
single planning issue, such as a green belt, that may cross local
planning authority boundaries. Stress was also laid upon the fact
that local plans '. . . must conform generally to the approved structure plan; they will develop the policies and proposals in it . . .'.[7]
This emphasis may be seen either as an attempt to reintroduce
central government control within the local planning system, or
simply as an early realisation that the authorities who were likely to
prepare the local plans were unlikely to be the same as those who
prepared the structure plan, as was first envisaged by the Planning
Advisory Group.
The Town and Country Planning Act 1968 was, however, repealed and replaced by the Town and Country Planning Act 1971
which established the current statutory basis for local plans.[8]

6 At the time the Manual, together with a few advice notes, was all the information to be had. The Circular 82/70, Structure and Local Plans: a Manual on
Form and Content, simply drew attention to the Manual. Regulations such as
SI 1974 No 1486 were obviously not introduced for four years.
7 Development Plan Manual 1970, para 7.4.
8 1971 Act, s 11.

Changes to the system of local government,[9] however, necessitated amendments to the 1971 Act, and their significance for local plans is fully explored in two Circulars.[10] Emphasis was clearly focused on the procedures of plan preparation, presumably as a means of ensuring the desired harmony between the newly formed county and district councils. From 1976 onwards, however, advice from the Department of the Environment concentrated for the first time on the content of local plans.[11]

It was made clear that the content of the early plans was far too wide and, in some cases, inappropriate, and that local plans should concentrate on what was seen as their prime role – providing the detail for development control. This has been suggested as contradicting the concept of these plans as envisaged in the Town and Country Planning Acts 1968 and 1971 and their related regulations, where they were seen as much wider policy documents.[12] Their prime role as development control documents was confirmed in a subsequent circular.[13] This Circular also added to existing advice by clarifying the purpose of the subject plan; emphasising the need for all types of local plan to be site or area specific; and urged that local plans be created as soon as possible to replace non-statutory plans and policies. Further advice[14] then concentrated on the need to make the plans concise, clear and precise documents, while what was considered to be appropriate, as opposed to unacceptable, content was mentioned, using the example of housing. In this context it was made clear that it was acceptable that only land should be allocated for housing, not that housing areas should be allocated to the public or private sectors, that is, that 'use' rather than 'user' should be the concern of the local planning authority.

It has been commented that there appeared to be some contradiction between this specific advice and the continuing suggestion that local plans should be flexible,[15] the inference being that if a local

9 Local Government Act 1972 introduced considerable changes to the counties and districts, with wholesale boundary reorganisation resulting in new county and district areas as well as new county names.

10 Circulars 74/73, Local Government Act 1972 – Town and Country Planning: Co-operation between Authorities, and 58/74, Local Government Act 1972 – Town and Country Planning: Development Plan Provisions; both are now superseded.

11 Circular 55/77, Town and Country Planning Act 1971: Memorandum on Structure and Local Plans, and two advice notes – Local Plans Note 1/76, Development Plan Schemes and Local Plans, and Local Plans Note 1/78, Form and Content of Local Plans.

12 Purdue M *Cases and Materials in Planning Law* (1977); Loughlin M 'Planning Control and the Property Market' Urban Law and Policy, 1980, 3, pp 1–22.

13 Circular 55/77, para 3.28.

14 Local Plans Note 1/78.

15 *Healey*, p 76.

planning authority was seeking to have its local plan adopted, a policy that was specifically expressed may be seen by the Department of the Environment as lacking the desired flexibility, while a policy that was expressed in a general fashion could also meet with disapproval for being not specific enough.

Further legislation in 1978[16] introduced minor changes regarding local plans, but this and other minor revisions of policy[17] were rapidly overtaken by events as a result of the new Conservative administration taking office in 1979. Immediately, the new Secretary of State initiated work on what was to become the Local Government, Planning and Land Act 1980, which introduced the start of the contemporary phase of local plan formation.

Part IX of the 1980 Act, which amends the 1971 Act, is specifically concerned with planning matters involving development plans. The majority of these provisions demonstrate the intention of the government to speed up the planning process by making the preparation of local plans somewhat easier. At the same time, the 1980 Act introduced a considerable devolution of real development control power into the hands of the district planning authorities, with the requirement that county planning authorities now had only to be consulted, rather than acceded to, regarding the likely effects of structure plan policies on the local plans themselves. As a consequence, central government control over local plan issues through the indirect medium of structure plan policy has been somewhat devalued. Circular 23/81, Development Plans, sought to restore the balance somewhat, not only by suggesting that consultation with the regional offices of the Department of the Environment in relation to local plan preparation was advisable, but also by revising slightly the role of local plans. The Circular suggested that local plans were not needed where there was little pressure for development as the structure plan policies would suffice, and also that the absence of a local plan was not a good reason for refusing planning permission.

Current advice on local plans is to be found in Circular 22/84, which offers the following comment on the all-important interpretation of the relationship between local plans and structure plans:

> Local plans are likely to be needed where the strategic policies in the structure plan need to be developed in more detail, the structure plan provision for development and other use of land needs to be related to particular sites and local planning issues need to be brought before the

16 Inner Urban Areas Act 1978 allowed local plans to be deposited for certain areas prior to the structure plan being approved.
17 Circular 4/79, Town and Country Planning Act: Memorandum on Structure and Local Plans.

public. Where provision for growth is proposed, local plans will be required to identify the locations of land . . . and to provide a basis for co-ordinating programmes for development, improvement and protecting the environment. Where restraint is necessary, local plans may be required to identify the limits of such growth as is to be permitted.[18]

The point noted in earlier circulars that local plans are not needed for all areas is reiterated, and the criteria for needing a local plan remain those of either controlling or encouraging development in specific areas. The question of informal plans is raised, and it is made quite clear that where such documents are to be used primarily for development control, they should be formalised into some form of local plan as soon as possible.[19]

The three forms of local plan are then described in the light of current policy.

(i) A general or district plan can be prepared to cover the whole or any part of the area covered by the structure plan, and contain proposals relating to as many or as few topics as seem appropriate. From this it seems quite clear that the old idea of a development plan covering everything in an area in detail is now a historic concept. This does not, however, overcome the practical problem that the local planning authority will be faced on a daily basis with development control decisions that are not covered in recent local planning policy.

(ii) The second form of local plan is the subject plan. Its '. . . purpose is to concentrate on the preparation of proposals for one or two issues across what may be an extensive area'.[20] Many green belt plans have been prepared under the subject plan title, seeming to fit in well with this concept, but Circular 22/84 also suggests that the general or district local plan may now be as appropriate a vehicle for such subject plan topics.

(iii) The final form of local plan is also specific, being an action area plan which is intended to indicate priority areas, which, in the opinion of the local planning authority, require extensive development or redevelopment within the immediate future. This form of local plan has a slightly different history from the other two, as prior to the Local Government, Planning and Land Act 1980 these plans were the only local plans mentioned in the structure plan. This meant that they had to be prepared as soon as practicable, a requirement which remains in being for those action areas specified prior to 1980, and which are

18 Circular 22/84, para 3.10.
19 Circular 22/84, para 3.12.
20 Circular 22/84, para 3.15.

still without approved plans. Since the Local Government, Planning and Land Act 1980 it is no longer possible for structure plans, approved after the commencement of the Act, to specify such action area plans, but they still can be created if there is a need for that type of local plan.

The relationship between these three types of plan and the structure plan is further explained in Circular 22/84, especially with regard to the possibility of policies within different local plans overlapping one another in a particular area. It is stressed that if each plan generally conforms with the policies within the structure plan, there should be no conflict. However, if conflict, or rather differences of policy, do occur in overlapping local plans, the Circular makes it clear that the most recently approved plan will prevail.

Possibly the best illustration of this relationship between local and structure plans is provided within Circular 22/84[1] when the content of both types of plan is considered simultaneously. For example, the advice on waste disposal suggests:

> The structure plan should set out the broad criteria to be applied in allocating land for waste disposal purposes. . . Where appropriate, local plans can set out site specific policies for the disposal, storage or treatment of waste.[2]

Several such examples of the general policies in structure plans being given a detailed local and site specific context in local plans can be found in the Circular, providing a good general indication of the relationship between the plans.

Content and scope   As to the content of a typical local plan, it is true to say that no such beast exists, as each plan, if it is fulfilling its planning purpose, must be specifically related to its own particular area and is therefore unique. It is possible, however, to consider the form that the content of these plans must take, as that is clearly stated in the Town and Country Planning (Structure and Local Plans) Regulations 1982 and reiterated in Circular 22/84.[3]

Local plans consist of a written statement and a proposals map. The written statement should clearly set out the local planning authority's proposals in such detail as may be appropriate, and which should be clearly distinguishable from the rest of the text. The remaining text should contain a justification of the proposals, including their relationship to the structure plan, and can include any such information or diagrams as are appropriate, providing that

1 Circular 22/84, s 4.
2 Circular 22/84, para 4.32.
3 SI 1982 No 555, part V; Circular 22/84, paras 3.22–3.29.

the latter do not confuse any information included on the proposals map. This map will be based on an ordnance survey map showing the grid lines and numbers, so that it can easily be placed in its geographical context, and at an appropriate scale that is large enough to indicate individual properties if any are to be affected by the plan's proposals. There will only be one such map which will define the area of the plan and indicate all the proposals in the written statement insofar as they relate to land use and development:

> Its purpose is to provide as comprehensive an index as possible of the plan's proposals in a form which may be used with assurance by the public to assess whether their property interests are likely to be affected.[4]

Finally, in the event of any conflict between the written statement and the proposals map, the written statement shall prevail. Local plans are clearly intended to indicate the specific land use proposals that will form the basis of development control in all its local detail. For example, it should be possible for a potential developer to refer to the local plan in order to ascertain what the specific land use proposals are for the site he intends to develop.

Returning to the content of such plans, it can be shown that, in practice, the range is very wide indeed. One of the best current synopses[5] briefly considers the content of seven local plans and gives examples of the policy statements that they contain. For example, the general employment policy from the Islington Development Plan states:

> The Council will carefully consider the employment implications of all proposals for development and change of use and will treat these as being material considerations in the determination of planning applications. Subject to the specific land use and environmental policies set out elsewhere in the plan sympathetic treatment will normally be given to developments which bring employment benefits to the borough.[6]

Much more specific policy statements can also be found within the plans, such as the example quoted by another source from the Hucknall District Plan (Nottinghamshire):

> 18 hectares of land will be developed for industry and/or warehousing over and above that already with planning permission for such including
> (a) 5.3 hectares south of Watnall Road,
> (b) 0.6 hectares besides the Ambulance Station, Watnall Road, ... [etc].[7]

4 Circular 22/84, para 3.26.
5 *Healey*, ch 7.
6 *Healey*, p 174.
7 *Telling*, p 64.

Many such examples could be quoted from any local plan, but all would be rather meaningless unless the reader was familiar with the specific area referred to within the proposals. This very point, however, serves to illustrate exactly what local plans are – very local policy statements relating to the ways in which the land might be developed – all contained within documents that may run to over one hundred pages, or consist of a single written page plus a map, that may be lavishly illustrated or contain no illustrations at all. 'One might say that the only common element about them is that they are on A4-sized paper',[8] and that they all consist of a written statement and a proposals map.

Approval To conclude this brief examination of local plans it is necessary to consider how they are formally adopted. The procedure is similar in many ways to that for structure plans. Adequate publicity must be given to the matters proposed for inclusion as policy within a local plan. Those parties likely to be either interested or affected, such as local amenity groups or local chambers of trade, must be informed in writing by the local planning authority of their right to make representations. All the plan documentation must be made available to the general public, and normally a period of six weeks is allocated for any representations to be made to the local planning authority. It should be noted that the general heading of interested parties is, of course, intended to include other local planning authorities at both district and county level, as well as any government department or other public body likely to be affected by any proposals.[9]

Having considered any representations received, the local planning authority then prepares what is effectively the first draft of the plan, together with a section 12 statement which simply confirms the steps taken regarding the initial consultation exercise. In certain cases, a certificate of general conformity is issued by the county planning authority, confirming that the draft local plan does conform to the relevant structure plan policies.[10] All these documents are then sent to the Secretary of State. At the same time, copies of the draft plan are made available for public inspection and also sent to any interested parties, together with a notice that any representations regarding the content of the draft plan must be made to the local planning authority within six weeks. At this stage, the Secretary of State has the power to call in the plan for his approval, but normally he will simply consider the section 12 statement and, if

8 *Healey*, p 128.
9 Circular 22/84, Annex C.
10 Circular 22/84, para 3.42.

satisfied, will allow the local planning authority to continue to the next stage. This consists of considering any objections and then inquiring of the objectors whether they wish to appear at a public inquiry to be held to consider the draft plan. If every objector agrees, then no public inquiry need be held. Normally a public inquiry will be held in the prescribed manner[11] in the presence of an inspector appointed by the local planning authority.[12] The fact that the local planning authority itself chooses the inspector to consider its own plan and report back to it, has given rise to comment that the authority is acting as judge and jury regarding its own plan. As a consequence, it should be noted that all aspects, such as the appointing of the inspector, the conducting of the inquiry and the report of the inspector's findings are very carefully controlled. Any failure to follow the correct procedures can result in the plan being called in by the Secretary of State and possibly rejected.[13]

At the close of the inquiry, the inspector reports his findings on the proposed plan and the objections to it, to the local planning authority. His report is then published. After considering the report, the local planning authority prepares and publishes a statement of its response, together with the justifications for any conclusions it may have reached. If, on the basis of the inspector's recommendations and its own findings, the local planning authority decides to substantially modify the plan, it has to repeat the public participation procedures that followed the first publication of the draft plan. This is, of course, necessitated by the fact that the modifications may have produced what amounts to a new draft local plan. Such events are unusual, however, and indeed, are discouraged by the Secretary of State, who is normally content if it can be shown that effective public participation and consultation have taken place. Nevertheless, it may be argued that this possibility of such a major set-back in the progress of plan approval encourages the local planning authority to prepare the initial draft plan with considerable care, especially in respect of taking fully into account any representations that may have been received.

A stage will eventually be reached when the local planning authority will want to adopt the plan, and normally only two things can prevent this. The Secretary of State still has the power at this stage to reject or modify the plan, or more unusually, an objection from the Ministry of Agriculture that has already been considered, can also prevent the plan's adoption unless specifically allowed by the

11 Department of the Environment *Local Plans: Public Local Inquiries — A guide to procedure* (1984).
12 1971 Act, s 13(1) and (2).
13 Ibid, s 14(3).

Secretary of State for the Environment. All being well, however, the authority simply gives notice that it intends to adopt the plan in 28 days and, after that period has elapsed, officially adopts the plan, again giving public notice of the event. Once adopted, such plans can be the subject of review by the courts, but only in very specific circumstances.[14] They are, of course, expected to be kept up to date, and can be modified, altered, repealed and replaced at any time if the local planning authority sees fit or is so directed by the Secretary of State, the procedures being practically identical to those used in adopting the plan.

Development plans in Greater London It should be noted that the system of structure and local plans had a slightly different form within the Greater London area, and details can be found in Schedule 4 of the 1971 Act. The main difference was that the Greater London Development Plan, even though it was in effect an 'old style' development plan approved in 1963, was to be taken as the structure plan. As such it could be amended using the same procedures available for any structure plan, and its specified areas of comprehensive development, redevelopment or improvement are to be taken as action areas as in any structure plan. The Greater London Council, prior to 1st April 1986,[15] therefore, acted as the equivalent of the county planning authority in relation to the Greater London Development Plan, this being the structure plan for its administrative area.

Regarding local plans, the system was practically identical with that existing elsewhere, with the London borough councils acting as the district planning authorities and preparing, where necessary, local plans. The Greater London Council was also able to act as a local planning authority in this respect, and prepare local plans. There were, therefore, very few differences, except that both the Greater London Council and many of the central London boroughs were able to exercise considerable influence over development as a consequence of the high land values, rather than any extraordinary planning powers. This was mainly achieved through the use of planning agreements often involving 'planning gain', an aspect of the planning system that will be fully explored in Chapter 8.

A useful summary of what constituted the development plan system in Greater London can be found in section 20(2) of the 1971 Act, and runs as follows:

> ... the development plan for any district in Greater London ... shall be taken as consisting of –

14 These circumstances are fully explored in a later section of this chapter.
15 On this date the Greater London Council was abolished as a result of the Local Government Act 1985.

(a) the provisions of the Greater London development plan as in force for the time being, together with the notices given . . . by the Secretary of State indicating his approval of any feature or element of the plan;

(b) any alterations to that plan, together with the Secretary of State's notices of approval thereof;

(c) any provisions of a local plan for the time being applicable to the district . . . ;

(d) any alterations to that local plan . . .

As may be noted, this is an almost identical list to that provided by section 20(1) which relates to all areas outside Greater London, but this situation has now changed because a new form of development plan has been introduced for all the metropolitan areas, including London, as will now be explained.

Unitary development plans   As a result of the Local Government Act 1985, which abolished the Greater London Council and the six metropolitan county councils on 1st April 1986, the whole of the system of structure and local plans as it applies to those areas will eventually cease to exist. In its place will be yet another type of development plan – the unitary development plan. The reasoning behind this abolition is to be found in the White Paper 'Streamlining the Cities'[16] which argued that the planning system in metropolitan areas was becoming unwieldy as a consequence of the actions of the county planning authorities, who had outlived their purpose.[17] However, as Schedule 1 of the Local Government Act 1985 makes clear, any 'old style' development plan, structure plan or local plan that was in force on the day of abolition, will continue in force until replaced by a unitary development plan, and it appears unlikely that these will make a rapid appearance.[18] Nevertheless, it is important to appreciate what these unitary plans are to consist of, and how they will be created, as they will undoubtedly figure in the development plan system in a few years.

These plans will be prepared either individually, or jointly by the planning authorities of the 33 London borough councils and the 36 metropolitan district councils in a manner and form detailed in the Local Government Act 1985.[19] As was the case with the structure

16 Cmnd 9063.
17 As a consequence of a variety of statutory changes the planning responsibilities of the metropolitan county planning authorities had dwindled to almost zero, and their real justification as the preparers of the structure plan was no longer valid.
18 It seems unlikely that the first unitary development plan will be approved before 1990.
19 Schedule 1, Part 1 of the 1985 Act sets out the procedure for the preparation of unitary development plans, and is to be substituted for Part II of the 1971 Act in those districts where unitary plans are to be prepared.

plan system, there will be slightly different arrangements in the Greater London area, where a joint planning committee has been established to advise the boroughs '...on matters of common interest relating to the planning and development of Greater London'[20] and other related factors, but as far as can be gathered at present, this body has no executive function.

The unitary plans shall be based on a survey, which effectively is to be the revised and updated survey inherited from the abolished Greater London Council and metropolitan county councils. When equipped with the necessary information, the local planning authorities will set about the preparation of the plan, but it should be noted that there is no time limit within which this should be undertaken, even though the Secretary of State may specify one. The plan will consist of two parts. Part I is a written statement, setting out the general planning policies and effectively appears to be the same as any structure plan. Part II is a little more complicated in that it is to consist of a written statement setting out detailed proposals for specific areas or topics, accompanied by a map indicating these proposals geographically – the standard local plan format. In addition, this information will be accompanied by a reasoned justification of the policies in both part I and part II, together with any explanatory diagrams that may be appropriate. Clearly, this is related to the explanatory memorandum that accompanies post-1980 structure plans, but is distinct in that it must include justifications of local policies at the level of detail expected in a local plan, and consequently, a somewhat complex document may be expected.

Procedures for approval of unitary plans are not dissimilar to those employed at present for local plans. One major difference is to be noted, however, and that is apart from his usual powers to direct aspects of, and call in plans, the Secretary of State is not required to approve either part of a unitary plan. Given the similarity of part II of the unitary plan to a local plan, this is perhaps not surprising, but bearing in mind the similarity of part I with a structure plan this lack of approval does seem strange.

Speculation as to how these plans will operate and the effects they will produce was rife even before the Act took effect in 1986.[1] At this stage, therefore, until such a plan is actively being produced, little of value can be added. Circular 30/85, Local Government Act 1985: Transitional Matters, gives some indication as to the likely content of unitary plans, and it is made clear that they should

---

20 Local Government Act 1985, s 5(2)(a).
 1 Comments were to be found in the professional journals, such as The Planner, Estates Gazette, Chartered Surveyor Weekly.

incorporate any existing local plans, or work that is currently being undertaken on the preparation of a local plan. To date, the early stages of local consultation as to the major policy topics that should be included in part I are being undertaken. These, at least, in the context of Merseyside, seem to be following very much the existing policies of the structure plan, while being somewhat more selective in that certain policies, such as inner city regeneration, are being concentrated upon to the exclusion of others.

Development plans and the law

The title to this section is somewhat misleading, as frequent references to legislative provisions have already been made elsewhere in this chapter. Development plans are a statutory concept whose creation and implementation is regulated by legislation. The purpose of this section is simply to describe the law's treatment of a development plan, once that plan has been approved. This needs to be distinguished from the way in which other individuals and bodies involved in the development control process treat a development plan. An inspector will refer to the policies in a development plan in the course of a planning appeal in order to determine whether those policies, coupled with the Department of the Environment policy and the specific characteristics of the site, militate for or against the granting of planning permission. Such a use of a development plan is not an infrequent event. In contrast, the contents of a development plan are subject to legal scrutiny in very specific circumstances, which occur only infrequently.

JUDICIAL REVIEW UNDER SECTION 244

The first of these occasions is when the details of a development plan, or any amendments to it, have been finalised and approved by the relevant authority. It is possible at this stage to challenge the validity of a development plan or a policy within the plan. This process is described as a review, since it is the task of the court to consider whether the content of a development plan and the procedures relevant to its making are in accordance with what is required by the law. If they are not, the court has the power to set aside the whole or a part of a development plan. It is not, however, the task of the court to consider the merits of the development control policies in a development plan. Section 244(1) of the 1971 Act provides as follows:

> If any person aggrieved by a structure plan or local plan or by any alteration, repeal or replacement of any such plan desires to question the

validity of the plan, alteration, repeal or replacement on the ground that it is not within the powers conferred by Part II of this Act or that any requirement of the said Part II or of any regulations made thereunder has not been complied with in relation to the approval or adoption of the plan, alteration, repeal or replacement, he may, within six weeks from the date of the publication of the first notice of the approval or adoption of the plan, alteration, repeal or replacement . . . make an application to the High Court under this section.

What is plain from this is that the judicial challenge contemplated in section 244 has to be made within six weeks, and on very specific grounds which do not permit the planning merits of any particular policy to be reconsidered. In addition, the challenge has to be made by 'a person aggrieved'. What that expression signifies is that only those individuals and organisations, for example, local authorities, property companies and amenity societies, who have been involved in the preparation and approval of a development plan, can take advantage of the opportunity offered in section 244(1).[2] Given the very specific nature of the challenge, not to mention the costs involved in taking a case to the High Court, it is hardly surprising to discover that few development plans have been scrutinised by the courts in these circumstances. Of the challenges which have occurred, however, certain points have emerged which deserve emphasis.

On the issue of observing the requirements of the 1971 Act and its associated regulations, what few cases there have been have focused on the adequacy of reasons given for accepting or rejecting the recommendations made at the conclusion of the public scrutiny of a development plan. For example, in *Great Portland Estates v Westminster City Council*,[3] it was alleged that the local planning authority had rejected, without providing adequate reasons, the modifications to its local plan suggested by the inspector. In considering this point, the House of Lords indicated that, in the words of the test in *Re Poyser and Mills' Arbitration*,[4] adequate, proper and intelligible reasons must be given. In addition, the House of Lords approved the decision of the High Court in *E H Bradley & Sons Ltd v Secretary of State for the Environment*,[5] which was to the effect that adequate, proper and intelligible reasons might also be

2 The preparation and adoption of a development plan can take several years and may involve hundreds of individuals. According to Purchas LJ in *Buckinghamshire County Council v Hall Aggregates (Thames Valley) Ltd* [1985] JPL 634 at 638, only procedural irregularities related to the adoption of a plan can be challenged under s 244, as opposed to all procedural irregularities. This, if correct, may limit those who can challenge the development plan.
3 [1985] AC 661, [1984] 3 All ER 744.
4 [1964] 2 QB 467, [1963] 1 All ER 612.
5 (1984) 47 P & CR 374.

brief reasons. Applying these two tests to the situation in question, the House of Lords decided that they had been satisfied, particularly in view of the fact that the Council had indicated its justification for adopting particular policies in the development plan itself.

Yet, however briefly the courts may allow reasons to be expressed, they will insist that some reason is given. In *Barnham v Secretary of State for the Environment*,[6] the Secretary of State had left untouched a policy in a structure plan which had been the focus of considerable argument at the Examination in Public. In so doing the Secretary of State appeared to contradict his own policy, as set out in a Departmental circular.[7] Consequently, in removing that policy from the structure plan, the court stated that in failing to give a reason, however brief, for its retention, the Secretary of State had failed to comply with the provisions of the 1971 Act.

When preparing a development plan a local planning authority must also be sure to include in the plan all relevant information relating to the operation of any particular policy. In *Great Portland Estates v Westminster City Council*, the Council had sought, as a development plan policy, to confine office developments to a central zone. Development outside the zone would not be permitted, save in exceptional circumstances. Guidelines would, however, be prepared, indicating what amounted to such circumstances. These guidelines would not be included as part of the development plan, but would be published separately. Since the House of Lords believed that these guidelines embodied an important aspect of the Council's policy, their omission from the plan constituted a failure to comply with the relevant provisions of the 1971 Act, and hence the Council's policy on office development was deleted from the plan.

Even if it can successfully be shown that the requirements of the 1971 Act have not been observed this is not an end to the matter. The court will agree to set aside a policy within the development plan which is affected, only if an additional factor can be proved. According to section 244(2)(b) of the 1971 Act, this requires the court to be satisfied that:

> ... the interests of the applicant have been substantially prejudiced by the failure to comply with any requirement of the said Part II or of any regulations made thereunder.

The reasons for including this provision are easy to understand. Given the relative complexity of the procedure which has to be observed in the production and approval of a development plan, it

6 [1985] JPL 861.
7 Circular 15/84, Land for Housing.

162

may be all too easy for mistakes to occur. If the most trivial of errors led to portions of the development plan being set aside by the courts, this would be out of all proportion to their likely effects. This explains the requirement that the applicant's interests must have been substantially prejudiced. In *Great Portland Estates v Westminster City Council*, the omission of the office development guidelines from the development plan had substantially prejudiced the interests of Great Portland Estates, since it had deprived the company of the opportunity to question those guidelines at the public inquiry into the plan.

Apart from procedural errors, proof that the powers in the 1971 Act have been exceeded constitutes sufficient grounds for challenging the validity of a development plan. The 1971 Act envisages that development plans are specifically intended to contain policy on planning. Therefore, any attempt to insert policies in such a plan which do not have a clear planning purpose may well be adjudged to be beyond the powers of the 1971 Act or *ultra vires*. There is evidence to suggest, however, that the courts will be generous in their interpretation of what constitutes a planning purpose. In *Great Portland Estates v Westminster City Council*, objections were raised to Westminster City Council's industrial policy contained in the development plan, which was devised in order to retain certain well-established industrial activities in the area. As a result of this policy, the Council had indicated that it would be reluctant to grant planning permission for the redevelopment or rehabilitation of property where such industrial activities were being undertaken, if it caused the activities to cease. It was argued that the effect of this policy was to make it exceedingly difficult for landlords to refuse new tenancies to industrial tenants in these properties. Since policies in a development plan should relate only to the land and its development in a planning context, it was argued that this industrial policy had wider social implications which rendered it *ultra vires*. On this issue, the House of Lords contented itself with saying that a policy having no objective other than the protection of the individual, might be considered *ultra vires*. Here, however, the policy in question had a definite planning purpose, namely the protection of various industrial uses. The fact that the tenants of certain premises would benefit from this policy was irrelevant, since it was a consequence of, not the purpose of, that particular policy.

Apart from alleging that a particular policy has no planning purpose, it is also possible to argue that the policies in a development plan, even though they have a planning purpose, are totally unreasonable. If, for example, a development plan contained a policy restricting the construction of new houses to a particular field in a particular village, and nowhere else in the area covered by the plan, the policy could have a planning purpose but this might not be considered a reasonable one. According to the courts, when a policy reaches the stage of being so unreasonable that no reasonable local planning authority would have adopted it, then that is proof that the power to create that policy has been exceeded, and the courts will intervene. In *Buckinghamshire County Council v Hall Aggregates (Thames Valley) Ltd*,[8] the reasonableness of a minerals subject plan was the issue. The alleged unreasonableness related to the way in which certain areas were designated as 'preferred areas' for mineral extraction, and others were excluded. This designation was made, it was suggested, without sufficient information on whether economically workable reserves existed in the 'preferred areas'. Here, the Court of Appeal made it clear that there must be overwhelming proof of unreasonableness, which was not apparent in this case. The suggestion that 'unreasonable' in this context be treated as the antonym of 'reasonable' was rejected. If it had not been, the courts might, in the future, have fallen into the error of substituting their view for that of the individuals or bodies charged with the duty of preparing the development plan.

Certainly, in the past, the courts' decision to set aside a development plan policy on the basis of its being unreasonable has been criticised. The conclusion reached in *Fourth Investments Ltd v Bury Metropolitan Borough Council*[9] is an example. Here, the West Bury Local Plan had allocated some land to be included in the green belt rather than be used for residential development. Although at the public inquiry the inspector expressed the view that insufficient land was available to meet Department of the Environment advice on the supply of housing land, he went on to confirm this particular allocation of land to the green belt. In the view of McCullough J the inspector's failure to explain his reasoning was a serious omission, since the inspector had made no attempt to assess whether, in the light of this shortfall, the land in question might be required for housing. On this basis McCullough J concluded:

> . . . on the inspector's findings (or his inability to make findings far enough into the future) about housing land requirements and upon his findings about the open land and green belt significance of the applicants' site, the chances that the applicants' site might be needed for housing before 1991 were sufficiently high for it to have been wrong to allocate a green belt notation to this site. This was not merely to say that he disagreed with the inspector's planning judgment. I believe that he had reached a conclusion which could not reasonably have been reached.[10]

8 [1985] JPL 634.
9 [1985] JPL 185.
10 Ibid, 187.

Although the inspector's reasoning might have been at fault, this hardly seems a basis for concluding that his decision was one which no reasonable inspector could have reached.

The difficulty of challenging the validity of a development plan under the terms of section 244(1) should now be apparent. If an applicant is successful, however, the courts have considerable discretion in the action they take. Section 244(2)(b) provides that a court may:

> ... wholly or in part quash the plan, alteration, repeal or replacement, as the case may be, either generally or in so far as it affects any property of the applicant.

In *Great Portland Estates v Westminster City Council*, the House of Lords deleted that policy within the local plan which related to office location. In contrast, the offending policy in the West Bury Local Plan was deleted in *Fourth Investments v Bury Metropolitan Borough Council* only insofar as it affected the applicants' land. What the court cannot do, however, is to rewrite any part of a development plan. In *Buckinghamshire County Council v Hall Aggregates (Thames Valley) Ltd*, for example, the judge at first instance concluded that there were grounds for a successful challenge under section 244. Instead of setting aside the minerals subject plan, he modified it in such a way that it was no longer acceptable to the local authority, a fact which was commented upon when his decision was set aside in the Court of Appeal.

JUDICIAL COMMENTS UNDER SECTION 245

Once the six-week period for challenge mentioned in section 244(1) has elapsed, a development plan, together with its policies, is incapable of direct review by the courts. Yet it can still be the object of judicial comment by virtue of the power given to the court in section 245 of the 1971 Act. Among other matters, this section allows the courts to set aside the Secretary of State's decision to either grant or refuse planning permission on appeal. This is done on the basis that his decision has been made in disregard of the relevant procedure, or in excess of his statutory powers. Since, in resolving planning appeals, the Secretary of State must take account of any relevant development plan, it is hardly surprising to find the courts commenting on the role of the development plan in cases arising under section 245. If an attempt is made to summarise what the courts have had to say they appear to take as their starting point section 29(1) of the 1971 Act. This provides that:

165

... where an application is made to a local planning authority for planning permission, that authority, in dealing with the application, shall have regard to the provisions of the development plan, so far as material to the application, and to any other material considerations.

On appeal, therefore, the inspector and the Secretary of State must have regard to the very same factors. In the court's opinion, however, all that section 29(1) guarantees is that if the development plan is relevant it must be taken into account, but once that has been done, it is perfectly legitimate to use some other source of policy to resolve the development issue.

The stance taken by the courts over the role of development plans is understandable when the terms of section 245 of the 1971 Act are recalled. All it allows the court to do is determine whether the correct procedure has been followed and the terms of the 1971 Act observed. The courts cannot ensure that the terms of the development plan prevail. This point is illustrated in *Greater London Council v Secretary of State for the Environment*.[11] This case concerned the development of the Coin Street area of London. After various schemes had been proposed, outline planning permission was granted to Greycoat Estates by the Secretary of State.[12] During this period, political power changed hands on the Greater London Council and an administration which had previously backed the Greycoat scheme was ousted in favour of one which wanted to see the site developed differently. Once announced, the Secretary of State's decision was challenged in the courts by the new majority party on the Greater London Council, on the basis that he had exceeded his power by failing to take account of a change in Council policy. This argument was rejected, since the court was convinced that the Secretary of State had taken into account all material considerations, including the change in Council policy. The fact that his decision disregarded that change and reflected the Secretary of State's own views on the proposed redevelopment of Coin Street, was immaterial. As Stephen Brown J said in the course of his judgment:

... the role of the court in proceedings of this nature was a limited one: it was to examine whether the Minister had acted within his powers. It had no jurisdiction to pronounce upon or, indeed, to comment upon the merits of the Minister's decision in the general sense. It could not assume the role of the Minister or act as a Court of Appeal from him on the merits of the proposals approved by him. It had been generally acknowledged in the course of this hearing that the Minister was entitled to have a policy,

11 [1983] JPL 793.
12 The application for planning permission had been called in by the Secretary of State.

even though it may be a policy which was objectionable to various parties.[13]

Throughout this dispute, little attention was paid to the relevant development plan and its policies on the redevelopment of Coin Street. These policies did not correspond with the opinions of either the Secretary of State or the Council. Arguably, there was little the court could do about this, since, once the development plan and every other material consideration had been taken into account, the Secretary of State was free to reach whatever conclusion he wished. In this fashion, the development plan, which was meant to play a major role in the development control process, had, so far as this particular area of London was concerned, become little more than a cipher.

Nor is this decision an isolated one. There are other decisions where some other material consideration has prevailed at the expense of the development plan, and the courts have upheld the decision.[14] In part, this can be attributed to the specific powers which the courts possess. In part, it reflects the nature of a development plan. As should be apparent, the policies in a development plan may be expressed in very general terms, they may be out of date, or they may be inapplicable to the circumstances of a particular case. Situations can exist which warrant the setting aside of a development plan policy in favour of other material considerations. The courts have acknowledged, therefore, that the development plan need not be adhered to slavishly. The real problem occurs in those cases where the development plan is relevant, is up-to-date and is still ignored in favour of some other policy document. Should this happen, there is nothing that the courts can do, once they are satisfied that the development plan has been taken into account.

The truth of this is illustrated in a case such as *Waverley Borough Council v Secretary of State for the Environment*.[15] Here, the Waverley Borough Local Plan contained a policy permitting a reserve pool of land to be maintained to meet housing needs. The idea was that should a five-year supply of land for residential development not be available, the possibility of granting permission for residential development on these reserve sites might then be considered. The local planning authority, therefore, refused planning permission for residential development on one of the reserve sites. On appeal, the Secretary of State, disagreeing with his inspector's recommendation, granted outline planning permission. He

13 [1983] JPL 793 at 798.
14 *Ynys Mon Borough Council v Secretary of State for Wales* [1984] JPL 646, *Philglow Ltd v Secretary of State for the Environment* [1984] JPL 111.
15 [1987] JPL 202.

did so on the basis that the policy in the local plan constituted 'arbitrary rationing of land' and so was contrary to the advice given in the Department of Environment Circular 15/84, Land for Housing. The fact that the local plan had been recently drawn up, and the policy in question approved by a Department of Environment inspector, was irrelevant, according to the court. All the court could consider was whether there were grounds for the Secretary of State reaching his conclusion that there was arbitrary rationing of land. In the opinion of Simon Brown J there were such grounds.

The *Waverley* case concerned a local plan which the Secretary of State is not directly responsible for approving unless the plan is 'called in'. In contrast, structure plans are scrutinised and approved by the Secretary of State. Yet, there would appear to be nothing in the relevant legislation to prevent a structure plan being approved by the Secretary of State on one day, and then ignored in favour of some other policy document on the next. Certainly, it is not un-known for structure plan policies to become incompatible with Department of the Environment policy. For example, some structure plans may contain policies which are out of line with policies in Circular 1/85 on planning conditions[16] and Circular 22/83 on planning gain.[17] Evidence also exists of the Secretary of State being willing to approve structure plan policies at odds with his own Departmental policy, as shown in *Barnham v Secretary of State for the Environment.*

Apart from their stress on the development plan as a material consideration, the courts have had to deal with cases which arise when a development plan is in the course of preparation or revision. An application for planning permission may thus anticipate policy decisions to be made in a development plan. An application to build one hundred houses on a green field site, for example, may raise the issue of whether that land should be developed or allocated to the green belt. A local plan which is in preparation may be dealing with the identical issue. In contrast, an application for a change of use from house to nursing home may have little significance in relation to development plan policies. The courts appear to take a pragmatic approach to the whole affair. If an application for planning permission is likely to have no repercussions upon a development plan in the course of preparation, then there is no reason for deferring a decision on the application. This was the opinion of the court in *J A Pye (Oxford) Estates Ltd v Secretary of State for the Environment.*[18]

16 Circular 1/85, The Use of Conditions in Planning Permission.
17 Circular 22/83, Planning Gain. Obligations and Benefits which Extend Beyond the Development for which Planning Permission has been Sought.
18 (1982) 261 EG 368.

If, however, issues are raised by the application for planning permission which it appears more appropriate to consider in the course of the public inquiry which accompanies the deliberations on a development plan, then it may be sensible to defer an immediate decision on the application. This is a matter for the exercise of judgment and not an automatic rule. As was said in *R v City of London Corporation, ex parte Allan*:[19]

> But it is wrong to say ... that a situation can come about where the holding of an inquiry into a proposed local plan creates a situation where it is wrong as a matter of principle for the planning authority to grant permission.[20]

As long as the court is convinced that a local planning authority has taken all factors into account, including the proposed development plan, and the impact that its decision may have upon the plan, then it would appear that a decision can be made whether or not to grant planning permission, which cannot be challenged.

It might be tempting to conclude from what has been said that development plans are not worth the paper they are printed on. This would be both a hasty and erroneous judgment. While there is no denying the importance of what the courts have to say, it should not be used as proof that development plans are consistently ignored or are totally out of step with Department of the Environment policy.

The future of development plans

Various studies[1] have been made of the current development plan system and all seem to agree that it works tolerably well with the exception of one or two aspects, which arguably are inherent in any system that attempts to indicate development policy for an area. The major problem focuses on the form and contemporaneity of the policies. Such policies are formed over the period in which the plan is being prepared, and may then be reformed during the adoption procedures, all of which inevitably takes time. As a consequence, the policies, when adopted, are always lagging slightly behind the

19 (1980) 79 LGR 223.
20 Ibid, 227.
1 For example: Department of Town Planning, Oxford Polytechnic *The Implementation of Planning Policies and the Role of Development Plans* (1986); *Healey*; Bruton M J 'Local Plans, Local Planning and Development Plan Schemes in England 1974–1982' Town Planning Review, 1983, 54(1), p 18; Town Planning Review *The Future of Development Plans: PAG Revisited* 1980, 51(2), p 131.

current situation within which they have to operate. This problem is then aggravated if the form that the policy has assumed is lacking in flexibility, which inevitably is the case if the policy is map-based as follows for all local plans. There appear to be two possible ways of alleviating these problems. The first would be to produce only the most general form of policy guidance relating to the widest of areas. Such policy would, therefore, be unlikely to become rapidly dated due to its general form, while being totally flexible as a result of its loosely defined area of implementation. This, however, does itself produce a problem, as the generality and flexibility combine to produce an almost total lack of guidance, which is one of the fundamental demands that must be placed on a development plan. The alternative is to produce the exact opposite to this flexibility, that is, a prescriptive zoning system where the development plans totally dictate the form of development allowed.

Apart from the policy issues, the other major problem associated with the present development plan system is the simple fact that it is not, in reality, a single system. As the sections of this chapter have explained in some detail, the present development plan situation in England and Wales is an amalgam of two major Town and Country Planning Acts, further complicated by other legislation, as well as informal policy that combine to produce a very 'patchy' coverage of the country. These and other less important issues have been considered in a Department of the Environment consultative paper entitled 'The Future of Development Plans'.[2] This document analyses the present situation and puts forward proposals for a new system, or rather an altered system, of development plans for England and Wales.

The main difficulties are seen to be the slowness of the processes involved in both structure and local plan preparation and approval, which it is suggested is mainly due to the complexity of both documents, and the range of policies covered, often in too much detail. These problems are then, according to the consultative paper, exacerbated by the fact that policies are often duplicated in both local and structure plans, which only leads to confusion and a further waste of time. The following proposals are consequently presented in the consultative paper as being necessary if the development plan system is to be improved: the overlap between county and district plans must be removed as it is unnecessary and wasteful; detailed supervision of plan approval by the Secretary of State must be reduced as it wastes time; the content of the plans should be simplified, as this will reduce approval time; preparation procedures should be made more effective by involving the public

2 Department of the Environment, 1986

at an earlier stage. The emphasis placed on saving time in all these suggestions should not be simply regarded as a government efficiency drive, although this undoubtedly plays a part. More constructively, these proposals may be regarded as attempting to solve one of the major development plan problems, as by speeding up the procedures in plan preparation, the plans and the policies they contain are more likely to be up-to-date.

A new system, or rather an altered existing system, is consequently proposed. At the top of the system, the input of national land policy in the present shape of Department of Environment circulars and other policy statements will remain. Immediately below this it is suggested that a type of regional policy input be introduced. This should not take the form of a regional plan, but rather consist of formalised policy statements. These would be prepared by local planning authorities on major land use issues that were clearly of a pan-county or regional nature, or as directed by the Secretary of State, who would also be involved in formalising the statements. At the next tier, the county planning authorities would also issue policy statements rather than produce development plans, on such county-wide issues that needed to be dealt with on the scale of the whole country, as well as such common county issues as directed by the Secretary of State. In all instances the regional policy would be taken into account where relevant. Rural policy is seen as being particularly important, and the county planning authority's powers in this context would be strengthened. Finally, the district planning authorities will produce a district development plan covering the whole area, and taking into account, where appropriate, policies from all these sources. These plans will be mandatory, and will supersede all other forms of plan and any informal policy, thus providing a simple and comprehensive guide to development.

These proposals are then considered in more detail, especially with regard to their proposed implementation.[3] What emerges very clearly from the consultative paper is the desire to make the development planning system less cumbersome and more efficient. The intention to retain development plans in some form is never in doubt as they are seen as ' . . . a vital part of the framework of development control . . . ',[4] and ' . . . an essential component of a rational land-use planning system'.[5] The proposals as they stand could improve, at least by simplification if by no other means, the present situation. If they were to operate as intended, a more

3 'The Future of Development Plans', Department of the Environment, 1986, ch 3.
4 The Future of Development Plans, para 6.
5 The Future of Development Plans, para 9.

logical system of development plans would emerge that parallels quite closely the philosophical ideals discussed in the earlier parts of this chapter. What does remain as a major concern, however, is that the consultative paper makes plain that there is no intention to repeal the Town and Country Planning Act 1971, and create a new Act containing the legislation needed to set up the proposed system. Rather, it is stated that the existing legislation will be amended, and this must be seen as a retrograde step in a process that attempts to simplify. The 1971 Act has been amended so frequently that many important sections now contain sub-subparagraphs which will hardly be improved by new amendments.

Chapter 5

Local policy and special controls

The problem with this chapter is that two distinct, yet related, aspects of local planning control have to be considered. Firstly, an examination must be undertaken of local policy, where it comes from, how it is used and the different forms that it can assume. Secondly, a detailed account will be given of those forms of local policy which manifest themselves as special controls. Essentially, special controls are part of the wider classification of local policy. In distinguishing between the two forms of policy the intention is to highlight the fact that some local policy has a statutory foundation, with the result that such policies, when implemented, are binding on those affected by them. The term special controls is, therefore, used to denote such local policy. In contrast, other local policy consists simply of informal planning documents whose status can vary in relation to the form in which it is presented. Finally, it should be made clear that, for the explanations contained in this chapter to be fully appreciated, it has to be read in conjunction with the previous chapter on development plans and the succeeding chapter concerning Department of the Environment policy. This is due to two important but distinct characteristics of the development control system.

Firstly, it must be appreciated that although a development plan will contain policy which is local in its application and has a statutory basis, it is a unique document which is given special emphasis in the development control process. The local policy which is discussed in this chapter is simply one of the 'material considerations' referred to in section 29 of the Town and Country Planning Act 1971. It is possible for such local policy to supplement a development plan or even, on occasion, substitute for one. Secondly, the various means whereby the Department of the Environment exerts an influence on local policy must also be borne in mind. This is considered in some detail in the next chapter, particularly the influence of policy such as circulars and policy notes. These also constitute 'material considerations' in the context of section 29, together with the less obvious influences, such as the decisions of the Planning Inspectorate. The more general influence exerted by central government will be considered within this chapter.

The significance of local policy and its relationship with the development plan can best be illustrated by a simple example. A district planning authority is considering its conservation policy. This policy, which has as its objective the conservation of buildings and areas of particular architectural interest or especial character, can take several different forms. The county structure plan may contain some general statement on the subject of conservation, even going so far as to indicate areas which the county planning authority considers are worthy of conservation. Such statements are, however, not binding on the district planning authority, which can consider them simply as policy advice. On the other hand, the district planning authority may have included some specific policies on conservation in its own local plan, if it has one. If this is the case, then such policy, since it is included in an approved local plan, would have considerable authority in relation to any proposed developments within the area. It is quite common, however, to find that a local plan will make no mention of any policies on conservation. The explanation for this lies in the fact that it is possible to implement a policy on conservation without utilising the development plan system. This raises the question of how a local authority will go about instituting such a policy.

Depending on the level of development control that a local planning authority wishes to achieve, it can tackle the problem in several ways. If its only concern is to protect specific buildings, or small groups of buildings, within its area from being developed in an unsophisticated way, then an approach can be made to the Secretary of State to list the buildings,[1] or as an interim measure, to place building preservation notices on those buildings.[2] Once the decision has been taken to list a building, no development can be undertaken without securing not only planning permission, but also listed building consent. This additional safeguard is prescribed in the 1971 Act and, if ignored, can result in a criminal prosecution.[3]

1 By s 54 of the Town and Country Planning Act 1971, structures can be specially protected from alteration and demolition by being listed. This procedure and its consequences are fully considered later in the chapter.
2 By s 58 of the 1971 Act, a structure can be protected for six months as if it were a listed building.
3 By s 56 of the 1971 Act, any unauthorised development of a listed building is an offence punishable by imprisonment and/or a fine. In theory the penalties are not inconsiderable, ranging from three to twelve months' imprisonment, while fines can be related to any benefit that has accrued to the developer as a result of the unauthorised development.

As a means of implementing local conservation policy, however, listing has the disadvantage that the power to list buildings lies in the hands of the Secretary of State not the local planning authority. Consequently, it is at the discretion of the Secretary of State, based on advice from his officials, whether or not he chooses to list a building. That said, it is important to remember that, once listed, the ability to control what happens to that building is transferred back into the hands of the local planning authority.

In contrast, the power to designate an area a conservation area as defined in the 1971 Act[4] rests with the local planning authority. When exercising its discretion to designate such an area, therefore, the local planning authority will base its decision on local planning policy which is produced by its planning department and has no statutory authority. Various sources may, therefore, have been tapped in formulating that policy. These include the planning officers themselves, especially if one of them is given particular responsibility for conservation, the councillors who comprise the planning committee, and the public who may work in, or, more probably, live in an area which has a character that may merit conservation. The end result will be a decision to designate a particular area within a specific boundary as a conservation area. The process of designation is simple, and there is no appeal, while the consequences are to activate special development control powers in the area. Therefore, by establishing a local planning policy on the creation of conservation areas, a local authority can achieve a great deal, since, though the policy itself has no formal standing, its implementation has certain very positive legal and development control consequences.

Once established, it becomes necessary for the local planning authority to produce a policy document for the conservation area,[5] setting out the reasons why the area merits conservation and what special features need protecting. This document, once produced, will rank as an informal policy statement in the sense that, although its production is required by statute, how it is produced, and the degree to which the three policy sources of planning officers, councillors and the public should co-operate in its production, is not specified. Consequently, such an informal policy document is less important in the development control process than if it had gone through some formal procedures, such as those described in relation to development plans. Matters may be further complicated if the local planning authority chooses to increase the importance of such a document by instigating a form of approval procedure that

4 1971 Act, s 277.
5 Ibid, s 277B(1).

mirrors, at least in part, the formal approval procedures that would accompany the production of a local plan. It may then be argued that the resulting document had been approved after due consultation, especially with the public, and this factor would be taken into account if the significance of such a document was being considered in a public inquiry.

Besides taking advantage of the procedures for listing buildings or designating conservation areas, there are other forms of special control that can be employed within a designated conservation area, or elsewhere within a local planning authority's district. For example, it is possible to protect trees.[6] This occurs automatically if an area is a conservation area, but any tree can be protected against felling or lopping, provided that the local planning authority decides it merits such protection. Another procedure often adopted in conservation areas of especial merit is for a local planning authority to issue an Article 4 directive. This enables a specified area to be excluded from enjoying the normal General Development Order rights[7] so that activities can be controlled which normally fall outside development control powers, such as the colour of external paintwork. In the case of an Article 4 directive, however, a policy document is mandatory, in order to explain exactly what is permitted and why the decision has been made. Outdoor advertising is also carefully controlled in conservation areas under another set of special procedures.[8]

Finally, it is possible for a local planning authority to have a totally informal local policy on conservation, using none of the special controls described. The local planning district may be a rural one, containing many small villages, none of which is significant enough to become a conservation area in its own right, but many of which have a pleasant character that may be thought worthy of protection. In this case an informal policy document may be produced by the local planning authority to stand in its own right, or possibly to complement some general policy existing within a formal local plan. As has already been noted, the importance of such policy would depend upon how it was produced, particular emphasis being placed on the level of public participation involved.

6 1971 Act, s 60.
7 As has been discussed in Chapter 3, the benefit of the General Development Order and its classes of permitted development may be withdrawn or redefined in relation to specified areas by virtue of the powers set out in article 4 of the Order.
8 1971 Act, s 63.

Local authority policy

It should be clear from what has already been discussed that local planning policy can take many forms and be derived from several different sources. What follows is a description and analysis of various sources that can contribute to the creation of such policy. There are four main sources – central government, local planning officers, local councillors, and the public – the latter either in the form of individuals, including the developer, or organised groups.

CENTRAL GOVERNMENT

The influence of central government on local planning policy can take many different forms, apart from recognised formal controls, such as development plans or circulars. The Department of the Environment obviously has the greatest impact, given its specific involvement with the planning process. Its Secretary of State can employ various means to exert an indirect or informal policy influence on local planning authorities. Changes of emphasis in policy can, and indeed often have been included in a speech, usually to the annual conference of some professional body, such as the Royal Town Planning Institute, or the Royal Institution of Chartered Surveyors. In his speeches, the Secretary of State often does little more than present some general comments on a current planning issue, but these are usually fully reported in the professional press, and thus may influence those who implement local planning policy.

One such example concerns green belt policy. The majority of towns and cities prior to the passing of the 1971 Act did not possess a formally approved green belt. Green belt policy had been outlined in a circular[9] and a policy note,[10] but green belts did not often figure as approved policy in development plans. The term 'green belt' was not infrequently utilised by local planning authorities as the natural argument when refusing planning permission for some proposed development that would have decreased the amount of open agricultural land around an urban area. In the mid 1970s, however, central government started to suggest that more land should be released for housing, especially in the South East, where the London Metropolitan Green Belt had been established as a result of approved planning policy within the Greater London Plan. Pressure was applied by central government in various ways, but was particularly evident in informal requests to the Standing Conference on London and South East Regional Planning, asking them

9 Circular 42/55, Green Belts.
10 Development Control Policy Note No 4, Development in Rural Areas, 1969.

177

to indicate land within the green belt that they thought could be released for housing.

This government pressure, on what was a formally approved green belt, consequently left local planning authorities in other parts of the country in no doubt as to the direction of central government thinking on this particular planning policy. This gave local planning authorities only two options. They could comply, and release land for housing in those areas where they had previously utilised the green belt argument to reject applications for housing developments. Alternatively, they could formalise their green belt policy by creating local plans incorporating such policy. The result was that in some areas, local planning authorities set about the creation of formal green belts, normally by use of the subject plan. It may, therefore, be argued that these plans were, in a sense, a negative response to central government pressure which seemed to be seeking to undermine green belt policy.

Taking this idea of a negative response by local planning authorities to central government policy a stage further, it naturally introduces the question of the political differences that will, in some instances, undoubtedly exist between the two levels of government. Possibly one of the best recent examples of this is the situation that developed in 1985 between a socialist-led Liverpool City Council and the Conservative government.

The episode started with the victory of the local Labour Party in the Liverpool local government elections in 1983. At first, the results of the change in political power were slight, but direct confrontation between the local authority and the government became inevitable, when the local authority was accused of overspending by central government. Liverpool City Council had decided on a policy of urban regeneration,[11] an approach which, in general terms, was in line with Department of the Environment policy.[12] As part of its plans for regeneration, the Council concentrated on a much needed house building programme to provide accommodation for its tenants. The sites chosen for such development were all close to the inner city in areas that were unlikely to be of interest to the private developer.[13] This policy, however, soon produced confrontation with the government, not because the

11 Liverpool City Council's Urban Regeneration Strategy became policy in December 1983. A synopsis of this policy and its progress was produced by Liverpool City Council in January 1986 entitled *The Strategic Approach: Urban Programme 1986–1987*.

12 For example, the city was actually working in partnership with the Department of the Environment's Urban Renewal Unit.

13 Nineteen Priority Areas were declared, fourteen of which are in the inner city and three on the outer estates.

Council had embarked upon a major house building programme, but rather, as a result of the financial demands that such a policy placed on the local authority. The regeneration programme thus caused the Council to 'overspend' in the eyes of central government which, as a result, attempted to impose financial restraints on the city. Liverpool City Council argued against such restraints on the basis that housing in the city was probably the worst in the country, a fact that had been recognised by many members of the government. Although it appeared that the Council had a strong case, confrontation with central government could not be avoided. This confrontation has, for the present, been resolved, but its effects on the planning and development of the area are far-reaching. The process of development control has suffered for several reasons. These include the uncertainty of the Council's financial future, the disinterest expressed by the majority of the members of the then ruling party in any development, other than their own schemes for house building, and the arbitrary 'rules' that were applied to applications for planning permission involving housing, such as a totally inflexible height restriction.

Central government policy can thus affect local policy by indirect implication and direct confrontation, especially when political differences are involved. Confrontation of the type described above, however, is less common than the influence that other government departments regularly exercise over local authority planning policy, especially in relation to agriculture, transport and mining.[14] In some instances[15] such departments may be directly involved, either in the procedures leading to the preparation of a formal development plan, or in a planning application, as has already been considered in previous chapters. What is more significant in the context of this chapter, however, is the effect that the general policies of other organisations can have on local planning policy. For example, the 'rationalisation' of both British Steel and the National Coal Board, involving the closure of steel works and pits throughout the country, has had an enormous impact on local planning policy in the areas affected. Yet, the closures were totally outside the control of the local planning authorities, who simply responded to such events as rapidly as possible, usually by producing some informal planning policy in an attempt to help alleviate the problems.

14 The wide-ranging influence of other government departments has been referred to in Chapter 2 and will also be mentioned later in this chapter.
15 For example, the Ministry of Agriculture, Fisheries and Food must be consulted over a planning application that involves development associated with agricultural production – the Town and Country Planning General Development Order 1977, SI 1977 No 289, article 15(1)(i).

LOCAL PLANNING OFFICERS

Local planning officers receive an almost endless stream of policy advice in one form or another from central government. Such advice is supplemented by suggestions from other sources, notably local councillors and the general public. In this section the intention is specifically to consider the planning officers as sources of policy in their own right.

The majority of planning officers employed by local planning authorities are professionally trained in some aspect of the property system. Indeed, in the vast majority of instances, planning officers will have been educated to the equivalent of degree level in some aspect of town planning. During the course of their education they will have been presented with a variety of theories and possible explanations regarding the land use system and its development, including some suggested ideal solutions for the majority of planning problems. Although these ideas will have undoubtedly been tempered by the realities of practical, local authority town planning, many of them remain, providing a conceptual foundation for the local planning officer's ideas on planning control within his area.

To attempt to analyse these concepts in any sort of detail is beyond the scope of this work, but it is possible to illustrate, by way of an example, the effect they might have on the planning officers' policy suggestions. It is well established urban theory that certain general patterns of land use develop in any mature urban area.[16] In particular, certain land uses will attempt to repel each other, in the sense that they are not well suited as neighbours due to the incompatible nature of their particular functions.[17] The obvious example is, of course, housing and industry, or rather what is termed 'special industry' in the Use Classes Order.[18] By way of contrast, however, other concepts suggest that the ability to travel to the place of work is an important factor,[19] since any attempt to isolate industry from housing may result in the 'working classes' being unable to bear the cost involved in transporting themselves to work. Immediately this introduces a new range of concepts, as the term 'working class' has

16 For a discussion of such theories see Carter H *A Study of Urban Geography* (3rd Edn, 1981) ch 8.
17 Harris C D & Ullman E L 'The Nature of Cities' Annals of the American Academy of Political Science, 1945, 242, p 7.
18 As has been considered in Chapter 3, the Use Classes Order 1987 distinguishes between General industrial, Class B2 and Special industrial, Classes B3–B7 on the grounds of the environmentally damaging, or simply unpleasant nature of the industrial processes in the special classes.
19 Duncan O D & B 'The Measurement of Inner City Locational and Residential Patterns' Journal of Regional Science, 1960, 2, p 37.

to be defined,[20] while the importance of urban transport with all its related mathematical modelling must also be considered.[1] It should, therefore, be obvious that a large body of theory exists concerning the location of industry and its juxtaposition to areas of housing containing inhabitants of different classes.

Many of these urban planning concepts may already have been incorporated into policies contained in the formal development plan, but they may also generate informal policy proposals. For example, using these theories as a basis, the planning officers may advocate a policy that seeks to develop a 'social mix' within or between certain residential areas.[2] To control such a mix directly would be beyond the ability of any planning officer, except where he may be able to influence the local authority's housing department in its choice of tenants for the council's own housing estates, but indirect planning controls may be feasible. A development control policy concerning the density and type of housing in various housing areas could effectively introduce controls, albeit indirectly, on the social classes likely to inhabit the houses, as could a transport related policy on road layout within the housing area. In these circumstances, the planning officer would be attempting, quite validly, to use the planning system to create the ideal environment that his extensive background in planning theory has suggested. Naturally, the uniqueness of the locations of his housing areas or industries would be of prime importance to any local planning policy decisions, but the general concepts would be drawn from such theories as those mentioned earlier.

It should also be appreciated that the body of planning theory does not remain static, but changes in response to new ideas. A variety of sources, such as professional journals[3] and conferences, offer the planning officer an opportunity to keep abreast of these changes. His views can also be influenced by exposure to a much wider range of information. This includes sources as diverse as official Department of the Environment guidance, to a chance conversation with a colleague from another local planning authority at a conference. In this fashion, the planning officer becomes a source of informed opinion, since he filters the information he receives and uses it to establish policy goals.

20 There is no standard accepted definition of any of the so-called social classes. For example, see the discussion in *Carter* chs 9 and 10, or, for a classic study, Cole G D H *Studies in Class Structure* (1955).

1 For example: Blunden W R *The Land Use/Transport System* (1971); Lane R et al *Analytical Transport Planning* (1971).

2 For a discussion of this and other social concepts, see Bassett K & Short J *Housing and Residential Structure* (1980).

3 For example, The Planner, The Chartered Surveyor Weekly and the Architects' Journal are all published by their respective professional bodies.

LOCAL COUNCILLORS

Councillors can effectively create policy in their own right, as well as direct and filter policy suggestions that may be received either from central government, or from their own planning officers. As was mentioned in Chapter 2, councils have become increasingly political in their make-up over the last two decades, with the numbers of independent or ratepayer councillors declining and being steadily replaced by those who belong to one of the major political parties. In the context of planning control and the production of local planning policy, this process appears to have had an effect which varies depending upon the nature of the planning issues that the local authority has had to face. Clearly, there is little political capital in a local policy which aims to regulate advertisements in different locations, or control the design details for shop fronts in certain streets. Political stances are more likely to be taken over the supply of housing land, or the development of office blocks, and this can be reflected in local planning policy.

In order to illustrate this process, reference will be made to Liverpool City Council's Urban Regeneration Strategy as published in 1984.[4] This policy must be viewed at several levels in order to appreciate fully its impact on development control within the city. Firstly, the general policy of attempting to provide more housing can be justified on basic planning, as well as political grounds, as there was an undoubted need for such housing in the inner city residential areas. Secondly, the selection of housing areas where the city chose to concentrate its own housing developments was also acceptable as a planning policy. The main criterion used for selection was simply those areas of housing which were in local authority ownership, followed by an assessment of their condition. Thirdly, the designation of these areas had the effect of diverting into them most of the city's housing efforts. This tended to produce a negative planning policy in the rest of the city, by implication rather than intent, as the other areas of housing suffered from a relative lack of positive policy. Finally, the city's concern for housing development extended to specific development control policy regarding the design of the 'right type' of housing. This had the effect of producing a development control policy which seemingly resulted in planning permission being refused for any form of housing development over two storeys in height. The justification for such a policy can clearly be seen in the disastrous tower blocks that Liverpool has been forced to live with since the 1960s, but the two-storey policy was seemingly applied, not so much as a guide,

4 The policy was never published as such, but documentation was produced by the City and made available to the general public. See footnote 11 above.

but as a rule that could not be broken, often with what was apparently little regard for the actual merits of the proposed housing development.

Political motivation can, therefore, produce local planning policy, but so too can local circumstances. Examples may be found within the Cumbria region where planning authorities have attempted to introduce policies designed to check the proliferation of second homes.[5] Such policy is probably motivated by the perceived needs of the area, rather than by any specific political goals, and in this sense can be seen as the local councillors creating policy as local men and women rather than as a political group.

The acceptability of some of these policies, whether produced by political motivation, local need, or a combination of the two, is sometimes put to the test, more commonly in a public inquiry, but sometimes in the courts. The public inquiry will assess the legitimacy of such policies as planning policies, which have to be weighed against other planning policies. Therefore, a local policy designed to restrict the number of second homes, will have to be viewed in the light of Department of the Environment policy, which is currently unsympathetic to any such attempts to regulate the housing market. In contrast, the courts are concerned solely with whether such policies can be regarded as valid planning policies which can legitimately be taken into account when a development control decision is made.[6]

To conclude this consideration of councillor produced policy, it should be realised that a 'crusading' councillor who adopts a particular cause, could influence or even create policy if he had the personality to carry the majority of other councillors with him. Such councillors may often be motivated by what they perceive to be public opinion, and it is probably more appropriate to consider the policy which is likely to be produced from this source under that heading.

THE PUBLIC

In considering the public as a source of local planning policy it is

5 The following condition was imposed by the Lake District Special Planning Board and appealed in 1985 (APP/5941/A/80/06966): 'The dwelling-house shall be occupied as a sole or main residence only by a person employed or to be employed or last employed locally and the dependants of such a person living with him or her and the widow or widower of such a person. "Locally" shall mean the area of the District Council of Allerdale. A "main residence" is a dwelling occupied for more than half of every year.' The condition was discharged.

6 See *Alderson v Secretary of State for the Environment* [1984] JPL 429. For a detailed study, see Loughlin M *Local Needs Policies and Development Control Strategies* (1984) School for Advanced Urban Studies, Bristol.

appropriate to tackle the subject under two headings – the public at large, and the public as organised groups – both of whom can have a definite but distinct influence on local planning policy.

The public at large tends to have a sporadic and largely unregulated influence on local planning policy, much depending on the attitude of the local planning authority. As the local planning authority consists of both the local planning officers and the local councillors, the public can exert an influence on either or both groups. Any attempt to influence opinion is normally focused upon the local councillors. As politicians, these individuals are dependent on public opinion in order to be re-elected, and are, therefore, likely to be receptive to public opinion on various matters within their ward. This can affect planning policy indirectly. If a local councillor is aware that public opinion is for or against a particular policy, then he can make these views known to his fellow councillors as well as to the local planning officers, in the hope that the policy might be changed. Certain issues are almost always contentious, such as the building of new roads, or the demolition of the older, 'much loved' parts of town centres, and on these the local councillor will undoubtedly be made aware of public opinion. In these circumstances, however, it would be common practice for a local planning authority to canvass deliberately the views of the public, thus ensuring a degree of public participation which could have a direct influence on policy. Much depends on the attitude of a local planning authority, however, as only in certain circumstances is public participation mandatory, such as in the preparation of development plans.

Public participation exercises that are not mandatory can take various forms depending on the circumstances. Undoubtedly the most common type is the public inquiry, but despite its name, this is not quite as public an exercise as might be imagined. Public inquiries are most commonly held to consider a specific planning application for which planning permission has been refused by the local planning authority. As such, the procedural guidelines[7] ensure that only interested parties are heard. This normally includes the local planning authority representatives, the would-be developer and his representatives and any other directly affected parties. The developer can be considered as representing an aspect of public opinion, but public opinion in its true sense is better represented in these circumstances by those people who own or occupy adjacent property, whose interests might be affected if the proposed de-

7 The Town and Country Planning (Inquiries Procedure) Rules 1974, SI 1974 No 419, as amended. Other Rules exist to govern other forms of special inquiry, for example, for enforcement.

velopment goes ahead. In general, the opinion of the man in the street will only be heard at a public inquiry if the inspector asks for comments from the public gallery. Such a request is frequently made, and the response can vary greatly, though its ultimate effect on policy is unclear. The public inquiry has been called, not specifically to determine general local planning policy, but rather to assess its effect on a specific development proposal. The outcome of the inquiry often has implications for local planning policy, but the question of how much influence the public will have had on any decision is difficult to evaluate.

On the other hand, public participation exercises can be designed to elicit a more positive response and exert a more direct effect on planning policy. For example, such exercises may be held with the aim of producing informal policy that is intended to supplement the general policy contained within the structure plan. Opinions can be canvassed on almost any planning topic from housing to leisure facilities. As has been indicated, the form of such public participation exercises can vary, but public meetings and a standing exhibition are often arranged. The aim of the planning officers will be to present the public with an explanation of the alternative policies so as to elicit a response. In order to achieve this, public meetings will be arranged when possible policies can be discussed. This is often accompanied by attempts to illustrate, by means of models and artists' impressions, the impact a proposed policy of development may have on an area. Planning officers will also be at hand to answer any questions from the public while the public, in turn, may be asked to complete questionnaires as well as to make any comments on the proposals. After a specified period, the planning officers will attempt to gauge public opinion from all the information and comments received, the aim being to formulate possible future policies which take account of those views as far as possible. In this manner, the general public can have a direct effect on the policy process.

Arguably, however, it is public opinion, as represented by various organised public groups, that has the greatest influence on local planning policy. These groups are of various types, and include local sections of national organisations, such as the Georgian Group or the National Trust; groups that are specifically local and long-term, such as amenity societies or residents associations; groups that are local but short-term, which may have been formed in response to a specific problem within the community; and groups that may be a mixture, changing their form in response to local needs. Standing apart from these 'organised' groups is the developer, whose influence on planning policy will be considered at the end of this section.

Organised public groups can have an effect on local planning policy in the same way as the general public influences such ideas, namely, through public inquiries and public participation exercises. The impact of the organised group in these circumstances, however, is much greater than that of the public at large, mainly due to the fact that a group is often regarded by the local planning authority as having more 'standing', but this varies depending on the type of group. For example, local representative groups of national organisations, such as the Ramblers' Association, would possibly have more attention paid to its opinions by the local planning authority, than a purely local group concerned with public rights of way. This is for the simple reason that the weight of the national organisation, in terms of its influence and lobbying potential, could be brought to bear on a local issue. On the other hand, some purely local organisations, such as conservation area amenity societies, may gain extra influence, simply due to the fact that they are affiliated to the Civic Trust, a national organisation with considerable influence on conservation matters.

The final party that exerts an influence on local planning policy is the developer. It would be naïve to assume that developers only respond to local planning policy, rather than play a part in its creation. Their involvement in that process can take two forms, the one passive and the other active. The passive form is represented by the developer's willingness to undertake some form of development. Once the developer chooses to apply for planning permission, he then becomes the focus of whatever planning policy exists in order to control development. In these circumstances, his influence on local planning policy in general is not likely to be very great, although any development control decision taken in respect of his application for planning permission can, as has already been mentioned, have an indirect effect on planning policy. Another aspect of the developer's passive effect on planning policy is to be found in those instances where planning permission is not applied for, despite the fact that the planning officers have attempted to implement a policy that seeks to attract a particular form of development. For example, if the local planning authority has decided, as a matter of policy, to designate an area as a science park, and to offer various advantages to developers to build within the area, any failure to attract, or possibly divert, the attention of such developers from other areas of the region or city, may result in the policy being re-examined or dropped altogether.

The active effect that developers have on the planning policy of local planning authorities is not very different from that exercised by other groups, in that they have as much right to express a point of view as any other interested party. Such influence can be increased if a developer belongs to a national organisation, for example, the National Housebuilders Federation. The 'size' of the developer may also be significant. A small local house builder who makes representations regarding a local planning policy is likely to have less effect on that policy than if a representative of a national building firm were to make a similar comment.

The forms and functions of local planning authority policy

As discussed in the previous section, various individuals have a contribution to make in formulating local planning policy. The example may be considered of a local planning authority district in which residents and local councillors alike are perturbed by the number of mature trees being felled to make way for new developments. Pressure will mount, therefore, from both groups, for a local planning policy relating to trees. Such a policy will aim to ensure the preservation of mature trees and encourage the planting of new trees. Consequently, on being instructed to produce such a policy, the local planning officers are faced with the problem that it is simply not enough to have a policy, but some effort must also be made to ensure that that policy has the desired effect. Various means exist which can give 'teeth' to such a local planning policy, and these means and the powers they involve will be discussed in the remainder of this chapter. What should be borne in mind, however, is that the local planning authority is given the option of whether or not to take advantage of these powers, although, as will be apparent, specific guidance is available from the Department of the Environment on how these powers might most appropriately be used.

This leaves the question of how such powers relate to the development control process as a whole. In some instances it will be found that they allow a level of control in addition to the need to apply for planning permission. For example, the developer of a holiday caravan site must, in addition to securing planning permission, also obtain a site licence. It is the licence in this case, that will be used by the local planning authority to control all the details of development on the site, such as the provision and siting of toilet facilities, or the creation of a suitable landscaped boundary to the site. In other instances, such powers also ensure that certain matters are given particular prominence as material considerations when a normal development control decision is being made. This is the case with any proposed development within a conservation area, when the special status of the area and its particular character will be a major factor in the development control issues under consideration.

Such powers thus play an important and fundamental role in the development control process in that they not only supply suitable vehicles for various policies, but also may be able to ensure that the policies can be effectively applied. In considering the forms and functions of these policy vehicles, however, the problem arises of how logically to group them for discussion. As has been suggested, their form and function is particularly varied, and can range from the protection of individual trees to a general policy that attempts to ensure, through the use of planning conditions, that only local agricultural workers occupy new residential developments. As far as the operation of development control is concerned, probably the most significant question about such policy vehicles is whether or not they can be applied throughout the whole of the local planning authority area, or only be involved in the development control decision in certain specific instances. On this criterion, therefore, it has been decided to group these policy vehicles in relation to their specificity. The specificity of a policy simply refers to how widely it applies. For example, the policy regarding conservation areas is focused only within such areas and may not be applied elsewhere, while the policy decision to impose planning conditions can be applied to any part of a local planning authority's area. As a secondary consideration it has also been decided to note the form of 'authority' for any policy vehicle. This is accomplished simply by noting whether the policy vehicle is given its existence within a particular statute or is derived from other sources, always remembering that such statutorily prescribed policy vehicles are not mandatory, but simply provide a specific form and function if the local planning authority chooses to utilise them.

There is, however, one important form of local planning authority policy that does not fit easily into either of these groups. This is what is normally termed informal local planning policy, which usually has two sources. The first may be some form of direction from another body. For example, a Department of the Environment circular may suggest that the local planning authority should prepare a policy document on housing supply. If the preparation of this document is not mandatory, then the local planning authority is free to ignore the suggestion. If, on the other hand, the document is prepared, then even if it is exactly on the lines suggested by the circular, it remains an informal policy document.

The second source is when the informal policy originates from within the local planning authority. If the planning authority decides that there is a pressing local issue, for example, acceptable designs for the modernisation of shop facades, which needs some form of policy direction, then if a document is produced, it becomes an informal policy document even though no circular has suggested its preparation. On some occasions, even when statute demands, as in the case of conservation areas, that local planning authorities should prepare policy documents in relation to these areas, such documents are also informal policy documents.

This is mainly because their 'informality' stems from the lack of any set procedure involved in their preparation. Consequently, informal policy documents can be imbued with increasing levels of authority depending on the way in which they are produced, and, in particular, the degree of public participation involved. If the document is produced exclusively by the planning officers without public consultation and then approved by the planning committee, it is acceptable as a statement of policy. On the other hand, if the proposed policy was discussed with members of the public at an exhibition within the planning department, or at a series of public meetings, or was based on the results of questionnaires involving major public opinion surveys, then its 'standing' as policy would be greatly enhanced.

Informal policy plays an important role in the everyday life of many local planning authorities and is an essential source of reference on any number of development control issues. As it is always produced solely as a response to local planning issues, extensive examples of such policy would be pointless but its significance cannot be over-emphasised. Equally clearly, the Department of the Environment is the other major source of planning policy and its role in this aspect of the development control system will be considered in detail in the next chapter.

Taking into account, therefore, the existence of informal local policy within the development control system it is possible to return to consider those suggested headings under which the remaining forms of local policy will be examined. Once again, it is worth emphasising that the local policies about to be discussed should be distinguished from those policies considered in Chapters 4 and 6. Undoubtedly connections exist between all these policy sources, which will be pointed out when appropriate, but the local policies discussed in this chapter should be considered as distinct, since they have an independent form and structure and produce a specific effect within the development control system.

Under the heading – Specific policies supported by statute – will be discussed those policy vehicles which, should they be activated, apply only to a particular area or object and have a procedure, form and function allotted to them by specific sections of an Act. The heading – Non-specific policies supported by various sources – will be used to accommodate those policy vehicles which may involve either a blanket coverage of the local planning authority's area, or rely on more indirect forms of support, such as statements made within the development plan or issues selected by the local planning authority.

SPECIFIC POLICIES SUPPORTED BY STATUTE

It is difficult to decide on the order in which to consider these policies and the different forms that they take, as the frequency of their use varies from one local planning authority to another. For want of a truly logical sequence, the intention is to consider first those policies and the special forms that they assume which relate to specific areas, such as conservation areas. This will then be followed by an investigation of those policies and their differing forms that can be applied to individual items, such as buildings, trees and advertisements. The sequence is not capable of remaining purely logical, however, as in the case of highways, the widening of a road may have a major effect on the transport system of the whole area, but at the same time raise quite specific planning issues in relation to the actual development operation.

In every instance, it is important to note, however, that policies relating to these issues may be included, often in some considerable detail, within the relevant development plan. The special forms that are about to be discussed, therefore, must not be seen as substituting for these development plan policies, but rather as applying an extra level of control. They can, of course, also be used to add to the policy of the local planning authority without the need to embark upon the lengthy procedure of amending the relevant development plan.

Conservation areas Areas of particular environmental character or historic association may be indicated in the local plan (if there is one) and any policy related to the control of development in the areas may be included in the plan. If, however, a local planning authority wishes to adopt a conservation policy in relation to a particular area, it is given powers under section 277 of the 1971 Act to designate an area a conservation area. Indeed, the same section makes it a duty of the local planning authority to review its area from time to time to determine if any areas, not already designated as conservation areas merit such treatment.[8] This task clearly re-

8 1971 Act, s 277(10).

190

quires that the local planning authority has some form of conservation policy. The initial task, therefore, must be to consider the derivation and nature of such a policy.

In this instance, some very specific policy guidance is to be found in the relevant Department of the Environment Circular 8/87, Historic Buildings and Conservation Areas – Policy and Procedure. According to the advice offered in this and previous circulars,[9] areas which, because of their special character, are worthy of designation as conservation areas, are to be found in almost every town and village.[10] Once a conservation area has been selected, a local planning authority then has to decide its attitude to proposed development within the area. In forming its views, the local planning authority is urged to take account of public opinion and in particular, to set up a conservation area advisory committee,[11] The membership of these committees should consist of local people, reflecting a cross-section of local opinion, together with, if possible, individuals with a professional background in planning or development. The purpose of the committee is to advise the local planning authority on planning applications within its conservation area, but it can also play a part in:

> ... helping to formulate policies for the conservation areas (including making positive proposals for their enhancement and measures for the general care and maintenance of the areas).[12]

In addition, the local planning authority is expected to:

> ... formulate and publish proposals for the preservation and enhancement of their conservation areas, and submit them for consideration to a local public meeting.[13]

While the policy guidance on the creation and subsequent treatment of conservation areas is quite clear, no guidance is given as to what constitutes the unique local character that justifies the designation of a conservation area in the first instance. Such designation will clearly depend on a host of uniquely local features, and the interpretation and importance attached to these features by both the local planning authority and other interested parties, ranging from national and local conservation organisations, to the developer. In addition, the number and size of conservation areas, or potential conservation areas within the local planning authority

9 Circular 23/77, Listed Buildings and Conservation Areas; Circular 12/81, Historic Buildings and Conservation Areas; Welsh Office Circular 61/81, Historic Buildings and Conservation Areas – Policy and Procedure.
10 Circular 8/87, para 54.
11 Circular 8/87, para 68.
12 Circular 8/87, para 68.
13 Circular 8/87, para 69.

district would have to be considered, as clearly the hardening of development control in these areas should be balanced by encouraging development in other areas. Circular 8/87 emphasises that conservation does not mean preservation.[14]

Given that there are currently approximately 5,500 conservation areas in England alone, the use of this statutory procedure to establish conservation policy is clearly widely used. The actual procedure for the designation of such an area is simple, once the area has been selected on whatever criteria the local planning authority thinks appropriate. The area becomes a conservation area by resolution of the local authority, and by formal notification to the Secretary of State, accompanied by publication of this information in the London Gazette, the local press, and an entry in the local land charge register.[15] The consequences of designation are complex, but can be appreciated by observing the effect they have on the local planning authority and the occupier of property in the area, particularly if the occupier intends to undertake any development.

Besides preparing policy proposals for the conservation area and setting up a conservation area advisory committee, the local planning authority has other decisions to make. There is the possibility of imposing even stricter controls on development within the area by using additional statutory powers. For example, an Article 4 directive[16] can be issued which modifies General Development Order rights, though the local planning authority is under no obligation to use this or any other power. When planning applications are received which are likely to affect the character or appearance of the area, the local planning authority is required to advertise them, both in the local press and near the application site, and in certain circumstances notice must also be given to the Historic Buildings and Monuments Commission.[17] Due regard must then be shown to any representations that are received, as is the case with any normal planning application.

The act of designating an area a conservation area also has certain important and automatic consequences for the occupiers of property in the area. For example, special permission in the form of conservation area consent must be obtained for the demolition of all or part of most buildings within the area even if the buildings are not specifically 'listed' in their own right.[18] Most trees within the

14 Circular 8/87, para 61.
15 1971 Act, s 277(6), (6A) and (7).
16 Circular 8/87, Appendix II.
17 1971 Act, s 28(2B); Circular 8/87, paras 27, 28.
18 1971 Act, s 277A; the Town and Country Planning (Listed Buildings and Buildings in Conservation Areas) Regulations 1987, SI 1987 No 349.

area are protected in the same fashion as if they were the subject of a tree preservation order.[19] This means that anyone wishing to undertake work on a tree, including lopping or felling it, must give six weeks' notice to the local planning authority, which has that period to prevent such work. Once the six weeks have expired, consent is assumed. The General Development Order rights are also modified within a conservation area, the main difference being that the amount by which a dwelling-house, industrial building or warehouse can be extended is less in a conservation area than elsewhere.[20]

To conclude, it is worth mentioning that grants are sometimes available to finance developments and improvements within a conservation area. These grants are available from both local and national sources and consequently the local planning authority is not always involved in awarding such funding.[1] Therefore, although the availability of finance can have an important impact on conservation policy, a local planning authority cannot always employ grants as an incentive to ensure its conservation policy is observed.

Caravans   It is no easy task for a local planning authority to devise a policy on caravans and the location and control of caravan sites. This is not from any lack of policy advice,[2] but rather because complications arise from the fact that caravan sites fall into a variety of categories – permanent sites for homes, sites for holidays containing static caravans, sites for holidays containing touring caravans and sites for gypsies, which form a special category. Clearly the planning implications for each category are different and may be subsumed, not only under the heading of planning policy but under some totally different policy. For example, policies relating to permanent sites for homes may quite justifiably be contained within the local authority's housing policies, while policies involving sites for holiday use may equally justifiably be found under tourism policy. On the other hand, it must also be admitted that all forms of caravan site pose common development control dilemmas, that

19 1971 Act, s 61A; Circular 36/78, Trees and Forestry.
20 Town and Country Planning (National Parks, Areas of Outstanding Natural Beauty and Conservation Areas, etc) Special Development Order 1985, SI 1985 No 1012, as amended.
 1 Circular 8/87, Part V, Financial Matters. This provides a good synopsis of the possible sources of funding.
 2 Circular 23/83, Caravan Sites and Control of Development Act 1960; Circular 57/78, Accommodation for Gypsies: Report by Sir John Cripps; Circular 12/78, Report of the Mobile Homes Review; Circular 28/77, Gypsy Caravan Sites; Development Control Policy Note 1969 No 8, Caravan Sites; Caravan Sites Act 1968; Caravan Sites and Control of Development Act 1960.

range from the obvious ones, such as access and the provision of services, to the aesthetic issues of appearance and even noise.

General planning policy guidance is still to be gained from Development Control Policy Note 1969/8, Caravan Sites. In this, caravans are considered under three headings – caravans as homes, caravans for holidays and caravan sites for gypsies – and policy advice is offered for each group. Where caravans are used as homes, the all-important policy issue is one of location, preferably near existing housing areas as the service requirements are the same, but for location on the periphery rather than in the centre of the housing area. A location deep in the country or in the midst of the green belt is not considered appropriate, but it is noted that caravans can often be accommodated on sites unsuitable for houses, in the sense that they can occupy land that, due to its physical features, is unsuitable for permanent buildings. Where caravans are used as holiday homes, concern is shown for the fact that demand is concentrated in the most popular holiday areas. This creates particular problems, the most obvious of which is the unsightly nature of the caravan parks themselves, and the danger that too many caravans will swamp local facilities. In general, therefore, it is suggested that all holiday caravan sites should be strictly controlled, with the emphasis on sites located in inconspicuous positions in areas already established as caravan areas. Where caravans are occupied by gypsies, the sites are also often used by the gypsies to pursue their occupations, such as scrap dealing, and this fact should be taken into account when locating and planning the sites.

This general policy has been supplemented with advice from other circulars[3] so that the present situation is one of very strict and largely standardised control for all the different groups. Effectively, this control is based on the fact that not only must planning permission be obtained in the normal way, but also a licence under the Caravan Sites and Control of Development Act 1960 must be secured from the local authority in whose area the site is proposed, which will be the same authority from whom planning permission would have been sought. A licence must be granted once planning permission has been given, but this seemingly pointless exercise is given a very real purpose since the site licence will contain a whole list of conditions that would be difficult, if not impossible, to attach to a grant of planning permission. The conditions, which are part of the site licence, will be concerned with such matters as densities and how they should be measured, spacings, water and toilet supply arrangements, landscaping, and establishing specific boundary features to the site. Examples of model conditions appropriate to the

3 Circulars 23/83, 57/78, 12/78 and 28/77.

various forms of caravan site are given in the circulars[4] and are generally adopted by local authorities. These controls are further complicated by a wide-ranging list of exclusions and exemptions relating to sites established before 1960[5] and to what are termed temporary sites.[6] In addition, local authorities are under an obligation, to provide accommodation for gypsy caravans.[7]

The need for a local planning authority to have a policy on the development and control of caravan sites varies from one authority to another, depending on the level and the nature of caravan use within the area. In some areas, such as parts of the Welsh coast, the control of caravans will be an important aspect of planning policy, while in others, the only concern may be to provide gypsy caravan sites. What should be clear, however, from the preceding paragraphs, is that guidance exists to help a local planning authority formulate a policy on caravan sites, as well as control the development of those sites for which it is prepared to give planning permission.

Mineral workings As is the case with the location and control of caravan sites, a local authority which is a mineral planning authority is provided with considerable powers and much advice regarding its policy towards, and control of, all forms of mineral working and extraction.[8] This advice concentrates upon the operations involved in the working and extraction of minerals but does not offer a definition of what constitutes a mineral in this context. Since the majority of mineral workings are undertaken in rural areas, with the possible exception of coal mining, it is normal for the mineral planning authority to be the county planning authority. As a result of the Local Government Act 1985, however, the mineral planning authority in metropolitan areas and Greater London is now a metropolitan district authority or a London borough.[9]

Local planning policy towards mineral working can normally be

4 Annex to Circulars 23/83 and 28/77.
5 Caravan Sites and Control of Development Act 1960, s 2, Sch 1.
6 Ibid, Sch 1.
7 Caravan Sites Act 1968, s 6.
8 Town and Country Planning (Minerals) Act 1981; Town and Country Planning (Minerals) Regulations 1982, SI 1982 No 975; Circular 11/86, Town and Country Planning (Minerals) Act 1981; Circular 2/85, Planning Control over Oil and Gas Operations; Circular 3/84, Opencast Coal Mining; Circular 21/82, Guidelines for Aggregates Provision in England and Wales; Circular 1/82, Town and Country Planning (Minerals) Act 1981; Circular 58/78, Report of the Committee on Planning Control over Mineral Workings; Circular 1/78, Report of the Committee on Planning Control over Mineral Workings. See also the new Minerals Planning Gains Notes, MPG 1 and MPG 2.
9 Local Government Act 1985, s 3(3).

found in three possible sources. These are, firstly, the structure plan which may contain general policy on mineral extraction. Secondly, a local mineral subject plan which, if it exists, could be expected to supply a considerable degree of development control detail, not only with regard to existing workings, but, more especially, to future developments. In metropolitan areas and Greater London, policy of this nature is to be found at present in any current development plan, but it will be revised and reissued in any unitary plan that is eventually produced. The remaining source of mineral working policy will emerge as a result of those periodical reviews that Circular 11/86, Town and Country Planning (Minerals) Act 1981, requires mineral planning authorities to conduct. Reviews are mandatory, in that they have to be undertaken periodically, and five-yearly reviews are thought to be the most appropriate.[10]

Since minerals are an important element of what is termed the national resource base, it is hardly surprising that there is a considerable amount of central government advice on the manner in which applications for planning permission to extract minerals should be considered. Such applications cannot be treated as raising solely local planning issues. Indeed, no fewer than three government departments – the Department of Energy, the Department of Trade and Industry and the Department of the Environment – all consider minerals policy to be within their remit. Their main concern seems to be to ensure that industry gets the materials and power that it demands.[11] Consequently:

> It seems to follow that authorities should be predisposed to grant extraction permission save where there are powerful environmental objections, or where an application is premature in that other sources of supply are economically available. In practice it is far from easy to decide when economic factors outweigh environmental ones.[12]

This predisposition towards permitting mineral extraction is ameliorated somewhat when considered in conjunction with the Department of the Environment Advice Note on the Minerals Content of Development Plans.[13]

This Advice Note urges that policies should be adopted by mineral planning authorities that attempt to maintain average levels of mineral production from within their areas as measured over the last few years. If such a policy involves opening up new areas of extraction, then a full examination of the development control consequences of the new mineral workings must ensue. This exam-

10 Circular 11/86, paras 7–10.
11 Circular 21/82.
12 Hughes D *Environmental Law* (1986) p 242.
13 Department of the Environment, 1981.

ination, which should allow for a considerable degree of public participation, must consider in detail the possible environmental and social impact of the new mineral workings, as well as taking into account the economic consequences these new workings might have on other mineral resources within the area. If the mineral planning authority has produced a minerals subject plan, it may contain policies of constraint, indicating situations or locations where planning permission for mineral extraction is not likely to be given. Specific policies on particular minerals may also be adopted, as may policies on appropriate environmental safeguards for mineral working sites, but these policies should not be so inflexible as to render real discussion on particular applications for planning permission pointless.[14]

Assuming that planning permission is granted, current practice is for the mineral planning authority to impose a whole range of planning conditions. The aim of these conditions is to regulate the way in which the site is to be worked, and also to ensure that the site is appropriately landscaped once extraction is complete.[15] Clearly, such conditions represent important policy controls over mineral working, but they have to be imposed with great care by the mineral planning authority if an appeal to the Secretary of State is to be avoided.[16]

Where it is the National Coal Board, as opposed to a private company, which intends to undertake the mineral working operation, the circumstances are somewhat changed. The National Coal Board can undertake new mining operations on land which is already being mined, or for which planning permission for mining has already been given.[17] In contrast, new coal mines require planning permission and this is an instance where local planning policy can have a direct effect on a nationalised industry. The situation regarding opencast mining is more complicated, however, but present practice seems to suggest that planning permission must still be gained in most circumstances.[18]

14 See *Buckinghamshire County Council v Hall Aggregates (Thames Valley) Ltd* [1985] JPL 634.
15 Circular 1/82, Annex, Section 5.
16 As with any form of planning condition, the conditions attached to a grant of planning permission for mineral extraction must comply with the 'rules' suggested for conditions in Circular 1/85, The Use of Conditions in Planning Permissions.
17 Town and Country Planning (National Coal Board) Regulations 1974, SI 1974 No 1006.
18 In some circumstances it may still be possible for the National Coal Board to undertake opencast mining without planning permission under powers granted by the Opencast Coal Act 1958.

197

Obviously any planning application involving mineral extraction is likely to raise contentious issues, particularly environmental issues, and attract the attention of many important national and local pressure groups. This emphasises the need for a clear mineral policy at local planning level if there is to be effective development control in the area. Such a policy will not solve all the problems or cover all the issues, but it will at least provide the parameters within which the inevitable discussion will take place.

Special areas In the context of development control there are at present three forms of area that should be noted. The first is the designated area of either a new town development corporation or an urban development corporation. Development corporations were mentioned in Chapter 2, where it emerged that, in relation to policy and development control, there is little distinction to be made between local planning authorities and development corporations. Within their designated areas[19] development corporations undertake all the normal duties of local planning authorities. Besides removing an area from the control of the relevant local planning authority, the main effect that such areas may have on local planning policy relates to the fact that various forms of financial aid may be available for development within the designated area. Consequently, this may have repercussions for development in those local authority areas adjacent to the designated area, as development may be drawn into the designated area rather than establishing itself elsewhere. Clearly, if this were to occur it would have a detrimental effect on local authority planning policy, but as the development corporations were specifically created in order to regenerate the general district as well as their designated areas, such occurrences can be guarded against.[20]

The second form of special area is the enterprise zone. These were established by the Local Government, Planning and Land Act 1980.[1] As with development corporations, such zones are intended to aid the regeneration of the area. Local authorities are invited by the Secretary of State to consider if an enterprise zone is needed in their area. If they conclude that such a zone is needed, then draft proposals are prepared and offered for public scrutiny in the manner required by the 1980 Act.[2] There are specified procedures for taking account of objections, and the draft proposals may be modified accordingly. Once these requirements have been observed,

19 Local Government, Planning and Land Act 1980, ss 148–150, Sch 29.
20 Ibid, s 136.
 1 Ibid, s 179, Sch 32.
 2 Ibid, Sch 32, Part I.

then the area may be designated an enterprise zone by the Secretary of State, normally for a period of ten years.[3]

The consequences of designation are mainly fiscal and bureaucratic, and so do not directly concern this work, but there is also a particular planning change that is relevant to development control. Within the zones, planning control is mainly dependent on the development scheme that has been specified by the local planning authority for the zone. This means that if a proposed development within the zone complies with the requirements of the development scheme, planning permission is deemed to have been granted.[4] Alternatively, if the proposed development does not comply with the scheme, then planning permission must be sought in the normal manner. Such development schemes need take no account of any existing local planning policies, and indeed, the 1980 Act requires that existing development plans be reviewed, if necessary, to take account of the scheme.[5] The content of the schemes has varied considerably between the many enterprise zones that have been established, with some local planning authorities allowing a very broad range of development within the zones, while others have been much more specific.[6]

The effect of the zones has not been assessed specifically with regard to their impact on local planning and development control, but reports have raised issues which throw some light on this aspect.[7] Rather than create new development as was intended, the zones have undoubtedly caused the short distance movement of existing enterprises. This has had a detrimental effect on the areas adjacent to the zones, virtually negating any existing local planning policy on commercial development. As many local planning authorities have also allowed the development of large retail units within the zones, this can undoubtedly have an adverse effect on existing shopping centres some distance from the zone, with the resulting disruption of existing retail and transport planning policies. It is obvious, therefore, that although the zones themselves involve quite specific areas within the local planning authority's district, the effects produced by the zone on the planning of the district or even the county are very wide-ranging indeed.

The final form of special area was introduced by the Housing and

3 Ibid; by implication the zones will last for ten years, which is the duration of the rate free period stipulated in Sch 32, para 27.
4 Ibid, Sch 32, para 17(1).
5 Ibid, Sch 32, para 23.
6 Grant M *Urban Planning Law* (1982, updated 1986) p 546.
7 Roger Tym and Partners *Monitoring Enterprise Zones. Year Three Report 1984* (for the Department of the Environment); Report of the Comptroller and Auditor General *Enterprise Zones*, HC 209; 34th Report from the Committee of Public Accounts 1985–86 *Enterprise Zones* HC 293.

Planning Act 1986, which provided for the setting up of simplified planning zones.[8] Simply stated, these appear to be zones in which identical development control concepts are employed to those found within enterprise zones. The local planning authority is again required to consider which parts of its area may be suitable for a simplified planning zone. As might be expected, the establishment of such a zone is an involved procedure calling for public participation. The final decision on the designation of such zones lies with the local planning authority and seemingly will not involve the Secretary of State. On its designation, each zone will have documentation setting out the form and classes of development permitted without the need for planning permission, together with all their related conditions. As with enterprise zones, the simplified planning zones will remain in existence for ten years.

The effect of such simplified planning zones on the local planning policies and development control of an area, is, at the time of writing, open to speculation, as no zones have yet been established. It seems doubtful whether they will have the 'attraction' of enterprise zones, either to the local authority or the developer, as they offer no obvious financial advantage apart from the speeding up of the planning process. On the other hand, such zones may be seen as a useful means of saving time by local planning authorities. This could be achieved by designating a simplified planning zone covering a large area of established residential suburb. All the necessary planning controls would be included in the zone's plan, which would result in the area effectively producing its own self-regulating development control system. As such areas would then be unlikely to produce many major development control issues, this would leave time for the local planning authority to concentrate on other more important development control matters. Whatever the effect of these zones on the development control process, they stand as yet another example of those parts of a local planning authority area in which the 'normal' development control procedures do not apply.

Trees The contribution that trees make to both the urban and rural environment has long been acknowledged. Trees:

> . . . enhance the quality of the countryside, provide a habitat for wildlife and soften and add character to built up areas.[9]

Consequently, local planning policy can quite legitimately be used to protect existing trees as well as to encourage the planting of new trees. Indeed, local planning authorities have the power to under-

8 Housing and Planning Act 1986, s 25, Sch 6; Circular 25/87, Simplified Planning Zones.
9 Circular 36/78, Trees and Forestry, Preamble, para 2.

take their own tree planting schemes.[10] In addition, when they grant planning permission, local planning authorities can impose planning conditions which may require the planting of young trees, and should stress the importance of selecting the right trees for the right location. It is also worth contrasting the role played by local planning authorities with that played by the Forestry Commission. Whereas local planning authorities use trees to enhance the environment, the Forestry Commission encourages large scale tree planting as a commercial proposition for the supply of timber.

If local planning policy requires the protection of existing trees, the local planning authority can resort to the use of tree preservation orders.[11] Individual trees or groups of trees are to be selected for protection ' . . . in the interests of amenity'.[12] This apparently means that the trees in question, which should be visible from a public place, have to provide some positive degree of public benefit, either by:

> . . . their intrinsic beauty, or for their contribution to the landscape; or because they serve to screen an eyesore . . . [or] by their scarcity . . . [or] as a wildlife habitat . . . [13]

Usually several of these criteria have to be present in order to merit the imposition of a tree preservation order. It is also suggested that trees need not be imminently at risk to merit such an order and that:

> . . . the preservation of selected trees by precautionary orders may therefore be considered to be expedient.[14]

The making of a tree preservation order by the local planning authority is not a difficult procedure, apart, that is, from the fact that the term 'tree' is not defined in the 1971 Act. Consequently, the courts have been called upon from time to time to provide a definition.[15] The results of their deliberations have not always been especially clear. The term apparently does not exend to all forms of woodland growth, but neither does it relate simply to plants of a certain maturity or size. It can include an area of woodland and may also be applied even if that area is being coppiced.

A tree preservation order can be made using the form prescribed

---

10 National Parks and Access to the Countryside Act 1949, s 89; Highways Act 1959, s 82.
11 1971 Act, s 60.
12 Circular 36/78, para 40.
13 Circular 36/78, para 40.
14 Circular 36/78, para 40.
15 The definition provided by Lord Denning in *Kent County Council v Batchelor* (1976) 33 P & CR 185, that related to size, was rejected in *Bullock v Secretary of State for the Environment* (1980) 40 P & CR 246 where the word 'tree' was seen to bear its ordinary meaning.

in the Town and Country Planning (Tree Preservation Order) Regulations 1969.[16] This requires that the trees to be protected be identified and indicated on a map at a scale large enough to show individual trees or woodland. Notice must be given to the owners and occupiers of the land containing the specified trees and they have 28 days within which to object. If no objections are received the local planning authority can confirm the order after 42 days. If there are objections, the trees can still be protected for a period of up to six months while the objections are being heard by the local planning authority. The effect of a tree preservation order is that any person wishing to cut down, top, lop, or uproot a tree must apply to the local planning authority for permission to do so. Failure to apply may result in prosecution and the imposition of a fine. Powers do exist to enable dangerous trees to be felled without going through the whole of this procedure. The application to the local planning authority to carry out work on a tree is treated in the same way as an application for planning permission, and the same procedures apply.

Listed buildings   The decision to list a building as being of special architectural or historic interest rests with the Secretary of State, not the local planning authority.[17] Although it cannot list buildings, the local planning authority can institute an interim measure, known as a building preservation notice.[18] This remains in force for six months, during which time it is intended that the building should be considered for listing by the Secretary of State. This power, however, must be used with discretion, as if the building is not listed the owner can apply for compensation for any loss or damage suffered as a consequence of the notice.[19] The process of listing is an ongoing one. Therefore, from time to time a nationwide review of the lists may be undertaken, county by county.[20] In this way the lists are brought up to date with buildings being added and removed. Guidance is available on the qualities which make a building worth listing[1] and there is nothing to prevent a local planning authority drawing the attention of the Secretary of State to buildings which it considers worthy of listing. In their way, therefore, the criteria for

16 SI 1969 No 17.
17 1971 Act, s 54 empowers the Secretary of State for the Environment and the Historic Buildings and Monuments Commission for England (English Heritage) to list buildings.
18 1971 Act, s 58.
19 Ibid, s 173(3) and (4).
20 At the time of writing such a review is being undertaken.
 1 Circular 8/87, Historic Buildings and Conservation Areas – Policy and Procedures, Appendix I.

listing are just as important to local planning authorities as they are to the Secretary of State, as those criteria form the basis for local planning policy on the issue.

The criteria effectively fall into two categories – the age of the building, and other factors. In relation to age, the guidance is quite specific, suggesting that all pre-1700 buildings still surviving in anything like their original form, and most dating from 1700 to 1840 will, or should be, listed. Between 1840 and 1914, however, criteria other than age are relevant, and quality will play a role, although the importance of group value is also stressed. Age, therefore, is an important criterion in selecting a building for listing, but even these apparently clear guidelines can, in reality, be blurred when a building has been altered and refurbished over several hundred years. In such circumstances the actual age of a building may be difficult to ascertain, and often its selection for listing will depend upon other criteria. Indeed, the real structural age of a building may not be known unless major works are undertaken.

Criteria apart from age are, therefore, of prime importance and Circular 8/87, Historic Buildings and Conservation Areas – Policy and Procedures, seeks to outline some important general issues. In all buildings dating from before 1914 it is suggested that group value should be assessed. Particular attention should also be paid to selecting buildings that are fine examples of their type by virtue of architectural or technological merit.[2] It is stressed that it is not simply the physical fabric of a building that should be considered, but also the building's economic or social associations with local history, or its standing as an example of the work of a particular architect. With regard to post-1914 buildings, all these factors are relevant, but the range of buildings to consider is greatly increased. English Heritage have selected 150 buildings as examples of what may be suitable for listing from this period. Once a building is listed, its grade of listing has to be determined. The advice within Circular 8/87 is again useful, though open to interpretation. Grade I, for example, is to include buildings of exceptional interest, and there is usually a consensus among all concerned as to which buildings are to be included in this group. Grade II buildings, on the other hand, are to be buildings of special interest, while particularly important examples of these are to be classed Grade II*. The distinction between these two grades is somewhat unclear but it is important, as the grade of the listed building is a factor taken into account when development is proposed that will affect a listed building.

Once the selection has taken place, the listed buildings come under the planning control of the local planning authority. Before

2 Circular 8/87, Appendix I.

considering what that entails, it is worth mentioning some consequences of listing which may not immediately be apparent. Although reference has been made to the Secretary of State and the local planning authority, no mention has been made of the owner of a listed building. This is because the owner is not consulted, but merely informed that his property is to be listed; nor does he have a right of appeal. This is because it is argued that having a building listed does not materially affect the owner unless he wishes to undertake development. In addition, the presence of a group of listed buildings in a particular area may persuade the local planning authority to designate the area a conservation area, with all the consequences that this involves. It is also possible that the presence of listed buildings, or listed buildings within a conservation area may actively discourage development in the light of the planning controls involved.

Any works being undertaken by either the owners or the occupiers, or indeed any other party, that will affect the character of a listed building require a special form of permission known as listed building consent, which must be obtained from the local planning authority before the works commence. The criteria on which a building was listed are to be found in the lists held by the relevant local planning authority, and usually contain quite detailed information. For example, the following extract is taken from Liverpool City Planning Authority's lists for 10–12 Rumford Place, a Grade II listed building found within a conservation area in the commercial sector of the city.

Office building c 1840. Stucco to ground floor and brick exposed above with stone dressings, slate roof. 3 storeys and 9 bays. All windows are tripartite sashes with glazing bars on ground and 2nd floors. Central rusticated cart entrance with pilasters and entablature. Parapet and cornice, sill bands between floors. 1st floor windows have marginal glazing bars only and central window with pediment, end windows with cornices on brackets. 2nd floor has 10 windows. Included for historical reasons as the headquarters of James Dunwoody Bullock the Confederate Agent who commissioned Confederate Cruisers to be built in England, mainly on Merseyside, under cover of the Southern Cotton Commissioners. The most famous of these ships was the CSS Alabama. This building was in effect the Confederate Embassy in England.

Listed building consent and whether or not to grant it are entirely independent of the need for planning permission. Indeed, it may be required even if planning permission is not needed, if the works in question do not constitute development.

Clearly, therefore, a local planning authority's response to an application for listed building consent will have direct consequences, not only for its own policies regarding conservation and the built environment, but will also affect its policies for encouraging development within its district. A range of possibly conflicting issues may thus be introduced. As Circular 8/87 notes,[3] the public is becoming increasingly concerned over the threats to listed buildings from the developer, but at the same time it should not be assumed that just because a building is listed it will eventually be preserved, but rather:

> ... it [the listing] does ensure that the case for its preservation is examined quite separately [from that for planning permission] under the listed building consent procedure.[4]

Applications for listed building consent will raise unique local issues as well as more general issues. It is on these general issues that advice is offered to the local planning authority.[5] Considerable stress is laid on the importance of considering thoroughly the possibility of a new use for a listed building, rather than permit its demolition, with the local planning policy being interpreted as flexibly as possible to allow the introduction of new uses if at all possible. The importance of the setting of a listed building is also stressed, together with the need to interpret widely what the term 'setting' means. This is illustrated by reference to an example:

> ... where a listed building forms an important visual element in a street, it would probably be right to regard any development in the street as being within the setting of the building.[6]

Specific advice is offered on individual elements such as the doors, windows and roofs. There can be little doubt, therefore, that the protection of listed buildings is considered to be an important aspect of planning policy from the point of view of the Department of the Environment.

Before assessing how this advice is acted upon by the local planning authority, it is necessary to point out that, as may already be evident, the protection of a listed building is supported by a considerable amount of legislative power which rests in the hands of the local planning authority. As the legislation relevant to listed buildings is quite complex and is more than adequately covered by other sources[7] no attempt will be made to examine it in any detail here. To summarise, therefore, it should be noted that the owner of a non-listed building can apply for a certificate from the Secretary of

3 Circular 8/87, para 38.
4 Circular 8/87, para 38.
5 Circular 8/87, paras 89–93.
6 Circular 8/87, para 27.
7 Apart from Circular 8/87, see, for example, Telling A E *Planning Law and Procedure* (7th Edn, 1986) pp 218–225, or *Grant*, pp 462–475.

State stating that the building will not be listed for five years;[8] that the local planning authority can undertake works to preserve an unoccupied listed building;[9] that loans and grants may be available from various sources, including the local authority, to help offset the costs involved in preserving the building; that it is an offence to undertake unauthorised works to a listed building;[10] that listed building consent can be granted with conditions if it is desired;[11] that certain buildings are exempt from listing; that listed building consent lasts for five years unless otherwise stated;[12] and that if listed building consent is refused and the building becomes incapable of reasonably beneficial use, a purchase notice may be served on the local authority.[13] Suffice it to say, therefore, that every possible action in relation to a listed building is regulated by statute.

From this brief summary of the legislation it is obvious that the local planning authority has both the power and the backing from the Department of the Environment to institute whatever policy it sees fit in relation to the listed buildings within its district. In reality, however, a comprehensive policy on listed buildings is not, with certain exceptions,[14] very often found within local planning authorities. This may not be due to any lack of concern on the part of the local planning authority, which may have a comprehensive conservation policy. That policy is likely to be quite specifically related to its conservation areas, and the listed buildings in those areas will be covered. Given the likely distribution of listed buildings throughout the whole of the local planning authority's area, however, a comprehensive policy for each and every building is almost impossible to produce. As a consequence, the treatment of listed buildings within a planning district is likely to be very much a matter of chance, and any application for listed building consent will usually be considered on its individual merits. How that application will be resolved depends upon a host of local circumstances that relate only in part to the reasons for the building being listed. For example, the local planning authority will have to consider how important the proposed development is in terms of new employment opportunities. This issue would then have to be weighed against the 'value' of the listed building in terms of its contribution to the history or character/architecture of the area. Such issues are,

8 1971 Act, s 54A(1).
9 Ibid, s 101.
10 Ibid, s 55.
11 Ibid, s 56.
12 Ibid, s 56A.
13 Ibid, s 190.
14 Such a policy may be expected in particularly important historic towns such as Chester, Bath and York.

however, impossible to consider in the abstract, rendering further discussion unproductive.

Advertising The control of outdoor advertising is yet another area where a local planning authority is presented with comprehensive guidance.[15] The Town and Country Planning (Control of Advertisements) Regulations 1984 define an advertisement as:

> ... any word, letter, model, sign, placard, board, notice, device or representation, whether illuminated or not, in the nature of, and employed wholly or partly for the purposes of, advertisement, announcement or direction, (excluding any such thing employed wholly as a memorial or as a railway signal), and (without prejudice to the preceding provisions of this definition) includes any hoarding or similar structure or any balloon used, or adapted for use, for the display of advertisements.[16]

The Regulations also distinguish between advertisements which are, and those which are not, subject to control. An advertisement is specifically not subject to control, if it is one which is:

(a) displayed on enclosed land, and not readily visible from land outside that enclosure or from any part of any public right of way over such enclosure or from any land on such enclosure to which the public have a right of access;

(b) displayed within a building . . . ;

(c) displayed on or in a vehicle;

(d) displayed on, or which consists of, a balloon flown at a height of more than 60 metres above ground level;

(e) incorporated in, and forming part of, the fabric of a building, other than a building used principally for the display of such advertisements or a hoarding or similar structure;

(f) displayed on an article for sale or on the package or other container in which an article is sold, or displayed on the pump, dispenser or other container from which an article is sold, being an advertisement wholly with reference to the article for sale, which is not an illuminated advertisement and does not exceed 0.1 square metre in area.[17]

All other outdoor advertisements are subject to the controls described in the Regulations and the accompanying circular.[18] An attempt will be made, therefore, to assess the implications of these controls for the development control process.

Normally, it is the district planning authority that is responsible

---

15 1971 Act, ss 63, 64 and 109; Town and Country Planning (Control of Advertisements) Regulations 1984, SI 1984 No 421; Circular 11/84, Town and Country Planning (Control of Advertisements) Regulations 1984.

16 SI 1984 No 421, reg 2(1).

17 Ibid, reg 3(1).

18 Circular 11/84.

for advertisement control. Any individual wishing to display an advertisement must, therefore, apply to the local planning authority for permission to do so. What is quite clear is that in performing that function a local planning authority cannot exercise any form of censorship over the subject matter of the advertisement. Instead, consent is being sought from the local planning authority for the use of a site for advertising. Effectively, the situation can be summed up by saying that those advertisements liable to control may only be controlled in the interests of amenity or public safety. In this context, public safety involves the positioning of advertisements in such a manner that they do nothing to detract from the safe use of the highway. The main criterion, therefore, for the control of advertisements in all other instances, is their effect on the amenity of the area. Clearly, this may be a contentious issue since, as has been indicated in relation to other issues of development control, exactly what merits control in the interests of amenity is difficult to define. The Regulations attempt such a definition, however, when they state:

> [. . . a local planning authority–] (a) shall, in the interests of amenity, have regard to the suitability of the use of a site for the display of advertisements in the light of the general characteristics of the locality, including the presence therein of any feature of historic, architectural, cultural or similar interest; and when assessing the general characteristics of a locality the local authority may disregard any advertisements being displayed therein.[19]

It seems that this wide definition of what may be considered in the interests of amenity places a considerable amount of development control power in the hands of the local planning authority. That power, however, is not entirely unregulated. For example, once the local planning authority has made a decision to permit an advertisement to be displayed, certain standard conditions have to be attached to the consent. These provide that the advertisement must be kept in a clean, tidy, and safe condition. In addition a local planning authority can impose any other conditions it sees fit, such as a requirement that the advertisement be removed at the end of a specified period.[20]

The Regulations also deal with the display of advertisements in what are termed 'Areas of Special Control'.[1] These are rural and urban areas whose definition as special areas is dependent on their need for particular consideration. Outdoor advertising is more strictly controlled in these areas on the grounds of their important

19 SI 1984 No 421, reg 5(2)(a).
20 Ibid, reg 19 and Sch I, Part I.
 1 Ibid, Part VII.

amenity value. The majority of open countryside has been so designated, but it is also possible to designate urban areas. Circular 11/84 does attempt to give some guidance on this point, by giving examples of what may be considered appropriate areas: '. . . the precincts of a cathedral, . . . or an historic market place, or a group of listed buildings and their immediate surroundings'.[2] Indeed, the Circular makes clear that this special status is intended to cover a wide range of areas. The criteria for selecting these special areas for advertising control is totally in the hands of the local planning authority. If it can provide reasons which justify an area being designated, on the grounds that an even greater control over advertising is needed than would normally exist, then the Secretary of State will approve the designation, as he has already done for over 40% of the area of England and Wales. The designation, which the local planning authority has to review every five years, effectively introduces even tighter controls over the classes of advertisements that can be displayed with or without express consent.[3]

In conclusion, it is interesting to note that despite all the regulations aimed at controlling advertisements, the interests of public amenity are often ignored, if not actually damaged, by advertising that is approved or allowed. A few examples will illustrate this point. Traffic signs are excluded from control, assent being assumed for their display,[4] but they can have a visually detrimental effect, especially when they take the form of overhead gantries. Certain forms of 'fly posting' also carry deemed consent, for example, election notices, circus and fair posters. The problem here is that they are seldom removed after the event and thus are taken as a sign to the true 'fly poster' that the wall or hoarding is 'fair game'. Approved advertisements can also cause problems in certain sensitive areas, such as conservation areas. Local planning authorities often seem unable, or possibly unwilling, to suggest that a 'standard' advertisement, such as a shop fascia used by a national chain store, is inappropriate in the area, perhaps on the grounds that they will be faced with the argument that it has been accepted elsewhere. Even such a strictly regulated aspect of development control is, therefore, not capable of achieving in every instance the desired protection of amenity.

Highways The importance of the transport network, particularly in relation to development control where a major issue is often the traffic implications of a proposed development, is self-evident. Yet,

2 Circular 11/84, para 36.
3 SI 1984 No 421, reg 26(4).
4 Ibid, reg 9.

the effective control, and indeed creation, of transport links is not simply a planning matter, since certain national responsibilities rest with the Secretary of State for Transport rather than the Secretary of State for the Environment. Furthermore, at a local level, some transport matters may be dealt with by the county planning authority and others by the district planning authority.

Trunk roads are major roads, including motorways, that are regarded as an essential part of the national highway system. Consequently, under the terms of the Highways Act 1980, the Secretary of State for Transport has the power to permit the construction of new trunk roads as well as the improvement, by widening or straightening, of existing trunk roads.[5] Clearly, such powers can have major implications for planning policy at both county and district level. As a result, when contemplating the construction of a new trunk road, particularly a motorway, the Secretary of State for Transport is obliged to consider the planning implications[6] and to adopt a special procedure. This involves publicising the proposals and, if there are objections, in normal circumstances holding a public inquiry. The procedure is outlined in 'Policy for Roads'[7] and represents the culmination of a process that may have taken up to ten years.

The construction of a new trunk road begins when a range of surveys is conducted which cover environmental and economic matters, as well as more specific traffic issues, such as traffic flows and destinations. Possible routes are then considered and the local planning authorities consulted, as are members of the public, as to their opinions on the likely effect of these routes. The information accumulated in this fashion is then considered by the Department of Transport which will, in time, announce a preferred route for the new road, or the form which any road improvements are to take. At this stage approximately three years will have elapsed from the initial surveys. The preferred route is then analysed in detail by the Department of Transport, and draft orders prepared, setting out precisely the possible effects that the road may have, so that these matters may be fully considered at a formal public inquiry. An inquiry can last for up to six months, if not longer, and the decision is often another year in preparation. At this stage, approximately seven years after its inception, the road proposal may be abandoned or approved. If it is approved, the process continues with the issuing of the relevant compulsory purchase orders. These orders enable the land needed for the building of the new road, or the improve-

5 Highways Act 1980, ss 1(1)(a), 18 and 24.
6 Ibid, ss 10(2) and 16(8).
7 Cmnd 7132.

ment of the existing road, to be acquired by the Department of Transport even if the owners of the land do not wish to sell. The acquisition of land is followed by the final stage, the road's construction, which can take another two to three years.

This protracted procedure obviously has policy implications for local planning in any area through which the proposed road will pass. For example, the period of uncertainty over whether or not the road will actually be built, lasts for seven years on average, and can cause severe blighting problems with respect to the land values and uses that lie in its proposed path. That is to say, the land on the proposed route will be regarded by prospective owners or developers as not worth developing. As a consequence, the local planning policies for the area may, at best, be disrupted, or, at worst, simply swept aside, while the local planning authority remains helpless to do anything to remove the uncertainty that is the cause of the blight. When making development control decisions the problems are just as real since, until the route of the road is confirmed, it will be extremely difficult for the development control officers to judge accurately its traffic implications for current planning applications.

It must be admitted, however, that the proposed construction of trunk roads and motorways is less and less likely to cause headaches in local planning offices in England and Wales, because the majority of such roads were constructed in the 1960s and 1970s. What is far more likely to be a recurrent issue is the continued, and often very necessary, work that is being undertaken on highways in England and Wales which are not classed as trunk roads; work that is being undertaken by the local highway authority which can be either the county or district council or, in very specific circumstances, the parish council.[8]

Briefly, county authorities have the responsibility for all classified roads[9] within their boundary that are not trunk roads or motorways. District authorities exercise responsibility over non-classified urban roads, footpaths and bridleways.[10] Effectively, therefore, a reference to a highway authority is, in most instances, a reference to the county authority. Consequently, a considerable amount of consultation will take place between the county highway authority and the district planning authority, since it is the district which will determine the great majority of planning applications, most of which will involve some highway or traffic issues.

8 Local Government Act 1972, ss 124–127.
9 Town and Country Planning General Development Order 1977, SI 1977 No 289, article 2.
10 Ibid, articles 11 and 12.

Transport issues of a lesser nature, such as the making of a new access point, or the supply of parking on a development site, constantly recur as factors in the development control process. In relation to many of these, there are quite specific guidelines supplied by the Department of Transport which the highway authority may observe when appropriate. For example, the splay of sight lines in the design of an access point into a new development is recommended, with variations relating to the speed at which traffic is likely to be travelling along the road onto which access is proposed. There are also various standards governing the width and materials used for the construction of roads within a development which are particularly significant if the developer wishes eventually to have the site roads adopted by the local authority.[11]

Overall, therefore, there are a whole range of transport factors that are directly related to the planning and development control issues of an area, but which are not under the control of the local planning authority. Some of these factors may be prescribed by the Secretary of State for Transport; others may be in the control of the county highway authority which has the power, in the event of its failing to reach a compromise on a transport issue with the district planning authority, to impose its decision. Even in relation to the specific development control powers held by district planning authorities, the highway issues may be largely prescribed by regulations and standards.

Waste land and waste disposal   It appears somewhat anomalous to consider the disparate subjects of waste land and waste disposal in the same section. Yet there is method in this approach. Section 65 of the 1971 Act permits a local planning authority to take action over land which is deemed to be in such a condition that it adversely affects the amenity of its area. A notice can be served on the owner of the land requiring him to take steps to rectify the situation, or the local planning authority can carry out the necessary work at the owner's expense. This provision, therefore, effectively allows a local planning authority to ensure that its area remains clean and tidy. Such a power can be compared with other local authority powers, contained within the Civic Amenities Act 1967, that allow the disposal of waste or rubbish.[12] These permit a local planning authority to remove rubbish, in the shape of abandoned cars or beds, and designate areas where members of the public can dispose of such unwanted items, rather than dumping them on any open space. In this fashion local planning authorities can devise policies

11 Highways Act 1980, s 38.
12 Civic Amenities Act 1967, Part III.

which will allow them to care for their area, rather than simply respond to others' actions.

While members of the public generally want to live in a pleasant area free of old mattresses and fish and chip wrappers, there is less agreement over where this accumulated rubbish should be dumped. It is hardly surprising, therefore, that the whole complex question of waste disposal is dealt with in a plethora of legislation, regulations and circulars.[13] Waste disposal is a county planning authority matter[14] and as such the policy relating to it will be found in the structure plan. Subject plans may also be prepared on issues which go beyond the location of rubbish dumps to the kinds of material being dumped and how it gets there. The most effective waste disposal power possessed by a local planning authority is to be found not in the development plans and related legislation, but rather in the Control of Pollution Act 1974.[15] This, together with related regulations and circulars,[16] clearly defines and controls the county planning authority's response to the issue. The matter can be complicated by the fact that the 1971 Act states that all forms of waste tipping, except, of course, those covered in the General Development Order, constitute a material change of use.[17] The development control functions in this instance are exercised by the county planning authority,[18] which is logical as it has prepared both the structure plan and possibly the subject plan relating to the issue, as well as the separate waste disposal plan demanded by the Control of Pollution Act 1974. It must, however, consult with the affected districts in the exercise of these functions, as well as with any water authorities which are similarly affected, and the Ministry of Agriculture, Fisheries and Food. This regulation and guidance apply to the disposal of any form of waste, but controls are even more

13 Depending on the form of waste involved, legislation ranges from the Control of Pollution Act 1974 and the Mines and Quarries (Tips) Act 1969 to the Health and Safety at Work Act 1974, and also includes various sections within the Town and Country Planning Act 1971, for example, s 22(3). Regulations proliferate, for example, SI 1971 No 1377, SI 1971 No 1378, SI 1976 No 732, SI 1980 No 1709, as do circulars – 55/76, 1/76, 29/78, 47/78, 4/81, 20/83.

14 Town and Country Planning (Prescription of County Matters) Regulations 1980, SI 1980 No 2010.

15 Control of Pollution Act 1974, Part I.

16 Control of Pollution (Licensing of Waste Disposal) Regulations 1976, SI 1976 No 732; Control of Pollution (Licensing of Waste Disposal) (Amendment) Regulations 1977, SI 1977 No 1185; Control of Pollution (Special Waste) Regulations 1980, SI 1980 No 1709; Circular 29/78, Control of Pollution Act 1974; Circular 55/76, Waste on Land.

17 Town and Country Planning General Development Order 1977, SI 1977 No 289, Sch 1, Class VI.

18 Except in Wales where the functions are undertaken by the district authorities.

specific in the case of what is euphemistically called 'special waste'. This is overseen by a Hazardous Waste Inspectorate.[19]

Little purpose will be served by examining in detail all the relevant legislation and guidance, as the development control issues effectively remain the same in all instances. Fundamentally, the problem can be summed up as an example of what has been termed the 'nimby' response – waste dumps are admittedly needed but 'not in my back yard' if I can help it. This response can come not only from individuals, but also from district planning authorities and even, in the case of nuclear waste, from the county planning authorities themselves. Depending upon the nature of the waste, the development control issues are likely to focus on the visual impact and size of the site, the duration of the proposed dumping, subsequent landscaping, screening the site, the safety of the site boundaries, traffic generated by the site and times when the site will be used, as well as pollution of all kinds, including noise and fumes. In all instances these issues will be solved only on a local needs and local factors basis that will take into account the unique effects of the proposed development on the local community and its area.

NON-SPECIFIC POLICIES SUPPORTED BY VARIOUS SOURCES

Apart from those aspects of planning policy which are site specific in that they are applied only to particular areas or objects, there are a whole range of other policies related to development control that a local authority can apply to a broad range of issues throughout the whole of its area. To cover all these issues and their related policies would constitute a book in itself, and would necessitate reference to a great deal of legal and regulatory detail which is not the focus of this work. The only possible solution is to make reference to a few examples and in this fashion to draw the reader's attention to the wide range of topics that may be covered.

Local authorities, for example, are responsible in part for the public health of the individuals within their authority boundaries.[20] Part of this duty includes a responsibility for controlling atmospheric pollution and noise. Both pollution and noise can be considered as planning issues, and can be directly controlled by the use of planning conditions in relation to new developments. Normally, however, alternative measures are relied upon to control noise and pollution, which are exercisable by some department within the local authority, other than the planning department.[1]

19 See SI 1980 No 1709 and Circulars 4/81 and 20/83.
20 For a synopsis of the local authorities' duties regarding public health see Webster C A R *Public Health Law* (1981).
 1 For example, under the Control of Pollution Act 1974 the local authority can effect various controls that are beyond its powers as a planning authority.

That is not to imply that these issues are not relevant planning issues. The pollution implications of any industrial development, for example, would obviously figure in any development control analysis. Rather, this indicates that pollution can be controlled by a whole variety of statutory provisions, of which the imposition of planning policy, in the shape of a planning condition, is simply one aspect.

By way of a contrast, local authorities are responsible for access to the countryside and the provision of country parks, both of which may feature in the planning policies relating to leisure facilities. As in the previous example, however, there are specific legislative provisions, which a local authority must observe, that are not to be found in the planning legislation but exist in their own right. The National Parks and Access to the Countryside Act 1949[2] and the Wildlife and Countryside Act 1981,[3] both provide local authorities with a range of duties and powers regarding the provision of access to the countryside. In addition, the Countryside Act 1968[4] confers on local authorities the power to set up and maintain country parks, which are areas provided for the public enjoyment of the country-side. These various statutory powers must be taken into account by the local planning authority when preparing its policy on leisure and recreational matters. Those powers will enable specific provision to be made for leisure facilities which might not otherwise have been the case if the local planning authority had simply relied on its ability to produce planning policy in respect of the issues.

Powers stemming directly from the Town and Country Planning Act 1971   While the local authority may use powers that are derived from a wide range of legislative sources to implement some particular aspect of its planning policy, it also possesses various general planning powers that can, in certain circumstances, serve the same purpose. Of these powers, the most significant are the ability of a local authority to acquire or appropriate land; to develop land in its own right; to dispose of land; to impose planning conditions on any development; and to enter into an agreement with a developer.

Compulsory purchase for planning purposes   This is a complex branch of planning law and administrative responsibility which is adequately covered in other works that concentrate specifically on the topic.[5] In essence, sections 112 and 113 of the 1971 Act give local

2 National Parks and Access to the Countryside Act 1949, Part V.
3 Wildlife and Countryside Act 1981, ss 53–58.
4 Countryside Act 1968, ss 6–10.
5 For a comprehensive and updated text see Denyer-Green B *Compulsory Purchase and Compensation* (2nd Edn, 1985).

authorities the right to acquire by compulsory purchase any land in their area for three possible reasons. They are that the land is needed to carry out (i) any form of development, redevelopment or improvement; (ii) the proper planning of the area; or (iii) a public service. Furthermore, once the land is acquired for a specific development, the local planning authority is free to undertake the development itself, or sell or lease it to a private developer to undertake the development, or work in partnership with the private developer to undertake the development. Similar powers are also to be found in sections 121 and 122 of the 1971 Act which allow local planning authorities to appropriate land by a somewhat different procedure than that of compulsory purchase. Naturally, all such actions are carefully prescribed by regulation and statute and all manner of safeguards to protect the individual are included.

In the context of this work, however, it is the implication that the ability to acquire land has for both the creation of local planning policy and development control, which needs to be considered. Realistically, that power is possibly not as significant as it may first appear, at least not in the past decade, as the desire, and indeed ability, of local authorities to participate in major development schemes either in their own right, or even in partnership with a private developer, is much reduced. In the 1960s and 1970s some local authorities became major developers of both housing, and, to a lesser extent, of retailing, often collaborating with a private developer to undertake major developments, such as the construction of large shopping centres. As far as the developer was concerned, the advantage of a partnership lay in the fact that a local authority could use its powers of compulsory purchase to assemble a development site relatively quickly. This was especially relevant in town centres where the fragmented nature of estate ownership made the job a nightmare for the independent developer. On the other hand, the advantage to the local authority was the dual one of sharing the risk, as well as gaining from the wider entrepreneurial expertise that a major developer could offer. In the housing field, however, local authorities tended to work alone, as the returns, if indeed there were any, were not attractive enough to interest the private developer, as much of the local authority housing built during these years was subsidised by central government grants. Besides being a prominent aspect of the development activity of those years, these schemes were part of the planning process, since the developments in question represented part of a declared planning policy usually contained within the development plans.

Today, however, although all the same options to purchase and develop land remain, the opportunity presents itself less and less frequently since neither the money nor the land is available. Local authorities have also become far more cautious due to some of the disasters, especially in the field of housing, that the flood of development produced, although even some commercial developments have failed to flourish as expected. In the majority of instances, therefore, development proposals found in newly produced local plans are unlikely to be implicitly supported by a local authority eager to use its compulsory purchase powers to enable a site to be assembled for development. On the other hand, this is not to suggest that local authorities are no longer prepared to enter into partnerships with developers for schemes they would like to see implemented.

Development by local authorities   Section 124 of the 1971 Act authorises local authorities to become developers in their own right of land that they own, or, alternatively, to allow the development of that land by another person. The connection between this power and the powers of compulsory purchase is obvious, but the important issue here is that the local authority gives itself, or, perhaps more significantly, may give the developer with whom it is in partnership, planning permission. This is not to say that planning permission is simply given without any consideration of the normal development control issues. Indeed, this is far from the case, as the Secretary of State, as empowered by section 270 of the 1971 Act, has established procedures which must be observed in these circumstances.[6] Essentially, the procedures ensure that the local authority makes public its intentions and involvement regarding the proposed development. Any representations received by the local authority must then be given due consideration. The second stage of the procedure is when the local authority decides whether or not to give either itself or the other party, who will be developing the site for the local authority, planning permission. It should not be assumed that this procedure in any way cuts short the normal development control debate undertaken by the planning committee in the process of reaching its decision. Provided those development control issues are properly considered, there is no way in which the local authority can be said to have prejudged the issue, as recent cases have shown.[7] It is a surprising procedure, however, made even more so when it is realised that planning permission can be granted

6 Town and Country Planning General Regulations 1976, SI 1976 No 1419, Part II.
7 *R v St Edmundsbury Borough Council, ex p Investors in Industry Commerial Properties* [1985] 3 All ER 234 and *R v Sevenoaks District Council, ex p Terry* [1985] 3 All ER 226.

even if the proposed development contravenes the proposals within the development plan, although admittedly this triggers another set of regulatory procedures.[8] Whatever the safeguards, the procedure allows the local authority to give itself, or the developer, permission to undertake almost any form of development[9] on land that it owns. As a last resort, members of the public alarmed by the power this places in the hands of a local authority can attempt to persuade the Secretary of State to call in the application for his personal consideration. However, this happens very infrequently.

As with compulsory purchase, this power must be seen in its true light where its use in relation to any major development is hardly a frequent occurrence. Notwithstanding this fact, however, it represents a significant weapon in the local planning authority's armoury of planning powers, as it clearly can be used to implement those developments that the local planning athority thinks are best for the area – a positive force amongst the negative regulatory powers that form the greater part of the day-to-day planning process.

Planning agreements, planning gain and planning conditions
Besides it being possible for a local planning authority to give planning permission to a developer about to undertake development on land that it owns, it is also possible for the local planning authority to enter into a planning agreement with a developer by virtue of section 52 of the 1971 Act. A section 52 agreement must be mutually agreed by both parties and be for the purpose of '. . . restricting or regulating the development or use of the land',[10] which in this instance, will be owned by the developer. Such agreements usually contain details about the clearance of a site prior to development, or the height of proposed buildings. Occasionally section 52 agreements are used as a means of obtaining from the developer what is known as planning gain. Planning gains are benefits for the community that the local planning authority seeks to extract from the developer (sometimes, but not always, by way of a section 52 agreement). Arguably, in certain circumstances, such as those related to commercial developments in the Greater London area, an attempt to extract planning gain may seem justifiable, as it provides the only direct and immediate means whereby some community benefit would accrue from the enormous profits developers may make from a commercial scheme. Events, however, appeared to

8 Circular 2/81, Town and Country Planning: Development Control Functions, Appendix D.
9 SI 1976 No 1419, reg 7.
10 1971 Act, s 52(1).

have got somewhat out of hand to the extent that a circular was issued in 1983[11] which attempted, somewhat unsuccessfully, to clarify matters. The whole issue of planning agreements and planning gain is examined in a more appropriate context in Chapter 8.

The ability of a local planning authority to impose planning conditions when granting planning permission is yet another power which clearly can be used to ensure that the proposed development observes the local authority's planning policy. This power is provided for in sections 29 and 30 of the 1971 Act and has been fully examined in Circular 1/85, The Use of Conditions in Planning Permissions. In essence, a local planning authority can grant planning permission subject to such conditions as it thinks fit, but these must have a planning purpose. This power gives the local planning authority a wide discretion in formulating conditions, and this will be used the better to implement planning policy. In every instance, however, as Circular 1/85 indicates, planning conditions must be shown to be relevant to the proposed development, enforceable, precise and reasonable, otherwise they may be the subject of an appeal by the developer to the Secretary of State, or of a challenge in the courts, as will be fully discussed in Chapter 8.

Policy formulated by other bodies   As may have already been gathered, the local planning authority is not the only body to either produce policy relevant to town and country planning, or influence in other ways development control within a local planning authority area. Other bodies, of which there are a considerable number,[12] can fulfil a similar policy generating role, but all exist on the fringes of what might be termed the 'normal' planning control of an area. That is to say, it is recognised that planning control generally rests in the hands of the local planning authority, but that in certain circumstances bodies, such as the regional water authorities, can have an effect on both local planning policy and development control. While reference may be made to the influence of such bodies in the planning legislation, their actual influence on the planning of an area is difficult to define. Given the number and range of these bodies, it would be impossible to consider each one in turn. Instead, by selecting what may be considered the most 'common', it is hoped to provide a series of examples of the possible effects that each can have on planning and development control.

The first of these examples concerns the Crown. Land belonging to the Crown, which includes land directly owned by any government department, is effectively exempt from the need to apply for

11 Circular 22/83, Planning Gain.
12 See Chapter 2.

and obtain planning permission.[13] Instead, the Crown is expected to consult with the relevant local planning authority before undertaking development, the detailed arrangements being set out in Circular 18/84, Crown Land and Crown Development. Here it is made quite clear that the consultation is not simply a matter of form, and that any objections made by the local planning authority must be duly considered. If they are not, these objections may then be upheld by the Department of the Environment and a public inquiry may be held.[14] However, this is only likely to occur when major developments are contemplated by the Crown. On the other hand, it is a matter of judgment for the Crown estate if a proposed development is covered by the General Development Order. This illustrates the anomaly of the Crown's position, since it is possible for a local planning authority to include proposals for Crown estate land in any of its development plans, just as it is possible for the Department of the Environment to list any buildings on Crown land, but it is impossible to ensure that any of these proposals are observed. Naturally, this can have an effect on local planning policy.

Another group of organisations that are likely to fall into the special case category, are statutory undertakers. These are defined in the 1971 Act by listing their various duties, which include;

> ... railway, light railway, tramway, road transport, water transport, canal, inland navigation, dock, harbour, pier or lighthouse undertaking, or any undertaking for the supply of electricity, gas, hydraulic power or water.[15]

Statutory undertakers are not beyond the reach of planning control, as is the case with the Crown estate, rather they are on the fringe. This means that any development that a statutory undertaker carries out which is directly related to its duty as a statutory undertaker is permitted development.[16] Therefore, if an electricity board decides that it needs to erect a sub-station at a particular location, it can do so without planning permission. What is not included, however, are related developments that arguably are not directly attributable to the statutory undertaker's specified duty. The Central Electricity Generating Board may build a dam to generate power without planning permission, but it would need planning permission to build accommodation for housing the maintenance staff of the dam. In this instance, if planning permission were refused by the local planning authority, and an appeal was made to

---

13 1971 Act, s 266.
14 Circular 18/84, Crown Land and Crown Development.
15 1971 Act, s 290(1).
16 Town and Country Planning General Development Order 1977, SI 1977 No 289, Classes XIII–XXI.

the Secretary of State, he must then consult with the relevant Minister, in this case the Minister of Energy, and they must jointly reach a compromise. The influence these events might have on a local planning authority's development control policy is obvious. They represent development that, besides being contentious, is effectively outside the local planning authority's control.

Central government Ministries can also affect local planning policy and development control. This has been discussed elsewhere, so a single example will suffice. The most obvious Ministry to mention is the Ministry of Agriculture, Fisheries and Food, which has a very wide remit covering agriculture as well as forestry, land reclamation, drainage, water supply and environmental pollution. In performing these tasks, the Ministry may well produce policy that is not specifically related to local planning policy, but the impact of that policy will be felt by most rural planning officers and their authorities. For example, the Ministry grades agricultural land according to its inherent food producing qualities.[17] Consequently, as high grade agricultural land has been effectively earmarked only for agricultural production, the ability of the local planning authority to produce proposals for alternative uses is severely restricted.

Finally, other bodies which can be mentioned because they may have some effect on planning include the Countryside Commission, the Forestry Commission, the Nature Conservancy Council, the United Kingdom Atomic Energy Authority, nationalised industries, and English Heritage. All of these are connected in some fashion with the government, while other groups, such as the Civic Trust, the Ramblers' Association, the National Trust, and the Georgian Group have no direct links with government, simply a considerable amount of influence regarding certain issues.

It is beyond the scope of this book to consider each of these in turn, but a single example may serve to illustrate their possible impact on the planning process. English Heritage have a large number of 'townscape' schemes that allow works within designated conservation areas to apply for grant aid to English Heritage.[18] That body may then provide finance for the works jointly with the local planning authority. Clearly, the local planning authority is involved in the schemes, and, indeed, any local planning authority may approach English Heritage to consider including one of its conservation areas in the townscape scheme. The final decision remains in the hands of English Heritage, however, and when taken it will have an obvious effect on local conservation policy.

17 Circular 16/87, Development Involving Agricultural Land.
18 Circular 8/87, Historic Buildings and Conservation Areas, Part V.

221

Chapter 6

Department of the Environment policy

In the opening chapter of this book it was acknowledged that land use planning is the '. . . art and science of ordering the use of land and the character and siting of buildings and communication routes so as to secure the maximum practicable degree of economy, convenience and beauty'.[1] The order of priority in which these objectives are arranged and the degree to which each is emphasised varies depending on planning policy. This policy varies from administration to administration and between central and local government, but in general terms represents the plan of action conceived in order to obtain the prioritised objectives. Within certain parameters, planning policy can have whatever content is thought most effective by the policy-making body to achieve a particular goal. If, for example, central government wishes to encourage new development, it can manipulate its land use planning policy in order to help achieve this goal. On the one hand, that policy may make more land available for housing, in the expectation that the opportunity to increase the number of housing starts will produce new development opportunities in the building industry. Alternatively, areas may be established where planning formalities are kept to a minimum, in the hope that new enterprises will be developed there and new jobs created. The land use policies are distinct yet their goal is the same. As for the parameters restricting such policy, basically, there are two. The need to observe the law and also to appreciate the basic constraints imposed by the theories of land use planning, such as those which attempt to explain the dynamics of urban structure.

This chapter is devoted to a study of central government policy, or more accurately Department of the Environment policy, as it relates to development control. In analysing that policy, a critic might say that little indication is given of what constitutes the content of that policy. Instead, this chapter concentrates on the

1 Keeble L *Principles and Practice of Town and Country Planning* (4th Edn, 1961) p 1.

form in which Department of the Environment policy is expressed, for example, legislation and circulars. There is, however, a simple explanation for this. In a sense, the whole of this book is a testimony to years of Department of the Environment and central government policy. The chapter on development plans is one such example. It was a central government policy decision that brought these plans into existence and, as that chapter explains, subsequent policy decisions have changed the nature of these documents and will undoubtedly continue to do so. The same can be said of the chapter on local authority policy, where a range of devices was considered which allow a local planning authority to initiate specific development control policies for its area. The origin of those devices is central government.

Yet, for all this power of central government to initiate policy, its relationship with the local planning authority is crucial, since it is the local planning authority which puts central government policy into practice, adapting that general policy to suit the specific needs of its area, and takes the bulk of the development control decisions. If it is correct to say that central government initiates and local government implements, what guarantees are there that this division of labour is observed? Briefly, they rely on the fact that central government policy is well publicised and, therefore, any attempt by a local planning authority to depart from that policy is likely to be apparent. In addition, there are, built into the development control system, opportunities for central government to monitor the activities of local government. Development plans, for example, may have to be approved, as does the creation of conservation areas, while a refusal of planning permission can always be the subject of an appeal. In this fashion central government can observe and, if need be, override a local planning authority which has been reluctant to implement central government policy.

Nor should it be imagined that only central and local government take an interest in Department of the Environment policy, as other individuals and organisations exist with an interest in development control to whom such policy is crucial. These range from property companies and the professional bodies, such as the Royal Institution of Chartered Surveyors, to members of the public. Central as well as local government policy will be used by them to estimate what type of planning application will be likely to succeed, or, alternatively, whether an appeal would be worthwhile.

The origins of policy

While no attempt will be made in this chapter to detail the content

223

of Department of the Environment policy, it seems sensible to consider the origins of that policy before listing the forms in which it can be expressed. Obviously the policy pursued by the Department of the Environment at any particular time is influenced by the political beliefs of the party which is in government. This may, for example, cause shifts in emphasis between private- and public-sector development. If the government of the day is trying to encourage private-sector development of housing and industry, it may contemplate policies that release more land for housing to private developers, create simplified planning zones for the establishment of industrial enterprises, and divert funds away from the public sector and, in particular, from local authorities. A government which wished to reverse such policies might behave in completely the opposite fashion, putting money into the public sector and controlling private-sector development, perhaps by the imposition of a tax on profits. Therefore, a good deal of Department of the Environment policy is shaped by political motives.

Leaving aside the influence exerted by a government's political beliefs, there are other factors which shape the policies pursued by the Department of the Environment. They include the expert opinions volunteered by professional organisations, such as the Royal Town Planning Institute and the Royal Institution of Chartered Surveyors. Pressure groups, such as the Council for the Protection of Rural England or the Civic Trust, can also shape policy. This is because the Department of the Environment normally canvasses a wide range of opinion while legislation or circulars are being prepared. Even if their views are ignored within the Department of the Environment, some pressure groups, for example the National Farmers Union, have considerable influence in Parliament, which can be mobilised in order to try to secure amendment to legislation. Indeed, on rare occasions the content of a circular has proved so unpopular that pressure of opinion has forced its withdrawal.[2] Therefore, pressures shape policy. Since governments wish to be re-elected, it is the Department of the Environment's task to balance these often conflicting views in order to achieve a policy which is politically and electorally acceptable. Quite obviously, not every section of an Act of Parliament or paragraph of circular is politically sensitive. Sometimes other considerations are uppermost, such as securing the most efficient way to administer a particular aspect of the development control process. Here policy takes a back seat. Attention will focus instead on the courts, and what they have to say on acceptable administrative behaviour. When Department of the

2 A draft version of a circular on green belts proved so unpopular that it had to be withdrawn and rewritten. The rewritten version is Circular 14/84, Green Belts.

Environment inspectors hear planning appeals, there are rules indicating how they must conduct such appeals in order to ensure procedural fairness.[3]

Making policy known

Once the content of a particular policy has been decided upon, the most appropriate way of implementing it has to be sought. The most obvious vehicle for putting policy into effect would seem to be legislation. It has the advantage of being publicly debated in Parliament, and will ultimately represent the law of the land which must be obeyed by all concerned. In the course of this book, Acts of Parliament have been considered which are statements of current Department of the Environment policy. They range from the Town and Country Planning Act 1971 to the Housing and Planning Act 1986. The overriding problem with using legislation to implement policy is that, once in place, legislation has either to be amended or repealed in order to take account of a change in policy. A space has to be found in the government's legislative programme and sufficient time allowed for the bill to pass through all its stages. Nor is there any guarantee that the original bill will remain intact and not fall prey to amendment. This apart, policy can be difficult to express in the precise language which legislation requires. It is not unknown for the courts to conclude that the meaning of a section in an Act of Parliament is either totally obscure, or the exact reverse of what was intended.[4] Nor is policy always capable of being expressed in absolute terms. Instead, it is subject to qualifications and exceptions which a parliamentary draftsman might be hard pressed to put into words. Legislation, therefore, is normally used to convey only the basic concepts of any development control policy.

In order to expand upon the role of legislation and to illustrate its relationship with other devices used to implement policy, it seems sensible to refer to an example. Sections 54 to 57 of the Town and Country Planning Act 1971 are concerned with buildings of special architectural or historic interest. Provision is made for the establishment by the Secretary of State of lists of such buildings, which cannot then be demolished, altered or extended unless special permission has been secured from the local planning authority or

3 Town and Country Planning (Inquiries Procedure) Rules 1974, SI 1974 No 419; Town and Country Planning (Determination by Appointed Persons) (Inquiries Procedure) Rules 1974, SI 1974 No 420.
4 See, for example, *Windsor and Maidenhead Royal Borough Council v Brandrose Investments Ltd* [1983] 1 All ER 818, where the Court of Appeal commented on the obscurity of s 52(3) of the Town and Country Planning Act 1971.

the Secretary of State. This is totally separate from the need to obtain planning permission. Failure to obtain consent can result in prosecution.[5] The policy behind these sections in the 1971 Act is the desire to preserve those buildings which are special, either because of their appearance or their history. Yet, apart from some very general comments in section 54(2), no detailed guidance is given in the 1971 Act on what constitutes a building of special architectural or historic interest. Further examination of these sections reveals that, while, according to section 55(2), listed building consent must be obtained before a listed building is demolished, altered or extended, there is only a passing reference to how to go about securing the same. This is to be found in section 56(6):

> Part 1 of Schedule 11 to this Act shall have effect with respect to applications to local planning authorities for listed building consent, the reference of such applications to the Secretary of State and appeals against decisions on such applications . . .

Although Part 1 of Schedule 11 provides some indication of the procedure to be followed on such occasions, it is not comprehensive. On the question of the form an application for listed building consent is to take, for example, provision is simply made for regulations to be produced.

Any individual, therefore, who wishes to know what makes a building worthy of listing or how to go about making an application for listed building consent must consult other sources apart from the 1971 Act. Circular 8/87, Historic Buildings and Conservation Areas – Policy and Procedures, supplies criteria for selecting listed buildings. The Town and Country Planning (Listed Buildings and Buildings in Conservation Areas) Regulations 1987[6] describe the procedure to be followed when making an application for listed building consent. From this brief illustration, it should be apparent that what the 1971 Act supplies is a framework for the policy which is supplemented with details from other sources. What those sources are, is not without significance. The Town and Country Planning (Listed Buildings and Buildings in Conservation Areas) Regulations 1987 represent delegated legislation. It will be recalled that Part 1 of Schedule 11 to the 1971 Act refers to provision being made ' . . . by regulations under this Act with respect to the form and manner in which applications for listed building consent are to be made'. When an Act of Parliament authorises the making of rules, regulations or directions on a particular matter, those regulations have the same status as any provisions which appear in the

5 1971 Act, s 55(1).
6 SI 1987 No 349.

original Act. Collectively such rules, regulations, directions or statutory instruments are known as delegated legislation.

It might occur to anyone reading this brief description of delegated legislation that regulations, such as the Town and Country Planning (Listed Buildings and Buildings in Conservation Areas) Regulations 1987, could just have easily been included in the 1971 Act. While this is no doubt correct, Ministers prefer to rely on delegated legislation because the procedure for introducing it, amending it or replacing it, is very straightforward indeed, and takes a fraction of the time required for amending an Act of Parliament.[7] The only limitations are that a power must exist in an Act of Parliament to make delegated legislation and it must be used correctly in accordance with the terms of the Act and certain general principles.[8] This apart, delegated legislation has the advantages of legislation without requiring a considerable period of parliamentary time to be devoted to its passage.

Given the convenience of delegated legislation, it might appear strange that the criteria for selecting listed buildings were not expressed in that form. The Circular which contains those criteria is not a piece of delegated legislation and, as will be demonstrated later, has no binding force whatsoever. The simple answer is that the 1971 Act gives no power to create regulations on this particular topic. While this is true, some further explanation is necessary for this apparent omission. According to Circular 8/87, age is a criterion for listing buildings. To quote from the Circular:

> Most buildings of 1700 to 1840 are listed, though selection is necessary. Between 1840 and 1914 only buildings of definite quality and character are listed, and the selection is designed to include the principal works of the principal architects.[9]

If an attempt had been made to express this passage in the form of binding regulations, then the result would have been less than helpful. This is because discretion is the essential factor in selecting buildings for listing. While, therefore, an indication can be given of what is important, for example, age, it is not possible to state

---

7 Once the content of delegated legislation has been decided upon and interested parties have been asked for their comments, most delegated legislation is put before Parliament for 40 days. The intention is that during this period motions can be made for the annulment of the delegated legislation. That 40-day period should be contrasted with the months it takes most bills to pass through Parliament.

8 The courts have a power to review delegated legislation in order to determine whether the correct procedure has been observed in its making. In addition, the courts can set aside delegated legislation where some unreasonable use has been made of the power to create it.

9 Circular 8/87, Appendix 1.

categorically that every building built between 1840 and 1914 shall be listed. In contrast, certainty as opposed to discretion is the keynote of the Town and Country Planning (Listed Buildings and Buildings in Conservation Areas) Regulations 1987. An individual needs to be certain of whom to apply to for listed building consent, what details must be given, who must be informed and what publicity is necessary. The Regulations supply that information and more besides. In this way they ensure that all concerned are treated fairly, and the fact that the Regulations are binding should guarantee this. To have used a circular in this situation would not have ensured compliance. Yet, the mere fact that circulars are advisory is not a reason for dismissing them without further comment. Theirs is a crucial role in disseminating Department of the Environment policy.

Circulars

Circulars have no binding force.[10] In that respect they are totally distinct from legislation, since their only purpose is to advise. That advice may be intended to explain the working of a particular piece of legislation, or even an individual section of an Act. Circular 19/86, for example, is devoted to an examination of the planning provisions of the Housing and Planning Act 1986. In contrast, Circular 1/85 analyses the circumstances where a planning condition may legitimately be imposed and, therefore, represents a commentary on section 29 of the 1971 Act. Alternatively, there may be no legislation which is relevant to the subject matter of a circular. Circular 22/83 on planning gain is just such an example, since it represents an attempt to regulate the process of bargaining for planning gain without the added sanction of legislation.

The use of circulars and comparable advisory documents is a practice which is not without its critics. There is no denying that the guidance which they offer is treated very seriously by those whose actions it affects. Consequently, the suspicion has been voiced that, on occasions, a circular may represent an attractive alternative to legislation, particularly if an issue is controversial. The dangers represented by such a practice need to be stressed, and should be kept in mind during the remainder of this examination of the role of circulars.

10 For all that, circulars in general and development control circulars in particular have an increasingly important role to play in the business of government. For a general assessment of the role of circulars see Baldwin & Houghton 'Circular Arguments: The Status and Legitimacy of Administrative Rules' Public Law, 1986, p 239.

THE PRODUCTION OF CIRCULARS

Circulars are the product of the relevant Ministry. On development control issues this is the Department of the Environment in England and the Welsh Office in Wales. Normally the same circular is issued jointly by the two Ministries. The impetus for producing circulars varies. It can include the necessity to explain the impact that a particular piece of legislation will have on the development control process, to give guidance on an issue that is proving troublesome, or to indicate a change of direction in policy. Given that the general purpose of circulars is to advise and inform, then their production could seem justified whenever guidance would prove helpful. Once the decision has been taken to produce a circular, then the comments of interested individuals and organisations may be sought on its proposed contents. Should such comment be unfavourable, then a circular may be modified or, on rare occasions, totally rewritten.

On average, between ten and twenty circulars are produced each year that have some relevance for the development control process. Once published, a circular represents current policy on a particular issue until it is cancelled or replaced by another circular. Circulars produced up to thirty years earlier can still be perfectly valid. Circular 14/84, Green Belts, for example, refers to Circulars 42/55 and 50/57 on the same topic. It says of those earlier Circulars:

> The policy advice that they contain remains valid but insofar as they relate to the earlier development plan system they are out of date and are replaced by the present circular.[11]

There are approximately 150 current circulars dealing with development control issues. The guidance they contain varies in length from a few paragraphs to pages of detail. With this in mind, the next task is to consider the content of circulars.

THE CONTENT OF CIRCULARS

The breadth of subject matter included in circulars can be illustrated by quoting a few examples at random. There is, for instance, Circular 28/85, Reclamation and Re-use of Derelict Land, or Circular 28/77, Gypsy Caravan Sites, or Circular 3/84, Opencast Coal Mining. Given the number of circulars it is impossible to consider the content of each one in turn. Instead an attempt will be made to indicate to the reader what circulars are, and how they are employed by the various parties to whom they are of interest. By approaching the topic in this fashion, the hope is that if the circulars

11 Circular 14/84, para 7.

mentioned in this book are superseded by new circulars, as often happens, a basic understanding of the significance of circulars will have been acquired.

However, in order to achieve this objective, something needs to be said concerning the content of circulars. All circulars are intended to provide advice, but that advice can range from the purely practical to deliberate policy statements.[12] This distinction is important and deserves further consideration. Some circulars concentrate on giving advice on how a particular situation should be handled. Circular 1/85 deals with the use of conditions in planning permissions. Much of the advice in the Circular is purely practical, dealing with legislative provisions relevant to the imposition of planning conditions, and tests laid down by the High Court to gauge the validity of conditions. In short, the Circular represents a compilation, derived from various sources, of information which a local planning authority should bear in mind when imposing planning conditions. Whether such a Circular can be described as a policy statement is open to doubt, since policy normally refers to a plan of action adopted by central government, rather than the dissemination of advice from other sources.

The problem is that even an informative circular, such as Circular 1/85, does contain passages which can be regarded as policy statements. Paragraph 77 of this Circular deals with domestic occupancy conditions, that is, conditions imposed in order to restrict the occupancy of a new dwelling-house to a particular type of person. Arguably, there may be good planning reasons why such a condition should be imposed, in order, for example, to prevent the proliferation of holiday cottages. Circular 1/85 makes it plain, however, that in the opinion of the Secretary of State such conditions are not acceptable, save in exceptional circumstances.[13] In addition, paragraph 88 of the Circular contains the following statement:

> The Secretaries of State recognise that some local authorities may have adopted development plan policies which may conflict with policies set out in this circular . . . Those authorities are invited to examine any such policies with a view to resolving any inconsistencies with the policy here stated.

The overall effect of this statement is that even though the power exists to impose such conditions, and they will not, as a rule, infringe any of the tests for legal validity devised by the courts, the

---

12 Currently, the Department of the Environment is producing Planning Policy Guidance Notes with the aim of making planning policy more accessible.
13 Circular 1/85, paras 77, 80 and 81.

Secretary of State, for the reasons stated in Circular 1/85, will not normally allow a domestic occupancy condition to stand. If, therefore, a local planning authority imposes such a condition, it may expect to see it removed if there is an appeal.[14] This may be so even though the relevant development plan contains policies to support its imposition, as the Secretary of State obviously intends that such policies should be removed from development plans if this is feasible.[15]

Circular 1/85, therefore, represents a circular combining information with policy statements. In contrast, Circular 15/84, Land for Housing, represents central government policy on the provision of housing land. No attempt is made in this Circular to summarise judicial decisions or legislative provisions. Instead, it presents the views and opinions of central government. This is apparent from the tone of the statements in the Circular. To take a single example:

> Local authorities should aim to ensure that at all times land is or will become available within the next 5 years which can be developed (or is being developed) within that period and which in total provides at least 5 years' supply in terms of the general scale and location of development provided for in approved structure and adopted local plans. Within this context the aim should always be at least 2 years' supply available on which development can start straight away.[16]

The emphasis here and elsewhere in the Circular is on ensuring that land is available for housing. Advice is offered on the appropriate way to treat applications for planning permission from private-sector house builders[17] as well as how to reconcile the policy in this Circular with other development control policies, such as those on conservation.[18]

This difference in content between circulars is important and should be borne in mind. While there is no denying that all circulars appear to be treated with deference by those involved in the development control process, viewed objectively a circular's content can dictate the weight it carries. Any attempt in a circular to summarise the impact of legislation or the significance of a judicial decision is not authoritative. The courts are responsible for statutory interpretation and they will have no hesitation in saying that a statement made in a circular is wrong, should this be the case. Policy

---

14 APP/5941/A/80/06966. This is a Department of the Environment planning appeal which discharged a condition imposed on a development in the Lake District National Park requiring that the property in question be occupied by a local person.

15 For example, when a development plan is amended.

16 Circular 15/84, para 12.

17 Circular 15/84, Annex A.

18 Circular 15/84, para 3.

statements, on the other hand, are neither right nor wrong, though the content of one policy may be inconsistent with another. In applying a policy a decision-maker has the discretion to decide that the policy is not appropriate to the particular situation, or that some other policy takes precedence. There can be, and often is, disagreement between central and local government over the appropriateness of a particular policy. In these circumstances, while it is possible to give one party the final say, this is not equivalent to deciding that the other party is wrong.

The legal significance of circulars

Department of the Environment circulars are not usually binding in the sense that legislation binds those individuals affected by its provisions. On very rare occasions, however, an Act of Parliament will give the Secretary of State power to create delegated legislation in this fashion. Circular 2/81[19] contains a direction from the Secretary of State to all local planning authorities detailing how planning applications, which would either conflict with, or prejudice, the implementation of a relevant development plan, should be handled.[20] Since that direction has the force of law local planning authorities have no choice but to obey it. This contrasts with the situation regarding most circulars where their content represents nothing more than current Department of the Environment development control policy.

The fact that circulars are policy documents and not legally binding has a number of important legal consequences. The first of these is that any statement made in a circular regarding the interpretation of a statute or the way in which the law is to be applied is, so far as the courts are concerned, an expression of opinion which may well be wrong. Nor should that advice have the effect of preventing development control powers possessed by the individual or body in question from being exercised. In *R v Worthing Borough Council, ex p Birch*,[1] advice was given in Circular 49/63[2] on the procedure to be followed when a government department disposed

19 Circular 2/81, Development Control Functions: Act of 1980.
20 This direction is made by virtue of powers conferred on the Secretary of State for the Environment by the Town and Country Planning General Development Order 1977, SI 1977 No 289, articles 7, 10 and 14.
1 (1983) 49 P & CR 53.
2 No longer a current circular. As a result of the decision in *R v Worthing Borough Council* the law was changed in the Town and Country Planning Act 1984, s 1. Planning permission in respect of Crown land can now be sought prior to its disposal.

of land. Here, a disagreement occurred between the local planning authority and the area health authority over how land being disposed of by the area health authority should be developed. Following the guidance in Circular 49/63, the dispute was resolved by the Secretary of State for the Environment in favour of the area health authority. When, therefore, planning permission was sought for the scheme sanctioned by the Secretary of State, the local planning authority, despite its misgivings, approved the proposed development. Local residents challenged this decision in the courts. They did so on the basis that for all practical purposes the effect of Circular 49/63 was to prevent the local planning authority from determining this application for planning permission in accordance with the terms of the 1971 Act. The court agreed with the local residents that the procedure set out in the Circular had prevented them from making effective representations against the scheme and the local planning authority from exercising its powers.

It might be thought that the stress placed upon the advisory nature of circulars is inconsistent with the views expressed by the court in the *Worthing* case. What needs to be appreciated is that, whatever their status, circulars are undoubtedly influential in the development control process. The court acknowledged this in the *Worthing* case, when it was thought inconceivable that the local planning authority would ignore the advice of the Secretary of State. The very same point was made in *Coleshill and District Investment Co Ltd v Minister of Housing and Local Government*.[3] Here, the House of Lords doubted the accuracy of the advice given in a circular regarding whether or not demolition could constitute development. Lord Wilberforce said of that misleading advice:

> ... the circular has no legal status, but it acquired vitality and strength when, through the years, it passed, as it certainly did, into planning practice and textbooks, was acted on, as it certainly was, in planning decisions.[4]

Therefore, the courts have not allowed the advisory nature of circulars to divert them from the true issue, which is whether the advice given in a circular is in accordance with the law. If it is not, then the presumption is that that advice will have been acted upon, unless the contrary can be shown. In *E C Gransden & Co Ltd v Secretary of State for the Environment*,[5] planning permission was refused for a residential development. On appeal, one of the issues was the instruction in Circular 22/80 that a five-year supply of land

3 [1969] 2 All ER 525.
4 Ibid, 538.
5 [1987] JPL 365.

should be available to meet the housing needs of an area.[6] If there was no identified five-year supply, then the presumption was that planning permission should be given for a proposed residential development unless there were clear planning reasons to decide otherwise. Here, the inspector had taken account of the fact that the shortfall in land for housing might have been made good when land at Chatham Dockyard became available for development. On this basis he refused planning permission for the proposed development. It was argued in this case that the inspector had misapplied the policy in Circular 22/80. The Court of Appeal dismissed this suggestion, believing that the policy had been correctly applied. In the first instance judgment[7] the court had considered the possibility that the intention of the Circular was to make a matter which was otherwise a material consideration an irrelevant consideration. If this had been the intention, and the Court of Appeal did not feel that it was, then the court of first instance was clear that this was not lawful.[8] Since, however, it was plain that whatever the Circular had said, the inspector had taken account of soon to be available land, then the court of first instance left his decision undisturbed.

Apart from the need for the contents of a circular to accord with the law, the courts have also made it plain on numerous occasions that the interpretation of a circular is a matter for them.[9] It might be thought that the sensible thing to do would be to ask the Secretary of State for the Environment exactly what he meant when drafting the circular. This the courts have shown no inclination to do. Instead, the same attitude is taken towards circulars as is taken towards legislation, that is, that their meaning is a matter for the courts. There are, however, a number of difficulties associated with this approach. Legislation is drafted in the knowledge that it may well be the subject of judicial scrutiny. In contrast, circulars are meant to provide guidance, and their language reflects this fact. It is the language of conversation rather than legislation. To subject this to rigorous scrutiny is to invite problems. As was said in the course of one judgment:

> These circulars were intended to provide local authorities with general guidance. Their paragraphs are to be read with common sense. Words are to be given their ordinary meaning and the sense and purpose of a

6 Circular 22/80, Annex A. This Annex is reproduced as an Annex to Circular 15/84.
7 [1986] JPL 519.
8 Ibid, 521.
9 See, for example, *J A Pye (Oxford) Estates Ltd v Secretary of State for the Environment* [1982] JPL 575, *Rockhold Ltd v Secretary of State for the Environment* [1986] JPL 130, *E C Gransden & Co Ltd v Secretary of State for the Environment* [1986] JPL 519.

paragraph as a whole, and indeed of a circular as a whole, is of greater importance than any individual phrase, or sentence contained in it.[10]

Whether this warning will be heeded remains to be seen. Circular 22/80, with its insistence on a five-year supply of housing land and its presumption in favour of development if none exists, has been the subject of two conflicting interpretations in the courts.[11] The difficulty is that circulars are essentially practical documents intended to spell out Department of the Environment development control policy. The more the courts intervene and 'interpret' that policy, the more confusing the situation becomes for those who have to make everyday use of those documents. In addition, the temptation is there for those unhappy with a development control decision to challenge it in the courts, on the basis that the policy in a Department of the Environment circular has been misapplied.

On this question of the practical significance of circulars, there is no doubt that when a development control decision is taken any relevant circulars should be taken into account. When, for example, a local planning authority is considering an application for planning permission, the 1971 Act directs that regard shall be had to the relevant provisions of the development plan and to any other material considerations. Undoubtedly those material considerations can and do include any relevant circulars, as well as other factors, such as local site conditions. The fact that a relevant circular cannot be ignored does not mean that its advice has to be followed. It may well be that the advice given in a circular is inappropriate, or that it conflicts with another policy document which a local planning authority chooses to follow, for example, the development plan. Circular 1/85 advises against the use of local user conditions, that is, conditions designed to restrict the occupation of houses or factories to individuals or firms in the locality. If a development plan were to contain a policy advocating the use of such conditions in appropriate circumstances, then a local planning authority might feel justified in ignoring the strictures of Circular 1/85. The fact that there is every chance that a condition of this nature would be the subject of an appeal does not prevent a local planning authority from imposing it. Nor is it evidence of bad faith on the part of the local planning authority, since there is always a chance that the Secretary of State might be persuaded to leave such a condition undisturbed.

If the local user clause mentioned in the previous paragraph were

---

10 *Mid-Bedfordshire District Council v Secretary of State for the Environment.* The decision is unreported, but a brief account of it is to be found at [1984] JPL 631.
11 Compare the judgment of Glidewell J, as he then was, in *J A Pye (Oxford) Estates Ltd v Secretary of State for the Environment* [1982] JPL 575, with that of Forbes J in *Rockhold Ltd v Secretary of State for the Environment* [1986] JPL 130.

to be the subject of a planning appeal, the likelihood is that the whole issue would be reconsidered, not by the Secretary of State, but by a Department of the Environment inspector. He too must have regard to all relevant considerations, including circulars and the development plan. The scope which an inspector has to ignore the policy spelt out in a relevant circular is unclear. On the one hand, the inspector is responsible for making the most fitting development control decision. On that basis he may believe that a local user condition is essential. On the other hand, he is a Department of the Environment inspector and might, therefore, be expected to observe Department of the Environment policy.

While it would appear legitimate for an inspector to behave in this fashion and favour a circular at the expense of a development plan, he must have evidence and reasons for acting in this fashion. This point was made in *Surrey Heath Borough Council v Secretary of State for the Environment*[12] where an unthinking application of the policy for economic regeneration in Circular 14/85 caused the court to set aside an inspector's decision. This was on the basis that since Department of the Environment policy is formulated in general terms, there must be local circumstances which justify its application as well as the abandonment of pertinent policies in a development plan.

On this issue of the role of the inspector, the courts have made a number of points. The most important of these is that, in the eyes of the courts, the inspector is not a policy maker. The point was made in *Sears Blok v Secretary of State for the Environment*[13] and repeated in *Chelmsford Borough Council v Secretary of State for the Environment.*[14] In the latter case it was said of an inspector determining a planning appeal:

> He was not, and should not be regarded as having any authority on behalf of the Secretary of State to lay down any general policy, or as giving a decision which should be treated as a precedent for other planning applications or other planning appeals in the area, save to a limited extent.[15]

It would appear, therefore, that a inspector does not create policy but simply applies established policy to the situation that confronts him. Yet, even in this role the inspector will have to interpret the general policy of a circular as well as make choices between what is said in a circular and what is said in the development plan. A choice which, once made, does not apparently bind another inspector,

12 [1987] JPL 199.
13 [1980] JPL 523.
14 [1985] JPL 316.
15 Ibid, 317.

who can make exactly the opposite choice provided he gives his reasons for so doing.[16]

As for those occasions when the Secretary of State determines a planning appeal, his decision would no more appear a precedent than that of an inspector. Where the two are distinguishable is that a circular represents the Secretary of State's own policy, and he can, if he chooses, abandon that policy provided he gives his reasons for so doing. Hence, in *Barnham v Secretary of State for the Environment*,[17] an amendment to the structure plan was approved which apparently conflicted with departmental policy as set out in Circular 15/84. While the Secretary of State's right to behave in this fashion was never in doubt, he must, according to the court, give his reasons for so doing.

From what has been said so far it would appear that for all practical purposes circulars are general statements of development control policy which are not to be slavishly followed. This would appear eminently sensible, since general statements are just that and cannot anticipate the uniqueness of individual situations. In particular, their generality also contrasts with that more specific policy document, the development plan, whose policy is drawn up with a particular area in mind. When development plans are prepared it is with Department of the Environment policy, as expressed in the circulars, as a background. It might be expected, therefore, that any differences would be resolved when the plan is in preparation, since the process is monitored by the Department of the Environment, although, as the decision in *Barnham*'s case shows, mistakes can occur. Indeed, in *Waverley Borough Council v Secretary of State for the Environment*,[18] the Secretary of State condemned a policy in a local plan as an arbitrary rationing of land and contrary to his policy, as set out in Circular 15/84. On that basis he proceeded to grant planning permission for a residential development. The fact that the local plan in question had recently been adopted without adverse comment from the Department of the Environment was apparently immaterial, and did not prevent the Secretary of State coming to that conclusion.[19]

However, what that decision and others like it represent, is a

---

16 *Rockhold Ltd v Secretary of State for the Environment* [1986] JPL 130.

17 [1985] JPL 861.

18 [1987] JPL 202.

19 Local plans do not have to be approved by the Secretary of State for the Environment, as is the case with structure plans. Their content is, however, monitored by the Department of the Environment, and some comment on this policy to arbitrarily ration land might, therefore, have been expected. For further discussion on how policy should be treated, see *Wycombe District Council v Secretary of State for the Environment* [1988] JPL 111.

determination on the part of the Department of the Environment that the policy of its circulars should be the equal of the policy in any development plan. The fact that development plans are specifically mentioned in section 29 of the 1971 Act is not seen as significant by the courts. They are simply regarded as one of any number of material considerations that can influence the making of a development control decision. As for the Department of the Environment, that has made its views plain in Circular 14/85, where the following statement is to be found:

> Development plans are therefore one, but only one, of the material considerations that must be taken into account in dealing with planning applications. Many development plans were approved several years ago, often several years after they had been prepared and based on even earlier information. The policies which they contain, and the assumptions on which they were based, may therefore be out of date and not well related to today's conditions. They cannot be adapted rapidly to changing conditions, and they cannot be expected to anticipate every need or opportunity for economic development that may arise. They should not be regarded as overriding other material considerations, especially where the plan does not deal adequately with new types of development or is no longer relevant to today's needs and conditions – particularly the need to encourage employment and to provide the right conditions for economic growth.[20]

This unequivocal declaration of intent from the Department of the Environment seems to make it plain to all those involved in the development control process that where there are inconsistencies between circulars and the development plan, the development plan is not automatically to be given precedence. It is worth emphasising that often the development plan may be the only policy document, or may be totally in line with Department of the Environment policy. Indeed, there have been occasions when the local planning authority has been just as eager to disregard the development plan as the Department of the Environment.[1] Circulars, therefore, enjoy the dubious privilege of being general policy documents, subject to little in the way of scrutiny, which can take precedence over documents prepared in accordance with the 1971 Act. They can be used by the Department of the Environment to initiate fundamental changes in development control policy which can have dramatic consequences for local planning authorities. Whether circulars are now being used in preference to legislation has yet to be proved. What is clear is that the courts show no sign of intervening in favour of development plans.

20 Circular 14/85, Development and Employment, para 5.
1 See, for example, *Greater London Council v Secretary of State for the Environment* [1983] JPL 793.

Development control policy notes

Apart from circulars, the Department of the Environment also publishes development control policy notes. The majority were issued in 1969 by the Ministry of Housing and Local Government, though the latest in the series was produced in 1985.[2] Each note is prefaced by the following statements:

> These Notes set out current ministerial policy and their purpose is to give general guidance to intending developers. Policies are not rigid and from time to time new Notes will be issued in this series taking account of changes in emphasis in policy or of new policy decisions.

> Each application or appeal is treated on its merits and the application of a general policy to the particular case must always be a matter calling for judgment. Any legal views stated in these Notes have no statutory force and should not be relied upon as authoritative interpretations of the law.

The advice given in the notes covers such matters as Development in Residential Areas, Rural Areas and Town Centres and Road Safety and Traffic Requirements. These notes must, of course, be read in the light of any guidance given in legislation, circulars and Ministerial statements. Policy Note 8, Caravan Sites, should, therefore, be read in conjunction with Circulars 23/83,[3] 57/78,[4] 12/78[5] and 28/77.[6] The aim of the policy notes appears to be to give general advice to developers. In contrast, circulars contain more detailed guidance designed to take account of current legislation and be of use to a far wider audience. Recently, the Department of the Environment has begun to produce Planning Policy Guidance Notes. These contain planning policy statements which in some instances supercede the advice in the development control policy notes. Their status appears identical to that of circulars or advice notes.

In certain respects, however, circulars and policy notes are exactly alike. Both are designed to offer advice to those engaged in the development control process. Though that advice must be taken into account, it should be viewed in the light of the specific situation to which it is sought to apply that advice. There can, therefore, be circumstances when it is judged inappropriate to apply a particular policy. This is perfectly acceptable, as long as it is made clear why this is so. That this is the case with policy notes as well as circulars was made clear in *Penwith District Council v Secretary of State for*

2 Development Control Policy Note 1985/16, Access for the Disabled.
3 Circular 23/83, Caravan Sites and Control of Development Act 1960.
4 Circular 57/78, Accommodation for Gypsies.
5 Circular 12/78, Report of the Mobile Homes Review.
6 Circular 22/77, Gypsy Caravan Sites.

the Environment.[7] A company, Main Street Marketing, had applied for planning permission to establish an amusement centre in St Ives. Their application had been refused, since their scheme was to open the amusement centre in an outstanding conservation area. On appeal, Main Street Marketing were granted planning permission by the inspector. The local planning authority challenged this decision on the basis that in its written submissions to the inspector, it had drawn his attention to Development Control Policy Note 11. This stated:

> As regards situation, amusement centres are not acceptable near residential property; nor are they good neighbours for schools, churches, hospitals or hotels. They are out of place in conservation areas or other places of special architectural or historic character except perhaps where these cover a really wide area.[8]

In his decision letter, the inspector made no mention of Policy Note 11. In the event, Woolf J, as he was then, was prepared to set the inspector's decision aside on the basis that:

> ... the Inspector should, if indeed he had taken the Circular into account, have indicated why it was he felt that his was a case in which he should depart from the general prohibition.[9]

The court was not prepared to assume, therefore, that the Policy Note had been taken into account.

It would appear that policy notes, if they are applicable, will be treated by the courts in the same way as circulars. As has already been mentioned, a more up-to-date circular may deal with the same subject as a policy note and should be read in conjunction with it. Indeed, if a criticism can be made of policy notes, it is that the advice they contain is too general and not in keeping with current trends in planning. This is a criticism that can also be applied to some circulars, but with less justification. In relation to policy notes, the following comment has been made:

> Given the commitment to economic recovery it is surprising the DCPN 3, 'Industrial and Commercial Development' which is both bland and hopelessly out of date, has not been revised as a matter of urgency, together with the treatment of non-conforming uses in residential areas in DCPN 2, 'Development in Residential Areas'. Despite extensive experience of the operation of 'superstores' in recent years, DCPN 13, 'Large New Stores' still contents itself with generalities which offer comfort in equal measures to the promoters and opponents of any proposal. These are but a few examples. They may be contrasted with the forthright and detailed

7 [1986] JPL 432.
8 Development Control Policy Note 1970/11, para 6.
9 [1986] JPL 432 at 433.

guidance contained in Circulars 23/77 and 12/81, in respect of listed buildings.[10]

Other sources of policy

Apart from legislation, circulars and policy notes, one other Department of the Environment policy source needs to be mentioned and that is the Secretary of State for the Environment himself. The Secretary of State may use occasions, such as speeches to professional bodies, to indicate his views or policies on a particular matter. It might be assumed that such views will later be translated into legislation or circulars, and on most occasions this will be so. Yet, keynote speeches should not be neglected, since they may give an important indication of shifts in Ministerial policy. A valuable insight into the significance of such speeches is given by Richard Crossman in his book *The Diaries of a Cabinet Minister.* His entry for 21st September 1965 reads as follows:

> The day of my speech to the A M C annual conference at Torquay. I had to prepare the speech yesterday and go down last night because I was speaking first thing in the morning. I had previously agreed with the Department that I would speak on two topics: local government press relations; and the ethics of the councillor. However, yesterday I suddenly decided that I would add a third topic, the reform of local government; and I would announce that the situation was now getting unworkable and I was thinking of winding up the Local Government Boundary Commission. What should the next step after that be? I called in J D Jones, who was very good indeed, and with his advice I came to the conclusion that I should propose a committee of inquiry with very great authority and with terms of reference that instructed it to lay down the principles of local government reform. I rang up Harold to tip him off that I was going to do this and he liked the idea. There was a great rush to finish before I caught the train with John Delafons. We were met at the station at eleven o'clock by Francis Hill, the secretary of the A M C, and taken back to the hotel for a drink. In the early morning I prepared the final draft fitting the new section in with the old sections, and I delivered it at eleven, answering questions for a full hour afterwards, and getting something like a standing ovation. I was quite sure that I had done well.

Ministerial statements and speeches, therefore, may be used in order to signal policy changes, or to emphasise an aspect of Ministerial policy which is seen as particularly important. Obviously, however, the reliance which can be placed on such statements varies, according to whether or not they have been translated into legislation or a circular. That said, it is as well to mention the decision of MacPherson J in *Dimsdale Developments (South East)*

10 Sullivan J M 'The Implementation of Ministerial/Departmental Policy and Objectives' Journal of Planning and Environment Law Occasional Papers, 1984, pp 115, 116. Planning Policy Guidance Notes have recently been produced on some of these topics.

Ltd v Secretary of State for the Environment.[11] Here, planning permission had been refused by the local authority for the erection of offices and residential accommodation in Brentford. On appeal, the refusal of planning permission was affirmed by the inspector, whose decision was then reviewed by the courts. In the course of the case, counsel for the developers drew the attention of the court to an after-dinner speech made by the then Secretary of State for the Environment, Patrick Jenkin. On the matter of whether such a speech was admissible, MacPherson J concluded that although he:

> ... wondered at first whether to receive it at all he had thought it best to take it into account, although he was bound to say that he doubted whether such manifestations should be used in argument.[12]

On analysing what the Secretary of State had to say, MacPherson J concluded that it did nothing to alter his opinion that there were no grounds on which to set aside the inspector's decision. It is a matter for speculation what the outcome would have been if the Secretary of State had announced some major shift in policy in his speech. Undoubtedly, if it was a change that required the introduction of new legislation, the court would have done nothing at that time except apply current legislation. As it was, the Secretary of State's speech registered his dislike of stale development plans, that is, ones long overdue for updating. In the case in question, the relevant development plan had been updated and, therefore, its policy to discourage office development of the type proposed, represented current policy. If this had not been so, the court might have taken the Secretary of State's speech into account, to the extent at least of considering whether the age of the policy made it less relevant.

As well as after-dinner speeches, the Secretary of State will sometimes make statements in the House of Commons in order to clarify his policy. This was the case with a statement on phasing the release of land for development. It was designed to augment and explain the policy set out in Circular 15/84, Land for Housing.[13] Undoubtedly, the significance to be attached to views expressed by the Secretary of State will vary. Factors, such as the occasion and the exact purpose of a statement, may well be relevant. Though the court may be uncertain exactly how to treat such statements, this does not mean that they can be discounted as a source of policy. Planners, inspectors and organisations concerned with the environment may well take their lead from what the Secretary of State has to say.

11 [1986] JPL 276.
12 Ibid, 277.
13 4th June 1986, Hansard, HC Vol 98, Col 569.

Chapter 7

The development site

In this chapter an attempt will be made to explore what is, in practice, one of the most important aspects of development control. This is the influence that the site, with its unique characteristics, and the surrounding area, exert on the planning application decision. Previous planning decisions involving the site also have to be taken into account, as they form part of its unique planning history. On every occasion the emphasis is on the word 'unique'. In this area of development control the local planning authority and developer are involved in a situation which necessitates the consideration of a particular set of development proposals for a specific site, in an equally specific location at a certain point in time. The problem is, therefore, of how adequately to analyse this important aspect of development control which is, in reality, comprised of a unique set of circumstances.

The site defined

It will be recalled that development can take two forms, either a material change of use, or a building, engineering, mining, or other operation.[1] In determining what constitutes 'the site', the type of development contemplated is crucial. If, for example, the proposed development involves the construction of new buildings, that is, a building operation, then the site is the equivalent of that piece of land within whose boundaries the building operation is to take place. The issue may be less clear when a change of use is contemplated. This is because, on any particular piece of land, there may be a number of separate uses. A piece of land, for example, may be being used with planning permission for the parking of lorries. Facilities may exist on the land for cleaning and repairing the lorries. Should the repair side of the business expand with motor cars being repaired in addition to lorries, then the planning officers

1 Town and Country Planning Act 1971, s 22(1).

may ask themselves whether there has been a change of use from storage, in the form of the lorry park, to vehicle repair. In such a situation what constitutes the site can be crucial, though in this context it is more usual to talk of planning units rather than sites. The explanation for this is straightforward. In the example, the terms planning unit and site are interchangeable, since allied to the main use of the land for parking lorries are the ancillary uses of cleaning and repairing them. The question facing the planning officers would be whether, having determined the extent of the planning unit, there had been a change of use within that unit, with an ancillary use becoming the prime use. In contrast, should a building on the lorry park have been rented to a manufacturer of pork pies, the terms 'planning unit' and 'site' would not be synonymous. The planning officers would then argue that there were two separate and unrelated uses on a single piece of land constituting two separate planning units. One planning unit would be the equivalent of the building used for the manufacture of pork pies and enforcement action against an unauthorised change of use might be contemplated. The other planning unit would be the lorry park on which no development had occurred.

Clearly, therefore, there is more to defining the site, or rather the planning unit, than is first apparent. The issue can be a complex one particularly when a single piece of land or a building is put to many individual uses. This explains why, in the past, the courts have found it necessary to pronounce on what constitutes the planning unit.[2] Their approach seems to be a commonsense one, reflecting the issues that would be pertinent to a planning officer when contemplating the problem. In *Burdle v Secretary of State for the Environment*,[3] three criteria were suggested to help determine the planning unit. In all instances it is the use that is the fundamental consideration. If there are distinct uses being carried out in discrete areas within a single unit of occupation for unrelated purposes, then each discrete area forms a planning unit. If there are distinct but related uses being carried on generally within the unit of occupation, then the whole unit forms the planning unit. If there is a single main use being supported by ancillary uses, then again, the whole unit is to be considered as the planning unit.

The development plan and other material considerations

Once it is appreciated that the meaning to be attached to the term

2 *East Barnet Urban District Council v British Transport Commission* [1962] 2 QB 484.
3 [1972] 3 All ER 240.

'site' can vary with the particular situation, it remains to be seen how far those factors which have been considered in detail elsewhere, impinge on the site. Section 29(1) of the Town and Country Planning Act 1971 directs a local planning authority to have regard to the development plan, as well as other material considerations, when deciding whether or not to grant planning permission. The relationship of any site to the development plan is perhaps the more obvious, as it will be possible to locate the site, either generally or specifically, on the maps or diagrams which form part of the development plan. In many instances, therefore, the preferred land use for the area containing the site will be indicated, as well, possibly, as other factors relating to the density or height of any development. Far from being binding, such information simply indicates the planning policy contained within the development plan.

On the matter of what will constitute material considerations, this varies in relation to the proposed form of each development. For example, the exact location and size of a proposed new entrance to the development site will always be considered a material consideration. The physical form of such an entrance, together with its width, and the sight lines that it affords for traffic using it, will also form material considerations, as indeed, would the amount and type of traffic that the site generates. Conversely, the costs of constructing such an entrance are unlikely to be considered material, as these will not be seen as planning issues.

Other more general factors directly related to the development and its site may also be considered as material considerations, particularly if they form part of local or even national planning policy. The question of whether the development is needed, both in relation to the needs of the area, and with regard to the appropriateness of the proposed use of the site itself, has often been accepted as a material consideration, especially in relation to proposed residential developments. These considerations concerning the need for the proposed development are not evaluated in isolation, however, as clearly they will often be related to other important issues. Consider an application for planning permission to develop a housing estate in a location that the local planning authority had decided was to be included in its green belt. The decision would be largely dependent on the developer proving that the need existed for such a development, not only in a general sense, in that more housing was needed in the area, but more particularly, in that such a development was needed on that site at that time. The local planning authority, on the other hand, would be considering the importance of maintaining its green belt policy. All of these factors are material considerations, and many will clearly be interrelated.

The planning history

Another important element that comes under the description of a material consideration is the planning history of the site. All the documented planning events from 1947 onwards that relate to either the whole or part of the site, constitute its planning history.[4] Since 1947, all activities constituting development, permitted development apart, should have been the subject of an application for planning permission or possibly a related permission, for example, listed building consent. Any such application will have been placed on record by the local planning authority and this information is available, together with any decisions reached, for examination by a member of the public.[5]

It appears possible to interpret these instances of past or existing planning permissions, or indeed refusals, in several ways. Consider, initially, the example of an existing planning permission for a one-acre site permitting the development of a four-storey block of sixteen flats, all with garages. This permission may not have been acted upon but is still current, the statutory five-year period having yet to elapse.[6] Arguably, this planning permission represents current planning policy for the site. If, therefore, a planning application is made to construct a workshop or small industrial development on the same site, the fact that planning permission has been granted for residential development is clearly not a material consideration and should be disregarded. In contrast, the fact that current planning policy favours residential, rather than industrial development on the site, is a material consideration, but reference should be made directly to the source of that policy, as well as to the planning permission that is based upon it. This necessity to refer, to both the policy as well as any previous planning applications, would be more imperative if a previous application for some form of non-residential development had been refused. Such a fact would be taken as an important material consideration, as the use relates closely to the use being proposed in the new application. In these

4 As the Town and Country Planning Act 1947 is seen as introducing the modern planning system, the planning history of a site is normally taken to start with this date.
5 The planning register has to be maintained in the manner specified by the 1971 Act, s 34, and the Town and Country Planning General Development Order 1977, SI 1977 No 289, article 21.
6 1971 Act, s 41.

circumstances, however, the reasons given for refusing the previous application would be most significant as they would probably contain reference, not only to the policy relating to the site, but also to the particular physical details of the development. Although the policy may still be current, it is likely that the physical details of the present application will be different, and it is this fact that should be emphasised. It is most important to remember that all planning applications must be considered on their own individual merits, and the physical features of the present proposed development may, therefore, be much more appropriate for the site than those presented in the application that was refused. It is factors such as these that will be considered by the local planning authority as being particularly pertinent, while the planning history of the site should be viewed as providing a background to any current applications for planning permission.

The planning history of the site may also consist of various planning permissions that have been acted upon and, as such, these are normally considered to indicate the sequence of policy that has affected the site. Consider the example of a building that was originally a Georgian town house which has been used for several years as offices by a firm of solicitors. In the past a planning application may have been approved to extend the building to the rear to allow for an increased demand in office space. An adjacent building may then have been acquired by the firm of solicitors, and planning permission granted to join both buildings in order to increase still further the amount of office space. Each of these approvals would be considered as relevant aspects of the building's planning history if yet another extension were proposed, possibly upwards, by the addition of a new roof structure on both properties incorporating two new floors. When planning permission is sought, reference would be made to the fact that the local planning authority had, in the past, always allowed office expansion on this site. Although this would be relevant to the present application, it in no way constitutes a precedent that is binding on the local planning authority. It is, therefore, free to approve the present expansion proposals or to reject them, possibly on the grounds that the change in the roof line is unacceptable, or indeed that such an expansion could be taken as an undesirable precedent in an area where many similar applications might ensue as a result. This does not contradict the statement just made that planning permission does not constitute a precedent. As a matter of law this is true. In practice, however, it would be far more difficult for a local planning authority to justify a refusal for a similar development, as presumably whatever policy justified approval in the first example would still be applicable. It is, however, important to remember that this would apply only if the two buildings in question were virtually identical, since each application for planning permission must be considered on its own individual merits, and other details will be relevant, apart from the fact that planning permission has been granted for a similar proposal on a similar property. Many of these details will stem from the significant features of the site and the proposed development, so it is now appropriate to initiate an examination of these.

The significant features

To provide some logic to what follows these features have been divided into three. Firstly, there are those features contained within the boundaries of the site that have an effect on the form of the development. Secondly, there are those features that are a direct consequence of the function of the development and the effect that they may have on the site. Finally, there are those features that derive from the general area in which the site is located. In all instances it is essential to remember that these three divisions are purely artificial and that, in reality, all these features would probably be considered as inextricably interrelated. The purpose of dividing them here is in order to simplify, by means of isolation, what amounts to a complex series of interrelationships. For example, it should be obvious that the size of a site will influence what can feasibly be developed upon it, and that the location of the site, perhaps in a residential area, or a city centre, will likewise affect the function of the proposed development. In addition, it should be clear that the different forms and functions of development will make different demands on any particular site in respect of transport or pollution or building height. The complex reality thus starts to emerge. By artificially isolating various factors, therefore, it is hoped that a better overall understanding will be achieved.

THE FORM OF THE DEVELOPMENT

Section 22 of the 1971 Act neatly encapsulates the basic form that any development must take, in that it must involve either a material change of use, an operation or both. The legal interpretation of this section has already been considered in Chapter 3. At this stage, therefore, it is simply necessary to evaluate what implications this definition has for the range of developments that would normally occur on any site. A change of use is considered as significant by the local planning authority when the new use will have a markedly different effect on the site and the surrounding area from any existing use. It is important to realise that this would be a development control issue, even if the proposed use is unlikely to have a detrimental effect on the site or its locality. It is the effect of a use, rather than its possible positive or negative consequences, that is the real issue.

Another change of use which may, on occasion, be encountered, is an intensification of use. Here, an already established use experiences a change in emphasis of such proportions that planning permission is required. In this situation, both the site and its location assume particular importance as development control considerations, since the proposed intensification could impose pressures with which the site and the area are physically incapable of coping. A site may be used for the manufacture of concrete blocks, the production of which may have been limited by the size of the original business. If the business changes hands and is consequently greatly improved, the number of concrete blocks manufactured on the site could be quadrupled. Such an intensification of the original use would then be evaluated by the local planning authority. It would be judged in relation to the physical size of the site and its capacity for containing the production machinery, taking into account the ground contours of the site rather than its simple plan area. Also of importance would be the changed appearance of the site with the new machinery on it, as well as the frequency with which the concrete blocks were moved on and off the site. This latter factor would obviously have an immediate effect on both the traffic flows and the amenity of the surrounding area.

Use changes or intensifications are often, in reality, accompanied by some kind of building operation[7] most commonly in the form of a new building, an extension to an existing building, an extensive refurbishment of an existing building, or the construction of site infrastructure, such as roads, hard standing or walls. In every instance, the site and its location are once again of paramount importance in reaching the appropriate development control decision. In the case of new buildings, their position in relation to the size and shape of the site will be considered, taking into account not only the probable visual impact of the proposed structures given their size or density, but also their design and the materials to be used in their construction. Similar considerations would apply in the case of any proposed extensions or refurbishments, while

---

7 Or any other form of operation involving development, such as an engineering operation.

accompanying features, such as roads and walls, would also be treated with the same degree of scrutiny.

Clearly the attention that will be paid to the physical details of any proposed development cannot be divorced from the use that is either being newly created, or intensified, as the two issues can often be realistically considered only as a single complex aspect of the proposed development. It should be remembered that the policy for the site, or its more general location, will also form part of this complex equation. A proposal to erect new industrial units will be considered, first, in terms of the industrial policy of the local planning authority, then the policy that relates to the proposed development site, then the suitability of the site in respect of its size and shape, the existing or proposed connections to the surrounding road network, the location of other such units in the vicinity, the uses being made of the surrounding area, as well as the size of the proposed buildings, the materials to be used, the fencing of the area and the parking or unloading space.

THE FUNCTION OF THE DEVELOPMENT

From the examples used in the preceding section, it should be obvious that the actual use or function of the proposed development is particularly important in assessing the likely effects it could produce, both with regard to the site and the locality. Even to the layman the concept of unneighbourly development is easy to comprehend,[8] but the assessment of the impact of a proposed use is far more subtle than the obvious incompatibility of a tannery in the middle of a residential area. The range of possible uses or functions likely to be encountered in a lifetime considering planning applications in various environments is enormous, but the majority can be classified under surprisingly few heads, thus permitting the possible implications of each function for a site to be considered.

Retail The impact of this common land use function on the site clearly varies depending upon its scale and intensity but, as with all of the succeeding functions, the central issue is the suitability of the site for the proposed development. In the case of retailing this involves an assessment of the accessibility of the site, the need for which usually increases with the scale of the proposed development. The site would be viewed, not only from the point of view of the placing of the building within it, but also with regard to its ability to cater for accessibility-related demands, such as car parking.

8 1971 Act, s 26; Town and Country Planning General Development Order 1977, SI 1977 No 289, article 8.

Clearly, these issues are further complicated when the enormous range of goods that might be offered for sale is considered, as the nature of the goods on sale is relevant to the number of people using a particular retail outlet. Retailing in all its many aspects has become a study in its own right and no attempt will be made here to cover even a fraction of the elements involved.[9] Instead, a few examples will be considered in the hope that they will illustrate some of the important development control issues related to the site.

A national chain of jewellery shops wishes to open a shop in a city centre location, on a site that is in need of redevelopment. Given the site's central location, and therefore its high market value, the developer will probably wish to build on the entire site. The local planning authority would probably insist on this, particularly if existing buildings abut onto the site. This raises the question of the appearance of the new building, especially its ground floor window designs and any advertising incorporated into the proposed design of the shop front. The local planning authority is also likely to express concern over the appearance of the upper floors, if, for security reasons, small windows or even windowless walls are suggested by the developer. These design issues apart, however, what implications does the proposed retail use have for the site? Jewellery is what is known as a 'high order' good in retail jargon.[10] This means that the demand is infrequent, or put another way, only one person in one thousand is likely to be needing the services of such a shop at any particular time. As a direct consequence, the number of potential customers that the jewellery shop needs for it to run at a profit is comparatively large, so a city-centre location with a large customer flow is ideal. These facts, although known to the planning officers, are, in one sense, incidental, as they do not give rise to important development control issues. This follows from the fact that, since the goods on sale are small and of a relatively high value, there is unlikely to be a demand from the developer for customer car parking, nor indeed for special delivery arrangements to be made on the site. The planning officers' concerns in this instance are, therefore, limited, as the function produces no undue 'stress' on the physical nature of the site and its location.

At the opposite end of the retail spectrum, at least in a planning context, would be the out-of-town or suburban fringe retail location

9 For example: Harrison M *People and Shopping* (1975); Dawson J A *Shopping Centre Development* (1983); *Urban Models in Shopping Studies* NEDO (1970).

10 Goods are ranked according to their cost and the frequency of demand for them. Those which are expensive and for which demand is infrequent, such as jewellery, are called high order goods.

selling furniture or carpets. Here, the planning issues affecting the
site are very different, caused, not so much by the 'middle order'
goods,[11] but rather by the form of retailing that has been selected. In
this instance the demands which the retail development will place
on the site include extensive car parking facilities, good access to
the surrounding major road network, as well as a large amount of
retail or possibly storage space. The incorporation of these features
of the proposed development onto the site will naturally concern
the planning officers. Clearly, the impact that such a development
would have on any site would be considerable, while the impact on
the surrounding area is not confined to the traffic and aesthetic
implications, but would also include the competition that such a
retail development could exert on similar retail establishments in
the more traditional town-centre locations. This last issue serves to
illustrate the interface between planning policy and the detailed
development of the site. The question of competition with other
retail outlets, and indeed the location of such outlets, is effectively a
policy issue that has to be judged in the context of both national
planning policy on out-of-town retailing establishments, and the
current local planning policy on retailing. These issues are, in turn,
related to the nature of the development, particularly its size, whilst
the immediate site issues are those concerned with its appearance
and times of use. It will be a matter for the expertise and judgment
of the planning officers considering the application as to which
combination of these issues they will see as of paramount importance in making their recommendation to the planning committee.

Offices The main site-related issue regarding this function is one
of scale. The impact an office development has on an area is
normally restricted to its design and the number of employees it
contains. The latter are significant for the impact they may have on
the transport system in the area containing the office. As is common
in many development control situations, these factors may be interrelated. Design may be affected by transport demands if these
involve providing car parking on the site. Scale is, of course, the
controlling factor, as the larger the office development, the more
significant these issues are likely to be. Clearly, the use of a
Georgian town house as a solicitors' office has very different development control implications as compared with the development
of a two-acre inner-city site with 700,000 square feet of net lettable
office space. The former would clearly have few design implications, unless the building was significant enough to be listed. Con-

11 Furniture, and other similar goods, although expensive, are more of a necessity
than the luxury high order goods and are thus ranked as a middle order good.

sequently, the main issue relating to the site would be the availability of parking for possibly a dozen cars, either to the rear of the site, or in the immediate vicinity. The nature of the surrounding uses, particularly if they were retail, would also be a relevant issue. In the second development, the issues of design and transport are clearly of considerable importance. The design would be dictated by the shape and location of the site in the context of the surrounding buildings, with particular regard being paid to their height, materials and other design features. The transport issue must be resolved in the light of the local planning authority's transport policy. Such a policy would, in turn, depend upon the nature of the urban area containing the office development. If the area is not suffering from a high level of traffic congestion or, alternatively, if the public transport facilities are inadequate within the vicinity, a high level of parking provision on the site may be required by the local planning authority. This would obviously have implications for the design of the development as well as having an effect on the generation of traffic in the immediate area. If, on the other hand, the public transport facilities are good, or traffic congestion is a serious problem in the area, then the local planning authority would allow very few parking spaces within the development, with a consequent lessening of their impact on the design of the development.

Other policies, apart from transport policies, are also likely to affect the proposed office development, and these too could have significant implications for the site and the design of the development. There may well be height restrictions regulating the number of floors that the development can contain,[12] or plot ratio requirements that control the bulk of the building.[13] Policy issues such as these are, however, usually related to specific parts of a town or city and are considered in a later section.

Residential Once more the major site-related issue is scale. Here, planning applications will range from proposals to extend a single residential property, or to develop one unit on a site, to the reshap-

12 Height standards may form part of local planning policy and are normally applied to certain forms of development in specific areas. They may suggest the maximum number of floors appropriate in certain areas, but this number is not in any way prescriptive and higher buildings may be allowed if there is seen to be sufficient justification.
13 A plot ratio is a form of density control usually applied to commercial developments in city centres. It is an aspect of local planning policy that attempts to control the bulk of a building by expressing the permitted floor space as a ratio of site area. For example, a plot ratio of 2:1 allows a two-storey building to be developed covering the whole site, or a four-storey building covering half the site, and so on. Plot ratios vary between cities and even within cities.

ing of an undeveloped area with the construction of hundreds of units in a range of sizes. In general terms the site issues remain constant regardless of scale, focusing on access and appearance as well as the existing facilities within the area. With a small domestic extension, the question of appearance and the distance of the extension from the boundaries of the site are likely to be more important than the question of access. This is not so when a single new building is erected on a small, previously undeveloped site. Here, the matter of access is likely to be crucial, especially if there is no existing access or access has to be shared with another dwelling.

When a new access has to be constructed, the surrounding road network must be studied in deciding where that access should be, and an estimate made of the number of cars likely to use that access. The larger the development, the more vital these issues become, while other factors, including the impact of the proposed development on existing facilities, such as schools and shops, begin to feature. With all new developments, regardless of scale, the physical nature of the site and its existing boundaries must be examined in detail, since they play a large part in determining the visual impact the proposed development will make. With a small-scale development, planning permission is more likely to be given if building takes place behind existing walls and hedges, assuming them to be in a fair condition, than on an exposed site. Similarly, with a large scale residential development, the contours of the site should be used to their best advantage, not only to provide views for the inhabitants but also to 'hide' to a certain degree the new development from the surrounding area, especially if that area is in a green belt.

Industrial   Here, questions of scale and the nature of the industrial use will be vital in assessing the suitability of the site for the proposed development. As has already been mentioned in previous chapters, there are regulatory provisions governing certain types of industrial use,[14] and these too must be taken into account in assessing the site. The amount and type of traffic generated by an industrial development is also crucial. For example, an industrial use that produces heavy goods traffic, even on an occasional basis, can be distinguished from the industrial use that relies upon small goods vehicles. The environmental impact of each type of transport on the area surrounding the site is likely to be very different. Indeed, this example can be taken a stage further to emphasise the uniqueness of each site. On a site in a flat area the level of noise produced by

14 The various industrial groups are defined in the Town and Country Planning (Use Classes) Order 1987, SI 1987 No 764, Part B.

heavy goods traffic is likely to be less than in a hilly area, where the constant use of low gears would produce considerable engine noise. On the other hand, it may be argued that in a flat area heavy goods traffic might be tempted to travel at greater speeds and thus increase the problem of road safety.

While the importance of these issues increases in proportion to the scale of the proposed operation, it should not be imagined that only large-scale industrial development produces planning problems. Indeed, given that large-scale industrial development is often located within existing industrial areas, or alternatively, within new purpose-built industrial parks,[15] the planning issues are normally reduced. In the case of small scale industrial development in inner-city or residential areas, the problems are often much greater, a major one being intensification. In these circumstances, an industrial use develops on an existing site in such a way that its presence becomes more and more intrusive. This is as a result of increased traffic, more noise, longer hours of work, or even the building of a new extension. These factors, depending on the location and size of the site, may obviously become a planning issue if the various forms of intensification begin to have a noticeable environmental effect. On the other hand, this growth of the industrial concern has then to be set against the fact that it is providing more employment in the surrounding area. Department of the Environment policy emphasises the importance of encouraging the growth of small industrial enterprises.[16] Against this local planning authorities will have to assess the environmental damage that may be caused by the intensification of the enterprise in that particular location.

Design issues may also be important when considering industrial development, especially if the scale of that development is such that it can be seen over considerable distances. The physical nature of the site is all-important. If it is on low ground, the development may be screened by suitable landscaping and trees. Should the site be such that landscaping will not offer an effective screen, the appearance of the industrial buildings will be an important consideration, especially if the site is located in a mixed or non-industrial area. The visual impact of related activities, for example, the storage of raw materials and the equipment used to handle them, will also be taken into account, though the chances are that such large-scale industrial developments are likely to be within established industrial areas where the impact of these elements is considered to be less significant.

15 See Circular 16/84, Industrial Development, for an explanation of the various
   forms of industrial area.
16 Circular 16/84, and Circular 2/86, Development by Small Businesses.

Storage This function raises those issues discussed in relation to industrial uses. Normally the main difference stems from the fact that processing does not take place on the site so eliminating problems with noise or fumes, although this very much depends upon what is being stored. There is considerable variety within this category, as storage includes the warehousing on an inner-city site of goods intended for retail sale in the commercial core of the city, the storage of cars for export on a dockland site, as well as the storage of oil and grain in purpose-built structures or immense stockpiles of minerals covering acres. Clearly, the impact of each form of storage on the site and surrounding area will vary enormously, especially on the matter of its visual impact and the form and frequency of transport which it generates.

The visual impact of an oil storage depot, or a pile of one million tons of coal is too obvious to mention, but what may be less obvious is the difference in the frequency of use which can occur between such sites. An oil storage depot, although visually intrusive and practically impossible to hide, may at least have the advantage of generating very little traffic, as what is stored may be pumped in and out by underground pipeline. Alternatively, the site could be used as a supply depot for oil tankers, which would then distribute petrol to garages in the area, thus creating very different planning problems from those in the first instance. The same is true of the coal dump. It could be that all movement in and out may be by rail, but, on the other hand, heavy lorries might be used to transport the coal which would raise a major planning issue.

Transport This category includes all aspects of transport from private taxi-cab bases, bus, coach and train stations, to airports and seaports. The site-related issues are clearly dominated by the level and type of traffic generated, which, in turn, is dictated by the scale of the operation. Design issues, although related to the scale of the transport operation, can depend on the location of the operation, and become more significant in environmentally sensitive areas.

As with some of the functions already discussed, planning problems related to the site do not necessarily increase in proportion to increases in scale. The use of a site in a residential area as a private taxi-cab base may cause many local planning problems regarding on-street parking, late night use and traffic noise. In contrast, the use of an inner-city site as a bus station may be far less contentious in the matter of its impact on its immediate locality.

Undeniably, the main issue in every instance is the level of traffic generated, and the effect this has on the surrounding area, rather than the site itself. This is due to the fact that the site will usually be physically suitable for the particular transport use. In the case of road transport, this means the site should be flat, large and with the necessary connections to the road network. The traffic generated by the use of the site is fundamentally important, bearing in mind that a single use may generate a wide range of different types of traffic. For example, the traffic at a bus station does not consist simply of buses, but includes private cars and taxi cabs, not to mention pedestrians. The environmental impact will naturally vary; an airport is likely to be more environmentally damaging than a railway station, but this should be reflected in its location. In other words, an international airport will have been planned and its location considered to a far greater extent than the building of a new suburban bus station. The whole question of the traffic generated by these different transport functions is an issue so complex that normally it is dealt with by specialist transport planners and traffic engineers,[17] and their findings can often be the determining factor in whether or not such developments should be permitted.

Leisure   Once again the range of possible leisure pursuits is so wide and their effect so diverse that it is almost impossible to generalise. The obvious initial categorisation is into outdoor and indoor leisure pursuits. As outdoor leisure pursuits associated with urban areas normally demand sites that are large and grassed, such uses may often by regarded by the local planning authority as contributing positive environmental benefits to the surrounding area. If this is so, any development control issues will tend to focus on the level and frequency of use. Obviously not all outdoor leisure facilities result in large grassed areas, but those which do not are in the minority, and arguably even hard surfaced tennis courts may exert a positive environmental influence by virtue of the open space they provide in what otherwise may be a densely built up area.

As mentioned, the main site-related development control issues focus on the level and frequency with which the site is used, as well as its physical size. For example, a golf course may cover many acres of pleasantly landscaped country but the planning issues go far beyond this positive environmental benefit. The very size of the site may be an issue as it may be taking up land that could be used more appropriately. This alternative use question is somewhat more complex than simply considering an alternative use for the land, since market forces normally ensure that the most economic use is the one favoured. Rather, the issues concern the overall supply of land within the planning district, and the impact that the loss of a

17 In most local authorities, especially at county level, there is a specialist transport department that handles all issues concerned with transport.

large site for a golf course would have on the remaining un-developed sites within the area. Such wider issues clearly require reference to be made to the local policy of the development plan, or even Department of the Environment policy, and again such policy will obviously be taken into account in arriving at the eventual development control decision.

Using the example of the golf course, it should be obvious that the intensity and frequency of its use will vary considerably daily, weekly and even seasonally. The focus of that use is likely to be the clubhouse and its related facilities, so the fact that the site covers many acres is not reflected in the manner in which it attracts traffic to a single spot. The traffic issues are similar to those that arise when any form of suburban development is contemplated, with much importance attached to the location of the golf course in relation to the road network.

With indoor leisure pursuits the issues are slightly different, but tend to focus mainly on traffic and the location of the site. The design of the facility may also be relevant, as sports centres can demand a relatively large building with few external features and many blank windowless walls. Obviously in this respect the location of such a facility and its site is crucial, as design problems may be overcome simply by appropriate landscaping, if this is possible. The same factors are important when assessing traffic generation and on-site parking. In a city-centre location the relationship with public transport facilities is crucial if on-site parking is limited. In the suburbs, attention may be paid to the amount of traffic likely to be generated if the site is located in a residential area.

The heading 'leisure facilities' encompasses not only sporting facilities, but also a wide range of other activities, such as amusement arcades, cinemas, restaurants and public houses. It is clearly very difficult, and arguably of little benefit, to consider the possible implications that each of these proposed uses would have for the site, nor can any general comments be made. All that can be done is to draw attention, once again, to the all-important issue of the likely effects that the proposed use will have, and the ways in which these effects may be moderated or intensified by the site and its location.

Institutional The range of functions under this heading is extremely diverse. It includes educational facilities from nursery school to higher education institutions, health facilities from the local general practice surgery to regional hospitals, as well as the facilities for central and local government, statutory undertakers and the armed forces. In many instances it is a public body or quasi-public body[18] undertaking the development, but this does not automatically guarantee that the implications which the development has for its site and the surrounding area will be handled sympathetically. Indeed, in the case of some institutional developments, such as hospitals, no planning permission is required as the land in question forms part of the Crown estate. Should this be the case, it is likely that the advice of the local planning authority will be sought and largely heeded, so control over institutional developments will, in reality, be much the same as with any other development. Of the site issues, the most important are scale, design and traffic generation. In the majority of instances there are likely to be clear policy statements from a variety of sources on the development of the various uses.[19] These need not necessarily be policies produced by the local planning authority. In relation to schools, for example, there should be a clear policy on education produced by the local education authority.[20] Such a policy obviously has development control implications, in terms of the number of schools needed and their locations, and will thus form part of the development control debate.

Agricultural Agricultural uses can cover anything from horticulture and horse breeding to forestry. When a proposed agricultural development is being considered, the situation is complicated by the fact that policy generated from sources other than the local planning authority and the Department of the Environment, notably the Ministry of Agriculture, Fisheries and Food, has to be taken into account. Added to this is the image that the majority of people have of the countryside and its use, which is often far removed from the realities of the situation. The basic problem is summed up in the dichotomy between the countryside seen as part of our landscape heritage which should be protected at all costs, and the countryside seen as a vital food-producing industry that should be as efficient as possible. Indeed, early in 1987, these issues came to the fore when Ministerial statements suggested that due to the success of the agricultural policy of the European Economic Community, food production should be cut back and surplus farm land

18 A British university, for example, may be considered as a quasi-public body in this context, as it will be financed largely by central government but not otherwise directly controlled by central government.
19 For example, regional health authorities will have a clear policy on the development of health centres, water authorities will have policies on water storage.
20 Legislation demands that local education authorities produce a wide range of education policies. See Taylor G & Saunders J B *The Law of Education* (1979, with supplement 1981).

be put to other uses, such as housing and industry.[1] This statement was badly received by groups such as the Council for the Protection of Rural England, who saw it as heralding a development free-for-all that would effectively destroy our rural heritage.

With this dichotomy in mind, the main issue that is likely to arise in relation to an agricultural planning application can be summarised as follows – how does the planning officer ensure that the correct balance is maintained between the efficient use of rural resources and the conservation of the rural environment? The problem is exacerbated by the fact that a considerable amount of development that is directly related to agriculture is permitted development, over which the planning officer has no control.[2] Where controls do exist, therefore, over development not associated with agricultural production and especially change of use, such as the building of a farmhouse extension for the purpose of taking in bed and breakfast guests, the planning officer may be tempted to be over-cautious to compensate for the lack of control over agricultural developments. The correct path is a narrow one, but if the normal development control considerations that would apply to the development of any site are analysed, the most appropriate decision can usually be reached.

In arriving at an appropriate decision, the site and its location become crucial. Consider, for example, a planning application by a farmer to establish a camp site in one of his fields. As has already been mentioned, if caravans are to use the site, then a whole host of regulations have to be observed, but this is incidental to the real development control issues related to the site and its location. The visual impact of the proposed development has to be assessed, and not only when the site is full, as the presence of even one or two bright orange tents may be considered unacceptable in certain sensitive locations. That visual impact must be examined from different viewpoints. It may be appropriate that the site is visible from the main road, as this will ensure that camping traffic will head immediately for the correct location. On the other hand, it may be inappropriate that the site can be clearly seen from a viewing point at the other end of the valley. On this issue, therefore, the physical features of the site and its immediate surroundings are crucial, as they may dictate whether or not the camp site can be effectively screened.

Using the same example, the likely frequency and intensity of use must also be assessed, not so much for their impact on the actual

1 Circular 16/87, Development Involving Agricultural Land.
2 Town and Country Planning General Development Order 1977, SI 1977 No 289, Class VI.

area of the site, but rather for their effect on the surrounding environment and the transport system. As the use is likely to be seasonal, the maximum capacity of the roads should be calculated, as well as the traffic implications of any new means of access that may, in the summer months, lead onto what is then a busy road. In addition, the need for the camp site has to be carefully assessed, taking into account any existing sites and the impact any additional site is likely to have on local services.

Mixed and other uses In respect of these, little, if anything, can be added to what has already been said. Obviously, when dealing with a mixed use the implications for the site of each aspect of each use should be considered, the fundamental question being whether the site is capable of sustaining not only the individual uses, but, more particularly, the proposed mix. The basic issue is the likely effect that such uses would have on the site and its location, an issue that can be decided in relation to a particular site in a particular location with a specific set of proposed uses.

THE LOCATION OF THE DEVELOPMENT

The significance that the location of the site can have for the development control issues raised by the use or function, has been constantly referred to in the previous section. This is as a result of the fact that the issues related to the development of any site, regardless of function, have also to be considered in the context of that part of the urban area in which the site is located.[3] Consequently, it is perhaps useful to consider the implications that the location of the site produces under some general location headings, starting with the commercial core of the inner city and moving outwards into the rural hinterland.

The commercial core or central business district This area is readily defined within any major urban area as consisting of the shop and office quarters, although in many smaller urban centres the shopping function may be dominant.[4] Whatever the size of the town or city, however, this area has certain characteristics, and an understanding of these is crucial for the way in which they may affect the use of any development site. First, the commercial core is always

3 It has long been observed that all urban areas larger than a village tend to subdivide into areas of distinct uses.
4 In smaller urban areas the development of the commercial core may not be so advanced that the office functions have separated themselves from the shopping functions. Consequently, many of the office functions tend to locate on the upper floors, leaving the ground floors to be dominated by retail uses.

relatively small in relation to the area of the whole town or city, so that vacant sites are likely to be small[5] and all forms of development opportunity scarce. Consequently, when development opportunities occur, the pressures for an intensive use of the site are likely to be great. Second, the area is always the focus, or possibly, as a result of pedestrianisation, the near focus, of the road transport network.[6] The uses of the area are, therefore, geared to gain the maximum benefit from this concentration of people. Any development site in the commercial core thus has the potential to exploit this central position, either by providing on-site parking provision, or by fully developing any frontage onto a pedestrianised precinct. Third, the area is likely to contain one of the highest concentrations of historic buildings within the town or city[7] which may impose certain conservation and design restraints on any new development.

The combined effect of these factors will make itself felt on the development proposals for any site within the commercial core, particularly on its design, as the proposed uses are invariably restricted to shops and offices. On the matter of design, the planning officer will often move from the general issues of plot ratio and building height, to particular issues of detail and materials. Particular attention will be paid to the specific location and size of the plot, as well as to the design of the surrounding buildings, unless the site is so large as to be considered independent of its surroundings.[8] In most instances, however, the proposed design will fall into one of three cateories: the pastiche, possibly the most acceptable publicly; the well-designed modern, which will always have its supporters and detractors; and the 'non-designed' modern, which appears to have occupied little, if any, of an architect's time and yet is frequently to be seen in the centre of many towns and cities. Recent Department of the Environment circulars have suggested that the planner should not attempt to exercise undue control over the aesthetic aspects of a development.[9] In the case of city-centre development, however, it is almost impossible for the local planning authority to follow that advice on all occasions. This is due to

5 Vacant sites are usually formed by the demolition of a single building, which, if it dates back to the nineteenth century, is unlikely to cover a large area, besides having a restricted frontage.

6 Urban areas almost always developed around a convergence of routes and this feature will have intensified as the urban area grew.

7 The centre of any urban area is normally the oldest part as most urban areas tend to 'grow' outwards, with the new buildings always being furthest away from the centre on the edge.

8 A large site, such as an area surrounded by roads on all sides, is isolated, to a certain extent, from the nearby buildings.

9 Circular 31/85, Aesthetic Control.

the fact that any new developments in this location will invariably be seen by the majority of the people using the city centre and so will, in effect, act as a form of advertisement for the development control efforts of the local planning authority. The more prominent and public the site, therefore, and the larger the development, the more crucial the decision becomes.

The inner-city fringe or transition zone   This location may have all the problems associated with the commercial core plus some characteristic ones of its own, because within the urban area it contains the greatest mix of functions.[10] In smaller towns, this area may be indistinguishable from the commercial core, but, in larger urban areas, it assumes a particular importance, since it can be the focus of major planning problems. As the zone surrounds, or partially surrounds, the commercial core, it obviously covers a much greater area. The transition zone, therefore, has the theoretical advantage of containing extensive potential development sites. The road network is often almost as dense as that in the commercial core, but the greater mix of functions in the transition zone generates a much wider range of traffic, including heavy industrial traffic. The area can contain a high proportion of historic buildings, though the likelihood is that any conservation issues will be aggravated by the fact that many of these buildings may be in a poor condition. Empty sites in this part of the city may remain undeveloped for long periods of time, and the threat of obsolescence and dereliction is a constant worry for the local planning authority.

The net effect of these factors on the development of any particular site can be many and varied. Depending on the location of the site in relation to the main traffic routes through the area, the generation of additional traffic may pose problems, usually concerning access and congestion. As compared with the commercial core, however, design, in terms of compatibility with fine buildings, is less crucial. If, however, the site is to be developed for residential use, as may occur within the transition zone, design factors can be important if the development is to be successfully shielded from the usually incompatible mix of uses that may surround the site. The main planning issue affecting any site in this part of the urban area is the question of the market demand for a particular form of development in a specific location. Due to the variable nature of the area,

10 The transition zone, as its name suggests, is that part of the urban area that is continually changing as the uses of the commercial core expand into it, or conversely, move out of it. Consequently, it contains a very large mixture of uses, to which may be added some residential uses, as a result not only of immediate post-war redevelopment by local authorities, but also as remnants of nineteenth century residential areas.

which creates zones of potential growth and decline,[11] market demand is likely to reflect these variations by being either inconsistent, weak or strong, depending on the exact location of the development site. This process of flux will consequently tend to favour certain locations and ignore others, mainly as a reflection of development opportunities that are being experienced within the commercial core. In a favoured location, therefore, demand for development is likely to be strong, and a proposed development should be judged on the same criteria as those used within the commercial core. On the other hand, in a location which is more remote from such changes, the major issue concerning any planning application is likely to be the potential dereliction or obsolescence of the site should the application fail. In such circumstances, it is quite likely that some of the normal site constraints may be given less emphasis, in the hope that the proposed development will be successful and contribute to revitalising the area.

The residential suburbs These cover the largest area in any urban complex but are unlikely to contain the widest range of sites, either in terms of size or use. Sites are usually limited in size except, possibly, in inner-city residential areas where large scale redevelopment may be undertaken by a public or quasi-public body. Although the great majority of development is likely to be residential in character, other functions are to be found, including schools, shops, libraries and other service functions. The main planning objective is to maintain the residential nature of the area, and this will be considered paramount when non-residential uses or different residential uses, such as sheltered accommodation, are being considered.[12] Site issues are normally related to access and design, both of which tend to increase in importance with the scale of the development. Access can be crucial, and may affect the development of a site large enough to accommodate only a single dwelling almost as much as a site that can hold fifty. Attention must be paid to the road network surrounding the site, as well as to the levels of traffic flow and the times that peaks occur. The positioning of an access point from the site onto the road is crucial, and its inadequacy can be sufficient reason for refusing planning permission.

In many residential areas design seems a secondary issue, presumably on the basis that the public have a very traditional image of

11 See Preston R E & Griffin D W 'A Restatement of the Transition Zone Concept' *Annals of the Association of American Geographers*, 1966, 66, p 339.
12 The Town and Country Planning (Use Classes) Order 1987, SI 1987 No 764, gives some indication of the limitations regarding non-residential uses in residential areas. See Class B1, Business.

a house and providing this is observed, then a proposed development is likely to be acceptable. Obviously in the case of large-scale developments, especially those involving the construction of multi-storey flats,[13] the design and the location of the site become far more significant. The question of how well visually the scheme fits within the immediate environment will be important, as will the retention of existing features, especially mature trees. If the site is located within one of the many conservation areas that are often to be found within the older suburbs, the design compatibility of the proposed development with existing buildings will be assessed, but even in these circumstances the access issue is, more often than not, the one that determines whether the application will be approved.

The urban rural fringe This is the area which is second only to the commercial core in the development pressures it experiences. Sites in this location may vary considerably in size, but they tend to be large, often comprising several hundred acres of previously farmed land. The functions to be found in this area may be varied, with a proportion of industry and some farming or horticulture, but the major pressure for development is almost exclusively residential. In this location, therefore, the central issue is the need for additional housing rather than any specific site factors, apart, that is, from the capacity of the chosen site to hold a specific density of housing. If the need for such housing is proved, therefore, and its provision is in accordance with both local and national planning policy,[14] the proposed development will then be considered in the light of other important factors, such as access and scale. Design in this location may also be significant if the development is large, and attempts may be made to ensure that the visual amenity of the area is protected by landscaping.

If the proposed use for a site in this area is an industrial use, other criteria related to the site apply. Access and the traffic generated remain important factors, with design a significant feature. As with a large-scale residential development, increasing emphasis may be placed on the landscaping of the site as the scale of the development increases.

Rural locations To date these have been the most carefully protected areas, with local planning authorities generally unwilling to consider development that does not consist of the in-filling of

13 Multi-storey flats tend to be typified by the residential tower blocks built during the 1960s and early 1970s, ranging from six to thirty storeys in height.
14 Circular 15/84, Land for Housing.

certain sites in specifically designated villages.[15] As has been mentioned, this attitude may be in the process of changing,[16] but the site-related issues are likely to remain constant. The questions of scale and access are of prime importance and are obviously related to the use, while the likely pressures that the development might exert on local resources will also be a significant consideration. The emphasis placed on design will vary depending on the location of the site. In certain areas, such as the National Parks,[17] design will be considered fundamental, while in other areas it will be given much less weight.

Some common issues

What follows is a summary of those common issues that affect the development of various types of site, many of which have already been referred to in the previous discussion. These issues may be broadly categorised into those that create a visual impact and those that create a local impact. In this context local impact refers to those issues that have an effect on the local environment as a result of factors not related to the appearance of the development.

VISUAL ISSUES

Foremost amongst visual issues must be questions related to the scale, size and site coverage of the proposed development. Clearly site size will be the fundamental factor, but the problem of an appropriate development scale is not simply a function of site area. Arguably scale, in the sense of the bulk and height of the proposed development, should also be related to any existing developments in the immediate vicinity, regardless of the maximum capacity of the site. Scale is very much an issue when an existing building is extended, and should be considered regardless of whether the existing building has any intrinsic architectural merit, as an inappropriate extension is unlikely to improve matters. Site coverage, or the amount of the ground area of the site that is to be built upon, is also important, as too few buildings as well as too many can produce an inappropriate development, regardless of the intrinsic quality of design. Clearly, in the commercial areas of town

15 Normal policy, especially in green belts (see Circular 14/84, Green Belts) is for the local planning authority to designate in some way certain villages in which growth will be allowed in preference to other village sites.
16 Circular 16/87.
17 Development Control Policy Note 1969 No 4, Development in Rural Areas, para 5.

centres, total site coverage will usually be the norm, while the scale of the development in terms of its bulk will have to be carefully considered in relation to the surrounding townscape.[18] Buildings which provide a contrast with, as opposed to matching, existing buildings, can sometimes prove more acceptable, and a local planning authority may require a tall building in order to contrast with the surrounding townscape.

The size of a proposed building, together with related issues, is obviously an important aspect of the overall design, and it is in this area that local planning authorities are forced, willingly or unwillingly, into considering architectural aesthetics. In Circular 31/85,[19] the Department of the Environment draws attention to the fact that design issues are the chief cause of many planning appeals, creating consequential delays in the development control process. The suggestion is made, therefore, that control over design should be exercised only when there is a justifiable reason for so doing. Apart, however, from acknowledging that some areas, National Parks, for example, are likely to need sensitive treatment in this respect, no guidance is offered on what constitutes a justifiable reason for attempting to control the design of a development. The design of the development and the environment of the site upon which it is to be built should be indivisible, but, in reality, this is not always the case as standard designs, especially for residential developments, are continually being used on a wide range of sites.

As should now be obvious, the location of the site is crucial, in that the design criteria and scope for the development of a city centre site are very different from those employed in the development of a residential site in the suburbs, or an industrial site on the urban fringe. The main difference is that the site in the town centre is likely to be small, probably confined between other buildings, and demands to be fully developed in order that the developer stands a chance of recouping costs, all of which allow little, if any, scope to arrange any development on the site in such a way that its effect can be enhanced with landscaping. The whole design impact relies on the building in terms of its bulk, the materials employed and the detail of its features. The range of possible materials and details, such as fenestration, is so enormous that little would be served by singling out any particular aspect. Perhaps all that can be said is that people seem to know what they like, but clearly everyone does not like the same thing in the same place. The planning officer's personal taste may be moderated by the way in which the

18 Townscape is the term often applied to urban landscape. See Johns E *British Townscapes* (1969).
19 Circular 31/85, Aesthetic Control.

planning committee chooses to act on his advice, but what remains certain is that it is more often than not the design of a building that most excites the general public, particularly those buildings that they see every day and associate with a particular part of the townscape. There appears little point, therefore, to the warnings of Circular 31/85, as planning officers seem doomed to satisfy neither the Department of the Environment nor the general public.

On non-central sites, the scope for design control may be enhanced simply because of the size of the site and the possibility this offers for suitable landscaping. The insistence of a local planning authority on the landscaping of a proposed development is less controversial than a direct attack on the design, and indeed landscaping requirements are often imposed quite routinely as a planning condition. In this way the nondescript designs of a considerable amount of both residential, industrial and out-of-town retail developments may be hidden from the sensitive eye, providing that the site is capable of being suitably landscaped.

The significance of the visual impact of any development on its site cannot be over-emphasised. It is likely to be the one issue that is considered potentially contentious by the general public, more so even than an inappropriate use, as the use may be only intermittently obvious, while the building remains visible all the time. The details of the design of a building, despite the advice of Circular 31/85, are likely to be just as contentious as its bulk or position. Materials often seem to generate strong feelings, with concrete being at the top of the public's hate list, closely followed by almost any form of ceramic tiling. Experience suggests that the public's aesthetic appreciation extends to the finer details of texture and colour, so that it is not enough simply to have brick walls and a tile roof, but rather to have the correct colour and texture of bricks and tiles. The visual impact of the developed site, therefore, may be as major a consideration in the development control process as is any issue of policy or other planning guideline.

LOCAL IMPACT

As important as the visual impact are those wider issues related to the potential local impact of a proposed development. Usually these include its transport implications as well as other factors associated with the proposed use, such as need, local competition and environmental issues, including noise and smells. Obviously these matters are inextricably interrelated, as the transport implications of a development cannot, in reality, be considered without reference to the proposed use which clearly affects the level and type of traffic generated. While acknowledging these relationships, however, it is easier to consider the implications of each issue if they are examined separately.

The transport implications of the proposed development are likely to raise some major development control issues. First, the specifically site-related issues of access and parking can be considered. The question of access has to be considered in conjunction with estimates of the amount of traffic likely to be generated by the proposed development. It should be emphasised that access for a single car can, in certain circumstances, be just as crucial as access for one hundred forty-ton lorries daily. The important factor is the exact location of access onto the site in relation to, not only the proposed development, but also the surrounding configuration of the road network. At issue will be questions of road safety, especially visibility, and the likely disruption to existing traffic flows. The visibility or sight lines for traffic leaving the site can be improved by controlling the width of the access point and the level of any surrounding structures.[20] If, however, the access point is at the top of a steep rise on the site, the problem may be an intractable one. The matter is further complicated if the road onto which the access is made is a busy one, or if the access itself is near to a junction.

Parking provision on the site is obviously related to the amount of traffic likely to be using the site, as well as the positioning of buildings. Indeed, demand for on-site parking may restrict the amount of development that the site can accommodate. Rules, or more accurately rules of thumb, tend to exist in different local planning authorities indicating the number of parking spaces that will normally be required given the nature of the development, its location and the size of site. The development control issues centre around the level of demand for parking spaces that the site will generate, and the way in which this demand will fluctuate. This obviously varies greatly from one form of development to another, but a typical example may serve to illustrate the general issues. Consider the parking demands that may be generated by a tennis club in a residential suburb. In calculating what might be considered adequate car parking provision, importance will be attached by the local planning authority to the number of courts, and the existence of a clubhouse, as well as the use made of them. Sufficient car parking spaces will be required to cope, not only with the average daily maximum number of cars, but also with any additional demand that might be produced if the clubhouse is frequently used for dances. Of course the number of spaces required will inevitably be a

20 See Development Control Policy Note 1969 No 6, Road Safety and Traffic Requirements.

compromise between the maximum demand foreseeable, and the constraints of the site. It would be considered unreasonable to demand a car park large enough to provide parking spaces for all the cars likely to be generated by the occasional dance.

The need for the use must be assessed by taking account of other similar uses in the immediate area, or, conversely, the lack of them. Consider, for example, the range of uses in a small village centre. One greengrocer's shop may not serve local needs adequately, so another shop may be permitted, but if planning permission were sought for a third shop, the question of the need for this additional facility and its effect on existing businesses could not be ignored. These questions are comparatively easy to determine in relation to retailing activities, but with other uses the difficulties may increase. For example, how many large houses within an established residential area is it appropriate to convert into old persons' residential homes? Once planning permission has been granted for one, this will be used as an argument in support of attempts to gain planning permission for others. A stage will be reached, however, when the local planning authority will have to decide whether its area has a sufficient number of residential homes. The grounds on which this decision is made are often vague. Obviously, if every other property in the area was converted it would be inappropriate, but to what level such a use should be permitted before it can be considered to have a detrimental effect on the area – 5% of the properties; 10% of the properties – can be judged only in relation to the specific sites in a particular area.

The environmental effects of a use, for example, noise, fumes or other forms of pollution, are also significant and can be treated separately from those of scale and design. They occur, not only in the more obvious industrial context, but in relation to other uses. The use of a property as a hotel in a residential area may raise the issue of noise if the hotel has drinking and dining facilities that are open to non-residents. In these circumstances noise might emanate from the building as well as from any adjoining car park, and at times which were regarded as particularly unacceptable. Once again, the nature of the site and its location is crucial, insofar as these problems may be virtually eliminated by landscaping or other design features, depending on the actual physical features of the site.

Fumes and other forms of pollution are, on the other hand, normally related to industrial uses, but arguably the fumes from a small brewery in a village centre may be just as inappropriate as the chemical emissions from a tannery. The site itself can have little effect on such emissions unless it is particularly large or isolated, as clearly it is not possible to diminish the impact of smell by any form of physical landscaping. Consequently, such uses are normally seen as inappropriate for any site that is not specifically allocated for industrial use. As with almost every aspect of development control, however, there are exceptions, the most obvious being the location of crematoria. These can hardly be located in industrial areas and tend to occupy sites adjacent to existing cemeteries which are inevitably close to residential areas, or new green field sites on the urban fringe.

This brief examination of some of the commoner site-related issues of development should have illustrated the significance that the site holds in the development control process. Despite the importance of policy in development control decisions, it is always a question of applying that policy in relation to a particular application for a particular site, and since each site is unique, any decisions must be considered with that in mind. It is specifically for this reason that the concept of precedent does not exist in relation to planning permission. Planning decisions arrived at regarding development on one site cannot be directly related to the decisions on the development of the adjacent site, even if it is for the same use and at the same scale. Naturally such decisions are not ignored for the purpose of comparison, but they should never be considered precedents.

Chapter 8

Planning permission – the decision

According to section 29(1) of the Town and Country Planning Act 1971, a local planning authority can, after considering an application for planning permission, either grant planning permission conditionally or unconditionally, or refuse it. Eight weeks is the period allowed for a local planning authority to reach its decision once a planning application has been received, though that period can be extended by agreement with the applicant.[1] Should a decision not be made in the requisite period, then that counts as a refusal of planning permission.[2] The purpose of this chapter is to consider the implications of these various alternatives. In order, therefore, to place the discussion which follows in context, a table has been prepared showing the number of applications for planning permission received each year for the past five years. Figures are also given showing how many of those applications were granted and how many refused. From this simple exercise it is plain that the majority of applications for planning permission are approved.

Year	No of Applications	No of Applications determined	No granted	No refused
1981/82	372,000	407,000	350,000	57,000
1982/83	411,000	382,000	332,000	50,000
1983/84	430,000	404,000	351,000	53,000
1984/85	421,000	399,000	343,000	56,000
1985/86	432,000	403,000	342,000	61,000

In one sense this is far from surprising. A glance at the current applications for planning permission advertised in a local newspaper will show that the developments in question are fairly low-key. Permission for a new house, or a kitchen or bathroom exten-

1 Town and Country Planning General Development Order 1977, SI 1977 No 289, article 7(6).
2 Town and Country Planning Act 1971, s 37.

sion, is the norm, not large scale commercial or residential developments. Yet this can be misleading, since the decision to build a new house in an established residential neighbourhood with the possible subsequent loss of trees and walls, and disruption to the architectural homogeneity of the area, may be just as damaging in its small way as the building of a sixty-house estate on a green field site. The problem is that local planning authorities are urged by central government to take a positive attitude towards development. This is best summed up in Circular 22/80, Development Control – Policy and Practice.

> The planning system should play a helpful part in rebuilding the economy. Development control must avoid placing unjustified obstacles in the way of any development especially if it is for industry, commerce, housing or any other purpose relevant to the economic regeneration of the country. It is, and should be seen to be, part of the process of making things happen in the right place at the right time. Local planning authorities are asked therefore ... to adopt a more positive attitude to planning applications; to facilitate development; and always to grant planning permission, having regard to all material considerations, unless there are sound and clear-cut reasons for refusal.[3]

Although elsewhere the Circular asserts the government's commitment to conservation, green belts, and protecting the countryside from encroachment by the city,[4] the emphasis is undeniably on a local planning authority granting, rather than refusing, planning permission.

In addition, what these statistics for planning applications cannot take into account is development that takes place without planning permission. The way in which such unauthorised development is treated is considered in a later chapter, but what needs to be understood here, is that development can and does occur without a local planning authority having the opportunity to scrutinise it, and, as a consequence, in some instances refuse planning permission. Nor should it be imagined that such unauthorised development is always insignificant. A business may completely change its character over the years. What was a depot for parking lorries may become a workshop for repairing them. What was an arable field may be utilised as a gypsy caravan site. When this happens a local planning authority has lost its initial development control opportunity to weigh up the pros and cons of a proposed development. Instead, it is in the unenviable position of having to decide what approach to take to a development which is already in being, a

3 Circular 22/80, para 3.
4 Circular 22/80, para 4.

situation which can involve considerations that are very different from those under discussion in this chapter.[5]

To return to the theme of this chapter, namely the various ways in which a local planning authority can determine an application for permission, it is, perhaps, sensible to begin the discussion by indicating why this chapter occupies the position it does in this book. It might appear logical that a chapter entitled 'Planning permission – the decision' should immediately follow the chapter 'Planning permission – the application'. The fact that it does not is deliberate. It is to emphasise that when a local planning authority is faced with an application for planning permission, it may refer to some or all of those factors discussed in the intervening chapters before reaching a conclusion. At the end of this process of examination the likelihood is that a planning application will fall into one of three categories. These are:

(i) applications for planning permission which, in the opinion of the local planning authority, are totally unacceptable because they are incompatible with some particular aspect of development control;

(ii) applications for planning permission to which, in the opinion of the local planning authority, there are no development control objections;

(iii) applications for planning permission to which there are, in the opinion of the local planning authority, development control objections but those objections are not so fundamental as to warrant immediate rejection.

In commenting on each of these categories in turn, a start will be made with those planning applications which are unacceptable on development control grounds. Various factors can conspire to make a proposed development unacceptable. A policy in a development plan, a statement in a Department of the Environment circular, the contents of an informal local policy document, the physical configuration of the site, or a combination of all these factors can persuade a local planning authority to refuse planning permission. Even if the proposed development has some points in its favour, these might, in the local planning authority's opinion, be outweighed by its negative aspects. In the event, should a local planning authority refuse planning permission, the applicant has a number of courses of action open to him. The first of these is to appeal to the Secretary of State.[6] Planning appeals are discussed in the following chapter so at this stage it is sufficient to mention that

5 The local planning authority can invite the developer to apply retrospectively for planning permission. Alternatively, it can start enforcement proceedings against the developer, a process that is considered in Chapter 9.
6 1971 Act, s 36.

the purpose of a planning appeal is to consider afresh the issue of whether or not to grant planning permission. The very development control issues that persuaded the local planning authority to refuse planning permission will be reassessed. An appeal to the Secretary of State, therefore, should be contemplated only if an applicant believes that his proposed development has some points in its favour.

If this is not the case, or if an applicant is simply unwilling to risk time and money on an appeal to the Secretary of State, he has the alternative of entering into discussion with the local planning authority. When it refuses planning permission a local planning authority is under an obligation to give its reasons for doing so.[7] By studying those reasons and discussing them with the planning officers, an applicant may be able to make modifications to his proposed development. In the light of those modifications, such as reducing the density of housing, a fresh application for planning permission may then be successful. Obviously, it makes greater sense to consult the relevant planning officers before any planning application is submitted. Should this not be the case, an applicant can always seek their advice at this stage. It should be made clear, of course, that even if any advice given by the planning officers is followed to the letter, it cannot guarantee the success of a planning application, as this decision normally rests with the planning committee.

Planning conditions

As for the two remaining categories of planning applications, those to which there are no, and those to which there are some, development control objections, the intention is to combine the discussion of the two. This is because both raise the issue of planning conditions. According to the terms of section 29 of the 1971 Act, when a local planning authority decides to grant planning permission it can impose whatever conditions it sees fit. This ability of a local planning authority to impose planning conditions is important, and raises a number of issues. The first of these is the role of conditions in the development control process. In order to begin to appreciate that role, an example may be helpful. A builder applies for planning permission to build five bungalows in what was formerly the orchard of a large Victorian villa. In one sense the application is unobjectionable, since the proposed development is situated in a residential area, and from the plans it appears that the development has been well designed. Vehicular and pedestrian access do not seem to pose any problems, nor does the site appear to be too small

7 Town and Country Planning General Development Order 1977, SI 1977 No 289, para 7(7).

for the number of dwellings proposed. There would seem to be every reason, therefore, to decide to grant planning permission.

If such a decision was taken the development, when complete, could have a far from favourable impact on the amenity of the area. For example, the sandstone wall enclosing the site could have been demolished and replaced with a white painted fence. Mature trees might have been felled. The bungalows might have been constructed using yellow London brick with tiled roofs whereas the commonly used building materials in the area are red Ruabon brick with slate roofs. There may have been no attempt to landscape the site when building had finished. As for the vehicular and pedestrian access, concrete and tarmac may have been employed in their construction in harsh contrast to the York stone paving commonly used in the area. The end result, therefore, could be a thoroughly unsympathetic development.

In order to prevent this happening, the solution is to impose planning conditions when granting planning permission. In the example just given, the following set of conditions would not be unusual.

(i) Samples of all materials to be used externally to be approved prior to building commencing.

(ii) All boundary walls to site shall be retained at their present height and repointed in a suitably coloured mortar.

(iii) All existing trees to be protected during work. Any tree damaged or which dies within two years to be replaced with agreed trees in first available season.

(iv) Details of all hard ground surfaces to be approved (wholesale tarmacing or concreting will not be acceptable).

In this fashion it should be possible to ensure that the proposed development is as compatible as possible with the existing environment. Indeed, the justification, in planning terms, for the imposition of these conditions will be to enhance the visual amenity of the area.

In the light of this example, it is now possible to consider the role of conditions in the development control process. Do planning conditions represent an avenue whereby a local planning authority can implement its development control policy? In a broad sense this is undoubtedly true. A local planning authority, particularly a rural one, may have a policy that new factories can be built in its area only if they are to be occupied by local firms. It is possible to attach a condition to a planning permission which seeks to guarantee that this policy is observed. That condition could state, for example, that 'the factories in question may be occupied only by local firms'. It should be obvious, however, that this is a far from satisfactory planning condition, since it gives the applicant for planning permission no guidance on what constitutes a 'local firm'. To refer, therefore, to planning conditions as a device for implementing development control policy is not totally accurate. This is because policies often have to be broad rather than specific, whereas conditions, in order to have a role to play, must indicate clearly what is required.

If planning conditions do not provide a means for a local planning authority to implement directly its development control policy, what is their role? A clue is to be found in Circular 1/85, The Use of Conditions in Planning Permissions, which states:

> The power to impose conditions when granting planning permission is very wide, and can enable many development proposals to proceed where it would otherwise have been necessary to refuse planning permission.[8]

The value of planning conditions, therefore, seems to depend on the scope they give a local planning authority to regulate the details of a proposed development. As was mentioned, an application for planning permission to construct bungalows in an established residential area may be perfectly acceptable in principle. What may be unacceptable is the loss of trees and walls, and the unsympathetic construction of the new buildings. This is where planning conditions come into their own. They can be used to ensure the retention of trees, of walls, of building lines and the use of materials which are compatible with existing buildings. To this extent, planning conditions are being used to implement development control policy, for example, the policy of enhancing the amenity of a pleasant residential area. The same is true of all conditions. Most local planning authorities will have development control policies on noise, on the opening hours of businesses, on the provision of car-parking spaces and on roads. Planning conditions allow the generality of such policies to be applied to the specific circumstances of a particular development. In that sense they are a means of implementing policy, not directly, but at one remove.

Having explored the relationship between development control policy and planning conditions, the next step is to discuss in greater detail the content of conditions. Circular 1/85 regards conditions as falling into two general categories, those concerned with regulating the development, and those which are applicable after the development has occurred. In the first category are conditions which impose time limits on the commencement of development, which

8 Circular 1/85, para 1.

ensure the provision of the necessary infrastructure, such as sewage disposal, access roads and parking spaces, and which provide for the landscaping of the development site. In this fashion, a local planning authority is attempting to guarantee that planning permissions are not acted upon, and that buildings are not occupied before the necessary services have been supplied. Conditions which are applicable after the development has occurred are more contentious. As Circular 1/85 points out, such conditions:

> ...will remain in force after the development has been carried out...They can place onerous and permanent restrictions on what can be done with the premises affected, and they should therefore not be imposed without scrupulous weighing of the balance of advantage.[9]

In this category are conditions which attempt to restrict who can occupy houses, industrial or commercial property, which allow temporary or seasonal development to occur, which attempt to control noise or which are aimed at restricting rights under the General Development Order.[10]

Obviously this question of the content of conditions is related to the circumstances in which conditions are imposed. It will be recalled that this discussion of planning conditions began with a reference to the fact that some applications for planning permission will raise development control issues, and others will not. Planning conditions are a way of dealing with those development control issues while, at the same time, letting a proposed development proceed. The logic of this is that planning applications raising no development control issues will be granted planning permission unconditionally, a possibility which section 29 acknowledges. There is, however, a slight flaw in this logic, besides the obvious flaw of whether all planning applications are bound to raise development control issues. Section 41 of the 1971 Act provides that, with some exceptions:

> ...every planning permission granted or deemed to be granted shall be granted or, as the case may be, be deemed to be granted, subject to the condition that the development to which it relates must be begun not later than the expiration of –
> (a) five years beginning with the date on which the permission is granted or, as the case may be, deemed to be granted; or

9 Circular 1/85, para 65.
10 The General Development Order sets out certain classes of activity which rank as permitted development, that is, those activities that can proceed without the need to secure planning permission. It is possible to impose a planning condition restricting such rights. Circular 1/85 gives some examples, while, at the same time, discouraging the use of such conditions unless there are valid planning reasons for their imposition. A planning condition may also be used to restrict rights under the Use Classes Order.

(b) such other period (whether longer or shorter) beginning with the said date as the authority concerned with the terms of planning permission may direct, being a period which the authority considers appropriate having regard to the provisions of the development plan and to any other material considerations.

It would seem, therefore, that all planning permissions will be accompanied by at least one condition. This is to the effect that development must begin within a specified period, normally five years.[11] Such a condition might be described as a standard condition, in that it is inevitably used, whatever the circumstances.

One other planning condition can also be described as standard. This is the condition, attached to a grant of outline planning permission, reserving certain matters for subsequent approval by a local planning authority. It will be recalled that where the proposed development consists of the erection of a building, outline planning permission may be requested. The local planning authority will be given certain basic details concerning the proposed building and, on that basis, will decide whether or not to approve the development in principle. If the authority does, it will grant outline planning permission subject to whatever conditions it thinks necessary. One of these conditions will invariably require local planning authority approval of certain details, usually termed 'reserved matters'. These can include the siting of the proposed building, its design and external appearance, access to it and the landscaping of the site on which it is to be erected.

Apart from these two standard planning conditions, Circular 1/85 states quite categorically that '... as a matter of policy, a condition ought not to be imposed unless there is a definite need for it'.[12] This would seem to suggest that the practice of imposing conditions automatically whenever an application for planning permission is approved, is to be avoided. Failure to observe this results in the development control system being brought into disrepute. There must, therefore, be a planning justification for every planning condition imposed. This is not to say, of course, that planning conditions do not exist whose use is exceedingly common. It may be seen as sensible development control practice to specify the hours when machinery can be used when planning permission is granted for a factory, or to make provision for landscaping whenever a major building operation takes place. A local planning authority,

11 In the case of a grant of outline planning permission, approval for reserved matters should normally be sought within three years, with development beginning two years from that date, or five years from the original grant of outline planning permission, whichever is later. The local planning authority has the power to vary any of these periods if it so wishes.
12 Circular 1/85, para 12.

besides being aware of the need to use common planning conditions intelligently, should also appreciate that the power to impose planning conditions is a wide-ranging power. It can be used to frame very specific conditions to deal with a particular problem.

In considering what limits there are on local planning authorities' powers to impose planning conditions, reference needs to be made initially to section 29 of the 1971 Act. This suggests that local planning authorities can impose 'such conditions as they think fit', indicating, perhaps, that the authorities have a totally free hand in the matter. In reality, both the Secretary of State for the Environment and the courts have formulated rules which broadly restrict the content of planning conditions. It is only logical that the Secretary of State should have devised such rules, since it is to him that an individual will appeal when the content of a planning condition is considered unacceptable. The tests applied by the Secretary of State are set out in Circular 1/85. They demand that a condition should be:

  (i) necessary,
 (ii) relevant to planning,
(iii) relevant to the development to be permitted,
(iv) enforceable,
 (v) precise, and
(vi) reasonable in all other respects.

Before considering the significance of each test in turn, a word should be said about their sources. Some of these tests have been formulated by the courts. These will be apparent from the reference to decided cases. In contrast, the Secretary of State has formulated tests to assess the development control merits of a condition. A local planning authority should observe all the tests.

The first test is that a planning condition must be necessary. Circular 1/85 states, by way of explanation, that the

> ... argument that a condition will do no harm is no justification for its imposition: as a matter of policy, a condition ought not to be imposed unless there is a definite need for it.[13]

When employing planning conditions, therefore, a local planning authority should tailor the condition to meet the specific problems of a particular development. Used in this fashion, planning conditions can permit development to go ahead, while keeping to a minimum any unfavourable impact it may have on a neighbourhood. That, of course, is the theory. Little direct evidence is available on whether local planning authorities use conditions

13 Circular 1/85, para 12.

intelligently, or simply attach the same standard planning conditions to each and every planning permission. Nor is there a great deal in the way of indirect evidence. If a planning condition is breached and a local planning authority commences enforcement proceedings, that is good evidence of how necessary that planning condition was. Unfortunately, there are no figures for the reverse situation, that is, of a planning condition being breached and no enforcement proceedings being taken.

Perhaps the greatest guarantee that a planning condition is necessary rests with the fact that a local planning authority has, under the terms of the General Development Order, to give reasons to the applicant for its imposition of planning conditions.[14] Circular 1/85 warns against giving vague reasons, such as to protect the amenity of the neighbourhood.[15] Instead, local planning authorities are advised that if:

> ... the reasons for the imposition of conditions are clearly explained, developers will be better able to understand the need for them and to comply with them in spirit as well as in letter.[16]

This should in turn, it is suggested, reduce the number of appeals to the Secretary of State.

The second requirement is that planning conditions should be relevant to planning. This is a test devised by the courts and its significance can best be appreciated by referring to the case of *R v Hillingdon London Borough Council, ex parte Royco Homes Ltd*.[17] Here, the Council attached conditions to the planning permission granted to Royco Homes, one of which was that the occupants of the residential development which the company were proposing to build should, for ten years, be drawn from the Council's housing waiting-list. The court found that such a condition was invalid. Basically, the reasoning which accompanies this decision is simple. Section 29 of the 1971 Act allows a local planning authority to impose whatever conditions it thinks fit. This would seem to suggest that a condition, such as the one under discussion, would be perfectly legitimate. This, however, is not the case. Since the power to impose conditions appears in the 1971 Act, then any conditions must further the purpose of that Act within the statutory framework it establishes. In other words, they must have a planning purpose. In the *Royco Homes* case, the court held that the condition in question had no such purpose. Instead, it appeared to be an attempt

14 Town and Country Planning General Development Order 1977, SI 1977 No 289, article 7(7).
15 Circular 1/85, para 8.
16 Circular 1/85, para 8.
17 [1974] QB 720, [1974] 2 All ER 643.

by the local authority to force Royco Homes to carry the financial burden of the local authority's duties as a housing authority.

Other decisions have confirmed this approach by the courts towards conditions which have no planning purpose.[18] Faced with such a condition, therefore, an applicant has several courses of action open to him. He can, if he wishes, accept the burden and act upon it, though this in no way alters the fact that a condition of this nature is invalid. Alternatively, the applicant can appeal to the Secretary of State, giving as his reason the content of that particular condition. In these circumstances, the Secretary of State may remove the offending condition, since the Secretary of State should, and indeed does, observe the tests for validity laid down by the courts and in his own policy.[19] By taking this course of action, the applicant runs the risk that, once the offending condition is removed, the Secretary of State may no longer feel able to grant planning permission. Finally, if all else fails, the applicant can refer the offending condition to the courts since they have the power to strike it out.[20]

In addition to having a planning purpose, the courts have also made it clear that, in order to be valid, a condition must be relevant to the development to be permitted. The significance of this test can be illustrated by referring to *Newbury District Council v Secretary of State for the Environment*.[1] Here, a company had applied for planning permission in 1962 to use two hangars on a disused airfield as warehouses for storing synthetic rubber. Planning permission was granted subject to conditions, one of which was that the hangars should be removed by 31st December 1972. When the company did not remove the hangars by that date, enforcement proceedings were begun. On appeal by the company, the Secretary of State set aside the enforcement notice. He agreed with his inspector's recommendation that the condition requiring the hangars' removal was void on the grounds that it did not relate to the purpose for which the original planning permission was sought. When subsequently this decision was reviewed by the court, its reasoning was vindicated, the court agreeing that the condition was not relevant to the proposed use.[2] Other examples of conditions which are

---

18 See, for example, *Hall & Co Ltd v Shoreham by Sea Urban District Council* [1964] 1 All ER 1, *M J Shanley v Secretary of State for the Environment* [1982] JPL 380.
19 The Secretary of State will, therefore, be judging a condition both on its development control merits and its legal validity.
20 1971 Act, s 245.
1 [1981] AC 578, [1980] 1 All ER 731.
2 Neither was the condition valid under the terms of s 30(1)(b) of the 1971 Act which permits planning permission to be granted for a specified period, at the end of which buildings must be removed.

unacceptable on these grounds are given in Circular 1/85.

> For example if planning permission is being granted for the alteration of a factory building, it would be wrong to impose conditions requiring additional parking facilities to be provided for an existing factory simply to meet a need that already exists, and similarly wrong to require the improvement of the appearance or layout of an adjoining site simply because it is untidy or congested; despite the desirability of these objectives in planning terms, the need for the action would not be created by the new development.[3]

While the logic of this caveat on the content of planning conditions seems to be reasonably clear, its relationship with section 30(1)(a) of the 1971 Act needs scrutinising. That subsection provides:

> Without prejudice to the generality of section 29(1) of this Act, conditions may be imposed on the grant of planning permission thereunder –
> (a) for regulating the development or use of any land under the control of the applicant (whether or not it is land in respect of which the application was made) or requiring the carrying out of works on any such land, so far as appears to the local planning authority to be expedient for the purposes of or in connection with the development authorised by the permission ...

It might appear on first reading that section 30(1)(a) provides the justification for such conditions. In reality this appears not to be so. The words ' ... so far as appears to the local planning authority to be expedient for the purposes of or in connection with the development authorised by the permission', mean that a condition made under the terms of this subsection must be as relevant to the development to be permitted as any condition made under section 29.

The next requirement is that a condition must be enforceable. In order to clarify what this entails, this test is best considered in conjunction with the fifth test that a planning condition must be precise. This is because if a condition is imprecise the chances are that it will not be capable of being enforced. In the case of *M J Shanley Ltd v Secretary of State for the Environment*,[4] for example, the debate was over a residential development in the green belt. The contentious condition demanded that the first opportunity to purchase the houses in the proposed development should be given to local people. The imprecision of this condition is obvious, and relates to what constitutes both a 'first opportunity' and 'local people'. In these circumstances the court had no hesi-

---

3 Circular 1/85, para 21.
4 [1982] JPL 380.

tation in setting the condition aside, since its imprecision rendered it unenforceable.

Views on what is or is not precise, depend on the particular facts of a case. In *Alderson v Secretary of State for the Environment*,[5] the argument centred again on the use of the word 'local' in a condition restricting the occupation of premises to persons 'employed locally in agriculture'. The Court of Appeal held that in this context the word had a perfectly intelligible meaning, so that the condition was sufficiently precise. This was fortunate, since the condition was in common use among local planning authorities who had relied on Department of Environment advice that it was acceptable.[6]

One damaging consequence of imprecision is that it brings the process of development control, and planning conditions in particular, into disrepute, although it is worth mentioning that, even if a planning condition is imprecise and thus invalid, it may still have a perfectly legitimate development control purpose. Faced with a vague condition a developer will be uncertain what is required of him. If that developer then chooses to do nothing, the local planning authority may find itself in an equal predicament, since it will be impossible to take action to enforce the condition. This is not to suggest that every planning condition which is unenforceable is imprecise. There are examples of planning conditions which are perfectly clear in what they require but are still unenforceable. Circular 1/85 gives the example of a condition, imposed for traffic reasons, restricting the number of residents at any one time in a block of flats.[7] What makes the condition unenforceable in these circumstances is the impossibility of monitoring whether or not it is being observed. For all the good it is doing, therefore, the condition may as well not be there.

The final test for a valid condition is that of reasonableness. This is by far the most difficult proposition to explain. It is possible to give examples of what might constitute an unreasonable planning condition and Circular 1/85 does precisely that.[8] To allow a factory for canning vegetables to be built and then restrict its hours of operation from 11 a m to 3 p m represents an unreasonable condition, since it defeats the purpose of granting planning permission. Another instance would be a condition that demands something of a developer which is beyond his control, for example, requiring him to carry out work on land that he does not own. Yet, examples, particularly extreme examples, do not adequately convey the essen-

5 (1984) 49 P & CR 307.
6 It was set out in Circular 5/68 which, at that time, was the current circular on planning conditions.
7 Circular 1/85, Appendix B.
8 Circular 1/85, para 30.

tials of unreasonableness. This is perhaps because, in the context of development control, the concept varies according to whether it is the Secretary of State or the courts which is employing it. The Secretary of State may consider a planning condition unreasonable on development control grounds, meaning that what is demanded is not conducive to good planning. The objection to local user conditions may fall under this heading. To grant planning permission for factories or houses, then restrict who occupies the property to local firms or residents is not something which the Department of the Environment encourages at present.[9] Basically, this is because, in the eyes of central government, there are no good planning reasons for the practice except on very rare occasions.

In contrast, the court's use of the expression 'unreasonable' is somewhat different, as the courts are neither equipped, nor do they have the authority, to make development control judgments. Their task is to ensure that the law is observed. Therefore, in a case such as the *Royco Homes* case, the decision to impose a condition which had no planning purpose was described as unreasonable by the court, indicating that it is unreasonable for a local authority to behave in a way for which there is no legal justification. Sometimes, however, the expression 'unreasonable' will denote activity on the part of a local authority which no reasonable local authority would engage in. A planning condition described in this fashion could have a planning purpose, and be precise in its wording, but could be so crass in its demands as to be totally unreasonable. A local user condition, for example, would not fall into this category unless it restricted the occupants of a proposed residential development to individuals who had been living in a particular village for thirty years. Unreasonable in this context should mean an unlawful use of power, though it has to be said that some decisions may demonstrate a failure on the part of the courts to appreciate this fact. Examples can be discovered of the courts performing the Secretary of State's role rather than the one specifically allotted to them.[10]

If a planning condition is a valid planning condition, judged by the six tests in Circular 1/85, then it is binding on the individual who receives the planning permission. Failure to observe the condition may result in enforcement proceedings. However, there would be no logic to the whole concept if a planning condition were binding on the developer who made the application for planning permission but no one else. That developer might sell the land or property in question before any work started. In order to overcome this par-

9 Circular 1/85, paras 74–80.
10 See on this point *Fourth Investments Ltd v Bury Metropolitan Borough Council* [1985] JPL 185.

ticular problem, conditions are regarded as part of the whole package of granting planning permission. Anyone, therefore, who decides to act on that grant of planning permission must observe the planning conditions. This rather obvious point, however, conceals a more important truth about the nature of planning conditions. This point relates to their duration. As Circular 1/85 indicates, planning conditions fall into one of two categories. There are planning conditions which regulate the development, and those which remain in force after the development has been carried out. In the former group are conditions specifying time limits for the commencement and completion of the development and the provision of certain basic services, such as sewers. Once the development has been completed, these conditions have been discharged.

On the other hand, conditions which are intended to remain in force after the development has been completed, may have no limit on their duration. In this category are conditions which restrict the hours of operation of an industrial development, or the level of noise it is permitted to generate. Here, the aim of the planning condition is to reduce for all time the impact a proposed development might have on the amenity of an area. Yet this is not all. The more contentious of these conditions have about them the air of social engineering, or seemingly infringe on an individual's right to dispose of and use his property as he wishes.

As remarked upon in Circular 1/85, conditions which remain in force after the development has been carried out 'can place onerous and permanent restrictions on what can be done with the premises affected.'[11] It seems hardly surprising to find, therefore, a reference in Circular 1/85 to the power to vary or remove the effect of conditions. Section 32(1)(b) of the 1971 Act is credited with this ability. According to the Circular:

> ... applications can be made for permission to retain buildings or works, or continue a use, without complying with one or more conditions imposed on the original permission.[12]

This seems to indicate that section 32(1)(b) is specifically designed to deal with conditions that take effect once a planning permission has been acted upon. A reading of section 32(1)(b), however, does not support this view, since the subsection seems to be designed to cope with retrospective applications for planning permission rather than the discharge of conditions. While planning conditions are mentioned, some writers suggest that the use of the section is appropriate only when a planning condition is being disregarded,

11 Circular 1/85, para 65.
12 Circular 1/85, para 4.

rather than as a means of seeking its discharge.[13] Indeed, at least one writer suggests that no procedure exists for discharging a planning condition, the solution being, it is said, to make a fresh application for planning permission.[14] Whatever the correct interpretation of section 32(1)(b) is, there does seem to be a need for a procedure which allows the reconsideration of planning conditions. The Housing and Planning Act 1986 has apparently clarified the situation by inserting a new section, section 31A, into the 1971 Act. This allows an individual with planning permission to apply to the local planning authority for permission to proceed without complying with the conditions attached to the grant of planning permission. In this fashion only the planning conditions are reconsidered.

In bringing to a close this examination of planning conditions, it will be recalled that the discussion arose out of an analysis of the various ways in which a local planning authority can resolve an application for planning permission. Yet even planning conditions have their limitations, and with this in mind, local planning authorities often make use of planning agreements as a valuable adjunct to planning conditions in controlling development within their area. Since planning agreements are normally negotiated at the same time as an application is being made for planning permission, it seems appropriate to consider them in this chapter. The aim is to assess their advantages and disadvantages as compared with planning conditions.

Planning agreements

The power to conclude planning agreements can be found in various statutes. The powers most commonly used are those in:

(i) section 52 of the Town and Country Planning Act 1971;
(ii) section 111 of the Local Government Act 1972;
(iii) section 278 of the Highways Act 1980; and
(iv) local private Acts of Parliament.

Before considering each of these powers in turn, some general points need to be made about the use of planning agreements. The term 'planning agreement' has no specific meaning and can be used to cover a great many transactions between a local authority and a developer. A local authority, for example, may own a plot of land which it is prepared to lease to a developer in order that he may construct a new supermarket on the site, subject, of course, to his

13 See, for example, Grant M *Urban Planning Law* (1982, updated 1986) p 208.
14 *Grant*, p 208.

obtaining planning permission. Obviously, an agreement of this nature has development control implications, but to all intents and purposes it is a business arrangement. There will be no reference in the agreement to development control details, no provision for the number of car-parking spaces, the size of the supermarket or access to the site. Nor should the agreement contain any undertaking on the part of the local authority purporting to guarantee the grant of planning permission. If it does, the likelihood is that this could invalidate any subsequent grant of planning permission.[15] Instead, the decision whether or not to grant planning permission should be taken separately, and on the development control issues only.

Apart from these business arrangements, the term 'planning agreement' can also relate to an agreement which has, as its sole purpose, the regulation of development. Here are some clauses from just such an agreement:

Now therefore it is agreed as follows: 1. For the purposes of this deed it is agreed between the parties hereto that the line marked 'XYZ' on the said plan is the boundary between the respective developments of the corporation and the developer. 2. The corporation and the developer hereby covenant in respect of the following rights and restrictions and by reference to the said plan and plan no. 2 attached hereto as follows: (a) the corporation hereby covenants and agrees with the developer that the developer may build up to the said line XYZ and along its length at levels B, D and E on the said plan no. 2. (b) the developer hereby covenants and agrees with the corporation that the corporation may build up to the said line XYZ and along its whole length at levels B and D . . . (c) The corporation hereby further covenants and agrees with the developer that above level E the developer may build as follows: (i) Between points X and to a level of 5.3 metres above level E or higher if the point is contained within an angle of 50 degrees measured from a point 5.3 metres above level E along the line XY as shown on section AA of the said plan no. 2. (ii) Between points Y and Z to a height contained within an angle of 50 degrees measured from a point 3 metres from the boundary YZ and at a height of 8 metres above level E as shown in section BB on the said plan no. 2. 3. The developer hereby further covenants and agrees with the corporation that the developer will not build on its land edged purple on plan no. 1 to a height exceeding 16 metres above the present ground level at point X shown on the said plan no. 1.[16]

What is immediately apparent is that a planning agreement of this nature is serving a purpose which is remarkably similar to that

15 See *J J Steeples v Derbyshire County Council* [1984] 3 All ER 468. A clause in a business agreement whereby a local planning authority promised to use its best endeavours to secure planning permission for its business partners, or else pay compensation, rendered the planning committee's decision invalid.

16 *Windsor and Maidenhead Royal Borough Council v Brandrose Investments Ltd* [1981] 3 All ER 38 at 42.

performed by planning conditions. While this is true, some explanation is needed of why this should be so. There appears to be a two-fold reason which is rationalised on the following basis:

> Although local planning authorities sometimes use an agreement in order to achieve a measure of development control which would otherwise be clearly impossible . . . by reference to the legal limits of planning conditions, it seems to be more frequently the case that an agreement is resorted to either in order to avoid the uncertainties of planning law or in order to reinforce development control, . . . there seems to be a feeling in practice that there is a greater likelihood that a developer will comply with an element of development control which is incorporated in a formal, legal agreement.[17]

On the point that planning agreements can be used in circumstances where a planning condition might not be valid, this proposition needs to be qualified. In the first place, planning agreements draw their force from the fact that some accord has been reached between a local planning authority and a developer. In this respect, planning agreements are distinct from planning conditions, which are imposed whether or not a developer is agreeable. If, therefore, a local planning authority is unable to impose a valid planning condition, it cannot, as an alternative, force a developer to enter into a planning agreement. The developer must agree. It may well be that a developer, faced with the prospect of being refused planning permission, will be prepared to enter into an agreement. This may not, however, always be the case. A developer may prefer to appeal against the refusal of planning permission rather than commit himself to an agreement he finds unacceptable. Devices to force a developer's hand, for example, a planning condition to the effect that no start can be made on a proposed development until a planning agreement has been concluded, have been held to be invalid.[18]

Apart from the necessity of securing a developer's agreement, it may no longer be accurate to suggest that what cannot validly be embodied in a planning condition can validly be embodied in a planning agreement. Obviously, much will depend on the precise terms of the statute which creates the power to enter into a planning agreement. In the case of *City of Bradford Metropolitan Council v Secretary of State for the Environment*,[19] the Court of Appeal upheld the view of the Secretary of State that a planning condition which required a developer to widen an existing road by one metre,

17 Hawke J N 'Planning Agreements in Practice' (Part II), Journal of Planning and Environment Law, 1981, p 96.
18 [1980] JPL 841 (ministerial planning appeal decision).
19 [1986] JPL 598.

was invalid. This was on the basis that it related to land which was neither owned nor controlled by the developer, and was thus beyond his control. It was, therefore, not a reasonable condition. In setting aside this condition, however, the Secretary of State had commented that its objective could have been achieved if its contents had been the subject of an agreement entered into under section 52 of the 1971 Act. Reacting to this suggestion, Lloyd LJ made the following remark:

> If the condition was manifestly unreasonable, and so beyond the powers of the Planning Authority to impose it, whether or not the developers consented, it had to follow that it was also beyond the powers of the Planning Authority to include the condition as 'an incidental or consequential provision' of an agreement restricting or regulating the development or use of the land under section 52.[20]

Consequently, in Lloyd LJ's opinion, the wording of section 52 made it impossible to embody the planning condition in its original form in an agreement concluded under the terms of this section. This is not to say however, that an alternative statutory power could not have been used, or a modified form of the original planning condition utilised.[1]

With these caveats in mind it is now possible to consider the various individual powers possessed by the local planning authority to enter into a planning agreement, beginning with section 52 of the 1971 Act.

TOWN AND COUNTRY PLANNING ACT 1971, SECTION 52

According to the terms of this section:

> A local planning authority may enter into an agreement with any person interested in land in their area for the purpose of restricting or regulating the development or use of the land, either permanently or during such period as may be prescribed by the agreement; and any such agreement may contain such incidental and consequential provisions (including provisions of a financial character) as appear to the local planning authority to be necessary or expedient for the purposes of the agreement.

What is immediately apparent is that the purpose of a section 52 agreement is to restrict and regulate, rather than to force a developer to undertake a specific task, except where this is incidental or consequential. A section 52 agreement could, therefore, be used to ensure that a large-scale development is undertaken in a logical

---

20 Ibid, 600–601.
1 For example, the power to enter into agreements under the Highways Act 1980, s 278. Alternatively, a condition of the sort used in *Grampian Regional Council v City of Aberdeen District Council* [1984] JPL 590 might have been more fitting.

fashion, with buildings being demolished as and when it is necessary, and rebuilding not being unduly delayed.[2] Provision might also be made in the agreement for a developer to make a financial contribution towards a road-widening or pedestrianisation scheme that has to be implemented as a result of the redevelopment. It also appears that a proposal to reserve a piece of land in a residential development for a school, or as a piece of open ground, could be incorporated into a section 52 agreement.[3] As for what cannot legitimately be included in such an agreement, undertakings to build a public car park for the local planning authority or transfer a piece of land into its ownership probably fall within this category.[4]

The explanation for this vagueness on what may legitimately form the content of a section 52 agreement is straightforward. Since a developer cannot be forced to conclude such an agreement, the presumption is that any section 52 agreement he does enter into has terms which the developer regards as perfectly acceptable. Therefore, the chance of his disputing the validity of the agreement before the courts is slim. Section 52 agreements tend to feature in the courts only indirectly. Consequently, the exact meaning to be attached to the terms of section 52, and how closely those terms are observed in practice, is a matter for conjecture. Those earlier remarks on what can legitimately form the content of a section 52 agreement refer to agreements which have featured in the courts without attracting adverse comment, as well as advice offered by the Department of the Environment.

Once concluded, various consequences accrue from the existence of a section 52 agreement, one of which is that the agreement is binding on any subsequent purchaser of the land.[5] Section 84 of the 1971 Act does allow the owner of land, affected by such an undertaking, to apply to the Lands Tribunal for it to be discharged or modified. The mere fact that the machinery exists for discharging or modifying section 52 obligations emphasises the burden placed on the developer by these agreements. It is open to argument whether corresponding burdens are placed on a local planning authority. In the past, doubt has been expressed over the ability of a local planning authority, which is a party to a section 52 agreement, to exercise other statutory powers and so negate the effect of that agreement. If, for example, a section 52 agreement has been con-

2 Such an agreement would avoid the possibility of a site being cleared, and then left in an undeveloped condition for a considerable period of time, possibly up to five years.
3 *Abbey Homesteads (Developments) Ltd v Northamptonshire County Council* (1985) 49 P & CR 263.
4 Circular 22/83, Planning Gain, Appendix B.
5 1971 Act, s 52(2).

cluded between a local planning authority and a developer, which is aimed at regulating the comprehensive development of a city centre, can that very same local planning authority then exercise its powers under section 277 of the 1971 Act, and designate the area of redevelopment a conservation area? The effect of this would be to require the developer to obtain conservation area consent before demolishing buildings.

It has always been regarded as a cardinal principle of English law that a public body cannot become involved in any activity that may hinder or fetter, in any way, the discharge of its statutory duties.[6] Any attempt, even if totally innocent, will be considered unlawful by the courts, and hence, of no effect. This is, of course, crucial to the lawful operation of a section 52 agreement, and the section itself takes account of the problem in the following fashion:

> Nothing in this section or in any agreement made thereunder shall be construed –
> (a) as restricting the exercise, in relation to land which is the subject of any such agreement, of any powers exercisable by any Minister or authority under this Act so long as those powers are exercised in accordance with the provisions of the development plan, or in accordance with any directions which may have been given by the Secretary of State as to the provisions to be included in such a plan; or
> (b) as requiring the exercise of any such powers otherwise than as mentioned in paragraph (a) of this subsection.

The interpretation to be given to section 52(3) of the 1971 Act was considered in *Windsor & Maidenhead Royal Borough Council v Brandrose Investments Ltd.*[7] Here, the developers and the local planning authority had entered into a section 52 agreement which made detailed provision as to how adjoining pieces of land were to be developed. Outline planning permission was granted for the proposed development. Two years later, however, the same local planning authority designated the area containing the site for development a conservation area. As a consequence, it appeared that the demolition of certain buildings could not be undertaken without first obtaining listed building consent.[8] The developer argued that consent was not necessary, since the section 52 agreement had, by implication, sanctioned the demolition of the buildings in question.

6 See, for example, *British Oxygen Co Ltd v Board of Trade* [1971] AC 610.
7 [1983] 1 All ER 818.
8 Buildings in a conservation area cannot be demolished without obtaining what is now termed 'conservation area consent'. This is provided for in the 1971 Act, s 277A. That section permits the Secretary of State to issue a direction exempting certain buildings. Among the buildings exempted are those required to be demolished by a section 52 agreement. In this case no mention was made of demolition in the section 52 agreement.

The local planning authority disagreed, and the issue was eventually resolved by the Court of Appeal.

According to the Court of Appeal, section 52 represents just one of a number of powers possessed by a local planning authority, which come under the heading of general planning control, and enable the authority to regulate development in its area. The aim of section 52 is to allow a local planning authority to impose 'conditions' on a developer, which it might not otherwise be able to do through the ordinary channels of section 29. This did not, in any way, compromise an authority in its exercise of other planning powers. Consequently, the Court of Appeal concluded that there was nothing in section 52, or in this particular section 52 agreement, to preclude a local planning authority from designating the area a conservation area and thus, requiring the developer to obtain conservation area consent.

It is to be expected that parties which have freely entered into a section 52 agreement will observe its provisions. However, this may not always be so. In *Avon County Council v Millard*,[9] a section 52 agreement had been concluded to regulate the working of a quarry. Certain provisions in the agreement, requiring the construction of an access road and a fresh application for planning permission, were not observed. The issue here was whether the local authority must rely on enforcement proceedings in order to rectify the breach. While enforcement proceedings are the appropriate remedy for rectifying a breach of planning control, a section 52 agreement represents a contract between the parties. In these circumstances, the Court of Appeal was prepared to affirm that the local authority might rely on ordinary civil remedies, including the injunction, to restrain the breach of the agreement. This would appear sensible given the nature of a section 52 agreement, and the delays which, as Chapter 9 will illustrate, can occur in the enforcement process.

LOCAL GOVERNMENT ACT 1972, SECTION 111

In contrast to the specific terms of section 52 of the 1971 Act, section 111 is far more general in its scope. It provides:

> Without prejudice to any powers exercisable apart from this section but subject to the provisions of this Act and any other enactment passed before or after this Act, a local authority shall have power to do anything (whether or not involving the expenditure, borrowing or lending of money or the acquisition or disposal of any property or rights) which is calculated to facilitate, or is conducive or incidental to, the discharge of any of their functions.

9 [1986] JPL 211.

The purpose of this chapter, it may be recalled, is to discuss the various ways in which an application for planning permission may be resolved. Planning agreements, and the power to make them, are being considered as an alternative to planning conditions. With that in mind, it is probably true to say that a local planning authority, contemplating an agreement with a developer to regulate a proposed development, would be unlikely to rely on section 111. From its terms, it should be clear that the purpose of the section is to validate actions on the part of a local authority which are not specifically mentioned elsewhere, but are crucial to the discharge of its functions.

The kind of transactions, therefore, which will have a bearing on the development control process, and will fall within the scope of section 111 are likely to be business transactions. This section may be seen as authorising a lease of land to a developer, or a business arrangement between a local authority and a developer to undertake some large scale project, such as the construction of a leisure park.[10] An anticipatory agreement of this nature, anticipatory in the sense that the whole transaction may depend on whether planning permission is granted or refused, can give a local authority a say in the development control process which it may not normally enjoy. An example will help to demonstrate the truth of this statement. A local authority owns a plot of land. It enters into an agreement with a company to build the English equivalent of Disneyland on the site. Some of the development will be undertaken directly by the local authority. The remainder will be financed from capital raised by the company. Obviously, as a business partner, the local authority will have a considerable say on how that project is undertaken and the final form it takes.

Yet business agreements with developers can be a source of considerable difficulty. The fact that such an agreement exists may mean that the developer finds himself applying for planning permission to that very local authority with whom he is in partnership. This can lead local residents to believe that, in granting planning permission, the local planning authority has not displayed that impartiality which is expected of it. In a series of decisions,[11] the courts have expressed the opinion that a local planning authority

10 For examples of such agreements see *R v St Edmundsbury Borough Council* [1985] 3 All ER 234, *J J Steeples v Derbyshire County Council* [1984] 3 All ER 468.

11 *J J Steeples v Derbyshire County Council* [1984] 3 All ER 468, *R v Amber Valley District Council, ex p Jackson* [1984] 3 All ER 501, *R v Sevenoaks District Council, ex p Terry* [1985] 3 All ER 226, *R v St Edmundsbury Borough Council* [1985] 3 All ER 234, *R v Carlisle City Council and the Secretary of State for the Environment* (1985) 276 EG 1161.

which behaves in this fashion is doing no more than it is permitted to do by law. The only exception would appear to be where an undertaking is given by a local planning authority to obtain planning permission for the proposed joint venture. In these circumstances a local planning authority will be regarded as rendering itself incapable of exercising its discretion to grant or refuse planning permission.[12]

HIGHWAYS ACT 1980, SECTION 278

Section 278 of the Highways Act 1980 authorises a highway authority, which is often the local planning authority, to enter into agreements whereby, in return for the authority undertaking highway works, an individual agrees to make a contribution to the highway authority towards the cost of those works and their maintenance, once complete. The idea is that the person who agrees to make the payment will be deriving special benefit from the works. The benefit can take a number of forms. The agreement in question may specify that the work should be completed by a certain date, or should, at the request of the individual, incorporate certain features. It should not be imagined, however, that the highway authority represents a mere contractor, doing exactly what the individual wants. The section makes it quite clear that agreements of this nature should be entered into only if they are going to be of benefit to the public.

The relationship between agreements of this kind and other planning agreements, as well as planning conditions, needs to be considered. It will be recalled that a planning condition is unlikely to be valid if it requires a developer to undertake work on land which is not his, and over which he has no control. If, therefore, a developer proposes to build a block of flats, a local planning authority may feel that a grant of planning permission is in order, provided the road which runs alongside the flats is widened to cope with the extra traffic entering and leaving the building. A condition requiring the developer to undertake this work will not be valid for the reasons given above,[13] though a condition which forbids a start being made on the development until the road works are complete

12 *J J Steeples v Derbyshire County Council* [1984] 3 All ER 468. Here the local authority had promised to use its best endeavours in order to obtain planning permission. Although the judgment refers to the decision of the planning committee as being biased, the better explanation would appear to be that the terms of the agreement were regarded as fettering the discretion of the planning committee to grant or refuse planning permission.
13 That is that it requires work to be undertaken on land not under the control of the developer. See *City of Bradford Metropolitan Council v Secretary of State for the Environment* [1986] JPL 598.

might be acceptable.[14] As for section 52 of the 1971 Act, this sanctions agreements only if the developer has an interest in the land affected, which would not be the case in the situation under consideration. Section 278, therefore, offers a solution to this particular dilemma, since the work is carried out by the responsible body but not without a financial contribution from the developer who is deriving particular benefit from it.

It should be appreciated that section 278 agreements will be very specific in their contents. As such, they do not represent a direct implementation of development control policy. If, on the other hand, a local planning authority makes it a general policy requirement that any new development should not overload the existing road system, section 278 offers the opportunity to ensure that, in specific instances, general policy is observed. In that sense, this particular planning agreement offers a means to an end.

LOCAL ACTS OF PARLIAMENT

It is not unusual for local authorities to sponsor local Acts of Parliament whose purpose is to give specific powers to a local authority to be exercised in its administrative area. The procedure for securing the passage of such an Act is distinct from that observed in the case of an Act of Parliament, which affects the population at large. These Acts are mentioned because sometimes they contain a provision along the lines of that in the Glamorgan County Council Act 1973:

7. – (1) The Council and any person having an estate or interest in any land within the county may enter into an agreement which may provide for all or any of the following:–

(a) determining the manner in which that land is to be developed and the order in which development of that land shall be carried out as between the different parts of that land and as between the different parts of the development of any part of that land;

(b) determining the time by which development of that land shall be completed or the times by which the parts of that development shall be completed;
. . .

(f) arrangements relating to the provision, maintenance or use of facilities for the parking of vehicles for or in connection with development of that land;

(g) arrangements for the maintenance of open spaces provided in connection with development of that land;

(h) arrangements relating to the provision, maintenance or use of means of disposal of foul or surface water or trade effluent or waste for or in connection with development of that land;

(i) any other related or consequential matters.[15]

14 See, for example, *Grampian Regional Council v City of Aberdeen District Council* [1984] JPL 590.
15 Glamorgan County Council Act 1973, s 7.

The extent of the powers may vary from Act to Act. What needs emphasising is the existence of yet another opportunity to enter into an agreement to regulate development. On the face of it, there may appear little to distinguish these agreements from section 52 agreements. While undoubtedly the underlying purpose is the same, the wording in a local Act of Parliament may authorise agreements which not only regulate or restrict development, but which also commit a developer to undertake a specific task. A local planning authority may, therefore, regard agreements entered into under such Acts as offering greater flexibility than agreements made under section 52 of the 1971 Act. This was borne out in one study on the use of planning agreements.[16]

Planning gain

The term 'planning gain' has achieved a certain notoriety in the annals of development control. It has been defined as:

> ... a term which has come to be applied whenever, in connection with a grant of planning permission, a local planning authority seeks to impose on a developer an obligation to carry out works not included in the development for which permission has been sought or to make some payment or confer some extraneous right or benefit in return for permiting development to take place.[17]

It seems appropriate, therefore, before concluding this chapter on the grant of planning permission, to make a reference to planning gain. This is because planning gain is sometimes seen as the price to be paid for granting planning permission.

With the majority of applications for planning permission the question of planning gain simply does not arise. It is usually only with sizeable development proposals that the issue arises. It does so in the following fashion.

(i) A developer is granted planning permission to build a two-storey block of flats in the grounds of an old house. The local planning authority imposes a planning condition to the effect that the grounds are to be landscaped in accordance with a scheme to be agreed with the local planning authority.

(ii) A developer is granted planning permission to construct an industrial estate. The traffic generated by the scheme will necessitate the widening of an access road. The local highway

16 Henty T 'Planning by Agreement: A Local Survey' Journal of Planning and Environment Law, 1984, p 395.
17 Circular 22/83, Planning Gain, para 2.

authority, therefore, enters into an agreement with the developer under section 278 of the Highways Act 1980 which requires the developer to make a financial contribution towards the cost of the works.

(iii) A developer is granted planning permission to erect an office block. Included in the plans for the scheme are two car parks. One car park is for the exclusive use of workers in the office block, the other is available for use by members of the general public.

(iv) A developer is granted planning permission to construct offices, shops and flats on a two-acre development site in the centre of a major city. One block of flats to be constructed will be handed over to the local authority for occupation by council tenants.

In each of these situations it can be argued that the local planning authority has gained. The gain ranges from a more pleasant environment to a 'free' block of flats. In the first two situations the gain is an officially sanctioned one, since both the planning condition and the agreement are perfectly legitimate. In situations (iii) and (iv) a planning condition requiring the provision of a public car park or a 'free' block of flats, would undoubtedly be invalid; indeed, even a section 52 agreement to this effect would be suspect. The problem of planning gain, therefore, is the dilemma of an advantage, which may or may not be freely offered, and which goes beyond what can legitimately be demanded.

Gains can be required of a developer when, as in situations (i) and (ii), their underlying purpose is a planning purpose, namely, to integrate the new development into the existing environment. In situations (iii) and (iv) the gain on offer could be viewed in two ways. It represents either a local planning authority's attempt to levy a 'tax' on development, or a developer's attempt to 'buy' planning permission. Whatever view is taken of planning gain, one thing is certain. Its presence should not allow an unsatisfactory development to go ahead, or its absence allow a satisfactory scheme to fail. This is the advice given in Circular 22/83, Planning Gain – Obligations and Benefits which Extend Beyond the Development for which Planning Permission has been Sought. That Circular discusses at some length the point already made, that planning gain is legitimate only if it reasonably relates to the development for which planning permission is sought.[18] What the Circular omits to give is advice on planning gain which clearly cannot be described in this fashion.

Obviously, if a developer is prepared to accommodate any

18 Circular 22/83, paras 5–7.

demands that are made of him, then it could be argued that there are no grounds for complaint unless, of course, this convinces a local planning authority to turn a blind eye to his scheme's short-comings. Indeed, in the past some local planning authorities have made a specific reference in their development plans to planning gain,[19] and their expectation that it will be forthcoming. In such circumstances, planning gain can be seen as the community's share of the profits to be made from a development. The flaw in this reasoning, though some might not acknowledge it as such, is the power it puts in the hands of local authorities to decide upon an appropriate 'levy' without parliamentary sanction for the practice.[20] In addition, there are discrepancies in England and Wales over the availability of planning gain. While a developer in the south of England may be willing to concede a gain, the same may not be true in the north of England where it is the local authorities which have to offer inducements to prospective developers.[1] Should, however, a developer not wish to co-operate, he can simply ask for a decision on his planning application. If he is refused planning permission, he can then appeal and the decision is taken out of the hands of the local planning authority, though the development may suffer a delay as a consequence.

Planning gain is, therefore, an issue on which it is difficult to be categorical since there can be an element of planning gain in any decision to grant planning permission. It is a controversial subject which has generated a great deal of literature.[2] What has still to be produced is an official view of where to draw the line. Circular 22/83 makes little contribution towards this end, though it has to be said that an outright statement condemning planning gain would be hard to word and harder still to police.

19 *Westminster Renslade Ltd v Secretary of State for the Environment* [1983] JPL 454.
20 It is a basic rule of constitutional law that taxes can be levied only with parliamentary approval. This has been upheld by the courts in cases such as *Attorney-General v Wilts United Dairies Ltd* (1921) 39 TLR 781.
 1 Due to the concentration of private commercial development in the South East, the local authorities in other parts of England and Wales have little opportunity to extract planning gain from the relatively few developments that take place in their areas. Instead, developers may have to be offered inducements to under-take work, such as those to be found within enterprise zones, as discussed in Chapter 5.
 2 See, for example, Jowell J and Grant M 'Guidelines for Planning Gain?' Journal of Planning and Environment Law, 1983, p 427; Morgan P H and Nott S M 'Planning Gain – Business as Usual' Local Government Review, 1984, p 47.

Chapter 9

The last resort – appeals and enforcement

In entitling this chapter 'The last resort' the intention is to emphasise that beyond the local planning authority there is a second level of decision making, capable of passing judgment on and reversing, either totally or in part, a local planning authority's development control decisions. This second level of decision making is undoubtedly the last resort, since from it there is no appeal on the development control merits of a decision. Challenge in the courts is reserved for determining whether or not the law has been observed. There are two occasions when the development control decisions of a local planning authority will be re-evaluated. The first of these will be when an individual, having observed the development control system, is unhappy with the decision he has received. His challenge to that decision will take the form of a planning appeal. The purpose of a planning appeal is to re-examine the very issues which were relevant when the original development control decision was made.

In contrast, enforcement is pertinent only when the development control process has been disregarded. This book has proceeded on the basis that the development control system is observed by every individual and organisation wishing to undertake development. On this basis, any development that occurs is as the result of a reasoned development control decision taken in full knowledge of the circumstances, by a local planning authority. Unfortunately, this is far from being the true picture. Development can and does occur without an application being made for planning permission. Alternatively, the terms on which planning permission is granted may be deliberately ignored. When breakdowns occur in the development control system a local planning authority is faced with the decision whether or not to take enforcement proceedings. Little space is devoted in this book to the mechanics of enforcement. This is because enforcement is a formal and legalistic process whose complexities would take chapters to describe. Instead, the sole objective in considering enforcement is to see what light it sheds on the development control process. An attempt will be made to do this in two ways. Firstly, by considering why individuals choose to ignore the development control system, and what convinces a local planning authority to take enforcement action. This can usefully be compared with a local planning authority's decision whether or not to grant planning permission. Secondly, a comparison can be made between planning appeals and enforcement appeals in order to determine what factors are relevant when challenging a local planning authority's decision to take enforcement proceedings. It remains to be seen whether they are the same factors that are relevant in the course of a planning appeal.

Planning appeals

There are several types of planning appeal. The commonest is the appeal which occurs when an individual is either refused planning permission, including a deemed refusal when a local planning authority fails to deal with an application for planning permission within the prescribed eight weeks, or is granted planning permission but subject to unacceptable conditions.[1] Since this is the most common, reference will be made to this type of planning appeal in order to illustrate the argument. Unless specifically stated otherwise, it can be assumed that exactly the same considerations apply to all other forms of planning appeal.

WHY APPEAL?

There is a dual purpose to the question – why appeal? Initially, it raises the issue of why a right of appeal exists. If a local planning authority, which is fully aware of national planning policy, the development control policies of its own area and the planning needs of the community, either refuses or grants planning permission subject to conditions, then it seems logical that that should be an end to the matter. In an ideal world that might be so, but in practice, the local councillors who make up the planning committee may, in reaching their decision, have neglected national planning policy, or placed undue emphasis on a single factor, such as the strength of local protest, while failing to take account of other material considerations. Furthermore, since development control and planning permission are inextricably linked to the ability of the individual to use his property as he thinks fit, then the appeal can be seen as a form of quality control. In this context it allows an official, who normally has no connection with the locality and the personalities

1 Town and Country Planning Act 1971, ss 36 and 37.

involved, to make a fresh determination of the issues, applying relevant development control policies. The official can either confirm a local planning authority's decision to refuse planning permission, or reverse it. In the case of an appeal against the content of a planning condition, the appellant might find that even more onerous conditions are imposed in addition to the one he originally found objectionable, while the conclusion that a condition is unacceptable could result in planning permission being refused outright. All this is a consequence of the fact that a decision on appeal is a fresh development control decision. It should not be imagined from this that a local planning authority is incapable of being objective or impartial. Instead, the appeal allows an applicant for planning permission to pursue the matter if the applicant feels that this is warranted on the merits of the application.

The right of appeal, if acted upon, can place a considerable strain on the resources of a local planning authority. Obviously, the longer the period which elapses between a decision and an appeal, the greater that strain can become. Circumstances can change, not to mention personnel, as well as fresh proposals being received for the building or land in question. In the light of these facts, the relevant legislation limits the time for making a planning appeal to six months from the date the decision was notified to the individual, or the expiry of any relevant period.[2] The only exception is an appeal to the Secretary of State against the decision of a local planning authority refusing consent for, or restricting the display of, an advertisement. Here, the relevant period is two months, the shorter period being justified by the very specific issues such an appeal will raise.[3]

This emphasis on the use of the appeal as a means of re-evaluating the merits of a planning application raises a second issue. Of the 403,000 planning applications which were determined in the year 1985–86, 61,000 were refused planning permission but only 16,000 went to appeal.[4] It is obvious, therefore, that a significant proportion of those individuals who are refused planning permission do not bother to appeal. Numerous explanations can be offered for why this is so. The applicant may be convinced that his application is so at odds with local or national planning policy, as to

2 Town and Country Planning General Development Order 1977, SI 1977 No 289, article 20. The relevant period referred to is the eight-week period mentioned in article 7(6) within which a local planning authority should reach a decision on a planning application.
3 Town and Country Planning (Control of Advertisements) Regulations 1984, SI 1984 No 421, reg 22(2).
4 Extracted from the planning statistics in the Journal of Planning and Environment Law.

stand no chance of success. Alternatively, it may be clear after consultation with the local planning authority, that if the scheme were modified in some way then planning permission would be granted, or an onerous condition removed. In such circumstances a fresh application for planning permission may be made instead of an appeal. In addition, the right of appeal may not be utilised because an applicant does not possess the resources, particularly the financial resources, to proceed. Appeals take time and cost money.[5]

Whatever the reasons for either choosing or declining to take advantage of the appeals process, the decision is one for the applicant to reach. It is, however, in the interests of both central and local government to have as few appeals as possible. This is because appeals stretch the resources of the local planning authority, since officials within its planning department will have to prepare a full justification of the development control decision. The Department of the Environment has also to provide adjudicators to listen to and resolve such appeals as speedily as possible. Circular 18/86, Planning Appeals decided by Written Representations, makes this very point:

> An appeal is an essential statutory safeguard within the development control system. But the process is costly to all the parties involved and also to taxpayers and ratepayers and anything that can be done to improve and expedite the process will be well worth doing.[6]

Advice given in the body of the Circular is designed to stress that appeals should be exceptional rather than routine:

> ... before a disappointed applicant for planning permission lodges an appeal there should be consultation and negotiation. Difficulties can be more quickly and cheaply resolved by discussions of this kind than if an appeal is made to the Secretary of State. An appeal is intended to be, and should remain, a last resort.[7]

Potential appellants are advised to:

> ... assess the merits of their case and the prospects of success and balance these against the costs and time involved in an appeal. In particular, careful study of the policy background – in development plans, Department circulars, advice notes and elsewhere – is essential. Clearly stated policies which have been endorsed through the structure and local plan

5 Circular 2/87, Award of Costs Incurred in Planning and Compulsory Purchase Order Proceedings, gives advice on the circumstances when the Secretary of State may award costs to one of the parties in a planning appeal. The appellant may obtain costs if a local planning authority gives a fresh reason for refusal of planning permission at a late stage in the proceedings.
6 Circular 18/86, para 2.
7 Circular 18/86, para 7.

system and which remain relevant to present day circumstances are unlikely to be set aside lightly.[8]

The Department of the Environment's view of planning appeals is a correct one in some respects. Obviously, if an appeal can be avoided this will save time and money. Yet the exhortation to look to policy may, on occasions, have a hollow ring. It may be precisely because an applicant has looked to all the appropriate policy documents that he is persuaded, in the first place to apply for planning permission, and then, to appeal. The structure plan may be vague, no local plan may exist and Department of the Environment circulars may appear to contradict what little local policy there is. Planning appeals may be symptomatic, not of the obstinacy of applicants, but of the shortcomings of the development control system, particularly with regard to policy.

APPEAL TO WHOM?

If an applicant does decide to appeal, then the next matter to be settled is who will determine that appeal. Normally, appeals are made to the Secretary of State. The sheer number of planning appeals means, however, that some machinery has to exist for others to hear appeals on the Secretary of State's behalf. The officials with responsibility for doing just that are the planning inspectors. Although they are officials of the Department of the Environment, it is the task of a Department of the Environment inspector to assess the development control arguments put forward in the course of a planning appeal, and not simply to enforce the Department of the Environment's policy. Planning inspectors are well qualified to perform this task. Some may hold formal planning qualifications, others may be professionally qualified in other fields, such as law or surveying.

The role of the planning inspector in resolving planning appeals has changed over the years. In the past, he would hear an appeal and then prepare a report containing his recommendations. These recommendations would then be submitted to the relevant Minister for him to take the final decision. If, therefore, the Secretary of State did not intend to adopt an inspector's recommendation, he had to explain why. As long as the ultimate responsibility for determining planning appeals lay with the Secretary of State, the inspector's role could be seen as one involving the gathering of evidence, the summarisation of argument and the preparation of recommendations. The Secretary of State was then free to reach a different determination on those facts and arguments.

8 Circular 18/86, para 8.

In terms of time and resources, such a method of proceeding can hardly be described as efficient. Therefore, the Secretary of State, using powers he possesses under Schedule 9 to the 1971 Act has sought to rectify the situation.[9] Regulations have been issued, specifying classes of appeal which may be determined not by the Secretary of State, but by a person appointed by him, that is, a Department of the Environment inspector. The current Regulations are the Town and Country Planning (Determination of Appeals by Appointed Persons) (Prescribed Classes) Regulations 1981.[10] Appeals covered by these Regulations include all appeals against the refusal of planning permission, or the content of conditions attached to planning permissions. Recently, the Town and Country Planning (Determination of Appeals by Appointed Persons) Regulations 1986[11] have prescribed further classes of appeal to be determined by an inspector. These are appeals in England against the refusal of listed building consent, or consent to demolish buildings in a conservation area.

Even though the purpose of the Regulations is to allow others to determine planning appeals on his behalf, the Secretary of State can, if he chooses, direct that an appeal shall be determined by him. At present, the Secretary of State is still responsible for considering appeals which involve the demolition of listed buildings, the alteration of Grade I or Grade II* listed buildings, as well as appeals in relation to buildings for which grants have been made under the Historic Buildings and Ancient Monuments Act 1953.[12] In addition, appeals which concern development by statutory undertakers will normally be determined by the Secretary of State.[13] Apart from any indication given in the Regulations, it is a matter of judgment for the Secretary of State whether he considers an appeal so important as to merit scrutiny by his Department. The factors which are relevant in persuading him of this fact have been identified as follows:[14]

(a) residential development of 150 or more houses;
(b) proposals for development of major importance and having more than local significance;
(c) proposals giving rise to significant public controversy;

9 Schedule 9, Determination of Certain Appeals by Persons Appointed by the Secretary of State.
10 SI 1981 No 804.
11 SI 1986 No 623.
12 Town and Country Planning (Determination of Appeals by Appointed Persons) Regulations 1986, SI 1986 No 623, reg 2(3).
13 Town and Country Planning (Determination of Appeals by Appointed Persons) (Prescribed Classes) Regulations 1981, SI 1981 No 804, reg 4.
14 Planning Appeals, Call-in and Major Public Inquiries 1986, Cmnd 43, para 36.

(d) proposals which raise important or novel issues of development control;
(e) retail development over 100,000 square feet;
(f) proposals for significant development in the green belt;
(g) major proposals involving the winning and working of minerals;
(h) proposals which raise significant legal difficulties;
(i) proposals against which another government department has raised major objections;
(j) cases which can only be decided in conjunction with a case over which inspectors have no jurisdication.

From this it is apparent that planning appeals will be singled out for determination by the Secretary of State which, because of their size, complexity or sensitive nature, raise important development control issues. Some of the criteria in this list are, however, far from specific. At what level opposition to a proposed development becomes 'significant public controversy' is a matter for conjecture. Nor is the list intended to provide more than a guide, the Secretary of State may always act and 'call-in' an appeal if he feels that the circumstances warrant it.

The consequence of transferring jurisdiction to determine planning appeals to Department of the Environment inspectors, is that the majority of appeals will be dealt with in this fashion. Exceptions, apart from those already mentioned, include appeals against a local planning authority's section 53 determination that a particular activity constitutes development. The explanation for their continued referral to the Secretary of State may lie in the fact that they call for an interpretation of the term 'development', rather than an interpretation of development control policy.[15] Appeals against the refusal or restriction of permission to display an advertisement also go direct to the Secretary of State.[16]

In principle, allowing inspectors to determine planning appeals on behalf of the Secretary of State seems unobjectionable. The inspector will, in all probability, have viewed the site and heard the arguments. There seems to be no good reason, therefore, why he should not finally determine the matter in the majority of cases. This makes even greater sense when it is recalled that in the days when inspectors were restricted to submitting their recommendations, those recommendations were, in the main, adopted. If

15 More prosaically, it may be because there are so few such appeals. In a fifteen-month period from January 1985 to March 1986 the Secretary of State determined only 174 sections 88, 95 and 53 appeals.
16 Town and Country Planning (Control of Advertisements) Regulations 1984, SI 1984 No 421, reg 22.

objections are to be raised to this practice they must surely relate to uncertainty over the exact role of the inspector when he determines appeals on behalf of the Secretary of State. In addition, this raises the related problem of consistency. According to the terms of Schedule 9 of the 1971 Act:

> A person appointed under this Schedule to determine an appeal shall have the like powers and duties in relation to the appeal as the Secretary of State . . .[17]

What this fails to explain, however, is the way in which the inspector is to make use of planning policy. For example, a builder refused planning permission to build fifty houses may appeal. The inspector conducting the appeal will listen to the arguments for and against granting planning permission. On behalf of the builder, reference may be made to Circular 15/84, Land for Housing, and the following statement, made in Annex A to the Circular:

> In the absence of such an identified five year supply [of land for housing] there should be a presumption in favour of granting permission for housing except where there are clear planning objections which in the circumstances of the case outweigh the need to make the land available for housing.[18]

This may be supported by the allegation that there is no five-year supply of housing land. In its turn, the local planning authority may attempt to refute this argument, as well as advancing clear planning objections to the residential development of the land in question. Any such objections may be reinforced by reference to policies in the development plan. In these circumstances, it is the task of the inspector to interpret the application of these policies to the land in question.

Since, however, the Secretary of State is an initiator of development control policy, it is always possible for him, when determining an appeal, to decline to follow his own policy guidelines. Alternatively, he might use the occasion to create new policy rather than rely on policy already set out in the usual sources. This may be exceptional, but it is perfectly feasible as long as the Secretary of State justifies his decision with adequate reasons.[19] The ability of an inspector similarly to create new policy, is more questionable. In considering his role in conducting an appeal the courts have had occasion to make the following observations. In their view, the

17 Schedule 9, para 2(1).
18 Circular 15/84, Annex A, para 3.
19 *E C Gransden & Co Ltd v Secretary of State for the Environment* [1986] JPL 519 at 521, affd on other grounds in *E C Gransden & Co Ltd v Secretary of State for the Environment* [1987] JPL 365.

inspector should not be treated as a policy maker.[20] Such an assertion seems incontrovertible if it merely points out that an inspector cannot totally disregard existing policy and attempt instead to produce his own policy on the day.

In contrast, the situation can arise where an inspector is faced with a circular or development plan whose wording is vague and needs clarification. In the course of determining an appeal he may seek to clarify or interpret that policy. In a sense, this too could be regarded as policy making. The difficulty is that if several inspectors are faced with the same problem they may not agree. In *Chelmsford Borough Council v Secretary of State for the Environment*,[1] the following view was expressed on the status of inspectors' decisions:

> He [the inspector] was not, and should not be regarded as having any authority on behalf of the Secretary of State to lay down any general policy, or as giving a decision which should be treated as a precedent for other planning applications or other planning appeals in the area, save to a limited extent.[2]

That limited extent would seem to entitle an appellant to bring to an inspector's attention other inspectors' decisions, including their interpretation of a particular policy. This does not mean that those decisions have to be followed, though presumably reasons should be given for distinguishing them.[3] In the event, this view of the role of inspectors could give rise to inconsistency in the way a particular policy is applied.

While making it clear that inspectors are not policy makers, the courts have been prepared to acknowledge that they may, by virtue of their background, possess considerable professional expertise. This may be used in evaluating expert evidence, and the arguments produced in the course of an appeal. In *Mason v Secretary of State for the Environment*,[4] an inspector was said to have misconstrued expert evidence on noise. In rejecting this contention, it was said:

> ... an inspector was not bound to follow expert evidence even if it was unchallenged. He had to bring to bear on the issues in the appeal his experience, his own expertise and his common sense. This might be particularly important where noise was concerned for it was common knowledge that the effect of noise on human beings was very variable. The measurement of noise emission by instruments was simply the best that science could do in a very subjective field.[5]

20 *Sears Blok v Secretary of State for the Environment* [1980] JPL 523.
 1 [1985] JPL 316.
 2 Ibid, 317.
 3 *Rockhold Ltd v Secretary of State for the Environment* [1986] JPL 130 at 131.
 4 [1984] JPL 332.
 5 Ibid, 333.

THE CONDUCT OF APPEALS

Planning appeals can be conducted in two ways, either by written representations,[6] or by local public inquiry.[7] Written representations necessitate the appellant and the local planning authority fully setting out their arguments in writing. Other interested parties can also submit their views in writing. The appeal is then determined, without the parties meeting, on the strength of that written evidence, though the individual determining the appeal can make a site visit beforehand.

In contrast, a public inquiry allows a personal confrontation between the parties. It resembles, in certain respects, a judicial hearing. Each party, who may or may not be legally represented, puts their case and can call expert evidence to support it. The inspector, who conducts the inquiry, takes note of the arguments produced and can seek any further clarification that he thinks necessary. Once the public hearing comes to an end, there is a site visit. After considering all the evidence, the inspector will determine whether, on the development control issues, to allow or reject the appeal. The decision is normally communicated to the parties by letter several weeks after the conclusion of the public inquiry.

There are advantages and disadvantages to these alternative methods of hearing an appeal. The advantages of written representations are that they allow an appeal to be dealt with more speedily and at less cost. When a public inquiry is to be held, a date for that inquiry has to be specified some time in advance in order to allow those concerned to prepare their case and to take account of the availability of an inspector to hold the inquiry. In contrast, where written representations are used the parties can work to a strict timetable.[8] That said, the advantage of a public inquiry is that it allows a direct exchange of views. Members of the public can attend and, if they are permitted to, can comment on the proposed development. In such circumstances what appear to be insignificant points can assume a new importance. The written representations method obviously lacks immediacy, and it is not accessible to the public at large.

In the opinion of the Department of the Environment, however,

6 For the procedure to be observed when a planning appeal is conducted by written representations, see the Town and Country Planning (Appeals) (Written Representations Procedure) Regulations 1987, SI 1987 No 701.

7 For the procedure to be observed when a planning appeal is conducted by public inquiry, see the Town and Country Planning (Inquiries Procedure) Rules 1974, SI 1974 No 419, and the Town and Country Planning Appeals (Determination by Appointed Persons) (Inquiries Procedure) Rules 1974, SI 1974 No 420.

8 That timetable is to be found in diagram form in Circular 18/86, Planning Appeals Decided by Written Representations, Appendix 2.

the advantages of the written representations method outweigh its disadvantages. This view is apparently shared by those involved in planning appeals since the majority are conducted by written representations. According to Circular 18/86:

> The written representations method is intended as a quicker, simpler and cheaper alternative to the public inquiry method of determining appeals. By 1985, the proportion of appeals dealt with by the written method had increased to about 85% of the total. In the 6 months up to June 1986 the median time for deciding transferred written representations appeals (ie those decided by Inspectors) was 19 weeks compared to 35 weeks for inquiry appeals determined by Inspectors. There are similar time advantages for decisions taken by the Secretary of State. The Departments will, therefore, continue to encourage the use of the written procedure whereever appropriate.[9]

The inference to be drawn from this statement is, that although the written representations method may be satisfactory in the majority of planning appeals, circumstances may exist where this will not be so. Obviously, the more complex a development appeal, the more issues involved and the greater the level of public interest, the more justification there may be for holding a public inquiry. As matters stand at present, the choice of procedure is determined by the parties. Hence, it is possible for either the local planning authority or the applicant to insist on a public inquiry however straightforward the appeal. Alternatively, the parties could agree to use the written representations method in circumstances where the complexity of the issues involved would suggest otherwise. When such situations arise, the Department of the Environment appears to have some discretion in the matter and, for example, rather than categorically refuse a request for a public inquiry, an informal hearing may be suggested as an alternative. This approach is discussed in Circular 18/86:

> It remains the right of both the appellant and the LPA to be heard by the Planning Inspector. They should continue to indicate whether they want an inquiry. The Departments will in addition occasionally conclude that an inquiry is necessary in the public interest, even though neither party has opted for one. There are also more straightforward cases where a hearing is sought, but which could be dealt with by informal hearing. The Departments will continue to suggest this process where they consider it to be appropriate.[10]

The informal hearing represents a halfway house. It satisfies the wish of one or both of the parties to be heard without the formalities of a public inquiry. It is ideal when the planning appeal is uncompli-

9 Circular 18/86, para 12.
10 Circular 18/86, para 13.

cated. A Code of Practice exists describing the arrangements for such hearings.[11] That Code accurately describes the purpose of an informal hearing:

> The informal hearing procedure is intended to save time and money for the parties, and to allow for the Inspector to lead a discussion about the matters at issue in an appeal. The aim is to give everybody a fair hearing and to provide the Inspector with all the information necessary in order to come to his decision, but in a more relaxed and less formal atmosphere than at a public inquiry.[12]

As to the correct procedure to be followed on appeal, that depends on how the appeal is to be conducted. If it is to be determined by the written representations method then a timetable is set by the Department of the Environment which indicates what information should be sent, to whom and when. A diagrammatic representation of that timetable is set out in Circular 18/86. The aim is to ensure that before a decision is reached:

(i) the appellant has notified the local planning authority of his reasons for appealing;

(ii) the local planning authority has informed the appellant of its reasons for arriving at the decision to which he objects;

(iii) each party has had the chance to comment on their opponent's case;

(iv) the views of interested third parties have been taken into account and commented upon when necessary;

(v) any exchange of views is as succinct as possible, though a local planning authority is given an opportunity to expand its argument beyond the reasons it may initially have given when determining the application.

By observing the timetable and these simple rules, it should be possible to guarantee that an appeal has been handled fairly and cannot, therefore, be the subject of a challenge in the courts on the grounds of some procedural impropriety.[13]

Where an appeal is conducted, not by the written representations method but by means of public inquiry, the procedure to be followed is set out in the Town and Country Planning (Inquiries Procedure) Rules 1974[14] and the Town and Country Planning Appeals (Determination by Appointed Persons) (Inquiries Procedure)

---

11 *Informal Hearing for Planning Appeals – Code of Practice*. The Code is published by the Department of the Environment and is reproduced in the Encyclopedia of Planning, Vol 2, in the notes accompanying s 36 of the 1971 Act.

12 *Informal Hearing for Planning Appeals*, para 1.

13 1971 Act, s 245.

14 SI 1974 No 419.

Rules 1974.[15] The set of rules to be followed depends on whether the Secretary of State or an inspector will finally determine that appeal. Each set of rules gives a description of what has to be done prior to the holding of an inquiry, the procedures to be observed in the course of the inquiry, and post-inquiry conduct. Broadly, the requirements of the two sets of rules are similar. The aim is to ensure, once again, that when a decision is reached, there are no grounds for challenging it in the courts on the basis that it was not fairly made.

Clearly, where an appeal is conducted by public inquiry the rules must anticipate such eventualities as a request for postponement, which will not arise when an appeal is determined by the written representations method. Consequently, the detail to be found in the Inquiries Procedure Rules is much greater than that to be observed in the timetable for written representations. It is also a truism, but one which deserves repeating, that the greater the detail, the greater the opportunity for errors to be made. A failure to observe the correct procedure can be a ground for challenging a decision in the courts, but only if it causes substantial prejudice to the person concerned.[16]

While no detailed account will be given of the Inquiries Procedure Rules, certain general points need to be made concerning their operation. Attention needs to be drawn to the fact that the procedure to be observed during the duration of the inquiry is largely, according to those Rules, a matter for the inspector's discretion.[17] For example, an inspector has discretion in the matter of who may appear at a public inquiry, apart, that is, from those parties who have a right to appear.[18] Where the Rules offer guidance on what should occur, on the issue of cross-examination,[19] for example, parallels are immediately suggested between a public inquiry and a judicial hearing. Whether such a comparison is appropriate depends, perhaps, on what a public inquiry seeks to achieve. A judicial hearing is an adversarial process with one party trying to prove, and the other disprove, a particular contention. In contrast,

15 SI 1974 No 420.
16 1971 Act, s 245(4)(b).
17 Town and Country Planning (Inquiries Procedure) Rules 1974, SI 1974 No 419, rule 10(1); Town and Country Planning Appeals (Determination by Appointed Persons) (Inquiries Procedure) Rules 1974, SI 1974 No 420, rule 12(1).
18 Town and Country Planning (Inquiries Procedure) Rules 1974, SI 1974 No 419, rule 7(2); Town and Country Planning Appeals (Determination by Appointed Persons) (Inquiries Procedure) Rules 1974, SI 1974 No 420, rule 9(2).
19 Town and Country Planning (Inquiries Procedure) Rules 1974, SI 1974 No 419, rule 10(3); Town and Country Planning Appeals (Determination by Appointed Persons) (Inquiries Procedure) Rules 1974, SI 1974 No 420, rule 12(3).

the purpose of the public inquiry is to allow the correct development control decision to be taken.

The use of judicial techniques, such as cross-examination, at a public inquiry has its critics, but the fact that these procedures are employed may be a reflection of the desire to treat each party fairly. This has not prevented calls being made for inspectors to adopt a more inquisitorial approach to the public inquiry procedure.[20] An inspector, it is argued, should actively seek information from the parties, rather than simply listen to argument. If, however, an inspector is minded to do just this, he should avoid doing so in circumstances that cause others to believe either that he has pre-judged the issue, or that he is not giving the other party a chance to rebut what 'his opponent' has said.[1] This is again a reflection of the need to be fair.

The same need to be fair also accounts for the quite detailed rules on the procedures to be observed once a public inquiry has ended. Should new evidence be offered by one of the parties and be taken into account, or a new issue of fact be raised, then both parties must be given an adequate opportunity to comment, including the option of asking for the public inquiry to be reopened.[2] The one positive point in favour of this apparent obsession with fairness, is that any judicial challenge is unlikely to succeed if the rules are observed. Whether, on the other hand, it leads to important development control issues being neglected or obscured is another question.

THE DECISION

Whether a planning appeal is determined using the written representations method or a public inquiry, and whether the responsibility for the decision rests with an inspector or the Secretary of State, the culmination of every appeal is a decision letter. The decision letter is exceedingly important, since it contains a summary of the arguments raised during the course of the appeal, as well as the reasons justifying the particular decision reached. Its contents have a twofold importance. They indicate to the appellant and the local planning authority what factors, including development control policy, were crucial in reaching that particular decision. In addition, that letter can provide the basis for a challenge to the courts. Although that process is discussed in the next chapter, it

20 Keeble L *Fighting Planning Appeals* (1985) pp 30–31.
 1 See, for example, *Halifax Building Society v Secretary of State for the Environment* [1983] JPL 816.
 2 Town and Country Planning (Inquiries Procedure) Rules 1974, SI 1974 No 419, rule 12; Town and Country Planning Appeals (Determination by Appointed Persons) (Inquiries Procedure) Rules 1974, SI 1974 No 420, rule 14.

should be appreciated at this stage that it is from the decision letter that evidence will be sought to support such a challenge.

This puts the writer of the decision letter in a dilemma. However carefully such a letter is drafted, there may be the occasional ambiguity or omission. If this occurs, and if it is made the subject of a judicial challenge, the courts have to assess whether its presence warrants the setting aside of that particular development control decision. In evaluating the decision letter the courts can either subject it to a detailed analysis, or regard it as unsuitable for such treatment, since the letter is intended to be read as a whole and against the background of the earlier proceedings. Evidence can be produced from the cases to illustrate each approach.[3] If one approach is to be preferred, however, it is to consider the decision letter as a whole. Not only does this appear the more sensible approach, but it seems to be the one favoured by the courts. Indeed, the courts appear to have gone even further by suggesting that the decision letter which determines an appeal by written representations can be briefer and more to the point than the decision letter which determines a public inquiry.[4] The distinction is justified on the basis that written representations appeals will be straightforward with no disputes over facts.

Enforcement

WHY DO BREACHES OCCUR?

Research seems to suggest that there are a variety of reasons why an individual may fail to observe the development control system.[5] Ignorance is certainly a factor. It can range from total ignorance of the existence of the development control system, to partial ignorance. An individual may not appreciate the significance of the term 'development', believing that the planned activity either does not constitute development, or is permitted development. Obviously, advice can be sought from the local planning authority, but this fact may not be appreciated. There is, of course, the additional burden of planning fees which are levied each time an application is made

3 Some judges examine a decision letter line by line, others take a more generous approach. See, for example, *Dimsdale Developments (South East) Ltd v Secretary of State for the Environment* [1986] JPL 276, *Chelmsford Borough Council v Secretary of State for the Environment* [1986] JPL 112.

4 *Sir George Grenfell-Baines v Secretary of State for the Environment* [1985] JPL 256 at 257.

5 Whether the complexity of the enforcement system is itself a reason is open to question.

for planning permission. Given these circumstances, therefore, an individual may prefer to trust his own understanding of the planning system. Ignorance apart, the instances where an individual deliberately decides to flout the development control system may be comparatively rare.[6] Much will depend on the particular circumstances of the case. Deliberate demolition of a listed building may make economic sense to a developer when compared with the fine that can be imposed for this particular breach of the development control system.[7] Other deliberate breaches of development control may simply be incidents in a wider set of events. The decision to establish a caravan site without planning permission may be seen by the instigator as a protest against the failure of a local authority to provide gypsy caravan sites.

Apart from dealing with failures to apply for planning permission or listed building consent, enforcement proceedings may occur when conditions attached to a grant of planning permission are deliberately flouted. Here, there is no question of ignorance. As has already been mentioned, an individual who believes a condition is unreasonable can appeal. The decision not to appeal, therefore, but simply to ignore a condition, is definitely premeditated, though it is possible that an individual may not fully appreciate the consequences of a condition until he has acted upon the planning permission, by which time it will be too late to appeal.[8]

HOW ARE BREACHES DISCOVERED?

A breach of the development control system will not automatically come to the attention of a local planning authority. Breaches become apparent in various ways – the most usual is a complaint by a neighbour. An individual may become self-employed, selling rustic bird tables from his home. As the business becomes more successful neighbours may become aware of lorries delivering materials to the house, noise from equipment, and individuals arriving to purchase bird tables. Once traffic and noise reach a certain level, neighbours may complain and it is at that stage that a local planning authority may be alerted to a possible breach of the development control system.

6 These are more likely to be associated with a situation where the individual has been warned of restrictions on his ability to act. For example, where a tree preservation order is in existence.

7 The fine cannot exceed £1,000 on a summary conviction. Provision is made in s 55 of the 1971 Act for a trial on indictment in which case the fine imposed can have some relationship to any financial benefit which has accrued to the individual. Besides fines a prison sentence is also possible.

8 Six months is the period allowed for an appeal – Town and Country Planning General Development Order 1977, SI 1977 No 289, article 20.

There is evidence that local planning authorities rely to a considerable extent on members of the public alerting them to breaches of development control.[9] The alternative is for local planning authorities themselves to have some systematic scheme for monitoring development in their area. How successful this would be, and how feasible in terms of manpower and resources, is a difficult matter. There is evidence that some local planning authorities do not have a single individual engaged in the business of enforcement.[10] Instead, breaches of development control are located mainly by chance, because of the efforts of members of the public, amenity societies or even local government officials investigating some other matter, such as noise.

While the difficulties of a local planning authority in pinpointing unauthorised development may be apparent, there seems less excuse for local planning authorities failing to investigate whether conditions attached to a grant of planning permission are being observed. Here, a monitoring system could be devised, and research conducted on this issue suggests this does sometimes occur.[11] Local planning authorities might also devise a system to focus special attention on listed buildings, or on trees which are the subject of tree preservation orders.

THE ENFORCEMENT PROCESS

Having described the circumstances in which breaches of the development control system can occur, it now becomes necessary to comment on the process of enforcement. A substantial portion of the 1971 Act is devoted to the topic, which, it has to be said, is far from straightforward. The power to initiate enforcement procedures is given to a local planning authority in section 87(1) of the 1971 Act:

> Where it appears to the local planning authority that there has been a breach of planning control after the end of 1963, then, subject to the following provisions of this section, the authority, if they consider it expedient to do so having regard to the provisions of the development plan and to any other material considerations, may issue a notice requiring the breach to be remedied...

The first point to note about the power to enforce is that it is discretionary. A local planning authority may act, 'if they consider it expedient to do so', having had regard to those very factors which

9 Jowell J & Millichap D 'The Enforcement of Planning Law: A Report and some Proposals', Journal of Planning and Environment Law, 1985, pp 482–498.
10 *Jowell & Millichap*, pp 482–483.
11 *Jowell & Millichap*, p 483.

are relevant when the local planning authority is determining whether or not to grant planning permission. Therefore, despite receiving numerous complaints about a breach of planning control, a local planning authority could choose not to act, provided it does so on grounds which are relevant, that is, on planning grounds. In practice, it appears that enforcement is regarded as a last resort. A local planning authority may try to resolve a problem by negotiation, or by accepting a retrospective application for planning permission. Indeed, minor breaches may be totally ignored if they appear to be causing no inconvenience.[12] Far from denigrating this approach, it has the support of the Department of the Environment in Circular 22/80:

> This permissive power [in section 87(1)] should be used, in regard to either operational development or material changes of use, only where planning reasons clearly warrant such action, and there is no alternative to enforcement proceedings.[13]

It has to be said, however, as, by implication, does Circular 22/80, that the arguments for ignoring breaches of planning conditions are less convincing. As Circular 1/85 stresses, planning conditions should be used only if they are necessary to permit a particular development to proceed.[14] If those very conditions are then neglected, arguably every effort should then be made to rectify the situation, including the use of enforcement proceedings.

If a local planning authority does decide to issue an enforcement notice, the object of that notice is to rectify the breach of planning control. Therefore, besides specifying the breach, the notice will also indicate the steps which must be taken to rectify it. According to section 87(9):

> In this section 'steps to be taken in order to remedy the breach' means (according to the particular circumstances of the breach) steps for the purpose –
> (a) of restoring the land to its condition before the development took place; or
> (b) of securing compliance with the conditions or limitations subject to which planning permission was granted,
> including –
>   (i) the demolition or alteration of any building or works;
>   (ii) the discontinuance of any use of land; and
>   (iii) the carrying out on land of any building or other operations.

12 This appears logical since the main reason for taking enforcement action should be to prevent damage to the amenity of an area.
13 Circular 22/80, para 15.
14 Circular 1/85, The Use of Conditions in Planning Permissions, para 12.

The notice should also indicate the period within which such steps should be taken.

It is very plain, therefore, that the object of an enforcement notice is remedial as opposed to penal. No punishment is to be inflicted on the individual who breaches planning control. This is in direct contrast with the position of an individual who fells a tree protected by a tree preservation order, or who demolishes or alters a listed building without authorisation.[15] In such a situation a criminal sanction, in the form of a fine, is immediately imposed, presumably on the basis that such actions may be much harder, if not impossible, to rectify.

While the principle underlying an enforcement notice seems comparatively clear, the procedure concerning the issue of such a notice is fraught with legal pitfalls which act as a trap for the unwary, and can render an enforcement notice ineffective. Cases abound on whether an enforcement notice specifies with sufficient clarity the steps which must be taken to remedy a breach, or the relevant key dates, such as the date for compliance.[16] This emphasis on precision in enforcement notices may seem unduly legalistic. Indeed, the evidence is that it may actively discourage local planning authorities from proceeding with enforcement action.[17] Its justification lies in the fact that the courts, by insisting on the presence of certain information, are doing no more than insisting on what the legislation itself requires. In addition, any individual, who is the object of an enforcement notice, may have to undertake activities which can involve a considerable financial burden. Arguably, it is only fair that he knows exactly what the breach is, and how and when it is supposed to be remedied. A vaguely worded notice may cause work to be undertaken which is not necessary, or indeed, which is not intended. Nor should it be forgotten that failure to comply with an enforcement notice is a criminal offence. Once again, the concept of fairness is seen as crucial, requiring very exacting standards of behaviour from a local planning authority.

Apart from requiring precision in the content of an enforcement notice, section 87 places two important restrictions on the initiation of enforcement proceedings. The first of these restrictions is the four-year rule set out in section 87(4):

> An enforcement notice which relates to a breach of planning control consisting in –

15 1971 Act, ss 55 and 102.
16 See, for example, *Metallic Protectives Ltd v Secretary of State for the Environment* [1976] JPL 166, *Rhymney Valley District Council v Secretary of State for Wales* [1985] JPL 27, *King and King v Secretary of State for the Environment* [1981] JPL 813.
17 *Jowell & Millichap*, p 484.

(a) the carrying out without planning permission of building, engineering, mining or other operations in, on, over or under land; or

(b) the failure to comply with any condition or limitation which relates to the carrying out of such operations and subject to which planning permission was granted for the development of that land; or

(c) the making without planning permission of a change of use of any building to use as a single dwelling-house; or

(d) the failure to comply with a condition which prohibits or has the effect of preventing a change of use of a building to use as a single dwelling-house,

may be issued only within the period of four years from the date of the breach.

From the terms of the subsection it is apparent that its aim is to ensure that enforcement proceedings must be taken within four years. The logic is that if no action is taken in that period, then that particular breach of planning control can hardly represent a threat to the amenity of the neighbourhood. Yet the point was made earlier in this chapter that a breach of planning control may not always be particularly apparent. Therefore, it is worth noting that the four-year rule does not apply to material changes of use, apart from those specifically mentioned in the subsection. Material changes of use can happen gradually over a period of years. The same is not true of building, mining, engineering or other operations. It seems sensible, therefore, to treat the two in a different fashion.

However, this has not always been so. Prior to the Town and Country Planning Act 1968, the four-year rule applied to all forms of unauthorised development. When the distinction was made in the 1968 Act, therefore, steps were taken to ensure that material changes of use which could not previously have been the subject of enforcement proceedings would not lose that immunity. This explains the reference to 'a breach of planning control after the end of 1963' in section 87(1). Any breach occurring before that date was immune, and so was not affected by the 1968 Act, nor the 1971 Act.

It should be plain at this stage that the decision to issue an enforcement notice is not one to be taken lightly. It requires many factors to be taken into account. Once an enforcement notice has been issued, however, then the individual receiving the notice can either comply or appeal to the Secretary of State. Section 88(2) sets out the grounds for appeal. They are:

(a) that planning permission ought to be granted for the development to which the notice relates or, as the case may be, that a condition or limitation alleged in the enforcement notice not to have been complied with ought to be discharged;

   (b) that the matters alleged in the notice do not constitute a breach of planning control;

   (c) that the breach of planning control alleged in the notice has not taken place;

   (d) in the case of a notice which, by virtue of section 87(4) of this Act, may be issued only within the period of four years from the date of the breach of planning control to which the notice relates, that that period has elapsed at the date when the notice was issued;

   (e) in the case of a notice not falling within paragraph (d) ... that the breach of planning control alleged by the notice occurred before the beginning of 1964;

   (f) that copies of the enforcement notice were not served as required by section 87(5) of this Act;

   (g) that the steps required by the notice to be taken exceed what is necessary to remedy any breach of planning control or to achieve a purpose specified in section 87(10) of this Act;

   (h) that the period specified in the notice as the period within which any step is to be taken falls short of what should reasonably be allowed.

There are two aspects to enforcement appeals. Those aspects are the grounds on which such appeals can be made and the form which such appeals take. Both of these will be discussed, starting with the grounds for appeal which were outlined in the previous paragraph. An initial reading of those grounds for appeal will reveal that the circumstances specified in paragraphs (b)–(e) need no further explanation. The grounds specified in paragraph (f), however, immediately raise questions as to the content of section 87(5) of the 1971 Act. This provides:

> A copy of an enforcement notice shall be served, not later than 28 days after the date of its issue and not later than 28 days before the date specified in the notice as the date on which it is to take effect –
>
>   (a) on the owner and on the occupier of the land to which it relates; and
>
>   (b) on any other person having an interest in that land, being an interest which in the opinion of the authority is materially affected by the notice.

Unfortunately section 87(5) cannot be read in isolation, but must be viewed in conjunction with other legislative provisions. For example, the term 'owner' is defined in the interpretation section, section 290, of the 1971 Act. Although a local planning authority uses its best efforts to serve everyone affected with an enforcement notice, someone with the necessary interest in the land may still be omitted. This then raises the question of who should appeal against such an omission – an individual who has been correctly served or the person who alleges that they should have been served, but were not. The answer appears to lie in section 88(1):

> A person having an interest in the land to which an enforcement notice relates may, at any time before the date specified in the notice as the date on which it is to take effect, appeal to the Secretary of State against the notice, whether or not a copy of it has been served on him.

Either of these individuals might, therefore, appeal. Nor indeed is their appeal confined to this particular ground set out in paragraph (f). A person with the relevant interest, whether or not they have received a copy of the enforcement notice, can appeal on any of the grounds (a)–(h).

This raises the confusing possibility that enforcement proceedings could be initiated against allegedly unauthorised development taking place on land owned by A, occupied by B and in which C has a relevant interest. A and B are served with a copy of the enforcement notice but not C. A, B and C could all appeal against the enforcement notice, but on totally different grounds. Any of the three could raise the failure to comply with section 87(5).

However, even if A, B or C successfully proves a breach of section 87(5), this would not necessarily have an effect on the validity of the enforcement notice. Section 88A(3) of the 1971 Act provides:

> Where it would otherwise be a ground for determining such an appeal in favour of the appellant that a person required to be served with a copy of the enforcement notice was not served, the Secretary of State may disregard that fact if neither the appellant nor that person has been substantially prejudiced by the failure to serve him.

It can be argued that failure to serve an individual with a copy of an enforcement notice may result in his not being alerted to his right of appeal, as well as rendering him liable to a criminal prosecution. This could be regarded as substantial prejudice. Where an individual appeals without receiving a copy of the enforcement notice, this can be regarded as proof that no substantial prejudice has been suffered. Therefore, the usefulness of paragraph (f) as a basis for appeal may depend on who exactly is making an appeal.

Grounds (g) and (h) are an attempt to question, not the validity of an enforcement notice, but rather, to allege that too much is demanded by the local planning authority. Too much, that is, either in the nature of the steps required to remedy the breach, or the time allowed in which to do it. Should the Secretary of State agree, then he is able to vary the terms of the enforcement notice under the powers given to him by section 88A(1) of the 1971 Act.

Finally, it is necessary to consider the grounds for appeal set out in paragraph (a), namely, that planning permission ought to be granted or a condition discharged. On first reading this appears a most unusual ground for appeal. Enforcement proceedings are normally taken only when a local planning authority is convinced that the unauthorised development poses an unacceptable threat to the amenity of its area. If the local planning authority had been willing to grant planning permission then presumably it would have asked for a retrospective application or, in other circumstances, the local planning authority would not have attached the condition which is being ignored. Perhaps the explanation for this particular ground for appeal lies in the fact that the local planning authority's decision to take enforcement action is regarded as being equivalent to the refusal of planning permission.[18] Therefore, this ground for appeal is the equivalent of the appeal to the Secretary of State when planning permission is refused.

Should an individual wish to appeal on the basis that planning permission should be granted, or a condition be discharged, then argument will centre on development control issues. It is interesting to compare an appeal on this basis with appeals which do not dispute the validity of the enforcement notice, but simply ask for more time, or for the remedial work to be modified in some way. In these circumstances, the most that can be expected is that the Secretary of State will vary the enforcement notice. This can in turn be contrasted with an appeal which disputes the truth of what is alleged in the enforcement notice. Success here will lead to the enforcement notice being discharged. Improprieties associated with the service of an enforcement notice may or may not result in its being discharged, depending on the degree of prejudice suffered.

It would appear, therefore, that an individual served with an enforcement notice has a host of alternatives open to him on appeal, not all of which will result in the enforcement notice being discharged. One ground for appeal appears, however, to be missing, that is, an opportunity to assert that the contents of the enforcement notice are defective since, for example, they do not give in sufficient detail the steps which have to be taken in order to remedy the particular breach of planning control. When this occurs, the relevant course of action is not an appeal to the Secretary of State. Since the enforcement notice is not drawn up in accordance with section 87 of the 1971 Act, it is a nullity, that is, of no effect. An appeal cannot correct something which, in the eyes of the law, does

18 In determining whether or not to take enforcement action a local planning authority has regard to such matters as the development plan and other material considerations. These are exactly the same factors which are relevant in determining a planning application. If, therefore, a local planning authority believes that the unauthorised development could remain, it would invite an application for planning permission. Its decision to take enforcement proceedings is, therefore, tantamount to refusing planning permission.

not exist. Consequently, action must be taken in the courts to have the enforcement notice set aside.[19]

Apart from the grounds for appeal, reference was also made to the procedure adopted on appeal. Briefly, the procedure is, in most respects, similar to that already described when discussing planning appeals. It is set out in section 88 of the 1971 Act and the Town and Country Planning (Enforcement Notices and Appeals) Regulations 1981[20] and the Town and Country Planning (Enforcement) (Inquiries Procedure) Rules 1981.[1] The idea is that once an individual has given notice of appeal, then there should be an exchange between the parties, that is, between the appellant and the local planning authority, of the arguments on which they intend to rely. The intention is that the exchange should take place as speedily as possible. The parties then have the choice between the appeal being heard at a public inquiry, or decided by written representations. Finally, the majority of enforcement appeals are determined, not by the Secretary of State, but by an inspector. This is by virtue of the Town and Country Planning (Determination of Appeals by Appointed Persons) (Prescribed Classes) Regulations 1981;[2] only enforcement appeals involving statutory undertakers will be considered by the Secretary of State.

Once an enforcement appeal has been determined, this is not an end to the matter. It is possible to pursue the matter further by applying to the High Court. According to section 246 of the 1971 Act, either the appellant or the local planning authority, or indeed any other person with an interest in the land to which the notice relates, can appeal on a point of law to the High Court. The powers of the court in such circumstances are limited. It is not possible for the court to quash an enforcement notice should an error have been made. Instead, if there is an error of law, the matter is referred back to the Secretary of State, who is expected to rectify the matter himself, by rehearing the appeal for example. In certain circumstances it may also be possible to question the validity of a decision made on an enforcement appeal under the terms of section 245 of the 1971 Act.[3]

19 The appropriate remedy to achieve this is an application for judicial review. See *Rhymney Valley District Council v Secretary of State for Wales* [1985] JPL 27.
20 SI 1981 No 1742.
 1 SI 1981 No 1743.
 2 SI 1981 No 804.
 3 Section 245 allows a decision to be challenged because the person making it has exceeded his powers, or not observed a relevant procedure. This contrasts with the right of appeal in section 246. According to section 245 read in conjuction with section 242, only the Secretary of State for the Environment's decision to grant planning permission or discharge a condition can be reviewed in this fashion.

What should be apparent at this stage is the delay which is possible between the issue of an enforcement notice, and its final confirmation after appeals to the Secretary of State and the High Court. Throughout the whole of this period the unauthorised development remains, possibly causing considerable disruption to the neighbourhood. Once an enforcement notice has been confirmed, if it is not then complied with, section 89 of the 1971 Act allows the owner of the land to be fined. Even at this stage, when the individual is the subject of a criminal prosecution, it is still possible to raise, as a defence, the argument that the enforcement notice is a nullity.[4] It is, however, not possible at this late stage to raise any of the arguments which are set out as grounds for appeal under section 88(2) of the 1971 Act. Any individual who, after that initial fine, still does not comply, can then become the subject of a daily fine.[5]

Undoubtedly, the enforcement process can be a long and complex one. Indeed, it is tempting to allow the complexities of the procedure to obscure the significance of enforcement for the development control system. That significance is a negative and indirect one. Development control concerns itself with restricting the right of the individual to use his property as he wishes. The justification for this is the good of the community as a whole. Rarely does the development control system go beyond this regulatory function and demand that an individual use his property in a particular way.[6] Enforcement ensures that an individual, who decides to ignore the system and do what he likes with his property, is brought back into line. What is important, if the integrity of the development control system is to be maintained, is why the individual decides to step out of line and the way he is then forced to comply.

Stop notices

As an addendum to this section on enforcement two additional methods of securing compliance with the development control system need to be briefly discussed: stop notices and injunctions. One of the difficulties associated with an enforcement notice is that a breach of planning control can continue while an appeal is made against the enforcement notice. In order to prevent this occurring,

4 If it can be shown to be a nullity then quite obviously it cannot have been contravened.

5 This is by virtue of section 89(4) – unauthorised operational development – and section 89(5) – unauthorised use – of the 1971 Act. The fines can continue until the enforcement notice is observed.

6 His property can be acquired from him using powers of compulsory purchase, so that some other individual can use it in a particular way.

section 90 of the 1971 Act allows the service of a stop notice. Section 90(1) describes the circumstances in which this can occur.

Where in respect of any land the local planning authority –
(a) have served a copy of an enforcement notice requiring a breach of planning control to be remedied; but
(b) consider it expedient to prevent, before the expiry of the period allowed for compliance with the notice, the carrying out of any activity which is, or is included in, a matter alleged by the notice to constitute the breach,
then... they may at any time before the notice takes effect serve a further notice (in this Act referred to as a 'stop notice') referring to, and having annexed to it a copy of, the enforcement notice and prohibiting the carrying out of that activity on the land, or any part of it specified in the stop notice.

From this it is plain that a stop notice can be used only in conjunction with an enforcement notice, in order to prevent allegedly unauthorised activities from continuing. Under the terms of section 90(2) there are certain activities which cannot be restrained by a stop notice. They include the use of any building as a dwelling-house, or a piece of land as the site for a caravan occupied as a main residence. Nor must activities be restrained which may be necessary to remedy the breach, or which commenced more than twelve months previously, excluding building, engineering, mining or other operations as well as the deposit of waste.

A stop notice can take effect almost immediately after it is served, namely within three days.[7] A stop notice ceases when the enforcement notice is withdrawn, or an individual complies with the enforcement notice. It is, according to section 90(7) of the 1971 Act, a criminal offence punishable by a fine to fail to comply with a stop notice. An individual charged with such an offence can, however, raise questions regarding the validity of the stop notice in the course of those proceedings. It can, for example, be argued that the activity in the stop notice falls within that list of activities which cannot be restrained by a stop notice.[8]

From this description, a stop notice would seem the ideal device to employ if a local planning authority wishes to restrain behaviour which is seen as damaging to the amenity of the area. It is puzzling, therefore, that surveys apparently reveal little use being made of the stop notice.[9] The explanation is, however, very straightforward. If a stop notice is issued and the enforcement notice which it is

7 1971 Act, s 90(3).
8 Ibid, s 90(2).
9 *Jowell & Millichap*, p 485.

designed to supplement is, for example, quashed or varied on appeal, relying on one of the grounds mentioned in section 88(2) (b)–(h) then compensation becomes payable.[10] Under the terms of section 177 of the 1971 Act, the payment made is to compensate for 'any loss or damage directly attributable to the prohibition contained in the notice'. It is certainly possible to imagine situations where a stop notice could cause considerable loss. Circular 4/87, for example, cites the following situations:

> The costs to a firm may vary from having to modify a production process, at little or no additional cost (at one extreme), to the complete cessation of a business (at the other), with consequent loss of jobs, failure to complete contracts, or bankruptcy.[11]

With these dire warnings ringing in its ears, and the prospect of having to pay considerable sums by way of compensation if a mistake is made, it may be a brave local planning authority which chooses to issue stop notices freely.

Injunctions

There is one remaining way whereby a local authority may attempt to restrain unauthorised development swiftly. This is by use of an injunction. As a result of the power given to a local authority in section 222 of the Local Government Act 1972, it is possible for that local authority to apply to the court for an injunction.[12] Once issued an injunction has the effect of restraining the particular activity mentioned in it. Failure to comply with an injunction is a contempt of court and can result in imprisonment. In the past the courts have been reluctant to grant injunctions to restrain behaviour which also amounts to a criminal offence.[13] The argument is that Parliament is responsible for fixing the punishment for a particular offence. To use an injunction might be to punish certain behaviour far more severely than Parliament intended.

In a recent pair of cases, *Runnymede Borough Council v Ball*[14] and *Runnymede Borough Council v Smith*,[15] the courts have indi-

10 The rules governing claims for compensation are to be found in the Town and Country Planning General Regulations 1976, SI 1976 No 1419.
11 Circular 4/87, Section 90 of the Town and Country Planning Act 1971: Provisions and Procedures for Stop Notices, Annex 2, para 3.
12 Provided a local authority considers it expedient for the promotion or protection of the interests of the inhabitants of its area.
13 See the comments of the House of Lords in *Gouriet v Union of Post Office Workers* [1978] AC 435.
14 [1986] 1 All ER 629.
15 [1986] JPL 592.

cated the circumstances when they might be willing to grant an injunction to prevent a breach of development control. The key to the courts' attitude is how great a threat the unauthorised activity presents to the amenity of the area and how easy the damage will be to reverse, if it should continue. In *Runnymede Borough Council v Ball*, the court was convinced of the danger to the environment and the difficulty of restoring the situation if the enforcement proceedings went their lengthy course. An injunction was granted without any proof, therefore, that, if the enforcement notice was confirmed, the notice would not be obeyed. In *Runnymede Borough Council v Smith*, the court was unconvinced that the situation posed a similar danger and, therefore, refused to award an injunction. Should it be awarded, an injunction is an extremely speedy and effective method of control. The problem is that the court may be willing to grant an injunction only in situations where the threat to the environment is seen as particularly serious.

Chapter 10

The courts: their role in the process of development control

The aim of this final chapter is an ambitious one. It is to analyse the role played by the courts in the development control process. Reference has regularly been made throughout this book to statutes and judicial decisions. The danger is that these frequent citations of the law in examining the development control process can cause its importance to be over-exaggerated and the role of the courts misunderstood. This book is an attempt to redress the balance. Policy, formulated from a mixture of political dogma, economic forces, planning theory and design principle, is revealed as the driving force of the development control process. Legislation, such as the Town and Country Planning Act 1971, is merely an engine to put that policy into practice or, alternatively, a barrier to be negotiated before a policy goal may be achieved.

If the content of planning legislation were to be analysed, much of it would be seen as concerned with procedural matters. Great importance is attached to having a procedural framework which specifies who must be consulted, when they must be consulted, and to what end. Although the value of certain procedural requirements, such as the need to consult, has been questioned from time to time, there is strength in the argument that, by its very nature, a procedural framework does much to ensure the making of reasoned decisions.[1] Instead of being applied in an arbitrary fashion, therefore, planning policy is forced to take account of the individual circumstances of each case, since the procedural framework operates with this end in view. Yet these procedural requirements are not responsible for creating the policy, but merely create a channel to prevent that policy overwhelming other relevant factors.

Other issues dealt with in planning legislation include the creation of powers which may be exercised at the discretion of a local planning authority. The power to designate conservation areas is one such example.[2] It is a matter for the local planning authority

1 Although in the case of enforcement proceedings, the procedural requirements may represent a disincentive. See Chapter 9.
2 Town and Country Planning Act 1971, s 277.

which specific areas will benefit from the exercise of such a power. Key terms, such as 'development', are also defined in planning legislation.[3] Yet, for all the thousands of words devoted to the analysis of such terms, they are merely a means to an end. Should a proposed scheme not fall within the legal definition of the term 'development', then this means that its quality will not be assessed in the light of a local planning authority's policy on development. Policy is rarely mentioned in planning legislation. Rather, reference to policy is implied, as in section 29(1) of the 1971 Act, which mentions 'any other material considerations'. However, a lack of any specific mention of the term should not obscure the fact that essentially planning legislation is designed to secure the application of development control policy.

The function of the courts

Before moving on to questions of detail, certain general points need to be made about the tasks performed by the courts. Essentially, the courts function as watchdogs. On the one hand, individual citizens may flout the development control system and development may go ahead without planning permission. In such circumstances, the courts are a last resort, with powers to punish the offender by fine or imprisonment.

On the other hand, those who administer the development control system can just as easily flout the system they are meant to observe. Statutory procedures may be ignored, or matters may be taken into account which have no relevance to the decision to grant or refuse planning permission. In such circumstances, while it is desirable that the courts intervene, punishment, in the shape of a fine, is not seen as appropriate. Instead, the courts will remedy the damage done by setting aside any decision which has been affected by an administrative body's oversight. What should be clear from this brief description of the courts' powers, is that it is not their task either to approve, or to disapprove of a decision on its merits. Rather, the courts are there to ensure that the law is observed by everyone, from the Secretary of State downwards, who is involved in the development control process. In performing that function the courts are said to act as a review body, that is, they review the legality of decisions. This should be contrasted with the courts' ability to function as an appeal body. When hearing appeals, the courts can substitute their decisions for those of another body. The power to review limits the courts to inquiring whether a decision has

3 Ibid, s 22.

been legitimately made. What follows is a more detailed analysis of what exactly that function entails.

REVIEWING THE ADMINISTRATION

The 1971 Act sets out the circumstances in which the courts can review the activities of those who administer the planning system. Section 245(1), for example, provides:

If any person –
(a) is aggrieved by any order to which this section applies and desires to question the validity of that order, on the grounds that the order is not within the powers of this Act, or that any of the relevant requirements have not been complied with in relation to that order; or
(b) is aggrieved by any action on the part of the Secretary of State to which this section applies and desires to question the validity of that action, on the grounds that the action is not within the powers of this Act, or that any of the relevant requirements have not been complied with in relation to that action,

he may, within six weeks from the date on which the order is confirmed or the action is taken, as the case may be, make an application to the High Court under this section.

Section 244(1) of the 1971 Act, which is concerned with questioning the validity of structure and local plans, is drafted in a similar fashion. From the wording adopted in these sections, it would appear that their common salient features are: the meaning to be attributed to 'any person aggrieved'; the fact that any challenge must be made within six weeks; the grounds for such a challenge; and the orders and actions affected by such powers. If these matters, such as who, what, why and when, are analysed, the hope is that the role of the courts will become clearer and the contribution which they make to the development control process will be better understood.

'Any person aggrieved' The fact that this phrase is used, as opposed to 'any person', indicates that only certain individuals, rather than members of the public in general, can take advantage of these legislative provisions. Over the years the courts have agonised over, and changed their opinions on, the question of who will constitute a person aggrieved. The rigid approach, that only those who had some legal right jeopardised by the development control decision in question could be considered persons aggrieved, has now been abandoned.[4] Fortunately for prospective litigants, the court revised

4 It was typified by the decision in *Buxton v Minister of Housing and Local Government* [1961] 1 QB 278, [1960] 3 All ER 408, a decision which has been overtaken by events, particularly the rules on who may appear at public inquiries.

its views in *Turner v Secretary of State for the Environment.*[5] It did so in the light of the interpretation given to the term 'person aggrieved' when it occurred in other legislative provisions. In addition, the appearance of the Town and Country Planning (Inquiries Procedure) Rules 1969,[6] with their provisions allowing individuals to appear at an inquiry at the inspector's discretion, was significant. It persuaded the court that it was only fair that those same individuals should be able to challenge before the courts the validity of the very procedure in which they had participated. Indeed, the judgment in *Turner v Secretary of State for the Environment* suggests that the classification of persons aggrieved can extend beyond those who participated in a public inquiry:

> On the other hand I see good reason, so long as the grounds of appeal are so restricted [by time], for ensuring that any person who, in the ordinary sense of the word, is aggrieved by the decision, and certainly any person who has attended and made representations at the inquiry, should have the right to establish in the courts that the decision is bad in law because it is ultra vires or for some other good reason.[7]

Subsequently, the term 'person aggrieved' has been held to include individuals and organisations, such as companies and amenity societies, who have made representations concerning the decision under scrutiny by the courts.[8] The term can also include a local authority.[9] If, for example, a local planning authority grants an individual planning permission, subject to certain conditions, the Secretary of State may modify or remove those conditions on appeal. It may be clear from the decision letter that the Secretary of State has failed to give adequate reasons for his decision. In these circumstances, the local planning authority can challenge his decision as a person aggrieved. However, should the Secretary of State have affirmed the conditions, then however greatly the local planning authority may have then taken exception to something said in the decision letter, the local planning authority cannot be regarded as a person aggrieved.

This very situation arose in *Greater London Council v Secretary of State for the Environment,*[10] where, on appeal, an inspector

5 (1973) 28 P & CR 123.
6 These Rules have been revoked and their place taken by the Town and Country Planning (Inquiries Procedure) Rules 1974, SI 1974 No 419.
7 (1973) 28 P & CR 123 at 139, per Ackner J.
8 See, for example, *Great Portland Estates v Westminster City Council* [1985] AC 616, [1984] 3 All ER 744, *Bizony v Secretary of State for the Environment* [1976] JPL 306.
9 See, for example, *Chelmsford Borough Council v Secretary of State for the Environment* [1986] JPL 112.
10 [1985] JPL 868.

refused planning permission for a proposed development. Although the Greater London Council was in agreement with this decision and had directed the local planning authority, Harrow London Borough Council, to refuse the original application for planning permission,[11] there were remarks in the inspector's decision letter to which the Greater London Council took exception. These related to the feasibility of concluding a section 52 agreement[12] to overcome objections to the proposed development, as well as the correct approach to be taken to the over-supply of offices. In this case, the court held that the Greater London Council was not a person aggrieved in relation to the inspector's decision. Rather the Greater London Council was aggrieved by the inspector's reasoning which it feared would have an adverse effect on future development control decisions. In the court's view, it was clear from the wording of section 245 of the 1971 Act that an inspector's reasoning could not be challenged in this fashion. Any other interpretation could result in a considerable increase in the number of applications under section 245. Instead, the individual or organisation aggrieved by an inspector's reasoning should make an application for judicial review. In this way the procedures under sections 244 and 245 are apparently reserved for those who take exception to a decision.

'Within six weeks' Any challenge must, according to the relevant sections, be made within six weeks. This immediately raises a number of questions. The two most obvious are why have a time limit, and within six weeks of what. The justification for the time limit is seen essentially as a practical matter. The period is short, certain in length and allows no exceptions. On occasions, the courts have interpreted legislative provisions designed totally to prevent access to the courts in such a way as to thwart completely any such restriction.[13] However, in *R v Secretary of State for the Environment, ex parte Ostler*,[14] the possibility of treating this provision in a

11 The Greater London Council possessed the power to act in this fashion by virtue of the Town and Country Planning (Local Planning Authorities in Greater London) Regulations. With the abolition of the Greater London Council these Regulations have been revoked.

12 Section 52 of the 1971 Act gives local planning authorities the power to enter into an agreement with the owner of land to restrict or regulate the development or use of that land.

13 See, for example, *Anisminic Ltd v Foreign Compensation Commission* [1969] 2 AC 147, [1969] 1 All ER 208. Here a legislative provision purporting to prevent any decision reached by the Foreign Compensation Commission from being considered by the courts was said to be of no effect by the House of Lords. This was on the basis that the Commission's decision was void and hence not a decision.

14 [1977] QB 122, [1976] 3 All ER 90.

similar manner was considered and rejected. This was on the basis that a distinction can be made between provisions which totally prevent access to the courts, and those which merely restrict the right.

Six weeks means exactly that. If the period were longer or not of any specific duration, then developers might have to delay the start of a scheme, or else face the prospect of having the legality of a development challenged when buildings had been demolished or foundations laid. It is also important to note that the six-week period does not run from the date when any decision letter is received. In *Griffiths v Secretary of State for the Environment*,[15] the House of Lords was of the opinion that the six-week period in section 245 runs from the time when a relevant decision is made. In this case, the decision under consideration was the Secretary of State's determination of a planning appeal. Once the letter recording that determination has been typed, signed and date-stamped, then, according to the House of Lords, the decision is complete and the six weeks begin to run. This means that, in reality, allowing for the vagaries of the post, an individual will have less than six weeks to challenge a decision.

'The grounds for challenge'   According to sections 244 and 245 of the 1971 Act, a person resorting to the courts must demonstrate either that the activity in question is not within the powers of the 1971 Act, or that relevant requirements related to that activity have not been followed. Each of these grounds for challenge needs further consideration. As will be seen, sections 244 and 245 cover a variety of activities and decisions. Two examples, however, should serve to make clear the purpose of these sections. An application for planning permission is refused. An appeal is made to the Secretary of State, who confirms the refusal of planning permission. That decision taken by the Secretary of State can be challenged under the terms of section 245. Alternatively, a local plan is drawn up and after being scrutinised at a public inquiry, is adopted by a local planning authority. The validity of that local plan can be challenged under the terms of section 244.

If the intention is to show that the powers of the 1971 Act have been exceeded, in either case the argument is the same. It is that either the contents of the decision letter, or the contents of the local plan, demonstrate one of a number of situations which are examined below.

(a) A relevant factor has not been taken into account   What is

15 [1983] 2 AC 51, [1983] 1 All ER 439.

relevant varies with the circumstances. Particular attention needs to be paid to policy statements, such as circulars, and the arguments advanced at a planning inquiry. If a decision letter fails to deal with a relevant factor, or the contents of a local plan fail to take account of a relevant policy, this may be evidence that the powers of the 1971 Act have been exceeded. In *Penwith District Council v Secretary of State for the Environment*,[16] an inspector's apparent failure to take into account a Development Control Policy Note on amusement centres resulted in his decision being set aside since it was a relevant consideration. If he had taken it into account, and that was not clear, he should have given reasons for declining to follow the advice it offered.

(b) An irrelevant factor has been taken into account   In this context an issue will be considered irrelevant, either because it is not a development control issue or, if it is, because it is one which is irrelevant as far as the matter in hand is concerned. In *Great Portland Estates v Westminster City Council*,[17] for example, it was argued that some of the policies in a local plan did not have a planning purpose but were designed to benefit certain individuals. If this had been so, these policies would have been removed from the local plan, since the local planning authority would have exceeded its powers by taking account of an irrelevancy when compiling its local plan. In the event this was found not to be the case.

(c) A decision is so unreasonable that no reasonable individual could have arrived at it   As compared with other methods of challenging the validity of a decision, this is by far the most difficult to prove. It does not mean that a decision is unreasonable in the sense that the court, faced with the same set of circumstances, might have come to a different decision. Instead, to be considered unreasonable the decision should be such that it is totally arbitrary and illogical. In the event very few decisions are capable of being described in this way. This cannot, however, obscure the fact that the courts have been known, on occasions, to use this reasoning as a way of substituting their development control decision for that of the relevant body or individual. Judicial decisions exist which have been criticised on those very grounds.[18] Undoubtedly, the practice, if it occurs, is to be deplored. The Court of Appeal made this very point in *Buckinghamshire County Council v Hall Aggregates*

16 [1986] JPL 432.
17 [1985] AC 661, [1984] 3 All ER 744.
18 See, for example, *Fourth Investments v Bury Metropolitan Borough Council* [1985] JPL 185.

(Thames Valley) Ltd.[19] Here, the decision of the judge at first instance that portions of a minerals plan were so unreasonable that they should be set aside, left a development plan which was acceptable to neither the local planning authority nor the gravel mining company.[20] In setting aside his decision, the Court of Appeal re-affirmed the specific meaning to be attached to the term 'unreasonable', namely an illogical, perverse or arbitrary decision.

(d) A decision is contrary to the rules of natural justice There are two rules of natural justice. Their aim is to ensure that a decision maker is impartial and arrives at a decision only when the parties involved have had a chance to state their case. In short, the rules of natural justice are designed to ensure procedural fairness. Obviously, there is a connection between the rules of natural justice and the procedures set out in legislation such as the Town and Country Planning (Inquiries Procedure) Rules 1974.[1] Normally, these procedures are drawn up with the rules of natural justice in mind, and in particular, the requirement that both parties should have an opportunity to state their case and respond to the argument against them. The rule that the Secretary of State, should he take account of fresh evidence after the close of a public inquiry, must allow the parties to comment on it or reopen the inquiry, is just such an attempt.[2] Therefore, compliance with the relevant procedures will normally guarantee compliance with the rules of natural justice. It is always possible, of course, that no procedure will have been specified. In these circumstances, the courts will still insist on compliance with the rules of natural justice. The question will be asked whether or not that particular decision has, in the circumstances of the case, been arrived at fairly.

While it can be comparatively easy to ensure, with or without a specified procedure, that each individual is given an opportunity to state his case, the rule against bias can present more, if less obvious, opportunities for its breach. The rule against bias is designed to ensure that a decision maker is impartial. This does not mean that an individual, seeking to show that this rule of natural justice has

---

19 [1985] JPL 634 at 643, 644, per Purchas LJ.
20 Ibid, 641–642.
 1 SI 1974 No 419. These rules govern the procedure to be followed at a planning inquiry where the final decision will be taken by the Secretary of State for the Environment. Where the final decision is to be taken by an inspector the relevant procedure is to be found in the Town and Country Planning Appeals (Determination by Appointed Persons) (Inquiries Procedure) Rules 1974, SI 1974 No 420.
 2 Town and Country Planning (Inquiries Procedure) Rules 1974, SI 1974 No 419, rule 12.

been breached, must prove actual bias.[3] It is sufficient simply to prove one of two things. If it can be shown that a decision maker has a financial interest in the matter before him – owning shares, for example, in the company making a planning appeal – that will be sufficient to persuade the court that any decision is biased.[4] Alternatively, if the behaviour of the decision maker is such as to convince the court that a reasonable man, aware of all the circumstances, would believe that there was a real likelihood or reasonable suspicion of bias, this too can lead to a decision being set aside.[5] The aim of this second objective test is to ensure that only those decisions are set aside where sufficient evidence exists to render them suspect.[6]

Financial interests apart, bias can take many forms. In the context of sections 244 and 245 of the 1971 Act, it normally involves allegations concerning either the inspector, or conceivably the Secretary of State. If, for example, it can be shown that an inspector is related in some way to one of the parties participating in a planning appeal, that may constitute a breach of the rule against bias.[7] Also included is behaviour on the part of an inspector which indicates that he has pre-judged the issue before him.[8] Even indulging in a conversation with an individual who is opposed to a particular development, has been sufficient to cause a decision to be set aside on the grounds of bias.[9] What is unclear, however, is whether bias can occur in a situation where a decision maker, by his actions, appears to have given himself no choice in the decision he will reach.

To explain this situation more fully, reference can be made to the House of Lords' decision in *Franklin v Minister of Town and Country Planning*.[10] Here, the Minister had designated Stevenage the first New Town. Local residents objected, a public inquiry was held and the Minister confirmed that Stevenage would be the first New Town. When this decision was challenged on the grounds that

---

3 It would undoubtedly be exceedingly hard to prove that a decision was infected by bias. What the rule against bias seeks to avoid is the suspicion of bias, though in reality a decision may have been fairly made.
4 *Dimes v Grand Junction Canal Co Proprietors* (1852) 3 HCL 759.
5 The courts often treat the two tests of reasonable suspicion and real likelihood as separate tests, though the chances are that they will produce the same result in the majority of cases.
6 If this were not so, then decisions might be set aside on the slightest pretext with considerable disruption to the administrative process.
7 *Metropolitan Properties (FGC) Ltd v Lannon* [1969] 1 QB 577. The case concerned not a planning inspector but the chairman of a rent tribunal.
8 *Halifax Building Society v Secretary of State for the Environment* [1983] JPL 816.
9 *Simmons v Secretary of State for the Environment* [1985] JPL 253.
10 [1948] AC 87, [1947] 2 All ER 289.

the Minister who made it was biased, the House of Lords disagreed. While the Minister had made plain his determination that Stevenage should be the first New Town, he had held a public inquiry and taken account of the conclusions which it had reached. The Minister's decision to affirm his original opinion could not, therefore, in the circumstances, be described as biased. In reaching this conclusion, particular emphasis was placed on the administrative nature of the task being performed by the Minister.[11] While labels such as 'administrative' can, on occasion, do more harm than good, the description serves to stress that the Minister's role was one where he might be expected to have a policy, rather than maintain judicial impartiality.

From this and other related decisions,[12] it would appear that a Secretary of State who adheres to a particular development control policy, and employs it in resolving planning appeals, cannot be described as biased. This is provided that an opportunity is given to those who oppose that policy to state their case, and to try to dissuade the Secretary of State from applying it. It is only if a particular policy renders the Secretary of State incapable of properly exercising those powers which he possesses that it can be challenged in the courts. A policy which, for example, requires all planning appeals involving agricultural land to be referred to the Minister of Agriculture for comment, may cease to be legitimate if the Secretary of State automatically defers to those comments.[13] This is on the basis, not that the Secretary of State is biased, but that he is no longer capable of exercising the discretion given to him by statute.

(e) The decision must represent an effective exercise of any discretion given by the statute As already indicated, an individual can exceed his powers by failing effectively to exercise a discretion entrusted to him. What the courts require is proof of some factor – an agreement, not necessarily a contract, or an unauthorised delegation – which convinces them that the discretion has not been properly exercised.[14] For example, the understanding between local

11 Ibid, 102, per Lord Thankerton.
12 *R v St Edmundsbury Borough Council* [1985] 3 All ER 234, *R v Sevenoaks District Council* [1985] 3 All ER 226.
13 It is very difficult on occasions to distinguish between the legitimate application of a policy and the complete surrender of a discretion. An important factor appears to be the willingness of the discretion holder to listen to argument.
14 The mere fact that a contract exists will not automatically prevent the exercise of a discretion. On this point note the ability of a local planning authority to enter into section 52 agreements and yet still exercise its development control powers. See *Windsor and Maidenhead Royal Borough Council v Brandrose Investments Ltd* [1983] 1 All ER 818.

planning authorities not to sanction development in close proximity to Jodrell Bank radio telescope fell into this category,[15] as did a Minister of Housing and Local Government's decision to defer to the view of the Minister for Agriculture on planning appeals involving the loss of agricultural land.[16] While, as has already been stated, the courts acknowledge the major role played by policy in the development control process, even policy can be so rigidly applied as to stifle the proper exercise of discretion. The court's task, therefore, is no easy one. It is to pinpoint those instances, rare though they are, when the freedom of choice which is implicit in the term discretion, has been surrendered.

(f) A mistake of fact may cause a decision to be set aside The principle that a mistake of fact can vitiate a decision has been repeated on several occasions, but rarely acted upon. The problem is that in order to warrant a decision being set aside, the mistake must be one which, in all probability, has caused the individual making it to arrive at a decision which is different from the one he would have arrived at, had the mistake not been made. In *Mason v Secretary of State for the Environment,*[17] for example, an error was made over the distance of a house from premises which it was proposed to use as a vehicle repair shop. The distance was said to be 250 feet when, in reality, it was 125 feet. The following explanation was given for refusing to set aside the inspector's decision:

> But to vitiate a decision the mistake of fact had to be material, that was, there must be grounds for thinking that the decision might have been different if the mistake had not been made.[18]

Since the inspector in question had viewed the site and had seen how far apart the buildings were, the mistake was not regarded as material.

(g) The terms of any relevant legislation must be observed It may be apparent from the terms of a particular piece of legislation that the powers which it confers on the Secretary of State are to be exercised only in certain circumstances. Any attempt to exercise those powers when such circumstances do not exist, can be challenged.[19] The power of the Secretary of State to grant or refuse

15 *Stringer v Minister of Housing and Local Government* [1971] 1 All ER 65.
16 *Lavender v Minister of Housing and Local Government* [1970] 1 WLR 1231.
17 [1984] JPL 332. See also *Jagendorf and Trott v Secretary of State for the Environment* [1987] JPL 771.
18 [1984] JPL 333.
19 *White and Collins v Minister for Health* [1939] 2 KB 838. Here land which was part of a park could not be the subject of a compulsory purchase order. Therefore an order made in respect of the parkland was quashed by the courts.

planning permission on appeal depends on development being undertaken. If the courts were to find that there was no development, then the Secretary of State is exceeding his powers by refusing or granting planning permission. Though it is the court's responsibility to interpret statutes, the Secretary of State's determination that a particular activity constitutes development will not readily be disturbed unless there is ample evidence that it is untenable. In *Coleshill and District Investment Company Ltd v Minister of Housing and Local Government*,[20] the House of Lords was not prepared to disturb the Minister's decision that demolition of a structure could amount to development.

Apart from the list of situations whose existence may cause a decision to be set aside on the grounds that the powers of the 1971 Act have been exceeded, one more item remains to be discussed. This is the separate ground for challenge, mentioned in sections 244 and 245, that a relevant requirement has not been observed. Relevant requirements are procedural requirements which must be followed when action is taken, or a decision arrived at, under the terms of the 1971 Act. Such requirements are to be found in the 1971 Act and regulations made under that Act as well as in the Tribunals and Inquiries Act 1971.[1] It is a provision of both sections 244 and 245 that, in order for such a challenge to succeed, the applicant must show that his interests have been substantially prejudiced by the failure to observe the relevant requirements.[2] This necessity to show substantial prejudice is a practical matter, designed to ensure that projects which may be a matter of urgency are not delayed and financial loss caused merely because a trivial procedural error has occurred.

As for the contents of these relevant requirements, they reflect the necessity to take any action or to arrive at any decision fairly. Parties are given an opportunity to state their case and refute their opponents' arguments. A conclusion, once reached, must be justified by reasons. Nor are the courts content merely to see the letter of the law being observed. Reasons, for example, will not be considered sufficient if they are unintelligible. Over the years, in a series of decisions, the courts have insisted that such reasons must be clear and intelligible,[3] as well as dealing with the major points

20 [1969] 2 All ER 525.
1 The provisions of the Tribunals and Inquiries Act 1971 are applicable to planning inquiries, and s 12 of that Act, for example, provides that reasons must be given for a decision, but only if requested.
2 1971 Act, s 245(4)(b).
3 See, for example, *French Kier Developments Ltd v Secretary of State for the Environment* [1977] 1 All ER 296, *Thanet District Council v Secretary of State for the Environment* [1978] JPL 250.

raised in the course of the arguments.[4]

In concluding this discussion of the grounds for challenge, it is worth stating that even though sections 244 and 245 mention two separate grounds for challenge, the courts have not maintained a rigid distinction between the two.[5] As has already been mentioned, there is common ground between the rules of natural justice and the procedural requirements of the 1971 Act. Rather than maintain rigid distinctions, the courts have, on the whole, been at pains to use sections 244 and 245 flexibly, in order to set aside decisions which are flawed, not by minor omissions, but by what amounts to serious neglect of the terms of relevant legislation.

'The orders and actions capable of being reviewed in this fashion' It must be clearly understood that the power of the court to review decisions under sections 244 and 245 is a limited power, in the sense that it affects only certain decisions and actions. Section 244 is concerned primarily with development plans – that is structure, local and unitary plans – and the actions necessary to bring such plans into existence, as well as amend them. Subsections 244(3), (4) and (5), however, extend the operation of the section to other activities. These include the Secretary of State's order to stop up or divert a highway, as well as to extinguish the right of vehicles to use a highway or a public right of way over land. The 1971 Act sets out the circumstances in which such orders can be made,[6] and provides in section 244 a means of challenging their validity. As well as the Secretary of State's orders, a local authority's orders to authorise the stopping up or diversion of a footpath or bridleway, or to extinguish a public right of way over land, can also be challenged in this fashion. Finally, the direction of the appropriate minister discharging a statutory undertaker from obligations imposed on it by the 1971 Act, but which are impractical to carry out,[7] is subject to review under section 244.

Section 245 is concerned with the activities of local planning authorities, mineral planning authorities and the Secretary of State. The impact of the section is selective and renders liable to review, not every action, but only certain actions of the bodies or individuals mentioned. Orders made by local planning authorities requiring

4 *Camden London Borough Council v Secretary of State for the Environment* [1980] JPL 31.
5 *Reading Borough Council v Secretary of State for the Environment* [1986] JPL 115.
6 1971 Act, Part X. Normally such orders are made in order to facilitate a development.
7 Ibid, s 235.

the discontinuance of a use,[8] or the alteration or removal of buildings or works[9] are subject to challenge, as are tree preservation orders.[10] The decision of mineral planning authorities to make an order prohibiting the resumption of the winning and working of minerals is equally susceptible.[11] A whole range of activities on the part of the Secretary of State is capable of challenge under section 245. They include the Secretary of State's decision on an appeal against a planning decision, as well as his grant of planning permission on appeal against an enforcement notice.[12]

The significance of this list of activities is twofold. What is included is subject to challenge in the manner already described. A question remains, however, regarding those activities which are excluded, by reason of the fact that they are not mentioned. One such example is the decision of a local planning authority to grant planning permission. If someone wishes to question the validity of that decision, on the grounds that there has been a breach of the rules of natural justice, the 1971 Act does not appear to provide a way of doing so. An appeal to the Secretary of State can only be made by the party applying for planning permission, not by a third party. Sections 244 and 245 are not applicable to the original decision of a local planning authority to grant planning permission. In these circumstances, the course of action open to an individual is to make an application for judicial review.

APPLICATION FOR JUDICIAL REVIEW

The application for judicial review is a remedy designed to control the public activities of public authorities. In contrast with the powers of review detailed in sections 244 and 245 of the 1971 Act, the application for judicial review is not confined to assessing the legitimacy of specific activities of particular individuals. Instead, it is a general remedy and a complex one.[13] Indeed, books have been written describing precisely how the remedy operates.[14] The description of the application for judicial review which follows, therefore, is intended only to highlight those points that the courts

---

8 Ibid, s 242(2) and (3).
9 Ibid, s 51.
10 Ibid, s 60.
11 Ibid, s 51A.
12 Ibid, s 242(3).
13 In particular the decision of the House of Lords in *O'Reilly v Mackman* [1983] 2 AC 237, [1982] 3 All ER 1124, has made it clear that the application for judicial review is normally available only when some public right is threatened. The problem is distinguishing between public and private rights.
14 See, for example, Aldous G & Alder J *Applications for Judicial Review, Law and Practice* (1985).

consider essential when determining whether or not to give a remedy.

The procedure which must be followed in order to make an application for judicial review is set out in Order 53 of the Rules of the Supreme Court. It consists of a preliminary application, made by the individual seeking judicial review.[15] The purpose of the preliminary application is to secure the court's leave to proceed with the action. In this way, the court can weed out frivolous applications, though it should be stressed that very few actions are halted at this stage.[16] Apart from this, the applicant then has to convince the court to award him a remedy. It is perhaps worth mentioning that the application for judicial review amalgamates, under a single head, what were previously six separate remedies.[17] The applicant must, therefore, specify what combination of remedies he wishes the court to award him. In order to obtain them successfully, the applicant must show the court that:

(i) he has sufficient interest in the matter in hand;
(ii) there has been no delay in bringing the issue before the court;
(iii) there are grounds for awarding a remedy;
(iv) the court should use its discretion to award a remedy.

Does the applicant have sufficient interest in the matter in hand? At first sight this question may make little sense. Its immediate origins may be found in the wording of Order 53, which indicates that only an applicant with sufficient interest in the proceedings may be awarded a remedy.[18] In *Inland Revenue Commissioners v National Federation of Self-Employed and Small Businesses Ltd*,[19] the House of Lords indicated that what constituted sufficient interest depended on a number of factors. These included the terms of the legislation under the authority of which the public body has purported to act, as well as, in the opinion of some of their Lordships, the merits of the particular claim.[20] The

---

15 Rules of the Supreme Court, Order 53, rule 3.
16 For the way in which the court should treat applications for leave see *Inland Revenue Commissioners v National Federation of Self-Employed and Small Businesses Ltd* [1982] AC 617, per Lord Diplock at 643–644.
17 Those remedies are certiorari, prohibition, mandamus, injunction, declaration and damages. Briefly the purpose of the remedies is to quash an invalid decision (certiorari); to prevent or restrain an invalid decision or action being taken (prohibition, injunction); to force the carrying out of a duty (mandamus) and to secure a statement from the court that an activity is unlawful (declaration).
18 Rules of the Supreme Court, Order 53, rule 3(5).
19 [1982] AC 617, [1981] 2 All ER 93.
20 Ibid, 647, per Lord Diplock.

court also paid attention to the fact that the application for judicial review is an amalgam of various individual remedies which, in the past, all had different rules governing who could claim them.[1] It may well be that the history of a particular remedy, even though it now forms part of the application for judicial review, can make it easier or harder to obtain. In short, there are many factors influencing the court's decision on whether or not an applicant can be said to have sufficient interest. That said, certain members of the House of Lords in the *Inland Revenue Commissioners'* case made it very plain that a public body should not be able to escape the consequences of its unlawful activities merely on the technical point of lack of sufficient interest. This flexible approach which the courts are prepared to adopt towards the requirement of sufficient interest, is certainly borne out in those cases involving development control issues and the application for judicial review. The parties involved in a proposed development,[2] a neighbouring landowner,[3] and members of an amentity society,[4] have all been held in the past to have sufficient interest.

There has been no delay   Since the application for judicial review is concerned with the public activities of public authorities, any challenge to the lawfulness of those activities needs to be made promptly. If this were not so, a local planning authority might face the prospect of having a decision which was made several years earlier, and indeed acted upon, challenged in the courts. As has already been observed, under the terms of sections 244 and 245 of the 1971 Act, six weeks was allowed for challenge. Under the terms of Order 53, any challenge must be made promptly, meaning, in normal circumstances, within three months.[5] The courts have a discretion to extend this period, provided that their decision will not imperil the rights of the parties or good administration.[6] The three-month period begins to run from the date when any irregularity

1 The remedy under discussion in this case was mandamus which has always been hard to obtain since it forces a body to carry out a specific duty – here the Inland Revenue to collect taxes. Therefore, the court will normally only award such a remedy to someone with a particular interest in the matter in hand rather than an officious bystander.
2 *R v Camden LBC, ex p Comyn Ching & Co* (1984) 47 P & CR 417.
3 *R v North Hertfordshire District Council, ex p Sullivan* [1981] JPL 572.
4 *Covent Garden Community Association Ltd v Greater London Council* [1981] JPL 183.
5 Rules of the Supreme Court, Order 53, rule 4.
6 The court has to balance the interests of the applicant against the possible administrative disruption which could be caused if a decision which has been acted upon has its validity called into question. On this point see *R v Stratford on Avon District Council, ex p Jackson* (1985) 51 P & CR 76.

became apparent.[7] Since, however, the emphasis is on any challenge being made promptly, it is possible for a challenge made within the three-month period to be dismissed, on the basis that it was not made promptly enough.[8]

Grounds for awarding a remedy Basically, the grounds on which the lawfulness of a public authority's decision may be challenged, are the same as those already considered in the context of the 1971 Act. An applicant must show that the public authority has exceeded the powers given to it, either in an Act of Parliament, or from some other source.[9] There are various ways in which this can be proved. It may be that the procedure, which has to be observed in making a decision, has been ignored. Alternatively, a public authority may have misinterpreted the legislation which gives it its powers, and arrived at a conclusion which it has no power to make. If the legislation in question gives the public authority a discretion, such as the power to attach to the grant of planning permission such conditions as it sees fit, the courts will insist that the discretion is exercised in a reasonable fashion. This means taking account of relevant factors, ignoring irrelevant ones, and not using the power to achieve an improper purpose such as acquiring land by compulsory purchase in order to make a gain rather than out of necessity. Nor must the exercise of a discretion be so illogical that no reasonable public authority could have arrived at such a conclusion. Finally, a public authority must not do anything, such as enter into an agreement, which prevents that authority from exercising its discretion. Nor must it, in reaching a decision, breach the rules of natural justice.

In short, the courts possess a whole range of powers, designed to ensure that any decision arrived at by a public authority is a lawful decision. The ever-present problem is, however, that the distinction between the courts ensuring that a decision is lawfully made, and simply substituting their decision for that of the public authority, is a narrow one. At what stage does a decision become so unreasonable that no reasonable public authority would have arrived at it? Is it when the decision is not one which the court itself

---

7 This need not necessarily be the date when any decision was taken. For example, circumstances constituting bias may not become apparent until some time after a decision is taken.

8 *R v Greenwich London Borough Council, ex p Cedar Transport Group* [1983] RA 173.

9 For example, powers derived from the royal prerogative. It was thought that such powers were unreviewable but in *Council of Civil Service Unions v Minister for the Civil Service* [1985] AC 374, the House of Lords indicated that this was not so. Prerogative powers are normally concerned with such matters as the administration of justice and national security rather than development control.

would have made if it had been in the position of the public authority? Although this concept runs counter to the way in which the courts should use their powers of review, examples of this occurring in practice can be found.[10]

The courts' discretion to grant or refuse a remedy It is as true of the application for judicial review, as it was of the power to review in sections 244 and 245 of the 1971 Act, that the courts have a discretion whether to grant or refuse a remedy.[11] The fact that little damage may have been caused, even though a public body has exceeded its powers, could persuade the court to refuse the remedy sought. A more difficult issue altogether is, however, presented by the following situation. A local planning authority refuses planning permission for works which, in its opinion, constitute development. If the developer believes that the work in question does not constitute development, he faces a dilemma. Should he appeal to the Secretary of State as provided for in the 1971 Act? Alternatively, should he make an application for judicial review in the manner just described? If he does request the court to review the lawfulness of the local planning authority's decision, will the court, in the exercise of its discretion, refuse him a remedy on the ground that an alternative remedy exists, namely an appeal to the Secretary of State?

The circumstances when the courts will refuse a remedy on this basis have themselves been considered by the courts.[12] Consequently, while some general principles can be suggested, the possibility exists that these principles may be adapted somewhat if, and when, they are applied to the development control process. In the few development control cases where the existence of an alternative remedy has been discussed, the emphasis has been placed on the need for speed.[13] Several months might pass before the Secretary of State, for example, would arrive at a decision which may or may not provide a remedy. In such circumstances, the courts will normally be prepared to hear an application for judicial review in order to expedite the matter. Hence, the application for judicial review, besides supplementing the remedies specifically provided in the 1971 Act, can also be an alternative to those remedies.

10 For this narrow line between review and appeal in the context of Order 53, see *Bromley London Borough Council v Greater London Council* [1983] 1 AC 768.
11 All the remedies which constitute the application for judicial review are discretionary. Even though it can be shown that a public body has behaved unlawfully, the court may feel that the applicant's conduct is so reprehensible as not to deserve a remedy.
12 See *R v Chief Constable of Merseyside Police, ex p Carveley* [1986] 1 All ER 257.
13 See, for example, *Runnymede Borough Council v Ball* [1986] 1 All ER 629, *R v Hillingdon Borough Council, ex p Royco Homes* [1974] 1 QB 720, [1974] 2 All ER 643.

As a postscript to this analysis of the application for judicial review, as well as the remedies provided by the 1971 Act, one important point remains to be made. Each of these remedies allows the court to assess whether a public authority has acted within its powers. If this is found not to be the case, then normally all that the court can do is to set the decision aside. A court cannot substitute its decision for the one found to be at fault, since this would constitute an appeal and not a review. In the case of section 244, this will mean that the offending policies will be struck out of the structure or local plan.[14] Should a decision or action be found to be invalid under the terms of section 245, then the court will set it aside and remit the matter to the individual responsible for a fresh decision.[15] Therefore, if the Secretary of State exceeds his powers when deciding a planning appeal, the court will remit the matter to him after setting his original decision aside. The Secretary of State will then arrive at a fresh decision, which must take account of any guidance given by the court. He is, of course, free to reach exactly the same decision as before, provided he can do so by acting within his powers.

It is only the application for judicial review which can offer a wider range of remedies. It has been pointed out that six individual remedies were combined to create the application for judicial review. Consequently, an individual taking advantage of this remedy can ask the court to do more than simply set a decision aside, though it has to be said that on most occasions this is precisely what the applicant will want. The application for judicial review can be used to restrain an anticipated breach of its powers by a public body, as well as to force an official to carry out his duties. Damages can also be recovered when appropriate by using this remedy.

Although a considerable amount of space has been devoted to review by the courts, it also needs to be stressed that of the countless development control decisions made during the course of a year, a very small proportion indeed are the subject of review by the courts. Consequently, it may be useful at this stage to mention an alternative to the courts, which is cheaper by far, namely the ombudsman.

Ombudsmen

If an individual is dissatisfied with either the behaviour of a local authority, or the Secretary of State for the Environment, it might be

14 1971 Act, s 244(2)(b). The policies may cease to have effect generally or as they affect the applicant's property. On this latter point, see for example, *Fourth Investments v Bury Metropolitan Borough Council* [1985] JPL 185.
15 1971 Act, s 245(4).

possible to refer the matter to the ombudsman. The ombudsman charged with the task of overseeing the activities of central government is the Parliamentary Commissioner for Administration. His local authority counterpart is the Local Commission for Administration. There is an English Commission with three commissioners and a separate Welsh Commission with one commissioner.

The task of the central and local government ombudsmen is broadly similar. It is to consider whether a central government Ministry, such as the Department of the Environment, or a local authority, is guilty of maladministration thereby causing injustice to a complainant. There is no definition of the term 'maladministration' in the relevant legislation. Instead, a working definition has been built up over the years.[16] Maladministration concerns itself more with the activities which lead up to the making of a decision than the quality of the decision itself. Therefore, the losing of a file, undue delay, failure to observe some undertaking have all, in the past, been accounted maladministration. The fact that a decision is judged illogical or perverse can also constitute maladministration,[17] even though the relevant legislation makes it clear that the merits of a decision are not a subject for consideration by the ombudsman.[18] In reality, however, little reliance would appear to be placed on this particular aspect of maladministration aimed, as it appears to be, at the totally unreasonable decisions.[19] That said, the term 'maladministration' is undoubtedly sufficiently broad and vague to include some of those activities which can be the subject of judicial review. Since it is a matter for the discretion of an ombudsman whether or not he investigates a complaint, much will depend on the way the original complaint is phrased. Vague allegations of unfairness will not be sufficient. An act or omission must be identified which has prejudiced the making of a fair decision.

In assessing their ability to offer an alternative to the courts, the term 'maladministration' is a source of strength and weakness to the ombudsmen. It is perhaps unfortunate that other aspects of the legislation which regulates their investigations are much clearer. The cumulative effect of these may be said to be to reduce the

16 A working definition which is to be discovered in the Annual Reports of the Parliamentary Commissioner and the Local Commissions.

17 *Annual Report of the Parliamentary Commissioner for Administration* (1970) p 96. Here a decision not to award costs to a company which had appealed against an enforcement notice and won was made by the Minister of Housing and Local Government. There was nothing wrong with the way the decision was made, it was simply illogical.

18 Parliamentary Commissioner Act 1967, s 12(3); Local Government Act 1974, s 26(1).

19 Probably because of the inherent difficulty in concluding that a decision is perverse or illogical.

effectiveness of the ombudsman as an alternative remedy. Into this category come the legislative provisions which prevent a complaint being made directly to the ombudsman. Instead, in the case of the Parliamentary Commissioner, a complaint has to be made through a Member of Parliament.[20] If the Parliamentary Commissioner does receive direct what appears to be a complaint worthy of investigation, he must return it to the complainant. It is, however, his practice to indicate to the complainant's Member of Parliament his willingness to investigate, should the complaint be referred to him in the proper manner.[1]

Local councillors are the agency for referring complaints to the Local Commission.[2] Should an individual be unsuccessful in locating a councillor willing to pass on a complaint, it is possible to make a direct approach to the Local Commission.[3] In both instances, the need for an intermediary is seen as having a twofold purpose. On the one hand, it prevents the ombudsman from being overwhelmed by complaints. On the other hand, it preserves the roles of the Member of Parliament and the local councillor as individuals charged with resolving their constituents' complaints.

Other restrictions exist which curb the freedom of an ombudsman to investigate. They include a time limit of one year which runs from the date when the circumstances giving rise to the complaint first became known.[4] A complainant is also under an obligation to exhaust alternative remedies, such as legal proceedings, before approaching the ombudsman.[5] Each of these restrictions can, however, be waived at the discretion of the ombudsman.[6] In contrast, only bodies designated in the relevant legislation are capable of investigation.[7] Here, the ombudsman has no choice in the matter. The Parliamentary Commissioner would, therefore, be forced to decline to investigate a complaint against a nationalised industry, since its activities are not subject to his scrutiny.

20 Parliamentary Commissioner Act 1967, s 5(1)(a).
1 *Annual Report of the Parliamentary Commissioner for Administration* (1977).
2 Local Government Act 1974, s 26(2).
3 *Commission for Local Administration in England, Annual Report* (1985) indicates that complaints received directly are sent to the civic head of the local authority in question. That local authority is expected to settle the complaint or refer it to the Local Commissioner.
4 Parliamentary Commissioner Act 1967, s 6(3); Local Government Act 1974, s 26(4).
5 Parliamentary Commissioner Act 1967, s 5(2); Local Government Act 1974, s 26(6).
6 Parliamentary Commissioner Act 1967, ss 5(2) and 6(3); Local Government Act 1974, s 26(4)(b).
7 Parliamentary Commissioner Act 1967, s 4(1), Sch 2; Local Government Act 1974, s 25(1).

Even though an ombudsman is restricted in what he may investigate, the same is not true of the manner of his investigation. Individuals can be questioned and documents inspected with a freedom that is the equivalent of that enjoyed by the court.[8] Indeed, in some respects the freedom is greater, since the ombudsman can ask to inspect any relevant files. In contrast, a litigant has to specify to the court the exact documents he wants produced, which is no easy task when he has little idea of what documents exist and whether they are relevant.[9]

On the other hand, when it comes to reaching a decision on a complaint, the courts have the advantage over the ombudsman. The courts expect their judgments to be obeyed and are rarely disappointed. The ombudsman has no power to enforce his judgments. Instead, he must rely on the willingness of central and local government to co-operate. In reality, there are few instances where the Parliamentary Commissioner has had a finding of maladministration rejected out of hand.[10] When this occurs, a special report is presented to Parliament, and this may result in a Minister being questioned in the House over his refusal to accept the recommendations of the Parliamentary Commissioner.[11]

Local authorities are, on the whole, more likely to reject an ombudsman's finding. Even so, in only a small proportion of those cases where a complaint is found to be justified, will an amicable conclusion not be reached.[12] A local commissioner can also issue a second report to try to force recalcitrant local authorities into action.[13] If this fails the local commissioner is, at present, powerless.[14]

Even if an ombudsman's findings are accepted, however, he lacks the courts' power to set aside a decision. A central government Ministry or local authority may agree to revise its procedures to prevent a similar incident happening in the future. An ex gratia

8 Parliamentary Commissioner Act 1967, s 8; Local Government Act 1974, s 29.

9 The process which is known as discovery is very strictly regulated by the courts in order to avoid the production of sensitive information as well as 'fishing expeditions'.

10 There was an adverse reaction by the government to the Parliamentary Commissioner's report on the Court Line Affair, 498 HC Debates (5th series) Vol 897, col 566, 6th August 1975.

11 Parliamentary Commissioner Act 1967, s 10(3).

12 In the *Commission for Local Administration in England, Annual Report* (1987), it is noted that 26 further reports were issued, meaning that in 26 instances a satisfactory remedy for maladministration had not been provided.

13 Local Government Act 1974, s 31(2).

14 In the report *The Conduct of Local Authority Business* (Cmnd 9797), it was recommended that complainants be given a right to apply to the court if dissatisfied with the remedy offered by the local authority guilty of maladministration. See paras 9.67–9.70.

payment may be made to the complainant, or the case may be reopened if this is still possible. Sometimes an apology has to suffice. The appropriate remedy varies and much will depend on the particular circumstances of the case. The ombudsman can and does offer guidance on what he considers appropriate. The problem is that the complainant may wish to have the situation return to the way it was before the offending decision was taken. In many instances this is simply not possible, because the decision has been acted upon in a way which makes it incapable of reversal.

For all the restrictions on the type of complaint that can be investigated, the ombudsman can offer a very satisfactory alternative to the courts, besides providing a remedy on occasions when the courts would be unable to intervene, where a file has been lost, for example.[15] An analysis of the subject matter of the complaints investigated, shows that planning is high on the list of complaints received by the local commissioners. For the year 1986–87, the English Local Commission recorded that planning was the second most complained about subject, only housing drawing more complaints. Typical of the kind of complaints received by the English Local Commission and judged to amount to maladministration were the following: failing to notify a complainant of an application for planning permission by his neighbour to extend the neighbour's house; providing incorrect advice about the planning position of land; and failing to advertise the details of a proposed development affecting the setting of a listed building.[16] The Department of the Environment does not figure so prominently on the Parliamentary Commissioner's list. In 1986, the Parliamentary Commissioner investigated seven complaints against the Department of the Environment. He did receive a great many more but these were not properly referred. Of the seven investigations, four concerned planning appeals. Even where the Parliamentary Commissioner was satisfied that no maladministration had occurred in the conduct of a planning appeal, he still obtained reassurances that the administrative machinery would be overhauled. In one case instructions to employees of the Property Services Agency on when they could act on another's behalf in a planning appeal were clarified. Where the Parliamentary Commissioner found there had been maladministration, when the Department of the Environment failed to inform an appellant that an inspector's decision appeared wrong in law, compensation was paid.[17] As for the impact such investigations

15 The aid of the courts can only be sought where it is possible to make a claim the basis of an action for negligence or breach of contract.
16 *Commission for Local Administration in England, Annual Report* (1987).
17 *Annual Report of the Parliamentary Commissioner for Administration* (1986).

will have on the development control process, this is a matter for conjecture. It is argued that, besides providing a remedy for the individual, the ombudsman raises the general standard of administration. This ensures that decisions are taken and individuals dealt with in the fairest way possible. There is, however, the possibility that the presence of the ombudsman discourages innovation. Local government officials, in particular, may abandon new procedures designed to ensure greater public involvement, returning instead to established routine.[18] In this fashion complaints to the ombudsman may be avoided but at a price.

Other functions of the courts

Until this stage discussion has centred on the role of the court as a review body. Under the terms of the 1971 Act the court has other functions to perform. In the previous chapter, for example, reference was made to enforcement proceedings and, in that context, the court has an appeal function as well as a policing role to play, punishing individuals who ignore enforcement notices. There are other occasions when the court is required to act as an appeal body. It has to be said, however, that it is rare for the court to be called upon to play this role in the context of development control. The explanation is simple. Since most development control appeals involve issues of planning policy, the court is not an appropriate body to resolve them. Section 247 of the 1971 Act provides a rare example of the court acting as an appeal body. Under the terms of section 53 of the 1971 Act, an individual can ask a local planning authority for a determination whether or not certain activities will constitute 'development'. The matter may then be referred to the Secretary of State, either on appeal, or because the Secretary of State has called in the application or been forced to consider it, since the local planning authority had failed to come to a decision in the requisite period. The Secretary of State's decision can then be the subject of an appeal to the courts. The appeal is said, according to the terms of section 247, to be on a point of law. This means that the court is being asked to indicate whether the interpretation given to the term 'development' by the Secretary of State is accurate. This is hardly surprising, since one of the prime concerns of the court is the interpretation of legislation. Even when exercising its powers of review, the court has to interpret the relevant legislation in order to

18 On the basis that it is better to be safe than become the object of an investigation by a local commissioner.

determine whether the correct procedure has been adhered to, or powers have been exceeded.

In concluding this discussion of the role of the courts in the development control process, various points have emerged. First, the main role of the court is as a review body but this is not an exclusive role. Other tasks are assigned to the courts by the 1971 Act, not to mention those general powers possessed by the court to award damages for the negligent performance of development control functions.[19] From this assessment of what exactly the courts do, emerges a second point. It appears that the courts have a peripheral, as opposed to a central, role in the development control process. Development control policy, its formulation and application in individual cases, is not their business. The courts can indicate whether the formulation or application of policy is lawful by determining whether a policy maker has the power to do whatever is proposed. The courts can punish those who fail to comply with development control policy. The appropriateness of that policy in planning terms is, however, not an issue which the courts can legitimately consider.

19 See for example, *Davy v Spelthorne Borough Council* [1983] 3 All ER 278.

Index

Action area plan
functions, 149
Administration
review of. *See* COURT
Administrative county
function, 45
Advertising
local planning policy, 207–209
Aerodrome building
permitted development, 95
Agreement
planning, 218–219, 287–297
Agriculture
development site, 259–261
meaning, 70
permitted development, 93
Agriculture, Fisheries and Food,
Ministry of
development control process,
involvement in, 43–44
special planning controls, 221
Alteration
planning permission, need for, 67
Amusement park
permitted development, 96
Appeal
conduct of, 309–313
decision, 313–314
development, interpretation of,
83–89
enforcement notice, against, 27
generally, 300–301
inspector,
appointment of, 23
decision, 24–25
public inquiry, 23–24
reasons for, 301–304
to whom, 304–308
written representations, 23

Application for planning permission.
See PLANNING PERMISSION
Approval
local plan, for, 155–157
structure plan, for, 142–145
unitary plan, for, 159
See also PLANNING PERMISSION
Assembly
Use Classes Order, 100

Blight notice
service of, 29
Breaches. *See* ENFORCEMENT
British Steel
planning permission, application for,
30
Building
listing of, 176, 202–207
temporary, permitted development,
93
war damaged, permitted
development, 94
Building operations
court, interpretation by, 74–76
development, as, 66
Business
Use Classes Order, 99

Caravan site
licensed, development on, 95
local policy, 193–195
permitted development, 95
Central Electricity Generating Board
special planning controls, 220–221
Central government
local authority policy, source of,
177–179
See also NATIONAL PLANNING POLICY

Chamber of Commerce
annual report, information relevant
to planning application, 19
Chamber of Industry
annual report, information relevant
to planning application, 19
Circulars
central government policy advice,
form of, 8
content of, 229–232
development, interpretation of,
89–91
generally, 228
information provided in, 34
legal significance of, 232–238
production of, 229
City
Victorian, free market forces and,
1–2
Civic Trust
local authority policy, source of, 186
planning policy, effect on, 221
Community councils
functions, 46–47
planning function, lack of, 48
Compensation
blight notice, service of, 29
developer, claim by, 27–30
purchase notice, service of, 29
Compulsory purchase
local planning policy, 215–217
Conservation area
designation of, 175–176
local policy, 190–193
Consultation
planning permission, application for,
104–109
Cornwall, Duchy of
land held by, development on, 30
Corporate body
planning permission, application for,
7
Councillors
local authority policy, source of,
182–183
local planning authority,
contribution made to, 8, 9
Countryside Commission
planning policy, effect on, 221
County councils
planning permission, application for,
48
responsibilities, 46

Court
development, interpretation of,
generally, 72–73
material change of use, 78–83
operations, 74–78
development control process, role
in, 62–63
injunction, application for, 326–327
role of,
administration, review of,
actions, 340–341
any person aggrieved, 330–332
challenge, grounds for,
discretion given by statute,
exercise of, 337–338
generally, 333
irrelevant factor taken into
account, 334
mistake of fact, 338
natural justice, decision
contrary to, 335–337
relevant factor not taken into
account, 333–334
relevant legislation, terms
must be observed,
338–340
unreasonable decision,
334–335
orders, 340–341
statutory provisions, 330
within six weeks, 332–333
generally, 328–329
judicial review. *See* JUDICIAL
REVIEW
ombudsman compared with, 349
other functions, 351–352
watchdog, as, 329
supervisory role of, 35
See also HIGH COURT
Crown
government department seen as
representing, 43
land, development on, 30–31,
219–220

Decision. *See* PLANNING PERMISSION
Demolition
courts, interpretation by, 77–78
Department of Environment. *See*
ENVIRONMENT, DEPARTMENT OF
Department of Transport. *See*
TRANSPORT, DEPARTMENT OF

Developer
compensation, claim for, 27–30
Department of Environment, role
of, 33–34
motives of, 54
principal party in planning system,
as, 8
private, 54–56
profit motive, 55–56
public, 9
role of, 9, 54–56
scrutiny of, 54–55
Development
activities not constituting, 67–69
circulars, 89–91
control. *See* DEVELOPMENT CONTROL
courts, interpretation by,
generally, 72–73
material change of use, 78–83
operations, 74–78
exceptions, 67–69
General Development Order. *See*
GENERAL DEVELOPMENT ORDER
meaning, 5, 66–72
plan. *See* DEVELOPMENT PLAN
planning appeal, interpretation in,
83–89
site. *See* SITE
Development control
analysis of, 2–3
examples, 11–31
exceptions, 30–31
generally, 2–5, 32
local government, role of, 49–54
planning permission. *See* PLANNING
PERMISSION
policy notes, 13, 239–241
self-explanatory term, 3
system at work, 5–11
town and country planning,
relationship with, 3–5
Development corporation
functions, 60
membership, 60
new town, 60
urban, 60
Development plan
development site, effect on, 244–246
formation and structure,
generally, 125–127
old style, 127–130

Development plan—*contd*
formation and structure—*contd*
under 1971 Act,
local plan,
action area plan, 149
approval, 155–157
content, 153–155
current policy, 152–153
district plan, 149
form, 148–153
functions, 145–148
scope, 153–155
town map, 149
village plan, 149
structure plan,
approval, 142–145
content, 137–140
form, 135–137
function, 133–135
generally, 132–133
scope, 140–142
survey, 130–132
future of, 169–172
generally, 114–115
Greater London, 157–158
ideal environment, indication of, 5
judicial comments, 165–169
judicial review, 160–165
law and, 160–169
local planning authority, legal
requirement to prepare, 5
meaning, 5*n*
planning application, example of, 11
policy document, as,
generally, 115–116
land policy, concept of, 116–118
Town and Country Planning Acts,
1947, 118–123
1971, 123–125
Secretary of State, scrutiny by,
37–38
significance of, 109–110
unitary, 48–49, 158–160
Distribution
Use Classes Order, 100
District councils
planning permission, application for,
48
responsibilities, 46
District plan
functions, 149

Drainage authority
  permitted development, 94
Drink
  Use Classes Order, 99
Dwelling-house
  development within curtilage of, 92
  single, use for two or more separate
    dwellings, 69
  Use Classes Order, 100

Enforcement
  breaches,
    discovery of, 315–316
    reasons for, 314–315
  generally, 300–301
  injunction, 326–327
  notice, appeal against, 27
  procedures, 26–27, 316–324
  stop notice, 324–326
Engineering operations
  courts, interpretation by, 75–76
  development, as, 66
English Heritage. *See* HISTORIC
  BUILDINGS AND MONUMENTS
  COMMISSION FOR ENGLAND
Environment
  bodies charged with protecting,
    61–62
  ideal, achievement of, 2
  planned, development of, 2
  Victorian, 1–2
Environment, Department of
  administrative organisation, 39
  circulars. *See* CIRCULARS
  day-to-day business, 39
  delegation within, 39
  developer, role as, 33–34
  development control,
    decisions, responsibility for, 34
    failure to define, 3
  establishment of, 3*n*, 35–36
  finance, distribution grant, 36
  inspector. *See* INSPECTOR
  land use policy, failure to materialise
    in cohesive form, 8
  metropolitan counties, abolition of,
    36
  national planning policy, 13–14
  Planning Inspectorate, 39–41
  policy. *See* NATIONAL PLANNING
    POLICY
  policy notes, 13, 239–241
  Property Services Agency, 33–34, 41
  responsibilities of, 33–34

Environment, Department of—*contd*
  role of, 35–41
  town and country planning,
    responsibility for, 37
  See also SECRETARY OF STATE

Financial services
  Use Classes Order, 99
Food
  Use Classes Order, 99
Forestry
  permitted development, 93
Forestry Commission
  planning policy, effect on, 221
Form of development. *See* SITE
Free market forces
  Victorian city and, 1–2
Function of development. *See* SITE

Gain
  planning, 218–219, 297–299
General Development Order
  aerodrome building, use of, 95
  agricultural buildings, works and
    uses, 93
  amusement parks, 96
  caravan site, use of, 95
  changes of use, 92–93
  drainage authority, development by,
    94
  dwelling-house, development within
    curtilage of, 92
  forestry buildings and works, 93
  generally, 91–92
  Historic Buildings and Monuments
    Commission for England,
    development by, 96
  industrial purposes, development
    for, 93–94
  licensed caravan site, development
    on, 95
  Local Act, development under, 94
  local authority, development by, 94
  local highway authority,
    development by, 94
  mineral exploration, 96
  mineral undertakers, 95
  mineral-working deposits, removal
    of material from, 96
  National Coal Board, development
    by, 95
  permitted development, classes of,
    92–99

General Development Order—*contd*
Private Act, development under, 94
private ways, repairs to, 94
recreational organisations, uses by members of, 93
services, repairs to, 94
sewage and sewage disposal, 94
statutory undertaker, 94–95
sundry minor operations, 92
Telecommunications Code System Operators, development by, 95
telecommunications development, 95–96
temporary buildings and uses, 93
unadopted streets, repairs to, 94
Use Classes Order distinguished from, 100–101
war damaged buildings, works and plant, 94
warehouses, 96
water authority, development by, 94
Georgian Society
development process, involvement in, 58
local authority policy, source of, 185
planning policy, effect on, 221
Government department
Crown, seen as representing, 43
development control process, freedom concerning, 42–43
impact on, 44
land held by, development on, 30
local planning authority, canvassing opinion of, 44
planning application, consultation as to, 108
See also ENVIRONMENT, DEPARTMENT OF
Greater London
development plans in, 157–158
local government organisation, 45
Greenpeace
development process, involvement in, 58

High Court
judicial challenge, 25–26
Highways. *See* ROADS
Historic Buildings and Monuments Commission for England
advice from, 14
function, 61
permitted development, 96
planning policy, effect on, 221

History
development site, of, 246–248
Hostel
Use Classes Order, 100
Hotel
Use Classes Order, 100
Housing and Local Government, Ministry of
planning, responsibility for, 3*n*, 35
transfer of functions, 35*n*
See also ENVIRONMENT, DEPARTMENT OF

Individual
planning permission, application for, 7
Industrial development
permitted, 93–94
planning application involving, 9, 18–22
site, 254–255
Industry
Use Classes Order, 99–100
Injunction
application for, 326–327
Inspector
appointment of, 23
decision of,
appeal, conduct of, 24–25
judicial challenge, 25–26
Planning Inspectorate, 39–41
Institution
development site, 258–259
non-residential, 100
residential, 100

Judicial review
application for,
applicant having sufficient interest in matter in hand, 342–343
delay, effect of, 343–344
generally, 341–342
remedy,
award of, 344–345
grant or refusal, 345–346
development plan, 160–169
inspector, decision of, 25–26
Secretary of State, decision of, 25–26

Lancaster, Duchy of
land held by, development on, 30
Land
Crown, development on, 30–31, 219–220
waste, local planning policy, 212–214

Land use planning
policy, failure to materialise in cohesive form, 8
Scottish Office, responsibility of, 41, 42
Welsh Office, responsibility of, 41–42
Leisure
development site, 257–258
Use Classes Order, 100
Listed building
alteration to, 67
Local Act
development under, 94
Local authority
development on own land, 31
permitted development, 94
planning policy. *See* LOCAL PLANNING POLICY
Local commissioner
function, 63
Local councillors. *See* COUNCILLORS
Local government
development control, role in, 49–54
organisation, 45–47
planning, responsibility for, 47–49
reform, 45–47
tiers, 45–47
Local highway authority
permitted development, 94
Local plan
action area, 149
current policy, 152–153
district, 149
form, 148–153
functions, 145–148
planning application, example of, 12, 19
town map, 149
village, 149
Local planning authority
blight notice, service of, 29
compensation, claim for, 27–30
councillors, contribution made by, 8, 9
development, decision on whether activity constitutes, 5–6
development plan, legal requirement to prepare, 5
government department, canvassing opinion of, 44
legal duties, 8
planning officer, contribution made by, 8–9

Local planning authority—*contd*
policy. *See* LOCAL PLANNING POLICY
principal party in planning system, as, 8
purchase notice, service of, 29
Local planning policy
conservation area, designation of, 175–176
examples, 11–13, 18–19
forms of, 187 *et seq.*
functions of, 187 *et seq.*
generally, 173–176
institution of, 174–176
listing buildings, 176
material considerations, 173
non-specific,
compulsory purchase, 215–217
local authority, development by, 217–218
other bodies, policy formulated by, 219–221
planning agreement, 218–219
planning conditions, 218–219
planning gain, 218–219
Town and Country Planning Act 1971, powers stemming from, 215–219
various sources, supported by, 214–221
planning permission, application for, 111
significance of, 174
sources,
central government, 177–179
generally, 177
local councillors, 182–183
local planning officers, 180–181
public, 183–187
specific,
advertising, 207–209
caravan, 193–195
conservation area, 190–193
highways, 209–212
listed buildings, 202–207
mineral workings, 195–198
special areas, 198–200
statute, supported by, 190–214
trees, 200–202
waste disposal, 212–214
waste land, 212–214
Location of development. *See* SITE

London borough councils
creation of, 46
unitary plan, responsibility for
preparing, 49
Maud Committee
findings of, 50
Merseyside Development Corporation
function, 60
Metropolitan counties
abolition of, 36
responsibilities, 46
unitary plan, responsibility for
preparing, 48–49
Minerals
exploration, 96
mineral-working deposits, removal
of material from, 96
undertaker, permitted development,
95
workings, local planning policy,
195–198
Mining operations
courts, interpretation by, 76
development, as, 66
**Ministry of Agriculture, Fisheries and
Food.** *See* AGRICULTURE, FISHERIES
AND FOOD, MINISTRY OF
**Ministry of Housing and Local
Government.** *See* HOUSING AND
LOCAL GOVERNMENT, MINISTRY OF
**Ministry of Public Buildings and
Works.** *See* PUBLIC BUILDINGS AND
WORKS, MINISTRY OF
**Ministry of Town and Country
Planning.** *See* TOWN AND COUNTRY
PLANNING, MINISTRY OF
Ministry of Transport. *See* TRANSPORT,
MINISTRY OF
Municipal borough
function, 45

National Coal Board
permitted development, 95
National Health Service
land held by, as Crown land, 30
National Housebuilders' Federation
local authority policy, source of, 187
National planning policy
circulars. *See* CIRCULARS
examples, 13–14, 19–20
generally, 222–223
making known, 225–228
ministerial statements and speeches,
241–242

National planning policy—*contd*
origins of, 223–225
other sources, 241–242
planning permission, application for,
111–112
National Trust
development process, involvement
in, 58
functions, 61–62
local authority policy, source of, 185
planning policy, effect on, 221
Nature Conservancy Council
function, 61
planning policy, effect on, 221
Non-metropolitan counties
responsibilities, 46
Non-residential institution
Use Classes Order, 100
Northern Ireland
exclusion from analysis, 3
Notes. *See* POLICY

Office
development site, 252–253
portakabin, use of, 87–88
Officer. *See* PLANNING OFFICER
Ombudsman
development control system, impact
on, 64
functions of, 63–64
reference to, 346–351
supervisory role of, 35
Operations
building, 74–76
demolition, 77–78
engineering, 75–76
meaning, 72
minerals, 76
other, 76–77
permitted development, 92
Organisations
development process, involvement
in, 59

Parish council
functions, 46–47
planning function, lack of, 48
**Parliamentary Commissioner for
Administration**
function, 63
Personnel of planning
court. *See* COURT
Department of Environment. *See*
ENVIRONMENT, DEPARTMENT OF
developer. *See* DEVELOPER

Personnel of planning—*contd*
development corporation, 60
environment, bodies charged with
    protecting, 61–62
generally,33–35
government department. *See*
    GOVERNMENT DEPARTMENT
local government. *See* LOCAL
    GOVERNMENT
members of public, 56–59
ombudsman. *See* OMBUDSMAN
other groups, 59–62
statutory undertaker, 61
Planning
agreement, 218–219, 287–297
appeal. *See* APPEAL
committee. *See* PLANNING COMMITTEE
conditions, 218–219, 275–287
gain, 218–219, 297–299
history of site in question, 14–15
parties to,
    developer. *See* DEVELOPER
    local planning authority. *See*
        LOCAL PLANNING AUTHORITY
permission. *See* PLANNING PERMISSION
personnel of. *See* PERSONNEL OF
    PLANNING
policy. *See* POLICY
Planning Advisory Group
planning system, recommendations
    on, 122–123
Planning committee
application, consideration of, 10
decision,
    appeal against, 23–25
    options as to, 22–23
    process of reaching, 7–8
membership, 9–10
political representation, 9
representations to, 10
role of, 9–10
Planning officer
local authority policy, source of,
    180–181
local planning authority,
    contribution made to, 8–9
proposed development,
    consideration of implications of,
    15–17
Planning permission
activity constituting development
    requires, 6

Planning permission—*contd*
application for,
    appeal, 23–25
    consultation, 104–109
    corporate body, by, 7
    decision. *See* decision *post*
    development plan, 109–110
    enforcement, 26–27
    examples, 11–31
    form of, 7
    full, 7
    impact of proposal, consideration
        of, 15–17
    individual, by, 7
    industrial development, involving,
        9
    judicial challenge, 25–26
    material considerations,
        central government policy,
            111–112
        generally, 110–111
        local policy, 111
        other considerations, 112–113
        site, 112
    outline, 7*n*
    planning committee, consideration
        by, 10
    procedure,
        examples, 11–31
        generally, 10–11, 101–104
    publicity, 104–109
    refusal, 274
circulars, 89–91
Crown land, development on, 30–31,
    219–220
decision,
    agreement, power to conclude,
        287–297
    conditions, 275–287
    gain, 297–299
    generally, 22–23, 272–275
    numbers, 272
    refusal, 274
development,
    courts, interpretation by,
        generally, 72–73
        material change of use, 78–83
        operations, 74–78
    meaning, 66–72
    planning appeal, interpretation in,
        83–89
development control system, lies at
    heart of, 6

Planning permission—*contd*
General Development Order. *See*
GENERAL DEVELOPMENT ORDER
generally, 65–66
need for, 65–66
Use Classes Order. *See* USE
Planning unit
meaning, 82
Policy
co-ordination, responsibility of
Department of Environment, 37
development plan as document of,
generally, 115–116
land policy, concept of, 116–118
Town and Country Planning Acts,
1947, 118–123
1971, 123–125
informal, 12–13
land use, failure to materialise in
cohesive form, 8
local. *See* LOCAL PLANNING POLICY
local plan, on, 152–153
national. *See* NATIONAL PLANNING
POLICY
notes, 13, 239–241
statutory, 12
unemployment, impact of, 44–45
Portakabin
office, use as, 87–88
Private Act
development under, 94
Private way
repairs to, 94
Professional services
Use Classes Order, 99
Property Services Agency
developer, as, 33–34
role of, 41
Public
inquiry, appeal in form of, 23–24
local authority policy, source of,
183–187
member of, role in planning process,
56–59
**Public Buildings and Works, Ministry
of**
transfer of functions, 35*n*
Publicity
planning permission, application for,
104–109
Purchase notice
service of, 29

Ramblers' Association
local authority policy, source of, 186
planning policy, effect on, 221
Rate support grant
distribution of, 36
Recreational organisation
members of, uses by, 93
Refuse
existing dump, deposit on, 69
Repairs
services, to, 94
unadopted street, to, 94
Representations
planning committee, to, 10
Residential development
planning application, example of,
11–18
site, 253–254
Residential institution
Use Classes Order, 100
Retail
development site, 250–252
Roads
local planning policy, 209–212
unadopted street, repairs to, 94
**Royal Institution of Chartered
Surveyors**
development process, involvement
in, 56
Rural district
function, 45

Scotland
exclusion from analysis, 3
Scottish Office
land use planning, responsibility for,
41, 42
Secretary of State
appeal, decision in,
inspector's decision distinguished
from, 25
judicial challenge, 25–26
reasons must be given, 24–25
development plan, scrutiny of, 37–38
Services
repairs to, 94
Sewage
disposal, 94
permitted development, 94
Shop
Use Classes Order, 99

Site
common issues, 266–271
development plan, relationship to,
244–246
generally, 243
local impact, 268–271
meaning, 243–244
planning history, 246–248
planning permission, application for,
112
significant features,
form of development, 248–250
function of development,
agricultural, 259–261
generally, 250
industrial, 254–255
institutional, 258–259
leisure, 257–258
mixed uses, 261
offices, 252–253
other uses, 261
residential, 253–254
retail, 250–252
storage, 256
transport, 256–257
generally, 248
location of development,
central business district,
261–263
commercial core, 261–263
generally, 261
inner-city fringe, 263–264
residential suburbs, 264–265
rural, 265–266
transition zone, 263–264
urban rural fringe, 265
visual issues, 266–268
Society for Protection of Rural England
development process, involvement
in, 58
Special areas
local planning policy, 198–200
Statutory undertaker
development on own land, 31
function, 61
meaning, 61, 220
permitted development, 94–95
special planning controls, 220–221
Stop notice
service of, 324–326
Storage
development site, 256
Use Classes Order, 100

Street
unadopted, repairs to, 94
Structure plan
approval, 142–145
central government approval, 8, 11
contents, 11, 137–140
form, 135–137
function, 133–135
generally, 132–133
planning application, example of,
11, 18
scope, 140–142
Survey
development plan, preceding,
130–132
unitary plan, preceding, 159

Telecommunications
permitted development, 95
**Telecommunications Code System
Operators**
permitted development, 95
Town and country planning
Department of Environment,
responsibility of, 37
development control, relationship
with, 3–5
goals, 3–4
meaning, 1
modern system, emergence of, 2
**Town and Country Planning, Ministry
of**
establishment of, 3*n*
Town map
functions, 149
Transport
development site, 256–257
Transport, Department of
road building programme, 42
Transport, Ministry of
transfer of functions, 35*n*
Trees
local planning policy, 200–202

Unauthorised development
enforcement procedure, 26
Unemployment
planning policy, impact on, 44–45
Unitary development plan
approval, 159
function, 158
operation, 159–160
preparation, 158–159
responsibility for, 48–49
survey, based on, 159

United Kingdom Atomic Energy Authority
planning policy, effect on, 221
Urban district
function, 45
Use
changes of, 92–93
Classes Order,
assembly, 100
business, 99
distribution, 100
drink, 99
dwelling-house, 100
financial services, 99
food, 99
General Development Order
distinguished from, 100–101
hostels, 100
hotels, 100
industrial, 99–100
leisure, 100
non-residential institutions, 100
professional services, 99
purpose, 78–79, 99
residential institutions, 100
shops, 99
storage, 100
material change of, 78–83
planning unit, meaning, 82

Village plan
functions, 149

Wales
local government organisation, 46
planning system, administration of,
35
Warehouse
permitted development, 96
Waste disposal
local planning policy, 212–214
Waste land
local planning policy, 212–214
Waste materials
refuse dump, deposit on, 69
Water authority
permitted development, 94
Welsh Office
land use planning, responsibility for,
41–42
White Paper
Department of Environment, on,
35–36
Widdicombe Report
conclusions, 50, 52–53
Written representation
appeal by, 23